More praise for *The Ecological Indian*

"Shepard Krech's learned, lively and courageous reportrayal of the Indians-in-nature is as timely as it is important. It is a major contribution to historical justice as well as environmental reform."
—James Axtell, Kenan Professor of Humanities, College of William and Mary

"Ground-breaking and myth-busting . . . brave."
—Jean Feraca, "Conversations with Jean Feraca," Wisconsin Public Radio

"*The Ecological Indian* is a stunning, provocative reassessment of the image of the noble Indian living harmoniously within nature. Krech provides a new picture of Indians as sophisticated humans who both changed the land and responded to its changing ecology. Anyone who cares about the past human role in transforming nature and its implications for today will find the book stimulating, indispensable, and timely."
—Carolyn Merchant, University of California at Berkeley, and author of *The Death of Nature*, *Radical Ecology*, and *Earthcare*

"Krech carefully separates romance from data. . . . This book is what good science should be."
—*Detroit News*

"A well-researched, carefully written exploration . . . a good story and first-rate social science. . . . This book teaches us everything we have wanted to know about American Indians and the environment."
—*New York Times Book Review*

"[The] subtitle—'Myth and History'—whets the appetite for revisionism . . . [but] Krech evidently has no axes to grind."
—*Wall Street Journal*

"Unexpected and provocative perspectives. . . . Not only does Krech shatter a romantic stereotype, he also forces us to think more realistically about environmental issues."
—*Booklist*

"Krech is interested most of all in stories about how American Indians changed the land, and how the land changed them."
—*The Chronicle of Higher Education*

"Compelling . . . examination of the historical truths and romantic myths about Native Americans and their relationship with nature."
—*Publishers Weekly*

"Thoroughly documented, this work corrects the stereotype of the passive ecological or environmentalist Indian, demonstrating that Indian people were and are actively engaged with their environment—adjusting to it, modifying it, and exploiting it."
—William C. Sturtevant, curator of North American ethnology and general editor, *Handbook of North American Indians*, Smithsonian Institution

ALSO BY SHEPARD KRECH III

Praise the Bridge That Carries You Over: The Life of Joseph L. Sutton

Indians, Animals, and the Fur Trade: A Critique of "Keepers of the Game" (editor)

The Subarctic Fur Trade: Native Social and Economic Adaptations (editor)

A Victorian Earl in the Arctic: The Travels and Collections of the Fifth Earl of Lonsdale, 1888–89

Native Canadian Anthropology and History: A Selected Bibliography, revised edition

Passionate Hobby: Rudolf Frederick Haffenreffer and the King Philip Museum (editor)

Collecting Native America, 1870–1960 (co-editor)

The ECOLOGICAL INDIAN

Myth and History

SHEPARD KRECH III

W. W. NORTON & COMPANY
New York • London

Printed in the United States of America
First published as a Norton paperback 2000

For information about permission to reproduce selections from this book, write to Permissions, W. W. Norton & Company, Inc., 500 Fifth Avenue, New York, NY 10110

The text and display of this book is composed in Waldbaum.
Desktop composition by Thomas O. Ernst
Manufacturing by Quebecor Printing, Fairfield, Inc.
Book design by Charlotte Staub

Library of Congress Cataloging-in-Publication Data

Krech, Shepard, 1944–
The ecological Indian : myth and history / Shepard Krech III
p. cm.
Includes bibliographical references and index.
ISBN 0-393-04755-5
1. Indian philosophy—North America. 2. Indians of North America—Public opinion. 3. Human ecology—North America—Philosophy. 4. Philosophy of nature—North America. 5. Indians in popular culture—North America. 6. Public opinion—North America. I. Title
E98.P5K74 1999
333.7'089'97—dc21 99-19425
CIP

ISBN 0-393-32100-2 pbk.

W. W. Norton & Company, Inc.
500 Fifth Avenue, New York, N.Y. 10110
www.wwnorton.com

W. W. Norton & Company Ltd.
Castle House, 75/76 Wells Street, London W1T 3QT

8 9 0

For Sheila

Contents

Preface

My interest in the environment, ecology, conservation, and American Indians is long-standing. As far back as I can remember I have gravitated to the outdoors. I grew up with a gun in one hand and a rod in the other and at ten was avidly watching and shooting birds.

I vividly remember being distracted by migrating chestnut-sided and other warblers in the elms outside the windows of my high-school classrooms. My father and grandfather (after whom I am named) made it seem normal to be both a sportsman and a conservationist. Besides taking me hunting and fishing, my grandfather urged me to improve my vocabulary, admonished me with "Too little Latin too late / May almost seal your fate," and insisted, with my mother, that I read a lot. I did, devouring books like Ernest Thompson Seton's *Wild Animals I Have Known;* I still have my grandfather's copy, in which he had inscribed his name on Christmas Day in 1899, a gift to him that he recycled to me. My father, a physician before he retired and for decades a low-impact farmer who has volunteered much time to the restoration of the Chesapeake Bay and to conservation organizations, made the desire to understand other people's lives and the human impact on the environment a logical one.

After spending four years at Yale and earning a B.Litt. at Oxford, I went to Harvard and, for doctoral research in anthropology, conducted ethnography over a period of fourteen months in 1971–72 among the Gwich'in who lived in and near the small town of Fort McPherson in Canada's Northwest Territories; I returned for several weeks in the fall of 1984. On both occasions I spent much time in the bush, traveling in winter by dog team to various camps, participating in the hunt for caribou, accompanying men on the trap line, shooting muskrats and ducks in spring, and netting fish, snaring hares, and shooting moose in summer and fall. Many Gwich'in and Métis whom I came to know patiently instructed me about their lives; the environment many knew intimately, understood systemically, and moved through effortlessly; and the animals and fish they shot, trapped, snared, and netted for their livelihood (and about which they told stories, including those of long-past times). They had a lasting impact on my interest in American Indian environmental knowledge, ecological thought, and conservation-related behavior—all at a time when the contemporary environmental movement, about which I felt passionately, was in full swing. To Chief John and Bella Tetlichi and their daughters, Mary, Alice, Sarah, and Bertha; Bertha's husband, Alfred Francis; John, Caroline, Selwyn, and Esther Kay; Johnny and Jane Charlie; John and Jean Marie Blake; Elizabeth Blake; Chief Johnny Kikavichik; William McDonald; William Vittrekwa; and others, all in abiding respect and lasting friendship, yet too many now in memory: *Maasi choh.*

Much of this experience laid the foundation for *The Ecological Indian.* In the course of researching and writing this book, I incurred debts to others, beginning with James Axtell, William Cronon, Raymond D. Fogelson, and William C. Sturtevant, who expressed confidence in this project (and faith in me) from the start, and the Woodrow Wilson International Center for Scholars and the National Humanities Center, where I held fellowships in 1992–93 and 1993–94, respectively. In colloquia, a seminar on the nature of evidence, other gatherings, and many conversations, my fellow Fellows, especially Edna Bay, Michael Burns, Denis Donoghue, David Flaherty, Paula J. Giddings, Richard Grove, Douglas Jesseph, Donald Kelley, Lawrence Lipking, George Moffett, Conor Cruise O'Brien, Fritz Ringer, Nicholas Rostow, David Harris Sacks, Leonard Smith, Kathryn K. Sklar, Alan S. Taylor, Dorothy and John Thompson, Luise S. White, and the late José Donoso, Joseph Hamburger, and A. Leon Higginbotham, Jr., made these centers ideal interdisciplinary settings in which to research a project as wide ranging as mine. Center staffs provided unstinting support: Michael Lacey, James Morris, and the late Charles Blitzer at the Woodrow Wilson Center, and W. Robert Connor, Kent Mullikin, Karen Carroll, Jean Houston, Jean Anne Leuchtenburg, Linda Morgan, Mary Donna Pond, Wayne Pond, and Alan Tuttle at the National Humanities Center deserve special thanks.

I am indebted to colleagues who generously agreed to comment on individual chapters: Douglas Anderson, Charles A. Bishop, Jennifer Brown, William Doolittle, Paul Fish (who also took me to Hohokam sites), Suzanne Fish, Donald Fowler, Patricia Galloway, Richard A. Gould, David W. Gregg, Alice Kehoe, Henry T. Lewis, Carolyn Merchant, Toby Morantz, Stephen J. Pyne, Daniel Odess, David Harris Sacks, Timothy Silver, and Gregory Waselkov deserve special mention. Others provided clippings, reprints, citations, assistance, advice, encouragement, or respite, including Peter Ammirati, John R. Bockstoce, Elizabeth Byers, Daniel Clement, Julie Cruikshank, Dena Dincauze, Ann ffolliott, Barbara Hail, Don Holly, Henning Gutmann, Steve N. G. Howell, Beth Hrychuk, Charles E. Kay, Mary Kell, Amy K. Knowles, Igor Krupnik, Philip Leis, David Lussier, Ann McMullen, Scott McWilliam, R. Grace Morgan, Tim and Rebecca More, Natalie Moyer, Sydney Nathans, Matt Nichols, Evan Peacock, Eleanor Pryor, Paul Rabinow, Joyce Seltzer, Elizabeth Sifton, Sandy Smith, Will Russell, Neal Salisbury, Tom Schaefer, Gene Stephenson, Julia Thorne, Marianna Torgovnik, Germaine Warkentin, Megan Waples, Arthur W. Wang, Larry West, Peter Wood, and Desiree Zymroz. Thanks also to Keep America Beautiful, Inc., for permission to reprint the image of Iron Eyes Cody as the Crying Indian.

For three weeks in the summers of 1996 and 1998, Carolyn Merchant, Timothy Silver, and I ran (and Richard Schramm and Crystal Waters administered) a National Endowment for the Humanities Institute at the National Humanities Center. Each summer, twenty selected high-school teachers came to the table (joined, one summer, by a National Park Service ranger) to discuss and debate "Nature Transformed: Imagination and the North American Landscape," and I am grateful to all for considering, in the week for which I was responsible, the ideas forming in several chapters of *The Ecological Indian.*

I appreciate comments from audiences at Duke University, the University of North Carolina, Chapel Hill, University of California, Berkeley, University of Arizona, Brown University, and elsewhere on presentations on work in progress. Earlier versions of Chapter 5 appeared in "Ecology and the American Indian," *Ideas* 3, No. 1 (1994): 4–22, and "Ecology, Conservation, and the Buffalo Jump," in *Stars Above, Earth Below: American Indians and Nature,* ed. Marsha

Bol (Niwot, CO: Roberts Rinehart Publishers for Carnegie Museum of Natural History, 1998), 139–64.

I am deeply grateful to my agent, Charles Rembar, for his timely advice and, at Norton, to Edwin Barber, vice-chairman, for his early support; editor Alane Salierno Mason for an incisive critique of the manuscript; and Ashley Barnes.

Finally, my wife, Sheila ffolliott; daughters, Kerry and Teal; son-in-law, Matthew Morrison, who is pursuing his doctoral degree at Yale School of Forestry and Environmental Studies; and granddaughter, Hannah, graciously and with humor put up with my often single-minded focus on this project. Teal, who is in the master's degree program at Northwestern University's Medill School of Journalism and is a stylist (in her prose), critiqued portions of the manuscript. As always, if my ideas possess merit it is in large measure due to Sheila's wisdom.

Providence, Rhode Island
January 1999

The Ecological Indian

Iron Eyes Cody as the Crying Indian, 1971.

Reprinted by permission of Keep America Beautiful, Inc.

Introduction

FEW FORGET HIS FACE. Not just the mournful expression and braided hair, but his liquid, tear-filled eye, welling up and brimming over. Clearly an American Indian. Visibly, and unexpectedly, crying. His direct gaze rivets the viewer, and his message is simple: "Pollution: it's a crying shame. Peoples start pollution. People can stop it."

Unveiled in 1971 by Keep America Beautiful, Inc., the Crying Indian, as he became known, appeared widely in print and on television. He instantly became the cornerstone of a campaign against litter. In the history of American environmentalism, the moment was auspicious. Just months before, between fifteen and twenty million people had assembled on Earth Day to create the groundswell for an environmental movement unprecedented in scale and zeal. For the first time, millions of Americans aggressively protested against the pollution of the environment and destruction of natural resources. They defined the 1970s as the Environmental Decade and led the attempt to convert America's attitudes toward the land and natural resources. In this context, Keep America Beautiful, whose goals were to halt pollution and clean up litter, flourished. Enlisting Iron Eyes Cody as the Crying Indian, this organization made the Cherokee actor's face one of the most recognizable in advertising over the next eight years, and his tear, which tumbled again and again down his cheek, perhaps the most famous visibly shed. Unsettling the viewer, his gaze—to use the language of advertising agencies—made fifteen billion people-impressions. As a noble ecologist, the Crying Indian became iconic.[1]

Through the Crying Indian, Keep America Beautiful cleverly manipulated ideas deeply engrained in the national consciousness. "Pollution: it's a crying shame" expressed the widely held perception, then and now, that there are fundamental differences between the way Americans of European descent and Indians think about and relate to land and resources. In what amounted to a powerful indictment of white Americans, the Crying Indian unequivocally implicated white polluters; they, not Indians, were the people who start pollution. He shed a tear for land and resources, which, by implication, he and other Indians treated kindly and prudently (as conservators might) and understood ecologically. But after arriving in North America, Europeans and their descendants ruined its pristine, unspoilt nature.

A noble image speaking to ecological wisdom and prudent care for the land and its resources, the Crying Indian is the paramount example of what I call the Ecological Indian: the Native North American as ecologist and conservationist. How faithfully it reflects Native North American cultures and behavior through time is the subject of this book.

Even though an invention of Madison Avenue, the Crying Indian is an effective image and advocate because its assumptions are not new. From the moment they encountered the native people of North America and represented them in texts, prints, paintings, sculptures, performances—in all conceivable media—Europeans classified them in order to make them sensible. They made unfamiliar American Indians familiar by using customary taxonomic categories, but in the process often reduced them simplistically to one of two stereotypes or images, one noble and the other not. For a long time, the first has been known as the *Noble Savage* and the second as the *Ignoble Savage*.

The Noble Savage, the first of the two stereotypes or images, has drawn persistently on benign and increasingly romantic associations; the Ignoble Savage, the second, on a menacing malignancy. The first has emphasized the rationality, vigor, and morality of the nature-dwelling native; the second, the cannibalistic, bloodthirsty, inhuman aspects of savage life. Often elements from the two stereotypes have been combined in a single portrait.[2]

The label *savage,* which English-speaking people used for North American Indians (and their imagery) for centuries, presents problems today. With its derivation from *silvaticus* (Latin), cognates *sauvage* (French), *salvage* (Spanish), *selvaggio* (Italian), and the related forms *silva, selva,* and *sylvan*—which have woodland, wooded, forest, and wild among principal meanings—*savage* connoted originally a state of nature.[3] But in their theories of social evolution, nineteenth-century anthropologists and sociologists positioned savages on the earliest and lowest rungs of human society. Overwhelmingly derogatory connotations effaced the original woodland meanings of savage and even survived the now-discredited evolutionary schemes. Today, North American Indians frequently say that they are members of a particular tribal group or nation, or that they are Native Americans, American Indians, or (in particular) just Indians. They also refer to themselves as *native* or *indigenous people,* and sometimes as *aboriginal people.* For these reasons, the term *Noble Indian* (one manifestation of which is the Ecological Indian) is used here for the stereotype or image that others have called *Noble Savage,* and *Indian, native, indigenous,* and other terms are used for the people.[4]

There can be no doubt about the depth of ideas implicit in the image of the Noble Indian. Always present for more than five hundred years (even if overwhelmed by ignoble imagery), Noble Indians have, however, changed in attributes.[5] In their earliest embodiment they were peaceful, carefree, unshackled, eloquent, wise people living innocent, naked lives in a golden world of nature. The origins of nature-dwelling nobles are deep in the ancient world. When Columbus speculated that he found the Islands of the Blessed and their natural residents, his readers were not surprised. They commonly linked several mythic places originating in pagan or Christian thought—notably the Islands of the Blessed, Arcadia, Elysium, the Earthly Paradise, the Garden of Eden, and the Golden Age (collectively ideas of earthly paradise, eternal spring, and innocent life removed in space or time). Allegorical for some but literal for others who located them in geographical space, these places were objects of fancy and search in the New World and elsewhere.

The potency of this imagery as a source of ennobling sentiment over two and one-half centuries simply cannot be overstated, as Europeans drew liberally on it to represent the New World and its inhabitants, in the context of a nostalgic longing for the past and a simpler life. Among many affected by Columbus was Peter Martyr, who compiled accounts of discovery and wrote of an American Indian golden world, and Martyr influenced in turn Amerigo Vespucci's famous depictions of New World lives. For centuries, they and others invoked Tacitus and other ancients, and classical analogs like Scythians (stamped by many as simple, frugal, honest, natural folk) in order to make the indigenous people of the New World comprehensible to themselves and their audiences. In Virginia, they depicted Indians leading "gentle, loving, and faithful" lives "void of all guile and treason," exactly "after the manner of the Golden Age." Elsewhere they associated primitiveness with virtue in similar scenes.[6]

The French, seizing on liberty and equal access to basic resources as characteristic of "savage" life and important virtues to emulate, were without peer over two centuries in developing an imagery of noble indigenousness. Michel de Montaigne, Baron de Lahontan, and Jean-Jacques Rousseau were especially influential in this process. Montaigne drew widely upon Tacitus, missionaries to the New World, and Tupinambas at the French court both to laud the naturalness of Brazilians and to condemn the French as corrupt, greedy, and vain. He used the New World, one historian remarked, "as a stick for beating the Old."[7] Lahontan invented a natural, noble "Intelligent Savage" named Adario as a literary device to critique the European scene (including those who left him without property). Others copied Lahontan widely, and in the second half of the eighteenth century the Noble Indian ruled, especially in Rousseau's major works presenting "savage" life as simple, communal, happy, free, equal, and pure—as inherently good, and exemplified by America's indigenous people.

Like other synthesizers with perfect timing, Rousseau was a lightning rod for charged feelings opposed to his, and a touchstone for many who subsequently portrayed Indians as gentle, egalitarian, free people living in pure nature—and in sharp contrast to life in the city and in civilization. One train of influence runs toward and converges with the nature poetry of William Wordsworth, Samuel Taylor Coleridge, and others, which located the Noble Indian's day in the past, and a nearly uninterrupted path runs from Wordsworth to James Fenimore Cooper, best-selling author from the early 1820s through the 1840s and arguably the most important nineteenth-century figure for development of the Noble Indian imagery. Cooper's heroes are all in and of nature. Nature herself, a heroine of unsurpassed dimensions, shares the stage with Leatherstocking, the protagonist of heroic proportions in Cooper's most famous novels. Every manner of Indian can be found in Cooper's novels, Noble and Ignoble, each taking on and reproducing the character of their tribes, and Cooper's most famous Indian heroes are dignified, firm, faultless, wise, graceful, sympathetic, intelligent, and of beautiful bodily proportions reminiscent of classical sculpture.

By 1900, skill in nature, an important attribute of Cooper's Noble Indians, encapsulated noble indigenousness. It fit neatly with the day's effort to reform policy in natural resources (water, forests, wildlife, and lands and parks, from which came managed use in the progressive conservation movement), American Indian affairs, and America's youth.

The most important writers for Noble Indians from roughly 1875 through 1940 were Ernest Thompson Seton and—for the first time—an Indian: Charles Eastman (Ohiyesa), a Dakota or Sioux. Their influence was pervasive. With Captain Seth Eastman, the famous soldier-artist, as his maternal grandfather, Eastman took the white man's road to Dartmouth College and Boston University Medical School. After marriage—his wife was a self-described Yankee nonconformist, avowed romantic, and vivid and accomplished writer—Eastman wrote more than ten best-selling books that ennobled Indians both by resurrecting romantic visions of lives long past and by emphasizing skills in nature, or woodcraft. Eastman sometimes pointedly apposed an idyllic past with a demoralizing present (even if the present was a way station to a positive civilized future), and contrasted Indians who kill animals because they need them with whites who kill them wantonly. In perhaps his most famous work, *The Soul of the Indian*, Eastman first paid homage to Coleridge, and then painted his boyhood with his relatives as natural, altruistic, and reverent, and his current life as artificial, selfish, and materialistic.[8]

Both Cooper and Eastman influenced Ernest Thompson Seton, first Chief Scout of the Boy Scouts and charismatic naturalist, artist, author, public speaker, conservationist, and youth-movement activist who reached millions through his writings and activities. One of Seton's major goals was to instill manhood in boys through woodcraft or outdoor life exemplified by Cooper's "Ideal Indian." Eastman's talk of the need to form character through fishing, signaling, making fire, constructing canoes, forecasting weather, and other skills—what he called the "School of Savagery" or the "natural way"[9]—dovetailed with Seton's aims. And Seton's Ideal Indian was like Eastman's: He was kind, hospitable, cheerful, obedient, reverent, clean, chaste, brave, courteous, honest, sober, thrifty, and provident; he condemned accumulation, waste, and wanton slaughter; and he held land, animals, and all property in common, thereby curbing greed and closing the gulf between rich and poor.

The imagery of Noble Indians shifted again during the extraordinary era of 1963–73, known primarily for violent antiwar and civil rights movements, assassination, and societal upheaval, when bitter battles were also waged over pesticides, oil spills, flammable rivers, industrial and human waste, and related environmental issues. It was during this period that the Crying Indian came to the fore, reinforcing both practical and ideological slants present in the work of Seton, Eastman, and other predecessors.

New Ecological Indians exploded onto the scene. As critics linked many current global predicaments to industrial society, spoke openly of earlier less complex times as being more environmentally friendly, and castigated Christianity for anthropocentrism, they marshaled Ecological Indians (as deployment of the Crying Indian makes clear) to the support of environmental and antitechnocratic causes.[10]

Ecological Indians constituted fertile soil for those seeking alternative "countercultural" lives. In the back-to-nature movement, many sought communal life shot through with American Indian tribal metaphors and material culture, as well as native religion—or any religious tradition, in fact, perceived as more in tune with ecology and in harmony with nature. Greenpeace marked the convergence of ecology, environmentalism, critique of the social order, and images of American Indians as ecological prophets. More widely, environmentalists joined American Indians in their vision quests and struggles, and thought of themselves as "tribalists." In their conscious antitechnocratic critique of Western society, Rousseau was reborn.

American Indians embraced the new shift in perception and actively helped construct the new image of themselves. At occupied Alcatraz Island, they argued for social and political rights and advocated forming an Indian center of ecology. A new canon emerged: best-selling native texts in which nature and the environment figured significantly, and that critiqued, implicitly or explicitly, white civilization. Several crossed over notably with the environmental movement, and the new canon's expressions of an animistic world have affected many. By far most influential was *Black Elk Speaks*, the nineteenth-century biographical, historical, and visionary reminiscences of a Lakota holy man as told to John G. Neihardt, a poet who believed that literature existed to show people how to "live together decently on this planet." Published in 1932 to no stir, this work was rediscovered in the late 1960s and propelled by events into a widely reprinted and translated instant classic.[11]

Since those tumultuous days, Noble Indians have saturated public culture. They grace the covers of fiction and nonfiction best-sellers, and pervade children's literature. They leap from movies and television screens, fill canvases, take shape in sculptures, find expression in museum and gallery exhibitions, animate dance and other performances, and appear on T-shirts. Time and again the dominant image is of the Indian in nature who understands the systemic consequences of his actions, feels deep sympathy with all living forms, and takes steps to conserve so that earth's harmonies are never imbalanced and resources never in doubt.

This is the Ecological Indian. Exemplifying him, the Crying Indian brims over with ecological prescience and wisdom. On matters involving the environment, he is pure and white people are polluting. He cries because he feels a sense of loss, as (he silently proclaims) other American Indians do also. And if he could cry because he and others lived in nature without disturbing its harmonies (or throwing trash upon it), then he possessed authority to speak out against pollution.

The immediate forces that brought the Crying Indian into existence, as well as the long history of images of nobility preceding this one, have borne considerable fruit. The Ecological Indian has influenced humanitarians concerned about the global environment and health, so-called deep and spiritual ecologists, metaphysicians and new biologists interested in the Gaia hypothesis of an organic earth, ecofeminists, the Rainbow Family and other alternative groups, and self-help advocates.[12] Historians and other scholars have called Indians "the first" American environmentalists or ecologists to "respect" environmental limits and the "need to restrain human impact," to possess "the secret of how to live in harmony with Mother Earth, to use what she offers without hurting her," and to "[preserve] a wilderness ecological balance wheel."[13] Finally (and not least), in Hollywood, the Ecological Indian has become today's orthodoxy to reach millions, as the creators of the Lakotas in *Dances with Wolves* or of the animated Pocahontas, who talks to Grandmother Willow, the tree, and sings about herons and otters who "are my friends" and the "hoop that never ends," play on their presumed closeness to nature, nobility, and ecological sainthood.

Few visual or textual representations of the Native North American have been as persistent over time as this one has, in one form or another, and few others are as embedded in native identity today. The Ecological Indian has embraced conservation, ecology, and environmentalism; has been premised on a spiritual, sacred attitude toward land and animals, not a practical utilitarian one; and has been applied in North America to all indigenous people.

Explicit at several notable moments in the history of Noble Indians (as in the eighteenth century and today), and in the gaze of the Crying Indian, is the fact that the image usually stands against, not alone. Habitually coupled with its opposite, the Nonecological White Man, the Ecological Indian proclaims both that the American Indian is a nonpolluting ecologist, conservationist, and environmentalist, and that the white man is not. "The Indian," Vine Deloria, Jr., a Lakota author and lawyer, has remarked, "lived with his land." In contrast, "*The white destroyed his land. He destroyed the planet earth.*"[14]

But what does it mean to say that Indians are ecologists or conservationists? Because they are the most consistent attributes of the image of the Ecological Indian, the concepts should be defined with care. Embedded in them are certain cultural premises about the meanings of humanity, nature, animate, inanimate, system, balance, and harmony, and their suitability for indigenous American Indian thought or behavior should not be taken as a given.

Ecology, to start with, which is concerned mainly with interactions or interrelations between organisms and the animate and inanimate environments in which they live, has a distinct disciplinary history in which systemic balance, stability, and harmony have been central to ecological metaphors and premises. The idea of a well-regulated nature or of a balance in nature derives from antiquity, and through the centuries has been linked with different divine plans. In the seventeenth century, the balance was connected to God's harmony, and from that time until the late twentieth century, balance and harmony have remained central despite a major paradigmatic change from religion to science in comprehending the natural world. When George Perkins Marsh published *Man and Nature; Or, Physical Geography as Modified by Human Action*, one of the most critical early works for the development of both conservation and ecology, in 1864, the title initially contemplated was *Man the Disturber of Nature's Harmonies.* For Marsh and many others, nature in the absence of man was self-regulating, in balance, or in equilibrium; and man if he were "imprudent" could "[disturb] harmonies," producing "exhausted regions."[15]

Over the last twenty-five years, ecology has been in ferment. For those who favor rigorous, quantitative methodologies and replicable results, proof that balance, stability, or harmony exists has been elusive. Ecologists have abandoned these and other long-held assumptions in favor of chaotic dynamics in systems, and long-term disequilibrium and flux. The ferment is due to the recognition that organisms are as likely to behave unpredictably as predictably; that in the absence of human interference (if that is possible), natural systems are not inherently balanced or harmonious; and that left alone, biological communities do not automatically undergo predictable succession toward some steady-state climax community, which is an illusion. Natural systems, today's ecologists emphasize, are open systems on which random external events like fire or tempest have unpredictable impacts. As the biologist Daniel Botkin emphasized, "Change now appears to be intrinsic and natural at many scales of time and place in the biosphere."[16]

The implications of this fundamental shift in thought for assumptions about the very people perceived as part of nature, the indigenous people of North America and elsewhere, are profound. In a balanced, harmonious, steady-state nature, indigenous people reproduced balance and harmony. In an open nature in which balance and climax are questionable, they become, like all people, dynamic forces whose impact, subtle or not, cannot be assumed.

Some who write about environmentalism use the term *ecology* where they mean "environmental"—as in ecology movement. This unfortunate confusion unnecessarily conflates a scientific discipline with a moral and political cause, and muddies the definition of *ecology*. In this book the two terms are kept separate. *Environmentalism* has distinct meanings ranging from the belief that the environment and its components have basic rights to remain unmolested, to the idea that technological change and sustainable growth are compatible with proper care for the environment. One of the most inclusive—and, because of its breadth, useful—definitions of environmentalism is "ideologies and practices which inform and flow from a concern for the environment."[17]

When speaking of Native Americans as ecologists, we do not necessarily mean that they used mathematical or hypothetico-deductive techniques, but we should mean that they have understood and thought about the environment and its interrelating components in systemic ways (even if the system, all increasingly agree, is more metaphor than hard and bounded reality). When we speak of them as environmentalists, we presumably mean showing concern for the state of the environment and perhaps acting on that concern.[18]

Conservation, the second major attribute of the Ecological Indian, has also acquired different meanings through time, some of which (like the very general idea of "prudent husbanding") have ancient roots. Moreover, as with ecology and environmentalism, *conservation* has often been conflated with *preservation*—as in conservation as "preservation from destructive influences, natural decay or waste."[19]

Yet it makes sense to differentiate conservation from preservation. At the turn of the twentieth century, at least two separate camps debated conservation and preservation issues (the debates continue today). The most famous pitted Gifford Pinchot, widely regarded as the founder of contemporary conservationist policy in America, against John Muir, the preservationist. The two fought over the fate of Hetch Hetchy, a canyon in Yosemite National Park that thirsty urbanites wanted to make useful by a dam and lake. Pinchot and Muir battled heatedly, Muir's preservation assuming the sacral pristineness of nature and Pinchot's conservation privileging rational planning and efficient use: two very different approaches to environmental relations. Pinchot, who was Theodore Roosevelt's forestry chief, won the day even though Roosevelt had left office by the time Congress legislated damming Hetch Hetchy.[20]

In 1910, Pinchot wrote that conservation's "first principle" was "development, the use of the natural resources now existing on this continent for the benefit of the people who live here now." The second was "the prevention of waste," and the third that "natural resources must be developed and preserved for the benefit of the many, and not merely for the profit of a few."[21] Conservationists, as one observer noted in 1970, were "fairly united in attacking instances of apparent waste or unwise use." Waste or unwise use included obtaining products in a manner that proved destructive to the environment when a nondestructive method would do, obtaining less than the maximum sustained yield from resources, ignoring useful by-products of extractive processes, and using energy resources inefficiently.[22]

Today, conservation is defined in different ways. Some regard it as management "of human use of the biosphere so that it may yield the greatest sustainable benefit to present generations while maintaining its potential to meet the needs and aspirations of future generations." Others emphasize that it means "all that man thinks and does to soften his impact upon his natural environment and to satisfy all his own true needs while enabling that environment to continue in healthy working order."[23]

Narrower definitions—by Bryan Norton and John Passmore, respectively, both philosophers—focus on conservation as using a resource "wisely, with the goal of maintaining its future availability or productivity," or as saving "natural resources for later consumption." The conservationist promotes careful husbandry and sustainable development; if he opposes anything, it is waste. The emphasis in preservation is quite different, "a saving *from* rather than a saving *for*" as in conservation, according to Passmore; specifically "the saving of species and wilderness from damage or destruction." For Norton, preservation is protecting "an ecosystem or a species, to the extent possible, from the disruptions attendant upon it from human use." The preservationist, in other words, seeks to keep habitats from further deterioration or use even for purposes of conservation.[24]

If we describe a Native American as a conservationist, we do not mean that he calculates sustainable yield into the distant future or, in a preservationist-like manner, leaves the environment in an undisturbed, pristine state, but rather that he does not waste or "despoil, exhaust, or extinguish," and that he does, with deliberation, leave the environment and resources like animal populations in a usable state for succeeding generations.[25]

People everywhere creatively construct meaningful frameworks for understanding their past; they everywhere actively invent tradition. "History," as Greg Dening, a historian, reminded us, "is both a metaphor of the past and metonym of the present." No matter who their authors may be, narratives about the Native American past must be read in this light. As Edward Bruner, an anthropologist, underscored, narratives about Native North Americans are contingent on the times in which they were created. They mirror relations between Native Americans and people of European descent. They reflect not just changing national governmental policies toward indigenous people, but understandings of native people that vary from one moment to the next. Given that traditions are often fashioned creatively, it seems unwise to assume uncritically that the image of the Ecological Indian faithfully reflects North American Indian behavior at any time in the past.[26]

Quite the reverse: For while this image may occasionally serve or have served useful polemical or political ends, images of noble and ignoble indigenousness, including the Ecological Indian, are ultimately dehumanizing. They deny both variation within human groups and commonalities between them. As the historian Richard White remarked, the idea that Indians left no traces of themselves on the land "demeans Indians. It makes them seem simply like an animal species, and thus deprives them of culture."[27] In a related vein, Henry M. Brackenridge, a lawyer with archaeology as his avocation, remarked some 180 years ago on a voyage on the Missouri River how "mistaken" are those "who look for primitive innocence and simplicity in what they call the state of nature." As he traveled along the Missouri, Brackenridge mused on the "moral character" of Indians he encountered: "They have amongst them their poor, their envious, their slanderers, their mean and crouching, their haughty and overbearing, their unfeeling and cruel, their weak and vulgar, their dissipated and wicked; and they have also, their brave and wise, their generous and magnanimous, their rich and hospitable, their pious and virtuous, their frank, kind, and affectionate, and in fact, all the diversity of characters that exists amongst the most refined people." One need not believe that moral or emotional or psychological traits are universal (like most anthropologists today, I would assert that to be human is fundamentally to be a cultural being) to appreciate that no simple stereotype satisfied Brackenridge, who refused to reduce Indians to silhouetted nobility or ignobility.[28]

Yet as its simplistic, seductive appeal works its charm, the Noble Indian persists long beyond memory of when or how it entered currency. At first a projection of Europeans and European-Americans, it eventually became a self-image. American Indians have taken on the Noble Indian/Ecological Indian stereotype, embedding it in their self-fashioning, just as other indigenous people around the world have done with similar primordial ecological and conservationist stereotypes.[29] Yet its relationship to native cultures and behavior is deeply problematic. The Noble Indian/Ecological Indian distorts culture. It masks cultural diversity. It occludes its actual connection to the behavior it purports to explain. Moreover, because it has entered the realm of common sense and as received wisdom is perceived as a fundamental truth, it serves to deflect any desire to fathom or confront the evidence for relationships between Indians and the environment.[30]

To what degree does the image of the Ecological Indian faithfully reflect Native North American ideas through time? To what extent have Native North Americans been ecologists or conservationists? These are the major questions posed in *The Ecological Indian* and explored in chapters that range from the Pleistocene to the present. The intent is not to be encyclopedic but to select specific cases that have been hotly debated and deserve a fresh look. Were human hunters responsible for the extinctions of many large animals at the end of the Pleistocene in North America? Why did people like the Hohokam disappear prior to the arrival of Europeans? Was the human population in North America large enough to make any lasting difference on land and animals? What are the implications of the widespread use of fire in North America? Were Indians who hunted buffalo, white-tailed deer, and beaver—all hunted almost to extinction—interested in conservation as well as in subsistence or commodities? Are native people today ecologists or conservationists?

The Ecological Indian does not pretend to be exhaustive. It is not intended as, nor will it be, the last word on a subject that has attracted an enormous amount of attention over the years. The hope, rather, is that by revisiting and newly analyzing some of the most important and roundly argued cases pertaining to conservation and ecology in native North America, this book will rekindle debate on the fit between one of the most durable images of the American Indian and American Indian behavior, and that it will spawn detailed analyses of the myriad relationships between indigenous people and their environments in North America.

Chapter One

PLEISTOCENE EXTINCTIONS

BEGINNING 11,000 YEARS AGO, at the end of the period known as the Pleistocene, many animal species that had flourished just a short time before vanished from North America. Men and women had been in the New World for only a relatively short time, and scholars have hotly debated the coincidence of their arrival and the extinctions. Paul Martin, a palynologist and geochronologist, spurred the debate more than any other person. When he proclaimed in the late 1960s that "man, and man alone, was responsible" for the extinctions, he set off a firestorm that shows little sign of abating. Branding the ancient Indians—so-called Paleoindians—as super-predators, Martin likened their assault on Pleistocene animals to a *blitzkrieg*, evoking the aggressive, assaulting imagery of the Nazi war machine.[1]

Martin could not have made a more apt word choice for grabbing the public imagination. Over the last three decades "American Blitzkrieg" and "Slaughter of Mastodons Caused Their Extinction" have defined headlines, and writers in popular magazines like *National Geographic* concluded confidently that scientists suspect "man the hunter" as the "villain" in Pleistocene extinctions.[2]

There is no room for the Ecological Indian here. As Martin himself wrote in 1967, "that business of the noble savage, a child of nature, living in an unspoiled Garden of Eden until the 'discovery' of the New World by Europeans is apparently untrue, since the destruction of fauna, if not of habitat, was far greater before Columbus than at any time since." For Martin, that realization is "provocative," "deeply disturbing," and "even revolutionary." To no surprise, Martin's findings fed the conservative press who argued that because of the (supposed) sins of their earliest ancestors, Native North Americans today lack authority to occupy the moral high ground on environmental issues.[3] Martin's ideas have found support and reached a wide audience for over thirty years, but how well do they stand up today?

For well over a century, the consensus in the scientific community has been that Paleoindians, the ancestors of today's American Indians, wandered eastward into North America from northeastern Asia. But among American Indians outside the scientific community, that idea has not met with universal acceptance. Some have taken issue with the idea that their ancestors came initially from Asia. Asked about the origin of the world and human beings, or about the migrations of their ancestors, Indians have sometimes responded that their communities were never anywhere other than where they were at the moment the question was posed. Their ancestors, they said, came into the present world from worlds preceding and beneath the current one, through mouths of caves or from holes in the ground. Other native people believed they had migrated from the east, west, or elsewhere. Some living in the interior of the continent thought that their ancestors once lived far away on the shores of salty seas. In days before they had incorporated European ideas of their origins into their own, American Indians answered questions about their origin and historical movements in as many different voices as there were nations with separate cultures.

Even today native people do not speak with one voice on these or any other issues. Some adhere to contemporary versions of their traditional beliefs. But not all do. Many instead have long since converted to the position favored by archaeologists, paleontologists, and other scientists, that Indians came to the New World from Asia thousands of years ago. Like all scientific explanations, this one is changing based on the steady accumulation of data. Each year new sites or dates offer fresh insight on how and when people came into and spread throughout North and South America. The nature of science is to debate theories and to test and confirm or falsify hypotheses spawned by theories. As with evolution, a long period of shared understanding may be suddenly punctuated by "fresh" insight fitting more seamlessly both new data and the broader historical context in which all scientific thought exists, and a new consensus begins to build. One recent example of this process is illustrated by debates concerning mass extinctions before the Pleistocene, for which there is growing widespread agreement that asteroids—a radical theory when initially proposed—and climate change spelled the end of major orders of living things.[4]

The scientific community's consensus is that when Paleoindians wandered eastward from northeastern Asia to North America, they came across a broad and vast land known as *Beringia.* At the heart of Beringia is a continental shelf that was exposed during lower sea levels of the Pleistocene and is today covered by the Bering and Chukchi seas. In short order, Paleoindians migrated south from Beringia along the west coast or through a corridor between two massive continental ice sheets and spread rapidly to the southern tip of South America.

There was ample time and opportunity during the Pleistocene for Paleoindians to wander from Asia to America through Beringia. The Pleistocene era lasted for two million years, and was marked by periods when temperatures were cool and glaciers advanced and by periods when temperatures were warm and glaciers retreated. During the warmer eras marked by glacial retreats, the sea level was essentially today's, and Asia and North America were separated by a strait as they are today. But during the cooler periods when glaciers advanced, the sea level was lower, continental ice sheets were more expansive, and Beringia was exposed. A drop in the sea of 150 feet below today's level was all that was required to remove the obstacle of a strait and expose Beringia as a landmass. At these times, Asia and North America were joined, even if continental glaciers imposed to the east and south.

The general scheme is not in dispute; the details, not surprisingly, are debated. For example, many discuss precisely when climatic and environmental conditions permitted Paleoindians to cross Beringia—how much earlier than the era of Paleoindian sites that have been securely dated (see below). Even though evidence for human occupation of Siberia during very early times is mounting, there is no evidence that human beings moved across Beringia prior to a cool era beginning some 80,000 years ago. Indeed from 115,000 to 80,000 years ago, the sea level was essentially today's and water blocked movement by land. But from 80,000 to 10,000 years ago there were long periods when temperatures were very cool and the sea level dropped more than 150 feet below its present level, removing the barrier of a strait; at other moments, temperatures were not as cold and a narrow strait remained as an impediment—not, however, if people possessed the technology to cross water or ice. There were two especially welcoming eras during this 70,000-year-long span. The first was from 65,000 to 23,000 years ago, when the strait—if there was one—was even narrower than today and continental ice sheets loomed but evidently were not joined to block passage toward the heart of the continent to the south (for those who headed in that direction). The second was from 23,000 to 10,000 years ago when the sea level was even lower, and a straitless Beringia grew into a broad plain measuring 1,000 miles from north to south.[5]

How inadequate the metaphor of bridge for the landmass that formed between Asia and North America! As a one-thousand-mile-wide plain, the "Bering land bridge," as it has been called, was surely attractive to generations of animals large and small, as well as to people following them. At different places and separate times, Beringia was probably a cold but productive steppe rich in fauna and a colder more barren tundra marked by much lower biological productivity. From 80,000 to 10,000 years ago, its vegetation changed from being adapted to wetter and milder conditions to being more suitable for colder and drier climate and longer ice cover. At the end of the Pleistocene, wetter and warmer conditions caused a rapid buildup of peat and an explosion in the numbers of birch trees in Beringia. At its greatest extent, this landmass was no doubt marked by different vegetation zones from north to south, and in the late Pleistocene by a mosaic of environments and species. For human predators, the most important characteristic may have been the abundant graze afforded by grassy vegetation for mammoths, bisons, and horses.[6]

For most of the time when Beringia was at its greatest expanse from 23,000 to 10,000 years ago, beyond it to the south and east coastal glaciers loomed and two massive ice sheets covered much of Canada. When they were at their maximum extent 18,000 years ago, the ice sheets encased Canada and the Great Lakes. But as temperatures warmed, they retreated, and waters released from them and from shrinking polar ice caps raised sea levels. After several thousand years, Beringia flooded, Bering Strait re-formed, and human migration between the Old and New World took place henceforth only across water or on ice. For the story of migration into the heart of

North America, however, these changes mattered little. Men and women were already in the New World, and the major problem they faced was how to move south. One route was along the coast; some archaeologists argue that this route was the major and the earliest one. Another was through an inland gap or corridor from interior Alaska through the Yukon Territory, British Columbia, and Alberta—along the eastern flanks of the Rocky Mountains. The corridor formed some 13,000 to 11,000 years ago as the continental ice sheets pulled back from each other, allowing men and women, when conditions were optimal, to migrate into the heart of North America. Both routes marked the way into environments like today's but for their location farther south. Bordering the ice sheet was a narrow zone of periglacial tundra, south of which was boreal forest and mixed coniferous and deciduous forests in the East and plains in the West, and desert farther south. Each of these major environments contained grazers, browsers, and predators that would soon be extinct.[7]

The extinctions were remarkable by any measure. Animals familiar and unfamiliar, widespread and local, and large and small disappeared. Some were well-known creatures like lemmings, salamanders, and various birds. But many were not, and they constituted a fabulous bestiary. The mammals, especially the ones that were unfamiliar and large, have attracted great attention. How many mammalian species disappeared will probably always be unknown because of uncertainty over species boundaries, but at least thirty-five mammalian genera vanished.

Mammals weighing more than one hundred pounds that became extinct have drawn intense interest partly because of their assumed attractiveness to human hunters. For one familiar only with today's North American fauna, these so-called megafauna (literally, large animals) were exceptional. They included exotic hulking tusked mammoths and mastodons that roamed prairies and boggy woodlands, respectively, towering elephant-like over almost all else. Several types of slow-moving, giant ground sloths ranging in size from several hundred pounds to twenty feet long in the same weight range as the mammoths also vanished. So did rhinocerous-sized pampatheres, a kind of giant armadillo, and armored two-thousand-pound, six-foot-long glyptodonts resembling nothing known today.

Many herbivores disappeared, including single-hump camels, stocky six-foot-long capybaras, five-hundred-pound tapirs, three-hundred-pound giant beavers, four-horned antelopes, horses, bison-sized shrub oxen, and stag-moose with fantastic multiple-palmated and tined antlers. Carnivores also died out, including dire wolves whose large heads and powerful jaws made them resemble hyenas and huge fearsome fifteen-hundred-pound short-faced bears that were slim and possibly very quick and agile. Two large serrated-toothed cats vanished: scimitar-toothed cats that fed on mammoth young, and great saber-toothed cats that could gape, shark-like, opening their jaws to a one-hundred-degree angle before stabbing or ripping open prey with their enormous canines.

All vanished. The end for many came between 11,000 and 10,000 years ago, a watershed millennium that opened with the disappearance of many members of the amazing bestiary and closed with the demise of the remaining camels, horses, mammoths, mastodons, and other megafauna.[8]

These species entered oblivion in a geological blink. The big question is why, which returns us to Martin's proclamation, "Man, and man alone, was responsible." Can we accept this? In his search for proof, Martin marshaled the power of simulation to his side. On the basis of assumptions about when Paleoindians arrived south of the continental ice sheets, population growth and movement, and kill rates, he and his co-workers simulated the rapid human movement and killings—the "blitzkrieg." In one scenario, one hundred Paleoindians arrived on the Alberta prairies some 12,000 years ago. Each year, they moved southward just twenty miles and killed only one dozen animals per person. They also reproduced, doubling their population every twenty years. Except for the reproduction rate, the assumptions underlying these figures seem fairly modest. Yet based on them, Paleoindians in only three hundred years numbered 100,000, spread two thousand miles south, and killed over ninety million one-thousand-pound animals. Using more conservative assumptions in other simulations, Martin and others argued that it still took relatively few years to reach first the Gulf of Mexico and then Tierra del Fuego at the tip of South America, and to hunt megafauna to their doom.[9]

The thesis has proved seductive—and resilient. Granted, the overwhelming image one gets from Martin's blitzkrieg is of restless Paleoindians constantly on the move. Hunting people, they were always on the go along a "front" (as in a military campaign). They expanded methodically, killing a mammoth here, a mastodon there, a glyptodont one day, a dim-witted giant ground sloth or cumbersome giant beaver the next. Martin argued that men (and women) arrived in the New World with knowledge of hunting large animals, but these same animals lacked experience with human predators and thus did not fear them, and so hunters left megafaunal extinctions in their wake. They ate little but megafaunal meat and wasted up to half of what they killed. Singularly focused on big game, they ignored fish, shellfish, plants, and other less dramatic sources of food. They moved fast, killed efficiently, and were fecund. Critics, scoffing at overly generous assumptions about kill rates, population growth, and population movement that depart from cautious, reasonable inferences from twentieth-century hunting-gathering peoples, complain that Paleoindians were too successful.[10]

Martin speculated that Paleoindians were successful in part because they were newly arrived in the New World, and animals lacked fear of them as predators and did not develop an awareness of how fatal their encounters with them would be until it was too late. When Martin first proposed his thesis some thirty years ago, archaeologists generally accepted that humans were in the New World 10,000 to 11,000 years ago but not much earlier. Today, as a result of a flurry of activity on early sites, it appears likely that Indians reached southern South America some 12,500 years ago, and a new consensus is emerging over an arrival date in the New World of 13,000 to 14,000 years ago. An arrival time of any earlier is sharply disputed. The lines are clearly drawn between most archaeologists, who are uncomfortable with dates earlier than roughly 14,000 years ago, and a vocal, persistent minority asserting that Paleoindians reached the New World 30,000 or 40,000 years ago. While linguistic, dental, and genetic theories lend support to the older dates, it is currently doubtful that a precise chronology can be derived from these theories. In the meantime, the earliest dated sites are plagued by various methodological problems. This debate will not be solved to everyone's satisfaction anytime soon, but at this stage it seems prudent to remain skeptical of dates earlier than 14,000 years ago.[11]

Animals like slow-moving, sluggish ground sloths must have been especially vulnerable to human predation, but animals with far more presumed agility than gigantic sloths disappeared too. Martin's argument that the superpredators killed them all easily and quickly because they lacked time to develop fear is weakened both by the likelihood that Paleoindians arrived 1,000 to 3,000 years before the watershed millennium when most megafaunal animals vanished and by the fact that prey do not always fear human hunters (animals like buffaloes or pronghorn antelopes survived into the modern era alongside humans, despite a reputation of being so bold or so intensely curious that hunters rather easily killed them). It is as reasonable to suggest that Paleoindians played a greater role in the extinctions the longer they were in North America.

If only there were numerous archaeological sites with associated extinct megafauna to test Martin's thesis of overkill. But there are only fifty or so sites—a mere handful. At them, Paleoindians killed and butchered mastodons, mammoths, camels, horses, four-horned antelopes, tapirs, and a couple of other extinct species. Amazingly, Martin used the paucity of sites to help buttress his claim that a blitzkrieg marked the onslaught: "Perhaps the only remarkable aspect of New World archaeology is that *any* kill sites have been found," he once remarked, reasoning from the assumption that Paleoindians killed animals whenever they came across them and therefore the kill sites were scattered and ephemeral. For Martin, a negative (the absence of sites) proves a positive (man killed fearless animals in a blitzkrieg). Martin's unequivocal certainty that man alone was responsible seems remarkable in light of this alone.[12]

For Martin's image of restless, relentless Paleoindians to ring true and for the overkill thesis to work, Paleoindians had to be everywhere, required to focus energy and time on megafauna. Unfortunately for Martin, this simply does not fit our most sensible speculations today about Paleoindian adaptations. For too long, archaeologists interested in this period focused myopically, if understandably, on one type of technology referred to as *Clovis*, whose archetypal artifact is an impressive spear point from three to six inches long and supremely adapted to wounding or delivering the coup de grace to large animals. Archaeologists looking for Paleoindian remains have been attracted most often to bone sites where they have found these fluted points and concluded (not surprisingly) that Paleoindians were hunters, and perhaps hunters only.

But we now know that Paleoindian technology cannot be reduced everywhere to spear points used by their makers in an exclusive search for megafauna. And it is inconceivable that in every climate and in every era, the makers of fluted points possessed precisely the same culture or practiced identical gathering and hunting strategies. For some years now the evidence has mounted for very different Paleoindian technologies and adaptive strategies in North America (indeed, throughout the New World). In the West, people used not only Clovis points but also a variety of large and small fluted and nonfluted projectile points. Undeniably, some Paleoindians may have been deliberate or opportunistic hunters of the megafauna that became extinct, but others were probably hunters of caribou, deer, beaver, and small animals. In the tundra, parkland, and mixed forest environments in the East, Indians killed many caribou and some mastodons. But in forested regions, they also exploited species like tortoises—which also disappeared—and other small animals. Many North American Indians were probably generalized foragers whose diet included seeds, roots, shellfish, and fish. In their adaptations they may well have been similar to their contemporaries in Chile, who gathered shellfish and plants and hunted small mammals—and lacked Clovis technology.

Because of inadequate or expensive techniques of archaeological recovery, as well as poor preservation, much remains unknown about Paleoindian life, including how near the fit was to our contemporary understanding of hunter-gatherers as people with extensive and variable interest in seeds, fish, roots, shellfish, birds, and other such foods. In the twentieth century, people who gathered and hunted for their livelihood (who provide one way to think about Paleoindians at the end of the Pleistocene) have shown quite extraordinary variation in subsistence and social patterns, especially in environments as different as the various North American ones. Foraging people possess food preferences, but rather than restrict their hunting strategies to single classes of animals, many hunt animals that minimize the cost of their effort relative to their gain. For them, the consequences of hunting for the viability of a species are as likely to be accidental as deliberate. There is no reason to assume that Paleoindians in North America were any different.[13]

Of no help either to Martin's argument that only man the megafaunal hunter figured in the Pleistocene extinctions is that minifaunal as well as megafaunal animals vanished. Some were possibly relevant to Paleoindian diets or habits if people were generalized hunters and foragers, and some seem completely irrelevant. Relatively little is known about insects and plants, but at least ten genera (and many more species) of birds disappeared. They ranged widely in size and type from a jay to a flamingo. One was a shelduck, which like other waterfowl was probably easily killed while undergoing molt, when it could not readily fly. Another was a lapwing and no doubt tasty. Other birds included a condor, caracara, and vultures, all probable scavengers of grassland carcasses. There were other raptors, including eagles or hawk-eagles, and jays and cowbirds. Martin tried to explain all the extinct birds away by analogy with contemporary scavenging species in commensal or dependent relations with animals similar to Pleistocene ones that became extinct. But the behavior of the extinct Pleistocene genera was not necessarily identical to that of the living birds presumably related to them. Curiously, approximately the same percentage of birds disappeared as megafauna, even though in Martin's theory Paleoindians were interested only in megafauna. This coincidence alone suggests that we look elsewhere for causes before we conclude that humans alone were responsible for Pleistocene extinctions.[14]

The relevance of climate to these events has at times been too casually dismissed. Climate changes were pervasive at the end of the Pleistocene. Temperatures warmed by roughly thirteen degrees Fahrenheit, and the climate became drier overall. Affecting animals and plants more than higher temperatures and increased aridity, however, was probably the rise in seasonal temperature extremes. Winters became colder and summers hotter. In these new conditions, grasses and other plants, insects, and other organisms most directly dependent on temperature and precipitation either flourished or did not, as did invertebrate and vertebrate organisms in turn. Entire habitats changed rapidly at the end of the Pleistocene. In the Upper Midwest, spruce forest became pine forest almost overnight in geological time. For animals with firm boreal forest associations, such as mastodons, the consequences might have been dire. In some areas, grasses withered under drier conditions. With climatic and vegetational changes, small animals altered their distribution, retreating to areas where conditions remained tolerable. Through death or emigration, some animals abandoned the southern, desiccating parts of their ranges; herpetiles (snakes and tortoises) in particular changed theirs. At present, there is much we do not know about the consequences of these climatic and vegetational changes. For some species, there may have been less food. For some, grasses may have become more difficult to metabolize, or even toxic. Perhaps gestation changed. Although hypotheses such as a failure of enzyme systems abound, the causal chain between climate change and extinction remains unclear. The sequences are not clear today. Despite the focus on biotic properties and dynamics, we simply do not know enough about the specific properties of particular extinct forms. We may never know enough.[15]

Although much is conjectural, the emphasis on climate and attendant vegetational changes focuses discussion of the extinctions away from communities and on each specific species or genus that changed its range according to its tolerance to the changes. If extinctions are considered on a case-by-case basis, then factors like biomass, reproductive biology, overspecialization, feeding strategies, dependencies, and competition between species come to the fore as being in part responsible for a particular species's vulnerability. Some species have low rates of increase and others high rates. Some have long gestation periods, others short ones. Some have long lives, others brief lives. Some, because of their reproductive biology or social habits, are more vulnerable to extinction than others in a changing climate. The replacement of wet plant communities by dry plant communities in montane habitats will eliminate certain species. Climate changes might have destroyed a particular patchiness in habitat supposedly enjoyed by species like mammoths (on which human hunters also focused their energies). The timing of extinctions was surely important but has not been adequately worked out. Did large grazing animals, for example, become extinct before smaller ones in the same habitat? In large numbers, herbivores weighing over one ton can transform the environment. Once they are extinct, however, the floral composition of habitats can change to affect smaller grazing animals to the point of extinction. That the answers to these questions are currently ambiguous does not mean that they should not be pursued, on a species-by-species, genus-by-genus, habitat-by-habitat, or ecosystem-by-ecosystem basis.[16]

Climate presents a formidable obstacle to the exclusionary nature of Martin's thesis. Climate, after all, has been linked to the rapid evolution of mammalian forms. Moreover, in earlier extinction episodes that closely rivaled the late-Pleistocene one but took place long before man the superpredator arrived on the scene, climate overwhelmed plants and animals. Six other extinction events marked the last ten million years in North America. None was caused by Paleoindians, who did not yet exist. But it is a good bet that climate was involved, and there are marked similarities in climatic deterioration and extinctions of the late Pleistocene and the preceding era, the late Pliocene. Even though causation is far from clear, temperature and other climatic and sea-level fluctuations are correlated with these other extinctions, and they and other episodes make extinction seem normal, not abnormal, in the history of life. Indeed, most species that ever lived are extinct.[17]

The climatic changes at the end of the Pleistocene alone must have been sufficient to overwhelm certain animals and plants unable to adapt under altered conditions. Desiccation by itself imperiled animals forced to come to the remaining sources of water. Either animals moved to where conditions remained favorable, or they were left susceptible to a Paleoindian coup de grace, or they were weakened to the point of eventual disappearance without helping human hands.

If climate fatally complicates the simplistic idea that humans alone were blamable for the extinctions, there is still too much we fail to understand about climate to ascribe responsibility to it alone. Perhaps we will be able to say one day with near 100 percent certainty that climate change triggered interactions that were ultimately destructive to the majority of extinct Pleistocene species. But that day has not yet arrived. In the meantime, because it is naive to think that any single factor was solely responsible for all Pleistocene extinctions, it is safest not to rule out a role for Native Americans altogether. To deny human agency would be as foolhardy as Martin's ruling out climate. Only strict adherence to the belief that modern industrial societies alone cause significant ecological change would lead us to that position. It makes as much sense to hypothesize that Paleoindians pushed certain species already heading toward their doom over the edge to extinction. After all, Paleoindians and a distinctive hunting technology were widespread, and the association of their artifacts with animal remains does show a taste for species now extinct.[18]

Another reason for the plausibility of a scenario in which Paleoindians played some role is that preindustrial humans have caused extinctions in other times and places. Throughout the Pacific, indigenous people had a severe impact on birds. They exterminated literally thousands of species well before the arrival of Europeans.[19]

The Hawaiian archipelago presents a classic case. There, native people altered the habitat so that it met their needs and conformed to their cultural expectations—so thoroughly that extinctions followed in their wake. Ancient Hawaiians cleared land with fire and diverted streams for irrigation, and crop plants and extensive grasslands took over what had been forested coastal areas. Fish ponds emerged where there had been mudflats. Hawaiians introduced dogs, pigs, chickens, and—inadvertently—rats and reptiles that had stowed away on their canoes. As a result of these introductions and radical changes in the habitat, over forty species of birds (well over half of all endemic bird species) became extinct. Some, especially those that could not fly, the ancient Hawaiians ate: petrels, flightless geese, ibises, rails, a hawk, and crow. Others like honeycreepers, other finches, and a thrush vanished as their habitats disappeared or as their feathers came into demand to ornament clothing.[20]

New Zealand presents a second compelling case. As in Hawaii, early Polynesian colonizers—the predecessors of today's Maori—deployed fire to transform New Zealand's environment. They also hunted at least thirteen species of moas—ostrich-like flightless birds, one of which towered over men and women—to extinction. They killed adult birds in large quantities and gourmandized their eggs. They left necks and skulls unused—wasted parts they discarded. In the end, no moas survived, and these ancient Polynesians turned their attention to what was left—shellfish, fish, seals, and small birds.[21]

The human hand is deeply implicated in the extinction of avifauna in Hawaii, New Zealand, and other Pacific islands. Of course, North America is not a small island. Nor were Paleoindian societies organized or structured in the same way as early Polynesian ones. Nor do we imagine that Paleoindians transformed or fragmented habitats, or introduced predators, as early Hawaiians did. Nevertheless, a human role should not be ruled out in any case, and there is no good reason to bar humans from at least a supporting part in North American Pleistocene extinctions.

Perhaps the very large island of Madagascar provides a better model than smaller islands for what happened at the end of the North American Pleistocene. After the Indonesian–East African ancestors of the Malagasy settled Madagascar, large flightless birds, giant tortoises, hippopotami, more than fifteen species of lemurs (some of which were the size of gorillas), and other animals disappeared. Although some have blamed humans alone for this loss, it seems more likely that men and women arrived on this island at a moment of drought in a long-term climatic cycle oscillating from wet to dry, and that this in combination doomed more species than either humans, desiccation, or vegetation changes alone could have.[22]

In view of the evidence that recently came to light to support these island cases, Martin's theory that humans played a significant role in Pleistocene extinctions in North America may be more readily understood, but his continued assertiveness insisting that theirs was the only role that mattered is not. The evidence for the human role in the late-Pleistocene extinctions is circumstantial, and climatic change was fundamental and potentially far-reaching. There is still much we do not know about how and why animals responded to climate changes, but on Madagascar and Hawaii and other Pacific islands, both climate and human-induced changes played a role in the demise of animals. Multiple causes provide the best explanation.

Vine Deloria, Jr., recently spoke contemptuously of "mythical Pleistocene hit men" (and angrily vilified scientific methodology and authority), preferring in their place earthquakes, volcanoes, and floods of Indian legend. He theorized that such catastrophes not only occurred but somehow had continental reach to cause the extinctions.[23] But the Pleistocene extinctions continue to defy sound-bite simplification. Closer to the time when a fuller historical record can significantly inform interpretation, we turn to a case that also involves disappearance, not of animals but of people: the Hohokam, who lived in urban communities where Phoenix and Tucson sprawl today in the Arizonan Sonoran Desert.

Chapter Two

THE HOHOKAM

NAMED FOR THE PHOENIX of Egyptian mythology, Phoenix, Arizona, drew its first breath in ashes. It took shape among the ruins of people known as the Hohokam, on the banks of the Salt River in the late-nineteenth-century Arizona Territory. Precisely who the Hohokam were is not clear. There is no written record of Indians ever dwelling in their ruins. The Akimel O'odham, who had been living for several hundred years along the Gila River to the south and rarely ventured to the Salt River, seemed to be of two minds: Some said that they were related to the Hohokam; others said that they were not and that the Hohokam disappeared long before Americans or Spanish arrived. The meaning of *Hohokam* is ambiguous; it is not the same as *'ó'odham*, "people" or "human beings," which the Akimel O'odham use for themselves. Translated as both "ancient" and "extinct" or "finished ones," the term *hohokam* might originally have been intended either for one's relatives or for unrelated people. The Akimel O'odham say that the dead are "hohokam," gone or vanished; that Hohokam towns—long since ruins—are "hohokam," all used up; that when a tire on a pickup truck is blown, it is "hohokam," finished. Perhaps, as the Akimel O'odham suggested, the Hohokam were "those who have gone," and their way of life and society "that which has perished."[1]

Why did the Hohokam disappear? They left behind the largest canal system in native North America. The most persistent explanation throughout the twentieth century is that they irrigated themselves to death by delivering saline waters to saline fields and destroying crops too salt sensitive for the man-made environment. The explanation has had remarkable staying power, reaching even the wider public through essays in periodicals designed for general consumption like *Journal of the West*, in which one archaeologist charged in the late 1980s that the Hohokam delivered "mineral-laden" river water to farmlands, causing a hard deposit of salts and other minerals called *caliche* to form. With soils rendered infertile as an "unforeseen" consequence of irrigation farming, the "onetime Hohokam success" ended and their way of life dissolved. Put otherwise, the Hohokam, uncomprehending the nature of their ecosystem, failed to understand the systemic consequences of their actions. They upset whatever balance existed between themselves and their environment—if indeed balance ever existed or is not itself illusory. "Were these America's first ecologists?," this archaeologist asked. His answer was a resounding "No."[2]

Not all agree. Focusing not on the disappearance of the Hohokam but on their centuries-long persistence in a demanding environment, a second scholar—Emil Haury, the best-known archaeologist of these people—proclaimed in the late 1960s and early 1970s that the Hohokam who lived in the urban setting called Snaketown possessed "an uncanny ability . . . to read the resources of the environment." That they disappeared inexplicably was irrelevant. What mattered was that they evolved a "nearly perfect adaptation to a desert homeland," which they were able to achieve because of irrigation—"the basis for inspiring the settlement and subjugation of the arid valleys of the Gila and the Salt Rivers."[3]

Does "truth" rest with either of these two positions? They present opposite images of the Hohokam. In the first, the Hohokam were blind to ecology. They were not, as popular culture would have Indians be, primeval ecologists. At best, they may have possessed an ecological (systemic) understanding of their environment but were unwilling or unable to act on their knowledge. Their disappearance is testament to their failure. In the second position, regardless of their final disposition, the Hohokam adapted for thousands of years and are accordingly held up as ecological exemplars.

All this in a region where the population has grown explosively in recent years, demanding housing, freeways, and services, and where archaeology has been lively due to federal and state laws requiring mitigation of the impact of construction on archaeological sites. Over the past two decades, the laws have not saved Hohokam sites destined for physical oblivion, but have guaranteed at least that sites be excavated before they are consumed by new construction. One project alone unearthed a small part of a Hohokam town called La Ciudad, which lay in the path of a freeway. Over the course of a year, a crew of fifty excavated more than two hundred houses and burials, more than one hundred trash pits, almost three hundred test pits, and a couple of canals, and another thirty people washed, sorted, and catalogued more than 700,000 artifacts. For over a century, archaeologists have had much to say about the Hohokam, but now they can say a great deal more than ever before about their environment, their subsistence, their population, their irrigation systems, and their demise.[4]

To the visitor today, the Sonoran Desert of southern Arizona is an imposing place. Summer temperatures regularly spike above one hundred degrees Fahrenheit. Only seven inches of precipitation falls each year. In these ways the desert today is probably the same as at the time of the Hohokam, but in other ways, much has changed. Today's restricted plant and animal life, as well as rivers noted for their dry beds, are cultural products of numerous forces, especially decades of overgrazing by cattle. At the time of the Hohokam, habitats were far more robust. Of defining importance were the rivers, especially the Gila, which was the major river flowing through the region, and the Salt, whose streamflow was five times greater than the Gila's yet was the latter's main tributary. Until the twentieth century, they were permanent throughout much of their reaches, and were swollen seasonally by sudden and violent summer storms or steady winter precipitation. They flowed through riparian communities of great richness, in which cottonwood trees, mesquite forests, and river-border savannas with reeds, marshes, and stands of willows were once common. These parklands were attractive to birds, and the rivers they bordered held seasonally abundant fish. Where major rivers joined, vast and rich marshlands formed. On heights of land away from the rivers, habitats were like today's and held abundant resources that could be gathered when droughts interrupted water flow and doomed irrigation-dependent crops.

Today, most of this is difficult to envision. In midsummer, the channel of the Gila appears like a "mile-wide scar of lighter colored sand" in a "heat blasted wilderness of sandy plains, rock pinnacles and ridges," as one ethnologist remarked, and the Salt is a dry riverbed. Upstream dams long ago impounded river waters. Currently, the thirst of Sun Belt Arizonans for water for domestic, leisure, industrial, and agricultural purposes draws on a water table falling away each year.[5]

The Hohokam had interests in a vast region. Centered on the lush valleys formed by the conjunction of the Salt, Gila, Agua Fria, Verde, and Santa Cruz rivers, and extending upward into the arid heights along and between the upstream reaches of these rivers where quite different ecological conditions prevailed, Hohokam country measured some twenty-five thousand square miles. Where they could, the Hohokam farmed and where possible, they irrigated, guiding water to fields as much as fifty feet above the river channel. Along heights from fifty to one hundred feet above the river channel, the Hohokam practiced various dry farming techniques, and away from the major river valleys, they used both dry and floodwater farming techniques. Throughout the region, they gathered plants.[6]

Because of the lack of trees of the right kind and age for tree-ring dating, debates over when the Hohokam first settled in this region have been inconclusive. In the past, opinions have been divided over whether the Hohokam evolved from people already present or came from elsewhere. Today the best guess is that sedentary, agricultural people were living in southern Arizona's Sonoran Desert twenty-five hundred years ago, and that Hohokam traits emerged during the first half of the first millennium AD and perhaps as early as during the first century. From their beginnings through the fifteenth century, the Hohokam went through several periods marked by distinct signatures in material culture, technology, architecture, demography, and social organization.[7]

While most archaeologists conclude that the Hohokam are indigenous to the Southwest, they have also attributed certain changes in pottery, architecture, and other aspects of material culture to people of different ethnicity who influenced the Hohokam. In a century-long search for the source of influence, they have typically looked northward to Pueblo villages or, more convincingly, southward to Mesoamerica, the presumed source not just of corn, beans, and squash but of knowledge of irrigation, ceramic figurines, worked shell, earspools, copper bells, tripod palettes, stone palettes, ballcourts, and other features exotic in the Southwest. How ideas or objects came north has been debated. Traders in search of raw cotton and cotton products to exchange for goods they carried might have been responsible. Some objects could have arrived through intermediaries, who changed them slightly in form and meaning, and subsequently became indigenized in meaning by the Hohokam. At a minimum, knowledge filtered north, and there is no lack of sites nearby—such as Casas Grandes in northern Chihuahua—for the origin of immediate influences on the Hohokam from the twelfth through the fifteenth centuries. In the Hohokam, one has the sense of people exposed to ideas from a vast region and experimenting in different periods, changing both as a result of internal factors and from taking part in an active exchange of products inside and outside the region.[8]

For years, conclusions about the Hohokam were based on interpretations of findings at a few large sites like Los Muertos, a Hohokam town that covered twelve square miles near today's Tempe, and other highly visible sites in the Salt and Gila River valleys. The most influential was an expansive ruin that the Akimel O'odham called Place of the Snakes or Snaketown (from rattlesnakes that fed on rodents attracted to trash mounds). The Hohokam founded Snaketown in the fourth century and after several hundred years, constructed irrigation canals and built the town into a center for the production of pottery and other goods. They deserted the town by the end of the fifteenth century.

Today there is greater appreciation for the variability in the location, size, permanence, and history of Hohokam sites. For over a millennium, their settlements increased in size and density. The Hohokam watered crops first through the natural action of floods and thunderstorms, and later by irrigation. After the seventh century, their communities expanded, and during the tenth and eleventh centuries their communities and canal systems underwent robust growth. Many aspects of their lives changed. For example, instead of leaving their pottery essentially undecorated, the Hohokam colored it red-on-buff and then polychrome. They began making larger ceramic storage vessels. They increasingly surrounded themselves with exotic objects: sculpted flat stone palettes and worked shell and ceramic bowls, jars, and figurines, many of which were incised, engraved, or painted with a variety of curvilinear, geometric, and naturalistic designs, such as small abstract images of birds, reptiles, and humans swirling inside the bowls. Both human figurines and depictions of birds were common.

Domestic architecture also changed. At Snaketown, the shift was from pithouses to above-ground houses with post-reinforced adobe walls, and from free-standing houses to houses associated with areas for cooking and burial in compounds or courtyard groups. Elsewhere, architectural styles narrowed from eclectic to rigorously rectangular floor plans, and from free-standing houses to walled compounds, platform mounds, and public structures in larger towns located along irrigation canals. Some towns contained structures whose architecture hinted strongly at specialized activities. Some were large elliptical depressions that are reminiscent of ballcourts in Mexico and may have been used for ballgames or as ceremonial spaces.

The ideas that found fruition in architecture, urban spaces, and artifacts spread regionally, perhaps along with a set of society-wide organizational principles. By the mid–thirteenth century there may have been as many as sixteen separate communities in the valleys of the Salt and Gila rivers, their boundaries defined by dependence on a network of irrigation canals. But some towns were already in decline and by the fourteenth and fifteenth centuries, Hohokam communities contracted sharply into collapse and final abandonment. The abandonments were not synchronized but unfolded over a lengthy period. The Hohokam left behind their ruins—as well as the graves and cremation urns containing their relatives' ashes, from which, as mentioned, came Phoenix's name.[9]

Today we know the Hohokam as farmers and canal builders, but how dependent they were on their irrigated fields has an obvious bearing on their fate. If they were more narrowly focused on irrigated, domesticated crops, they would have been more exposed when crops failed; conversely, if their subsistence were more broadly based, they would have had more alternatives to turn to if forced, for whatever reason, to abandon their fields. The traditional focus on canal irrigation tended to eclipse Hohokam gathering, but recently, new appreciation of the use of desert foods by the Hohokam has come from both ethnographic analogy and archaeology. For example, there is renewed admiration of Akimel and Tohono O'odham traditional knowledge. These Sonoran Desert residents have gained a deserved reputation for their adaptations in a demanding environment. Well versed, like many indigenous people, in the nutritional and medicinal properties of the plants in their environment, at one time they met many of their nutritional needs through gathered plants. It is no stretch of the imagination to suggest that the Hohokam probably possessed similar knowledge of their far more lush region.[10]

Archaeological pollen and faunal remains reveal a range of forty to fifty species of domesticated and wild plants, as well as animals, in the Hohokam diet. Among domesticated plants, the Hohokam grew corn and beans as well as cucurbits (a member of the squash-pumpkin-gourd complex), perhaps in two plantings each year. High-protein, drought-resistant beans and salt-resistant tepary beans were probably of greater importance than the archaeological record indicates. They also raised agave, tobacco, and cotton and probably cultivated amaranths, chenopods, little barley, and other native grasses. The Hohokam also either grew cholla and yucca or gathered these two succulent desert perennials along with saguaro fruit, prickly pear, and mesquite pods. From May through October, the Hohokam harvested or collected fruits, buds, seeds, and pods from a variety of plants, and stored for late-fall and winter consumption what they did not eat on the spot. For animal protein, they ate jackrabbits and cottontail rabbits, mule deer, antelope, and other animals—but apparently not much fish and beaver. They probably traded meat—the choice parts going to town centers where animals presumably were more scarce—as well as cotton and agave.[11]

Hohokam farming strategies varied with their distance from rivers, their techniques being suited to topography and water control. Irrigation, while crucial, was not the only means of supplying water, and not all Hohokam settlements were associated with canals. There is no reason to doubt that the Hohokam were sufficiently knowledgeable of their environment to take advantage of moist areas suitable for floodplain, floodwater, or runoff farming. Perhaps, like indigenous people in Sonora today, they planted "living fencerows"—a remarkable feature of floodwater farming composed of brakes of willow and cottonwood that limit stream erosion and channel cutting, filter and enhance the deposition of rich silt, shelter animals and plants, and provide wood for fuel.

Some of the Hohokam farmed "dry"; that is, they captured rain and runoff by building gravel banks on terraced fields, low stone walls, and rock or cobble clusters, which guided and slowed the velocity of water and prevented excess water accumulation. They captured runoff where, from past experience, it was certain to flow—on slopes below rock escarpments, on valley floors, and at arroyo mouths—the last technique called "ak-chin" and practiced extensively by the Tohono O'odham. The Hohokam also stored water in reservoirs, wells, and depressions or catchment basins.

In any single year, some of the Hohokam were probably engaged in irrigation agriculture and others in floodwater farming or dry farming, and if any single year brought failure somewhere because of floods, drought, insects, or disease, then in other areas subsistence systems were left intact. But much remains unknown, including whether Hohokam farmers living in a single community simultaneously practiced dry, floodwater, and irrigation farming techniques, each suited for a particular location, or reverted to less favored methods when climatic and ecological conditions changed.[12]

Notwithstanding the importance of these various strategies, the Hohokam have been most strongly associated with their canals—the most extensive in pre-Columbian North America. Scholars have dubbed them "the Canal Builders." Some who wrote in the nineteenth and early twentieth centuries claimed that the Hohokam accomplished "an engineering triumph which dwarfed the mounds of Ohio and Missouri" only because they were taught irrigation by the Spanish, just as some argued that the people responsible for the mounds must have been unrelated to contemporary Indians. In both cases, the arguments were wrong. Over time, it became clear that Indians alone had designed and constructed these works of large-scale engineering (even if their precise link to native people living near the ruins remained unclear). There was no question about the Hohokam effort; explorers, missionaries, farmers, and archaeologists have all in their own way been awed by what they found.[13]

The Hohokam were building canals by the sixth century (and perhaps much earlier), and used them last in the fifteenth century. They drew heavily upon the permanently flowing Gila and Salt rivers. The two rivers had very different channels: The Salt's channel, along which canals were twice as extensive, shifted horizontally in its desert-surface bed and the Gila's channel cut deeply in the streambed. Hohokam canal systems were quite variable. Mature systems consisted of an intake to divert water from the river, a main canal, distribution canals—some branching off at forty-five-degree angles and others at ninety degrees—and lateral canals delivering water to the fields. The Hohokam often located intakes, which were headgates formed by barriers of stone slabs or posts that could be dropped or lifted (or more ephemeral woven mats and reed bundles and stakes), near bedrock where water was available at the lowest points of flow (when it was presumably needed most for agricultural purposes), a reflection, perhaps, of uncertain water flow during droughts. Individual main canals were as much as seventy-five feet wide from one crest of their bank to the other and seven feet deep, and up to fourteen miles long. Some canals left the river diagonally and then ran parallel to the course of the river, with short laterals spinning off like veins of a leaf. Others left the river and headed away into the flat desert.

Some systems were impressive in scale. There were 85 miles of main canals at Casa Grande near the Gila River and 75 miles at Los Muertos. With densities of up to forty canals per square mile, some sites resembled spiders' webs. In the valley of the Salt River alone, the Hohokam may have built as many as 350 miles of main canals and 1,000 miles of distribution and lateral canals along the Salt River. But even though we know that some systems were extensive, the aggregate length and total number of Hohokam canals remain unknown. Estimates of aggregate length vary, in fact, by 200 percent, in large measure because many canals have been obliterated and it is difficult to ascribe contemporaneous use to many others. The Hohokam seem not to have added branches to systems in the same way everywhere, but to have abandoned entire systems in favor of others. Long-term use of canals rested ultimately on long-term stability of river channels, which depended in turn on the resistance of underlying bedrock to erosion. Floods had dramatic effects on the systems: Channels often migrated laterally in riverbeds or were cut more deeply by the heavier volume of water, in some instances leaving intakes high and dry once the floodwaters receded.

How much acreage the Hohokam irrigated alongside the Salt and Gila rivers depended on the annual flow of the rivers, the success and simultaneous use of canals, and the moisture needs of the crops in acre-feet of water per acre. It also hinged on water velocity and flow in the canals, which in turn were linked to canal size, grade, lining (if any), and other morphological features. Some Hohokam canals are quite well known from cross-sections. Most were unlined and probably lost from 15 to 45 percent of the water flowing through them, which might have been recognized as a problem because a few canals were evidently lined with clay impervious to such high seepage. Canal grades, which controlled velocity, seepage, sedimentation, and erosion and were crucial to water delivery, varied considerably from a steep ninety-five feet per mile to negative grade. Some grades were impressively near today's ideal of five and one-quarter feet per mile. Some canals brought water to terraces above the level of the riverbed along which they ran and others ended up above the level of the fields they served. Hohokam canals so impressed Mormon settlers that they took some over without alteration, thereby saving themselves considerable labor, and their grades continue to astound today's hydrologists and engineers.

Although few estimates of the total amount of acreage irrigated are truly reliable, in specific cases, one canal probably carried enough water to irrigate approximately 500 to 800 acres, two canals together transported enough water to irrigate 650 acres, and one large canal was sufficient for almost 1,600 acres. "Highly speculative" estimates of the total amount of irrigated land have ranged up to 450,000 acres along the Salt, and far fewer along the Gila. The most recent estimates for the Salt River are much lower, based on reconstructed river flow and discharge estimates: roughly 7,000 to 10,000 acres. Regardless, the Hohokam appear to have been able to deliver in at least one canal system the requisite five acre-feet of water per acre per year to ensure the success of thirsty domesticated plants, enough, as one scholar imagined, to "[turn] the alluvial plains" near one creek "into a virtual garden."

Many scholars including Harold Gladwin, an archaeologist, regard the canals as the "outstanding accomplishment" of the Hohokam. But once built, the canals required maintenance; how much depended on how long they were used. Over time, silt collected and weeds grew in them, compromising grades and bottom hardness. Entire systems—intakes and canals—were vulnerable to sudden rushes of water and catastrophic floods; indeed, distinct channels in some canals reveal the signatures of flooding and siltation. Archaeologists who have studied canal morphology and canal systems caution that Hohokam canals were "technologically simple and relatively inefficient," and that the absence of drop structures, drainage canals, and (with minor exceptions) linings "prevented the Hohokam," as W. Bruce Masse put it, "from achieving the level of sophistication necessary to deal successfully with various environmental hazards such as field waterlogging and salinization and the destructive effects of catastrophic river flooding."[14]

In the last one hundred years, estimates of the size of the Hohokam population have varied greatly. At first, the estimates matched the awe inspired by Hohokam ruins and irrigation networks. Some claimed that some 200,000 to 300,000 Hohokam lived along the Salt River alone; others estimated that the canal systems supported farming for 130,000 people in the region. These estimates are controversial in part because the sites are unevenly distributed in the region as a whole. They are dense where irrigation or floodplain agriculture was possible, and densest in the lower Salt River valley, where eight communities existed along the banks of a twenty-mile stretch of river. But even where towns sprawled impressively over many acres, not all houses were simultaneously occupied, and open spaces were common. Population changes can be inferred from changes in the size of the towns and irrigation networks—and both expanded noticeably from the sixth through the eighth centuries and again in the tenth and eleventh centuries—but how many Hohokam lived at any single time in any single town is simply not known.

Early estimates of Hohokam population size were partially based on the assumption that very large numbers of laborers were required to build and maintain Hohokam irrigation canals. That assumption no longer holds; fewer people than initially estimated could do the job—although how many fewer is the question. At the same time that archaeologists have recovered evidence of more houses in Hohokam urban centers, they have come to question whether all the residential structures were used at one time. The initial estimate of the population of Snaketown at its height was 2,000; one recent estimate was 300. But other central villages are now believed to have been larger than initially thought. Today a few archaeologists suggest that there were only 12,000 people in the Salt River valley and 20,000 to 45,000 in the entire Hohokam region; but most think that the Salt River population was closer to 50,000 and the total for the region correspondingly higher.[15]

How the Hohokam were organized socially and politically is also uncertain. Some archaeologists argue that the great expansion of irrigation during the tenth and eleventh centuries could not have been accomplished without central political authority. Cooperation was required to move tens, if not hundreds, of thousands of cubic yards of earth to construct canals. Wider coordination of effort and shared sentiment were probably demanded for canals that served clusters of residences strung out along them or more than one town. Furthermore, in many towns the Hohokam erected imposing architectural features, which seem to have been both private and public spaces. Late in Hohokam history, most communities had at least one massive mound with an adobe retaining wall, evidently used for residential purposes. Over forty platform mound sites, each spaced with some regularity from others, existed along the Salt and Gila rivers in the mid–thirteenth century. The forty were grouped in sixteen discrete communities, each tied to a canal system—a spatial arrangement implying some form of water distribution. Ballcourts were widespread, their orientation alternating from one town to the next, a reflection, perhaps, of some sort of town-linking ceremony.

Many of these features lend support to the idea that the success of the Hohokam enterprise was dependent on strong leaders. Swayed by knowledge that other irrigation-based societies possessed state-organized political systems, some scholars have been predisposed to see hierarchy and centralization in an extensive irrigation system, towns with platform mounds and associated residential compounds, and nearly two hundred ballcourts. But the reconstruction of political or social organization is highly speculative, and there is no obligatory causal connection between irrigation on the one hand, and hierarchy and centralization on the other (with either as a cause). We do not know, and might never know, the degree to which upriver and downriver communities competed or cooperated with each other. The archaeological record does not contain unambiguous signatures of a society organized as a multitown community dependent on a single network of canals and strong centralized leadership. Moreover, while canal construction involves a substantial initial effort, routine maintenance does not necessarily require a large workforce. That much can be inferred from Akimel O'odham activity, but whether their political organization can serve as a model for the Hohokam is very much an open question.[16]

After the beginning of the fifteenth century, the Hohokam no longer lived in the major town centers or alongside irrigation canals. Some four centuries earlier, they had started to abandon their densely settled communities. Snaketown's residents, for example, left between the late eleventh and early fifteenth centuries after using their canal system for three hundred to seven hundred years. In Hohokam country as a whole, the abandonments were uneven.[17]

Why the Hohokam vanished is the puzzle we began with. Frank Hamilton Cushing, an ethnologist, offered one of the earliest explanations. Over one hundred years ago, fresh from ethnographic work with the Zuni, Cushing stood in the ruins of Los Muertos (The Dead), a Hohokam town near Tempe. Awed by "the arteries, veins and ganglions," as he called them, of Hohokam irrigation networks, he looked about and noticed not only canals and the burials that gave Los Muertos its name, but also tumbled-down houses. He also found artifacts resembling objects used by the Zuni to influence earth tremors. Musing on the resemblance, Cushing seized on the idea that earthquakes explained the Hohokam demise.[18] If nothing else, his theory was timely. On May 3, 1887, at the very moment Cushing was deep in thought, the largest earthquake ever recorded in the region rocked the Sonoran Desert. With a magnitude of 7.2, it devastated several small towns at its epicenter in Sonora, where forty people died. Three hundred miles north, Phoenix, just west of Tempe and Los Muertos, vibrated and many people, hearing a deep rumbling noise to the southeast, rushed into the streets.[19]

Cushing's theory of cataclysmic earthquakes was intriguing, but it and later hypotheses proposing a collapse of leadership and internal dissent, or the invasion of outsiders like Athapaskans or Puebloans, remain unsupported by convincing evidence. In contrast, the most compelling explanations of the fate of the Hohokam begin with their relationship with their desert environment and in one way or another concern water. The Hohokam had to solve four environmental problems: drought, a high water table, salt-laden waters and soils, and floods.

Did drought play a role in the demise of the Hohokam? They lived in a desert, after all, where less than ten inches of precipitation fell each year. In 1854, drought forced the Akimel O'odham to rely almost exclusively on mesquite pods, and many have suspected since that drought, the most important of the "forces of nature," defeated the Hohokam. Prolonged drought alone, or drought on the heels of flooding, might indeed have had dire consequences. In their mythology, the Akimel O'odham tell of a time when the Sun punished the Hohokam for gambling, first by causing a flood that deepened river channels and then by bringing drought, making it impossible for the Hohokam to guide water from those channels through intakes and canals to their fields. In the twelfth century, the Salt River Hohokam might have expanded their canal systems beyond the reach of drought-depleted rivers—a local explanation, perhaps, for some abandonments.

The evidence for drought is elusive in large measure because there are few trees in the Sonoran Desert suitable for tree-ring and climatological analysis. Nevertheless, when climatologists extrapolate from pollen sequences on the Colorado Plateau to the north or from Pacific Coast rainfall patterns, they detect fluctuating moisture throughout Hohokam times. From the eighth through the fifteenth centuries, long periods of "normal" precipitation were punctuated by brief but occasionally severe intervals of drought. Two extreme periods evidently occurred in the final decade of the ninth century, when one year in three was dry, and in the third and fourth decades of the twelfth century, when three years in five were arid. Perhaps the twelfth-century droughts spelled the end of irrigation-based life in some Hohokam towns.[20]

The difficulty finding evidence firmly linking drought to demise returns us to the remaining three environmental problems requiring solutions—a high water table, salt-laden waters and soils, and floods. In the Salt River valley, the water table was high and in many places clayey subsoil inhibited drainage. Irrigation waters probably nowhere evaporated totally from the surface of the land. Rather, an estimated one-fifth of the total volume of water went into the ground to add to the water table—and where clay halted drainage, the already high water table was brought closer to the surface. In other words, irrigation was potentially destructive. In these watery conditions, plants simply rotted.

The river that the Spanish branded Rio Salado, and the Americans the Salt, did not help. Many considered its waters saline in taste and even unpalatable. Moreover, many noticed that the valleys of the Salt and Gila rivers contained extensive salt (also called alkali) flats detrimental to irrigation farming. Europeans noticed these conditions the moment they arrived. One of the earliest Spanish explorers spoke of "sterile plains" and lands that "appear as if they had been strewn with salt." A mid-nineteenth-century American expedition encountered saline springs and cakes of pure salt near Akimel O'odham towns on the Gila River. In the late nineteenth century a water and irrigation survey report mentioned lands near Tempe "impregnated with alkali," and after the turn of the twentieth century, the ethnographer Frank Russell mentioned that in places, alkali "rises to the surface in an efflorescence that resembles snow in appearance."

Farming was impossible on or near alkali flats. It was problematic when irrigation waters contained (and delivered) significant concentrations of sodium and quantities of soluble salts. If the water table was low enough to allow runoff to disappear into the ground, then salts could periodically be flushed from soils, either deliberately or through floods. But if the water table was too high, as in the valley of the Salt River, the problem could not be mitigated. Here, the one-fifth of irrigation waters that seep into the ground was fatal. Irrigation brought not just water to the surface but also the salts in the groundwater, to be compounded by the salts in the irrigation water. Drought magnified the problems: More waters were required for irrigation and flushing away accumulated salts but were seldom available.

In the nineteenth and early twentieth centuries, American settlers who used Hohokam canals or built new ones to irrigate their farms discovered extensive stretches of land too saturated with water to farm. They irrigated nevertheless, and over the space of two decades in the late nineteenth century, water table levels rose forty feet in the valley of the Salt River. At the same time, these farmers realized that salinization was a severe problem where waterlogging occurred. To continue farming some fields longer than ten years, they had to install deep-well pumps and excavate drainage ditches to take water away from the top of the rising water table. Still, salinity and waterlogging continued to plague them. Within a half-century, salts too toxic for plant life left one-third of the irrigated lands useless. Salt River valley farmers continued to leach salts by flooding and draining lands, and by the 1940s were pumping off over 300,000 acre-feet of water annually.

The argument that Hohokam lands became waterlogged because of irrigation and lack of drainage, and that they were simultaneously salinated to a degree toxic to crop life, emerged forcefully in the 1920s to 1930s. It is easy to understand why. The idea that the Hohokam doomed their farms through irrigation just as Americans doomed theirs made sense. The Hohokam had neither pumps nor drainage canals to drain away the toxicity, and the high rate of evaporation in this arid climate would have left behind salts encrusted on the surface and fields beyond repair. Moreover, salts brought to the surface in flooded conditions tended to rise in moisture in adobe walls, shattering and eroding them after the moisture evaporated. Perhaps, some thought, the Hohokam constructed twenty-foot-high mounds in their towns in order to store food or keep themselves above damaging salt-laden waterlogged earth.[21]

One reason for the durability of the argument that waterlogging and salinization account for the end of the Hohokam is the long-standing appreciation of these two problems in desert environments worldwide. In arid regions, crop growth is problematic when the water table is near the surface because dissolved salts, as Daniel Hillel, a soil physicist, put it, "poison the root zone." Perhaps the best-known example is ancient Mesopotamia, where siltation of canals and salinization of lands watered by the Tigris and Euphrates have been linked to the decline of civilization. Through irrigation, Mesopotamians transformed desert into productive fields of grain. But the lands irrigated were near or below the riverbeds and irrigation waters were saline. As a result, the water table rose and the lands became waterlogged and accumulated salts, except where water was channeled off the surface or pumped away from underground wells. One key to farming success was fallowing land in alternate years so that weedy plants could replace nitrogen and soak up water, and another was to grow salt-resistant barley on lands where salinization and unleached salts compounded problems for sodium-sensitive wheat, the preferred grain.

In desert regions like Mesopotamia and the Sonoran Desert, farmers cannot count on rain to leach out accumulated salts. Irrigation water must do. Yet the more one irrigates, the more the water table rises, and with surface evaporation, even more salts are left in topsoil. Irrigation, as others have said, can "make the desert bloom." But it is a lethal blossom. Waterlogging and salinization are twin evils in desert regions, dooming crops and the men and women dependent on them. Removing ground cover—cutting down trees—can hasten the salt-laden rise of the water table in low-lying, riverine areas. For all these reasons, locating the explanation of the demise of the Hohokam in waterlogging and salinization.[22]

Compelling, popular, close to dogma, invoked even today—the argument nevertheless has been extraordinarily hard to prove through archaeology. Changes to the environment in the six centuries since the time of the Hohokam, especially at the hand of American settlers, have made it impossible to reconstruct conditions in most of the fields farmed by the Hohokam. There is no reason to doubt that the Hohokam also had to contend with poorly draining alkaline soils, as well as with a high water table in the valley of the Salt River reached with wells only ten feet deep. Moreover, if we can extrapolate from late-nineteenth-century events, the process of salinization and abandonment can be rapid. Yet there is and was much variability in the region as a whole. The Salt and Gila valley soils were not uniformly but variably permeable or saline; for example, concentrations of salt are greater downstream than upstream. There were probably differences at the level of specific fields, with saline levels moderate in one part but toxic in another. In other words, the soil saline pattern is and was mosaic-like, as would have been its influence on crops.

Of the two major river basins, the Salt and Gila, farming in the Salt was probably especially challenging. The water table was in all probability higher. Silt, quantities of which ended up on agricultural fields, had very poor nitrogen and potash content. Soils in this river valley were especially impermeable and saline. To farm successfully here, the Hohokam needed to irrigate frequently or raise salt-tolerant crops (or do both). Their major crops (corn, beans, cucurbits, cotton, and tobacco) varied in saline sensitivity and tolerance, from highly sensitive beans and less sensitive corn to moderately tolerant cucurbits and highly tolerant cotton.

How much a factor waterlogging and salinization were and whether the Hohokam recognized what was happening and knew what corrective action to take are unknown. Some scholars have estimated that one-half of Hohokam land was partly or wholly unfit for farming. One archaeologist thought that the Snaketown Hohokam "probably" flushed accumulated salts from the fields, but provided as his only evidence this town's "long life." The early-twentieth-century Akimel O'odham recognized the adverse effects of salt accumulation and flooded their fields to leach out salts. But it may be incautious to project knowledge also shared by their white neighbors to their Hohokam predecessors.[23]

For as long as they have traveled and lived along the Salt and Gila rivers, people have known that the rivers could rise destructively and without warning. Some floods were so destructive that Akimel O'odham historians recorded them as annual events in notches on sticks known as calendar sticks. They recalled one especially ruinous flood in 1833 with a distinctive notch, saying that it was brought upon them either as punishment for breaking taboos or by an angered and vengeful shaman. Another flood remembered was produced by four successive days of rain in September 1868, when the Gila River bloated from 150 yards in width to over a mile and obliterated a store (the event notched into the calendar) as well as three Akimel O'odham towns. A third flood remembered not on a calendar stick but in the written historical record occurred in March 1867, when both the Salt and Gila, which were "usually sluggish, half-dry" rivers, were described as "swollen and turbid" and "booming." Mesquite groves lay four feet under water, houses and towns were submerged, and travel was practically impossible. John Wesley Powell, the explorer and ethnologist, described the onset of a flood on the Salt as "terrific": "Coming without warning, it catches up logs and boulders in the bed, undermines the banks, and tearing out trees and cutting sand-bars, is loaded with this mass of sand, gravel and driftwood—most formidable weapons for destruction."[24]

Given these descriptions, it comes as no surprise that floods could ruin irrigation architecture and networks: Following five days of rain in January 1874, floodwaters swept away canal headgates; the next year another flood moved the channel away from canal intakes; and in 1891, a great flood, its effects perhaps compounded by overgrazing and deforestation, altered the channels of the Salt and Gila, destroyed irrigation systems and fields along both rivers, and forced the Akimel O'odham then living near the Salt River to high ground.[25]

Appreciation of the power of nineteenth-century floods initially produced the idea that catastrophic flooding caused the Hohokam demise. In the late 1920s, one archaeologist recycled a late-nineteenth-century suggestion and proposed that the Casa Grande mounds, like the mounds of the Mississippi, "were formed to meet the recurring menace of floods" and used to store food out of harm's way. The theory of salinization—and dams on the Salt and Gila rivers that made floods largely a memory—soon eclipsed this tentative idea. Yet "monumental floods" in April 1980 reminded many of descriptions of the "savage and unpredictable floods" of the past, and the idea reemerged.[26]

Over the last fifteen years, the notion that catastrophic flooding caused the demise of the Hohokam has come into its own, as archaeologists, climatologists, and other earth scientists have attempted to reconstruct climatic and fluvial processes in the Southwest and to link regional climatic and atmospheric circulation changes with floods. From known relationships between modern tree-ring series and streamflow volumes, scientists have inferred streamflow histories of the Salt River and its major tributary, the Verde, from tree-ring calibrations on the Colorado Plateau to the north. Moreover, in the colors and textures of deposits in irrigation canals, they have read a complex history, including floods that destroyed not just through the force of water but by silting-in processes. Alternating coarse- and fine-grained sediments, for example, suggest alternating slow and fast waters, or cyclical rushes of water produced either by floods or by the deliberate manipulation of water flow.

Scientists have inferred Salt River "streamflow events" from

Colorado Plateau tree-ring series dating from AD 740 to 1370. If in fact these data reflect both streamflow and specific "events," then several times in this 630-year period, a spate of destructive floods affected the Salt River basin. In eight years at the turn of the ninth century (AD 798–805), floods of 25-, 32-, 57-, 211-, and 316-year magnitudes occurred, and the Hohokam evidently abandoned at least one canal system. (A 25-year flood is one whose level is reached once every quarter-century on average.) In two successive years (AD 888–889), a 90-year flood and, astoundingly, a 632-year flood struck. Some of the Hohokam might have fallen back on alternative farming methods away from river bottoms. Then in a period of six years (AD 1197–1202), 30-, 42-, and 79-year floods swept the valley. Finally a 158-year flood overflowed the Salt River in AD 1356 and the three years AD 1380 to 1382 might have been comparable to AD 889 (the 632-year flood) in the amount of precipitation, but that awaits further study.

Some of these events might have had a catastrophic impact on canals and fields, and caused river channels to shift. Five-year floods could destroy intake structures, 25-year or 50-year floods possibly silted in some canals, leaving them inoperable for a time, and 100-year floods were potentially more destructive yet. But floods were sometimes separated by long periods of eighty to three hundred years, when drought—which affected rivers one in every five years in this period—presented the major problem. In the fourteenth century, however, only twenty-four years separates AD 1356 (a major 158-year flood) from AD 1380 (the start of three high flood years).[27]

But the evidence for this scenario consists of what many including George Gumerman, an archaeologist, call "proxy data." They come from the Colorado Plateau north and west of Hohokam territory. They infer precipitation from annual tree rings silent on whether or not moisture fell so that it became a flood. We should be wary of reading too much into the data, especially for a people who also lived in habitats away from riverside canals. It is difficult to conclude that flooding alone was responsible for the disappearance of the Hohokam.[28]

For years archaeologists depended on Snaketown and other centers for insights into the Hohokam as a whole; a myopic focus, it led inescapably to the conclusion that as the town centers went, so went the Hohokam. Thus, when Snaketown and other towns were abandoned, the Hohokam "disappeared as a viable culture."[29]

But rather than assume that the Hohokam disappeared, it may make as much sense to hypothesize that they vacated riverine town centers on major irrigation canals and took up residence elsewhere. The Hohokam were distributed over a wide area. They exploited different ecological niches, tailoring their adaptations accordingly. Perhaps they did not disappear entirely but simply left the town centers and abandoned irrigation farming for strategies more suited to the stable nonriverine portions of the Sonoran Desert. In this light, the abandonment of towns spelled the end not of the people but of irrigation-based society whose centers were linked to each other. Dispersed, with ecologically appropriate adaptations and social contact with other groups, perhaps the Hohokam joined others speaking related tongues, and through time their descendants became the O'odham speakers described several centuries later by the Spanish.[30]

For the past century, ethnologists have sought answers to these questions in archaeology, oral history, archives, and material culture. Some have always held to the opinion that the Hohokam merely moved, changed, and left descendants who live today. There is a limited range of candidates for descendants of the Hohokam. In the late seventeenth century, Indians speaking Uto-Aztecan, Athapaskan, and Yuman languages greeted Spaniards in the Arizonan Sonoran Desert. On the Gila River, where the newcomers settled, they found the O'odham (Uto-Aztecan)-speaking Akimel O'odham. But for the ruins and ashes of the Hohokam, the valley of the Salt River stood empty—and it remained deserted three centuries later when Americans arrived. The only exceptions were a few Akimel O'odhams and Maricopas who ventured there to fish, despite the danger posed by hostile neighbors like the Yavapai and Apache.[31]

Of all these Indians, only the widely scattered Akimel and Tohono O'odham have seriously been considered descendants of the Hohokam. Related linguistically and culturally, the Akimel and Tohono O'odham differed greatly in adaptations. In the seventeenth century, the Tohono O'odham exploited the southern Sonoran Desert, relying heavily on seeds, buds, fruits, nuts, roots, bulbs, greens, rabbits, deer, and other animals, supplemented by crops cultivated in fields positioned to receive and trap rainfall and runoff. The Akimel

O'odham, in contrast, lived two to three thousand strong in one-half dozen towns along the Gila River, and thousands of other river-dwelling O'odhams lived in villages along the Santa Cruz and San Pedro rivers. There they grew corn, beans, and squash in irrigated fields, supplementing their diet of domesticated crops with many gathered foods like mesquite, screwbean, and agave; with animals like bighorn sheep, rabbits, deer, beaver, birds, and small animals that did well in agricultural field borders; and with larvae and fish. They were far more sedentary than the Tohono O'odham because of their relationship to water, which allowed for irrigation and provided a riparian richness where foods could be gathered, small game hunted, and fish caught. But in times of drought, they became like the Tohono O'odham in their focus on gathered foods.

The Yumans, Apache, and Spanish all had an impact on the Akimel and Tohono O'odham. From the late seventeenth through mid–nineteenth centuries, the Apache raided indigenous Sonoran Desert people, whose response was to gather in defensive, compact towns. Prior to the Apache threat, the Akimel O'odham were living along a fifty-mile stretch of the Gila River. By the end of the eighteenth century their villages were concentrated along a far more easily defended twenty-mile stretch of the river, and resident with them were Yuman-speaking Maricopas who had sought refuge from their own enemies. The Spanish had a far-reaching effect on the Akimel O'odham, inducing them to plant and irrigate wheat and barley as well as their indigenous corn and cotton. Spanish-introduced diseases might have affected them in the sixteenth and seventeenth centuries but the evidence is inconclusive. In time, the Akimel O'odham grew crops for domesticated animals and to sell to newcomers, and engaged Tohono O'odham laborers at the time of the harvest.[32]

Are the Akimel O'odham the descendants of the Hohokam? If they are, there is no doubt that the forces of history that brought them into contact with various outsiders, from Apaches to Spanish and American settlers, changed them greatly. They shared with the Hohokam a preference for riverside communities and irrigation farming, as well as styles of domestic architecture, burial customs, and other traits. But in other ways, in particular in the sheer scale of Hohokam towns and irrigation networks and major architectural and ceramic features, the connection between the Hohokam and Akimel O'odham seems tenuous.

In the last one hundred years, the Akimel O'odham themselves have lacked consensus on their relationship to the Hohokam. In 1883, according to the historian and geologist A. F. Bandelier, some Akimel O'odhams spoke of their history as beginning with their creation on the Salt and Gila rivers, and of subsequent events including a flood that left only one man alive; the growth of their population on the Gila; the construction of Casa Grande, a multistoried ruin from very late in the Hohokam period, by the chief Civano (*siwañ*, chief); and the settlement of the Salt River by that chief's son. Then came intertribal war or perhaps even disastrous intratribal feuding, as well as epidemic disease, in the wake of which some Akimel O'odhams remained on the Gila while others dispersed. Casa Blanca and other ruins south of the Gila River, they said, had been built by their forefathers called *vipisat* (great-grandparents) or Hohokam. Bandelier concluded that "the gist of these traditions is that the Pimas [Akimel O'odham] claim to be the lineal descendants of the Indians who built and inhabited the large houses and mounds on the Gila and Lower Salado [Salt] Rivers, as well as on the delta between the two streams."[33]

One generation later, when Casa Grande was being excavated, the story recorded by ethnologists and archaeologists was less clear. Some Akimel O'odhams professed to know nothing whatsoever about who built the ruin. Others, perhaps struck by the similarity between archaeological artifacts like stone balls, hoes, small reed tobacco smokers, and wooden paddles and objects used by the oldest among them, said that one of their culture heros named Morning Green built Casa Grande after learning irrigation techniques from related people on the Salt River.

The lack of unanimity was striking. In 1907, J. Walter Fewkes, the archaeologist who excavated Casa Grande, suggested that hostile "invaders," whose relationship with the indigenous people is obscure, forced the residents of Casa Grande to abandon this and other indefensible compounds, and to subsequently adopt the inconspicuous housing and lifestyles that the Spanish described as characteristic of the Akimel O'odham. According to Thin Leather, Fewkes's main informant, the ancient people who lived in Casa Grande "were of Pima [Akimel O'odham] blood and spoke the

Pima [Akimel O'odham] language." The following year, the ethnologist Frank Russell stated that "however ready" the Akimel O'odham "may have been in the past to claim relationship with the Hohokam or relate tales of the supernatural origin of the pueblos, they now frankly admit that they do not know anything about the matter." Perhaps some Akimel O'odhams guarded information closely while others, influenced by their employer-archaeologists, told them what they thought they wanted to hear. In the quarter-century since Cushing and others started to excavate the ruins and inquire into the origins and fate of the Hohokam, the Akimel O'odham "have long since grown accustomed," Russell observed, "to being interrogated concerning the builders of the great stone and adobe pueblos."[34]

More recent texts are no more help in solving the problem of the connection between the Hohokam and the Akimel O'odham, even assuming that they spoke similar languages. Because they are ambiguous, often local, and focused on a few characters or lineages, oral traditions may never solve the problem. Many Tohono and Akimel O'odhams today believe that they are descended from the Hohokam, whom they construct as spiritual people in tune with the earth, but even if we could say for certain that the O'odham are greatly changed descendants of the Hohokam, it begs the question of why the Hohokam abandoned their towns and irrigation canals.[35]

In the archaeologist Emil Haury's portrait, the Hohokam had adapted in a "nearly perfect" manner to their environment and were therefore candidates for ecologically aware sainthood.[36] Haury elided that they disappeared or the possibility that they induced any significant environmental change as they adapted to their surroundings. Yet there can be no doubt that they cleared, irrigated, and cultivated fields, actions with consequences: fewer trees, more ragweed, a higher water table, possibly oversalinization. They also demanded wood for use in domestic consumption in a region where there was not much of it. If their demand was equal to the Akimel O'odham demand for fuel and construction, then they might have deforested areas where there were few trees, as along the Gila River, especially during periods of prolonged drought. If the Hohokam cut down mesquite groves, which were most readily available for fuel and construction, then they altered the habitat for the animals and birds dependent on mesquite and destroyed the food value of mesquite pods. But much concerning demand and consequences is frankly unknown. For example, mesquite groves recover rapidly from cutting, with trees reachieving maturity in the space of only four decades. And the Hohokam might even (as others have speculated) have extended wet, riparian communities beneficially as the Akimel O'odham have in recent times with their "living" fencerows of live trees and bushes that provide dense habitat for plants, animals, and birds.[37]

Haury surely had in mind that no matter how great the impact of Hohokam farmers on the landscape, they were outdone by European and American newcomers, who have had a marked cumulative effect on the Arizonan Sonoran Desert since the sixteenth century. Initially few in number, the Spanish brought epidemic diseases north from Mexico. Jesuit missionaries, who were the first Europeans to settle this region, established themselves on the Gila in the last two decades of the seventeenth century and were soon forced to withdraw—but not before introducing products that had a lasting effect on Sonoran Desert ecology, including wheat, peaches, sheep, and goats. Most destructive of all imports were cattle, which remained and flourished despite Apache predation, and were later nurtured on large land grants during the nineteenth century.

American settlers who went West to pursue their destiny had the greatest impact of all on the Sonoran Desert. Early in the nineteenth century, trappers exterminated beaver from the region's rivers, and the loss of beaver architecture hastened the erosive effects of flooding. Ranchers, miners, and other settlers who came in the wake of trappers demanded far more lumber than the region could supply. With Apache raiding under control, cattle operations expanded steadily until the land was overgrazed to the point of exhaustion. Cattle and men assaulted wetlands. They cut down riparian forests, which induced erosion, flooding, and desertification. Ciénegas—rich marshlands—were especially affected. Formerly abundant ecosystems with low-banked, slow-flowing, nonerosive streams at their heart, they supported lush grasses as well as canopy forests of cottonwood, mesquite, willow, and walnut trees and provided habitat for birds, fish, beavers, and other animal and plant life. Many were destroyed.

These changes came to a head in the last decades of the nineteenth century and first decade of the twentieth as cattle, mining, and farming interests grew. In the 1870s to 1880s, the cattle industry grew explosively at a time of drought and the effect on Arizona's Sonoran Desert was abrupt and devastating. Where five thousand cattle grazed in the Arizona Territory in 1870, over one million tried desperately to find grass in 1890. Luxuriant grasslands disappeared under the onslaught. With cover stripped away, erosion quickened. A fierce drought killed many cattle in the early 1890s but by then numerous ciénegas had been destroyed and a cycle of erosion, incised streams, and arroyo formation was firmly established. New immigrants placed heightened demand on wood and wildlife, and as trees fueled fires or shored up mine shafts and animals were consumed, mesquite forests and native wildlife were obliterated.

Yet another set of major changes came about as extensive irrigation was reintroduced in the late 1860s, in part through the use of abandoned Hohokam canals, and within the space of fifty years, the Salt River valley became a major producer of grapefruit, dates, cotton, lettuce, melons, and winter-grown salt-tolerant grains. Eventually, the water table dropped precipitously, and the Sonoran Desert spread to river-border lands to desiccate moisture-bearing riparian plant life except for what was under irrigation. Finally, the rivers were dammed into submission, the Salt in 1910 with Roosevelt Dam, and the Gila nineteen years later with Coolidge Dam, leaving dust swirling in dry riverbeds.[38]

Each age, it seems, reads something different into the demise of the Hohokam. In his day, Cushing was convinced that to explain Hohokam culture one need only know a contemporary culture like the Zuni's. Cushing's followers envisioned Hohokam cultivated fields surrounding "a cluster of cities," each with a central "massive structure" seven stories high—a "temple, the dwellings of the hierarchy of hereditary priests" headed by the Priest of the Sun. In their imagination, the Hohokam were "industrious, peaceable and contented folk" who knew how to subordinate individual interest to the common weal and whose "every movement, however significant or however slight, has its religious act and significance." Some thought that the Hohokam abandoned their towns because they thought they lived at the center of a world that they should abandon if it became unstable. As for Cushing's related proposal that earthquakes caused the demise, his evidence was slight—a crushed skeleton, some artifacts interpreted as related to the ritual control of earthquakes—and of far less significance than the impact on him of rumblings from the most powerful earthquake in recent Sonoran history at the very instant he was in the field.[39]

Not only does each age have an explanation, but each pushes into the shade explanations that had seemed reasonable to their adherents. This is what happened to the idea of earthquakes after American farmers experienced firsthand what happened to crops grown in saline soils on waterlogged fields irrigated with saline water. The saline qualities of the Arizona desert waters and soil had been remarked on since the seventeenth century, but the idea that the Hohokam disappeared because they oversalinated waterlogged fields came into its own only after American immigrants discovered they could not control the spread of salts in their own irrigated fields. Buttressed by knowledge of salinity and waterlogging in other arid zones, the argument has been popular for a very long time, but nevertheless has been difficult to prove.

Perhaps because the archaeological evidence on oversalinization is so soft, catastrophic flooding shoved it into the background when in the 1980s the Salt and Gila valleys were inundated to an extent rarely witnessed in this century. Flooding as the cause of the Hohokam's disappearance was actually an old theory whose explanatory power was related to the force of nineteenth-century floods. But this theory too has drawbacks, and it is just possible that as the archaeology of the Hohokam continues, some new explanation will rise to the surface. For example, if late dates for the occupation of Hohokam sites accumulate, then it may make sense, as Paul Fish, an archaeologist of the Hohokam, suggests, to consider a role for European-introduced epidemic diseases in the collapse of some Hohokam communities.[40]

As for Haury's remarks about the Hohokam becoming "a part of the ecological balance instead of destroying it" or having achieved "a state of long-lasting equilibrium," or that they "came to grips with, but did not abuse, nature," one can, like Haury, reflect on the history of Spanish and American relations with the Sonoran Desert environment, as well as the transformations that continued apace in Arizona in the twentieth century.

Yet these statements seem as problematic as others. Haury wrote at the very moment when American Indians everywhere became ecological exemplars. Published nine years apart in 1967 and 1976, his thoughts signaled an awareness of global environmental lessons. In 1967, Haury was explicit about the moral of his tale: "For our own generation, with its soiled streams and fouled air, its massive and abrupt changes in environment, its shortages of water, its rampant misuse of shrinking open space, the achievement of Snaketown holds a profound meaning."[41] As, for that matter, does his analysis. As historically contingent as others put under the lens here, it reveals far more about the time when it was written than it does about the Hohokam.

Chapter Three

EDEN

IN 1630, the Reverend Francis Higginson struggled for words to describe the natural bounty in Massachusetts. "The abundance of Sea Fish are almost beyond believing," he wrote, and wood was "no better in the World." On land and sea, a "store of blessings" awaited English emigrants. Perhaps anticipating skeptical readers, he assured them that he spoke "the naked truth." But he needn't have worried. Other Europeans as awestruck by North America's natural world also labored to describe what they encountered. Never had they seen birds and other animals in such profusion, fish and shellfish so large, or forests so expansive. Trees towered above them, producing prodigious quantities of nuts, and all about them bushes hung heavy with berries. Extensive beds of shellfish blanketed estuaries and shorelines. Fish schooled, spawned, or beached themselves in countless numbers, and birds darkened the sky and eclipsed the sun. Life teemed.

Along the eastern seaboard, many Europeans reacted as Higginson had. On the Virginia coast they were flabbergasted by the "incredible aboundance" of wildlife on islands "most beautiful and pleasant to behold, replenished with deer, conies, hares and divers beasts, and about them the goodliest and best fish in the world, and in great abundance." Throughout the seventeenth century, boggled by what they saw, they depicted a lush and abundant natural world. In New England, William Wood spoke of herrings that "come up the fresh water to spawn in such multitudes as is almost incredible" and of "no country known that yields more variety of fish winter and summer." John Josselyn encountered "ample rich and pregnant valleys as ever eyes beheld" as well as such "infinite numbers" of fish throwing themselves on shore that they lay on one another "half way up" a man's leg. Thomas Morton likewise saw "fowls in abundance" and "fish in multitude" in an environment that "made the land to me seem paradise." Massachusetts, Morton thought, was "Nature's Masterpiece," a land equal to "the Israelites' Canaan."

The quantities of birds—not just migratory waterfowl and shorebirds, which flocked seasonally in enormous masses, but passenger pigeons for which numbers were insufficient—awed many: Morton spoke in terms of millions, and Wood saw "neither beginning nor ending, length or breadth of these millions of millions" of pigeons. Even after several decades of netting by colonists "greatly diminished" the flocks, Josselyn remarked that millions upon millions remained. Farther south in the Carolinas in the early eighteenth century, John Lawson was stupified by flocks that "in great measure, obstruct the Light of the day."

Observers used similar language for land and animals in the eighteenth- and early-nineteenth-century South and West. On travels through the South in the early 1770s, the great naturalist William Bartram discovered soils that were "naturally fertile" or "exceeding fertile, loose, black, deep and fast"; he roamed through "grand forest[s] of stately trees," and saw waters that "abound with a variety of excellent fish" and bays and inlets "stored with oysters and varieties of other shell-fish, crabs, shrimp, &c." He visited an island with "a great number of deer, turkeys, bears, wolves, wild cats, squirrels, racoons, and opossums," and elsewhere witnessed "squadrons of aquatic fowls." In all it was an unimaginable cornucopia; "marvellous scenes of primitive nature," Bartram thought, both "sublime" and pregnant and overflowing with "a superabundance of the necessaries and conveniences of life."

Farther west, the scenes of abundance were similar; on his voyage of discovery up the Missouri River and beyond in 1805, Meriwether Lewis wrote, "The whole face of the country was covered with herds of Buffaloe, Elk & Antelopes; deer are also abundant, but keep themselves more concealed in the woodland. the buffaloe Elk and Antelope are so gentle that we pass near them while feeding, without appearing to excite any alarm among them; and when we attract their attention, they frequently approach us more nearly to discover what we are, and in some instances pursue us a considerable distance apparently with that view."

From the sixteenth through the nineteenth centuries, Europeans and European-Americans discovered the Garden of Eden somewhere in North America. Not all who did should, of course, be taken blindly at their word. Some deployed hyperbole to entice settlers to North America for commerce or to encourage those in search of religious freedom. What better way to spur on mercantilists than to emphasize the commodity value of resources, or to encourage colonists with snapshots of "strawberry time" from late spring through early fall, when plants and trees were flowering, waterfowl, passenger pigeons, and other birds were migrating, and berries hung heavy on bushes? In New England, late winter and early spring were often more hostile than hospitable, with resources in short supply or difficult to procure for those unused to them. Moreover, from many Puritan pens flowed not visions of paradise but dark images of a howling wilderness inhabited by savage heathen outside the orb of Christian influence and eager to fall upon them.

Nonetheless, to many the continent appeared as a bountiful land with inexhaustible resources, and their arcadian and cornucopian images captured the imagination of contemporary readers, as they do today. Time and again, they reported mammals, fish, shellfish, nuts, fruits, trees, and other living things as present in greater numbers or of a larger size than ever experienced before; and resources of many kinds as abundant, fertile, extraordinarily rich—and aboundingly present in great quantities, great stores, or multitudes. Reaching for comparative if imaginative sensibility to make the present comprehensible, Samuel de Champlain gave the name "Bacchus" to one grape-laden island off the coast of Maine, and Giovanni da Verrazzano stamped "Arcadia" onto the land of "great woods" along the eastern seaboard. In similar fashion, others worked the names *Canaan* or *Eden* into their lands and books, as a reflection of comingled ideas of a paradisiacal, bountiful, beautiful, blessed, delightful, rustic land of supreme happiness and promise.[1]

Yet how can America be simultaneously paradise seemingly untouched by human hands and—as archaeologists and other scholars have often proposed—inhabited by people who, prior to the arrival of Europeans, exploited lands and animals in order to live, cut down forests for fuel and arable land, and perhaps oversalinated fields and helped animals to an early demise? If accurate, the two images are not easily reconciled.

According to archaeologists, American Indians often so pressured or depleted basic resources like land and trees that they had to switch from one type of food to another or move the locations of their villages. Native farmers throughout North America transformed landscapes (as farmers everywhere did), not just by burning and clearing woodland for conversion to agricultural land, but through the steadily escalating demand for wood for fuel and construction matching growing populations supported by domesticated crops. In the East, they cleared fields by slashing and burning forests, then hoed the fields into washboard-like ridges or small hills in which they cultivated crops. If they had a total of one to three acres per person either under active cultivation or in fallow, as has been estimated, then in 1500, at least one-half million acres (and perhaps many more) showed the effects of agriculture in the East alone. In many places, farmers used fields year after year, until declining yields pushed them elsewhere. With soils rendered infertile, fields choked with weeds, fuel exhausted, and game scarce, Indians left their villages behind for more favorable habitats (perhaps in the knowledge that they could return one day when the ground and trees recovered). Iroquoian people apparently moved their villages every ten to twelve years for these and other reasons, including insect infestations. Wood, one of the most crucial resources, seemed particularly susceptible to overuse. In the Northeast, more than one observer was awed by its extensive use for domestic fuel. The newcomers from Europe were no different; Narragansett Indians theorized that the English came to Rhode Island because they had no firewood in England.[2]

The depletion of wood might hold the key to the disappearance of some notable people: the Anasazi, who lived in the Southwest, and the residents of Cahokia, a site located across the Mississippi from modern-day St. Louis, Missouri. Many scholars use superlatives in speaking about both people. The Anasazi are renowned for multistory villages in Chaco Canyon and in striking cliff-site locations at Mesa Verde and elsewhere, and for their interest in the solstices and equinoxes.[3] Cahokians, who inhabited the largest pre-Columbian site (part of the most densely settled community) in North America, are admired for the construction of large-scale works, including 120 mounds. One mound measuring 700,000 square feet at the base and one hundred feet high, and containing twenty-two million cubic feet of earth, is the most massive earthen structure in pre-Columbian North America.[4] Some nineteenth-century observers mistakenly considered these cliff dwellers and mound builders (especially the latter) as mysterious races unrelated to contemporary Indians. But these Indian people were farmers who supplemented diets based on maize, squash, and beans with other domesticates, gathered foods, and animals and fish. The Mississippi floodplain was much richer than the arid Southwest, and the leaders of Cahokia were powerful people who guided massive public projects and, following death, were interred with lavish care.[5]

The Anasazi abandoned their sites in the twelfth century; Cahokians, theirs from the twelfth through fourteenth centuries.[6] Explanations have ranged widely; with disease, feuds, warfare, and other ideas new and old unsupported convincingly by evidence, they have settled in recent years on environmental change, population pressure, and resource depletion. In the arid Southwest, where trees take many human generations to grow, an expanding Anasazi population could easily have stripped their lands of trees for house and kiva construction and for fuel, and to produce arable fields, bringing about a deforestation with various adverse repercussions on all aspects of their lives, just prior to debilitating drought. In Chaco Canyon alone they used over 200,000 trees in multistory buildings and denuded the land, inviting erosion and destruction of arable lands.[7] At Cahokia, full canopy forest was probably rare and trees inadequate to meet the estimated demands of a rising population for fuel, construction, and other ends. When the population was near and at its height, Cahokians imported wood. Perhaps they had no choice. They could easily have stripped the estimated 600,000 floodplain trees growing within a six-mile radius of the Cahokia center in a matter of decades, inducing deforestation-related runoff, erosion, sedimentation, and silting. Their population was in sharp decline before they fell back on local wood. Abandonment provided ample time for trees to replenish the Mississippi floodplain before Europeans first laid eyes on this great center's ruins.[8]

Perhaps demography is an important key to solving the paradox of paradisiacal plentitude despite human exploitation. If the human population was relatively low in most parts of the continent, then its relatively modest demands could be met without severe degradation in the environment. If in some places the population rose with demands that could not be met, then ultimately people vanished, releasing the pressure on land and resources. This was the most likely scenario for the Cahokians, Anasazi, and Hohokam, whose rising desire for wood or water might have proved their undoing.

Population pressure was not a constant everywhere. In demography as in other aspects of their lives, North American Indians differed greatly from one another. Settled throughout the continent for thousands of years by the time Europeans arrived, Indians lived in hundreds of distinct sovereign societies, each drawing its identity from being principal or real human beings and each possessing its own tongue, technology, economy, polity, beliefs, and so on.[9]

Some indigenous people lived in scattered communities relatively small in size. Others lived in densely settled circumstances, in some places circumscribed by deserts, infertile uplands, or other physical or social boundaries. But were population size and density great enough anywhere to constitute significant pressure on the environment? Given the relatively low-impact technology of these preindustrial people, it may be that except in a few notable cases, their few numbers trod so lightly as to leave bounty for European eyes almost everywhere.

Populations large enough to have made some difference might have declined from their failure to perceive (or halt) the consequences of their demands for wood or water. Moreover, most if not all North American Indian populations declined for another reason: After Europeans arrived, many indigenous people died from new microbes transported from Europe, to which they had no natural immunity. However slight their pressure on land and resources had been, it lessened until new technologies and commodifications tipped the scales of environmental pressure in the other direction. In other words, perhaps the North American Eden described by Europeans resulted both from aboriginal demography and—darkened by epidemic disease and death—from post-European epidemiology.

To investigate these ideas we need to arrive at an estimate for the size of the aboriginal population in North America. Firm population figures simply do not exist prior to European arrival, and the statistics after that point are often poor. The most important means of estimating the size of the aboriginal population is to determine the mortality of the epidemic diseases that arrived with Europeans—the most visible demographic process—and project backward to the moment before those diseases arrived.

America was not a disease-free paradise before Europeans landed on its shores. Today, scars on bones hold the memory of pre-Columbian endemic pathologies. Treponematosis, a disease complex manifesting itself in yaws, pinta, and endemic and venereal syphilis, affected many who lived in densely settled sedentary farming communities along the mid-Atlantic seaboard and in the South. Both forms of syphilis were present in North Carolina and Virginia. Nutritionally stressed from their reliance on maize, whose protein is of remarkably low quality, these farming people were especially vulnerable to the spread of infections. Tuberculosis (long associated with cattle in the Old World) was also present in the New World—in Peru and perhaps elsewhere.[10]

But the demographic effect of these endemic infectious diseases paled compared to the impact of the Old World microbes that were transported by Europeans and even traveled in advance of them, carried by infected Indians to more distant indigenous people who sickened and died before actually encountering white people. In 1585–86, Thomas Harriot wrote from Virginia that Indians in some towns "began to die very fast, and many in a short space," but never suspected how often others would sound a refrain. Thereafter, some contagion swept away native people somewhere in North America in almost every decade. The litany is overwhelming. In 1616–19, bubonic plague or some other disease decimated Indians in coastal Massachusetts and beyond, and Pilgrims took note of the "good hand of God" sparing them but not the Indians. Other diseases followed, among them the destructive virus smallpox, which ravaged the Huron in the 1630s and became especially virulent in the eighteenth century, when local outbreaks every decade or generation virtually destroyed Indians in southern California missions in 1709–10 and 1729–32, the Catawba in 1759, and many Plains Indians in 1779–83. From 1600 to 1900, there were at least twenty major epidemics of smallpox. In 1763, a zealous aide of the British commander Sir Jeffrey Amherst carried out his admonition that Indians be sent smallpox-infested blankets, and deployed the virus as a biological weapon.

Other recurrent afflictions included influenza, which hammered New England in 1647 and reached pandemic dimensions in 1761; and measles, which especially devastated people who took sweat baths, a traditional remedy for fever, and brought on bronchopneumonia. Other diseases plagued indigenous people—typhus in California in 1742, some unknown affliction along the Columbia River in 1782–83, and cholera in the Upper Midwest in 1832–34. Often, two or more diseases arrived simultaneously or in quick succession, or hunger and starvation dogged those laid low by sickness. Time and again, in a virtual viral, bacterial, and protozoal assault, smallpox, chickenpox, influenza, measles, mumps, rubella, yellow fever, common cold, pneumonia, scarlet fever, whooping cough, diphtheria, typhus, dysentery, cholera, bubonic plague, malaria, and amebic dysentery killed not dozens but hundreds and thousands of people. The written historical record is abundant and clear.[11]

Because of the microbes they carried, Europeans who arrived in and spread throughout North America were an invading force that took no prisoners. There is no need to accuse Europeans, as some have, of mass continental genocide—assuming that requires intent. These diseases did not need conspiracy to spread. They arrived on new ground, on undisturbed "virgin soil" where Indians lacked immunity and experience in dealing with them. All were susceptible, entire communities became sick at once, and people of all ages and both sexes died from primary or secondary infections or the effects of starvation.[12]

It is difficult for most of us to imagine what it is like to lose, through horrible death, one-quarter, one-half, or more of one's community overnight. Yet that is what happened, not in one but in hundreds of communities. There is no debate over what must have been the sheer terror of each major epidemic. The memories of Indians themselves make each case poignant and tragic.

Consider, for example, the scenes of utter desolation during the winter of 1837–38, which for Sioux historians was the year of smallpox. In what they called "winter record" or "winter count," Yanktonai Sioux historians painted small pictographs in spirals onto buffalo and elk hides and canvas and muslin, each image representing a year's significant happening. Read counterclockwise, the whole served as a mnemonic device through which the Sioux recalled event-based history. Many events worthy of historical notice were raids and killings. Others called up the death of important leaders. Still others remembered unusual or hazardous events: harsh climatological conditions, such as a winter when snow was so deep that snowshoes were needed for hunting; unusual meteoric or celestial phenomena like a meteor shower; the killing of a white buffalo. For 1837–38, the Yanktonai drew a human figure in outline, with heavy spots all over its body. That year, said John K. Bear, a Lower Yanktonai historian whose winter count was in his memory, "Smallpox big." He did not exaggerate. Over the next two years, Blood, Hidatsa, Kiowa, Mandan, and Teton Sioux historians all remembered the smallpox epidemic in their winter counts.[13]

For these and other people, the summer of 1837 was horrific. The central event is not disputed: An American Fur Company steamer carried smallpox-infected men and women up the Missouri River, and they in turn infected others each time they stopped. Bent on exchanging trade goods for robes and furs obtained over the winter, the steamer *St. Peters* left St. Louis in mid-April 1837 for upper Missouri River posts. After ten or eleven days on the river, a deckhand became feverish. Several days later, the steamer's captain and others discussed the reasons for the fever. Smallpox was raised as a possibility. Some advocated stranding the man ashore as a necessary preventive measure. But the symptoms were ambiguous and the captain, doubting smallpox and needing his hand's labor, refused.

By the time there was no doubt that the deckhand's sickness was due to smallpox, it was too late to isolate the disease. The deckhand had infected others aboard, including three Arikara women. On June 5, the *St. Peters* reached Sioux Agency and distributed trade goods to awaiting Yankton and Santee Sioux. Fourteen days afterward, the Arikara women left the boat at Fort Clark, a busy trading post, for a nearby Mandan village, and five days later the *St. Peters* arrived at Fort Union, where it remained briefly before its return downriver to St. Louis, stopping at the same posts en route.

Everywhere, Indians died. They succumbed in their villages alongside the Missouri River, and away from the river. They died that summer or when the disease reached them in the next two years. Some, like the Yankton Sioux at Sioux Agency, were partly protected by immunity gained through exposure to smallpox in 1819–20 or by inoculation following an epidemic of smallpox on the central Plains in 1831. Most were unprotected. The Santee Sioux had refused to be inoculated and died agonizingly and in droves. The Yanktonai living in more than sixty lodges—perhaps four hundred people in all—died. The Mandan, Gros Ventres, and Arikara living together in packed village lodges near Fort Clark presented ideal conditions for the spread of the disease. Eyewitnesses spoke about the "greatest destruction possible" among these people. Four Bears or Mató-Tópe, an accomplished Mandan warrior whose likeness Karl Bodmer, the artist accompanying Prince Maximilian of Wied on his excursion into the West, had painted just four years before, went "crazy" after his entire family perished, and died. George Catlin, the artist, was told that the Sioux boxed in the Mandan, who subsequently "destroyed themselves" with their own weapons and "by dashing their brains out by leaping head-foremost from a thirty foot ledge of rocks in front of their village." In one village only fourteen of six hundred Mandans survived. The Blackfeet and Assiniboine at Fort Union died in the thousands. With unfortunate timing, the Skidi Pawnee attacked their enemies the Oglala Sioux in the fall, returned to their village with smallpox-ridden, contagious prisoners, and subsequently died in the thousands. No action or ritual helped the Pawnee, not a Morning Star rite or human sacrifice. On the greater Plains, the tragedy was beyond description. The Mandan practically disappeared. Three-quarters of the Blackfeet, one-half of the Assiniboine and Arikara, and one-quarter of the Pawnee died. In all, perhaps seventeen thousand people perished.

Some have been tempted to try to pinpoint "blame" for this horrendous epidemic, but the exercise is futile. The symptoms were at first vague and subject to different interpretations, and by the time the illness was recognized as deadly, it would have been practically impossible to prevent its transmission. No one involved—not Indians, not white people—wished to see smallpox spread. While this was not the first or last time that traders transported microbes with trade goods, they had only mercantilism and profit in mind and understood that sick Indians brought fewer furs and robes, and dead Indians none. Had the symptoms been more clear-cut, they might have acted in everyone's best interest. Indians themselves also figured unwittingly in the disease's spread, beginning with the Arikara women who left the boat for the Mandan village probably harboring the virus. Some Indians refused inoculation and died (unluckily others accepted inoculation at one post whose traders, lacking cowpox vaccine, naively used the live smallpox virus with disastrous results). At Fort Union, whose gates the traders had locked, hoping to keep Indians outside away from infected people within, the Assiniboine angrily demanded access to goods. They succeeded—but got smallpox in the bargain. The Blackfeet and Piegan insisted that a smaller smallpox-infested boat continue its voyage so that they could get trade goods. In the end, Indians, who possessed far more reason than whites to abhor smallpox, were as shackled as whites—by desires for trade and beliefs about illness.[14]

Given the scope of the tragedy, it seems that the population of North America must have been very large prior to the arrival of virgin-soil epidemics. But over the last one hundred years, estimates have ranged as low as 500,000 and as high as eighteen million people. For over fifty years the most influential figure was one million, which went largely unquestioned. Then in 1966, Henry Dobyns, an anthropologist, drawing on the historical demography of Mexico and the Caribbean, estimated that the aboriginal population of North America ranged from ten to twelve million.[15]

Dobyns threw down the gauntlet with this revisionist and, to many, inconceivable estimate; many responded with new local, regional, and continental analyses. The most notable new continental estimates are (in rounded figures) two million, four million, seven million, and twelve million. Their authors share a healthy appreciation for both epidemic devastation and variability in the course of disease and the archaeological and historical record. Meanwhile, deciding that epidemics were more deadly, populations less able to recover, and the continent able to carry or support more people than he earlier imagined, Dobyns trumped his earlier estimate with a new one of eighteen million. Fifty percent higher, it made his earlier attempt appear timorous.[16]

Since the 1960s, pressure to look favorably upon high estimates like twelve and eighteen million has produced what one historian has called an "ideological morass," as estimating numbers has become sharply politicized. A generation ago, Francis Jennings and a few other scholars argued passionately that ideas of the size of the aboriginal population affect characterizations of American Indians and vice versa. Since then, native scholars Lenore Stiffarm and Phil Lane noted that "it has always been expedient for non-Indian 'experts' to minimize the size of aboriginal Indian populations, while denigrating the level of socio-economic attainment that presumably resulted in such sparseness of human presence." Those who think that the population was small risk being linked with theorists of an earlier day who tied population to social progress, arguing that low numbers went hand in hand with simple technology and a less evolved "savage" state of society absent progress and intelligence. If people were "savages," then their populations must have been small; if their populations were small, then they must have lived in a state of savagery. It was with understandings like these that missionaries and governmental agents found justification for conversion, civilizing programs, land appropriation, and imperial conquest.

Those who settle on a small number for aboriginal North America risk being branded anti-Indian; those who opt for a large number do not. In the year of the Columbus Quincentenary, David Stannard stated in his book, *American Holocaust*, that "few serious students" put the size of the aboriginal population at less than eight to twelve million. Seduced by the putative "accuracy" of Dobyns's eighteen million estimate, which meshed with the provocatively titled *American Holocaust*, Stannard preferred an estimate ranging from eight to eighteen million. Stiffarm and Lane also preferred Dobyns's estimate of eighteen million. Apparently swayed, however, by the work of Russell Thornton, a sociologist (and Cherokee), they have settled on fifteen million as a "real number." Thornton's own estimate was a much lower seven million; perhaps because he did not subscribe completely to Dobyns's methodology, Stiffarm and Lane regarded him as "somewhat confused." Worse than being labeled confused is being linked by implication to racists: Stannard regarded the relationship between European-Americans and North America Indians as genocidal and analogous to Nazis and Jews—and would not denying the highest numbers leave one complicit with the murderers?[17]

Was the aboriginal population of North America ever as high as Dobyns proclaimed (and was Stannard right about what "serious students" think)? In order to decide on a sensible estimate for the size of the aboriginal population, we do not need to trivialize the horror of the toll of the epidemics or doubt that disease was the most dramatic and significant source of biological and ecological change introduced by Europeans. But to agree with the highest estimates assumes that diseases arrived early, spread widely, and were invariably fatal; that populations did not recover between epidemics; and that diseases can actually be identified, a necessary step in order to say anything with confidence about their behavior.[18]

But misgivings come from almost every quarter—in particular on whether or not diseases arrived as early and spread as widely as supporters of the highest estimates argue. In the Northeast, for example, estimates of the aboriginal population range widely, depending on whether one believes that epidemics reached that region in the sixteenth or seventeenth century. The high-enders argue that European explorers and fishermen who landed on the coast in the sixteenth century, carried on a trade in furs, and captured native people and carried them back then to Europe also necessarily transported epidemics. They assert that an epidemic of smallpox in Mexico in 1520–24 and another disease in Virginia in the 1560s spread to the Northeast to cause thousands of unreported deaths. They believe that when sickness was reported to have felled fifty St. Lawrence Iroquoians in 1535, thousands actually perished. But there is no evidence for these or other assertions. In contrast, it is well documented that in 1616–22, a major "plague," which might have been bubonic plague, yellow fever, or viral hepatitis, decimated coastal Indians; eleven years later, in 1633–35, measles followed by smallpox ravaged people throughout the region; and thereafter various diseases including smallpox, measles, influenza, and undiagnosed fevers struck episodically during the century. By 1700, then, the population might have been reduced by 60 to 90 percent of its size one hundred years earlier—but there is no reliable indication that that size was itself reduced from the century before.[19]

The American Southwest presents a parallel case. Those who argue that smallpox preceded the arrival of the Spanish in 1539 to fell three-quarters of the aboriginal population base their assertion on abandoned pueblos. But abandoned pueblos are common in the pre-epidemic history of the American Southwest—and this region was separated from Mexico (the supposed source of the smallpox) physically, socially, and economically at the time the disease was supposed to have come. Diseases did indeed travel north in Mexico with the Spanish in the sixteenth century—far to the south, measles and perhaps dysentery, typhoid, malaria, and typhus ravaged Nayarit and Sinaloa on the Pacific Coast in the 1530s to 1540s—but there is no evidence whatsoever that they went farther north.

At the end of the sixteenth century the picture changes. In 1593, smallpox and measles hit Sinaloa hard—and from then on disease arrived in that region every five to eight or so years. Some afflictions trickled north, reaching the Rio Grande in 1598, and several decades later, in the 1630s, many people died from smallpox. They succumbed not uniformly, however, but in a ragged mosaic-like pattern, influenced, perhaps, by iron-deficiency anemia and tuberculosis, which were the signs of nutritional stress from a maize-based diet and crowded living conditions. Famine, emigration, and conflict all complicated the epidemiological picture, as some communities plunged into oblivion. Between 1539 and 1640, the population decline may have been on the order of 60 to 70 percent and a downward trend continued through the mid–eighteenth century.[20]

Contemporary reports of epidemics are not always reliable even in identifying diseases, because the chroniclers did not always understand what they were looking at; the problem is continental in scope. The behavior and demographic impact of disease depends on matters ranging from a microparasite's incubation period and the length of latent and infectious periods to how a particular disease is transmitted and how deadly it is alone or with complications. For an accurate idea of any disease's effect on an afflicted population, we ideally need to know how many individuals are immune or susceptible, and how many susceptible individuals are infected or uninfected, and then what happens both in the short term (life or death) and in the long term (effect on immunity or reproductive capability, for instance).[21]

In the late eighteenth century, European fur traders established a network of trading posts in the vast Mackenzie River region in the Canadian Subarctic, the homeland of a number of Northern Athapaskan–speaking people. Each summer they transported manu-

TABLE 3.1: *Diseases in the Western Canadian Subarctic, 1800-1860*

DATE	DISEASE*†	GROUPS AFFECTED†
1800	The pox	Denesóline
1802	Disorder	Dunne-za
1803	Stomach complaint	Denesóline, Dunne-za
1803–4	Endemical disorder	Denesóline, Dunne-za
1804	Sick all summer	Deh Gáh Got'ine
1805–6	Sickly state	Deh Gáh Got'ine?, K'áshot'ine?, Sahtúot'ine
1806	Diseases rage	Deh Gáh Got'ine?, Tlicho?
1808	Sickness very prevalent	Deh Gáh Got'ine?
1819	Measles	Denesóline
1819–20	Measles	Denesóline, Dunne-za
1820	Measles, dysentery	Denesóline, T'atsaot'ine?
1821–23	Malignant contagion	Dunne-za
1822–24	Dysentery, cough, flu	Denesóline, Deh Gáh Got'ine, T'atsaot'ine
1825–26	Contagious distemper	Denesóline, Deh Gáh Got'ine, T'atsaot'ine?, Tlicho, Shíhta Got'ine, K'áshot'ine, Sahtúot'ine?, Gwich'in
1827–28	Whooping cough	Dunne-za, Deh Gáh Got'ine
1830–31	Severe cold	Deh Gáh Got'ine
1834	Influenza	Deh Gáh Got'ine, Shíhta Got'ine, Sahtúot'ine?, Gwich'in
1835–36	Influenza	Denesóline, Dunne-za, T'atsaot'ine?
1837–38	Influenza	Denesóline, Deh Gáh Got'ine, T'atsaot'ine, Tlicho, Shíhta Got'ine, Sahtúot'ine
1839	Fatal disease	Sahtúot'ine
1843	Influenza	Deh Gáh Got'ine, Tlicho?, Shíhta Got'ine, K'áshot'ine, Gwich'in
1845	Whooping cough	Denesóline
1846	Measles, influenza	Denesóline
1849	Cough, sore throat	Gwich'in
1851	Influenza, dysentery	Dunne-za, Tlicho, Deh Gáh Got'ine, Gwich'in
1852	Mumps	Gwich'in
1852–53	Sickness	Denesóline, Gwich'in
1854	Sickness	Deh Gáh Got'ine, Tlicho?, Shíhta Got'ine
1855	Cold	Deh Gáh Got'ine
1856–57	Epidemic	Denesóline, Deh Gáh Got'ine, Tlicho
1858	Influenza?	Denesóline

* Diagnosis by fur traders and contemporaries.
† The question marks indicate uncertainty.

factured goods as well as microbes into the region. For the first six decades of the nineteenth century, afflictions called the pox, measles, dysentery, whooping cough, severe cold, cough, sore throat, influenza, mumps, disorder, stomach complaint, malignant contagion, or contagious distemper (Table 3.1) left a stark impression, even though the particular diseases may not have been accurately diagnosed or described.[22]

A "very disagreeable disorder, the Pox" killed at least one Denesóline and made others sick in 1800, but what was it? If it was smallpox (and related to an epidemic on the Columbia River two years before), it is curious that it did not attract more attention. It could not have been *variola major*, the deadly form of smallpox that killed roughly one-third of those who contracted it. Perhaps it was the less virulent *variola minor*, which killed less than 5 percent of those afflicted, or some other disease with a symptomatic rash often confused with smallpox in its earliest stages, like scarlet fever, measles, rubella, or meningitis. Or maybe it was chickenpox—even though the rashes for smallpox and chickenpox develop on different parts of the body and at different rates—whose pox can be caused by the recurrence of an infection in an older person with shingles or herpes zoster. There are far more questions than answers.[23]

Another disease identified by a familiar name is dysentery, which invaded the region several times. An intestinal dysfunction with bloody and mucus-filled diarrhea as the primary symptom, dysentery may be more clear-cut than "the pox," but nevertheless comes in two forms: bacillary dysentery, which is commonly spread by contact or flies and is far more common in temperate zones, and protozoan-caused amebic dysentery, which spreads by water and has high infection rates and increases in severity as it goes from host to host. Which arrived is not known but it coincided with influenza, measles, and a "consumptive disorder."[24]

In the case of a "disorder," "stomach complaint," disease that "raged," "prevalent sickness," and "malignant contagion," we are on even shakier ground. They are frustratingly vague in symptoms, yet contemporary observers called them fatal, virulent, or dreadful and said that they killed not the odd person but from one-quarter to one-third of the population. In 1803–4, one "endemical disorder" that killed people within two weeks of onslaught amounted to a "stomach complaint with great lassitude & shortness of breathing," with additional symptoms including a "gathering in the throat" or a "burning pain in the mouth and upper stomach." Infected Indians could neither eat nor sleep, and some "linger[ed] to death," including some three dozen Denesólines, which was considered a "great number." Perhaps this was typhoid fever, whose systemic symptoms include fever, malaise, and anorexia; or diphtheria, a rapidly spreading acute febrile infection that can involve paralysis of the palate muscles and is sometimes mild and in one form (*gravis*) severe, its virulence at times increased by invasive bacteriophages. Typhoid fever or diphtheria gravis can kill one of every ten people affected.[25]

"Distempers" twice crossed species boundaries, first killing animals like moose and then turning on people; on one occasion, dogs that ate dead animals also died. The epidemics sound horrendous but the actual mortality is unknown. One "rag[ed] with astonishing fury"—with only a small number reported dead. Traders said that the other was a "dreadful sickness" or "contagious distemper" that "indiscriminately" killed "a great number of men, women, and children" who came to one post for the exchange. These diseases might have been tularemia, a bacterial zoonotic disease that begins in wildlife and is transmitted between animals and humans. Significantly, rabbits, which often play a key role in transmission, were at a population peak at the time of both distempers. Tularemia affects the blood and tissues of infected animals, so that eating contaminated food, as dogs did, results in death. Tick-borne tularemia can be virulent, highly infective, and pathogenic, with "sudden and prostrating constitutional symptoms." Fatality rates can measure 5 percent or more but vary greatly. There is much we may never know for certain, however, about these particular diseases—beginning with their identity and how infective or pathogenic they were. Others were even more obscure.[26]

There is no problem identifying some diseases—like whooping cough (pertussis), whose hallmark symptom is a paroxysmal, repeatedly violent cough lacking an intervening inhalation and followed by a high-pitched inspiratory whoop. An acute bacterial infection, pertussis is typically mild and confined to children today, but on virgin soil in the nineteenth-century Subarctic, all were susceptible, many became sick, and hunger dogged the families of hunters who depended on stealth to stalk moose and other animals. Even if we do not know how many people pertussis killed in the Subarctic, one or more of every twenty people affected can die from it, and others are sometimes felled by complications from bronchopneumonia, enteritis, or convulsions.[27]

Measles, also readily identified, was the second most common affliction during this period and had more serious consequences. A viral disease of high but brief infectiousness, one attack confers lifelong immunity, but in populations lacking immunity, all are susceptible and develop measles, which, for at least four days, is extremely debilitating. In severe cases the rash affects all epithelial surfaces, in respiratory and gastrointestinal tracts and elsewhere, which can bring on bronchial pneumonia and diarrhea.

Fatalities are numerous in virgin-soil measles—a rate of 7 percent in two twentieth-century Arctic villages whose inhabitants were adversely affected by their nutritional status and evidently as high as 50 percent elsewhere. Most deaths are due to epidemiological factors and, especially, cultural and social responses to the disease. When all are affected simultaneously, village life collapses, food is lacking, and the afflicted may not be cared for appropriately or at all. A fatalistic response by people convinced that they will die, or a therapeutic sweat bath for a disease complicated by bronchopneumonia and dehydration from diarrhea in its final stages, is likely to produce the same result: death. Mortality is enhanced when measles occurs with bronchopneumonia or influenza. In Alaska in 1900, the year of the combined measles-influenza "Great Sickness," the death rate ranged from 13 to 74 percent and in interior Athapaskan Indian villages was 25 percent.[28]

In the north, disease and starvation coincided several times. The behavior of disease in an individual is often shaped by his or her nutritional state, and nutritional deficiencies reduce resistance and increase the severity of disease. The effects are not constant: Malnutrition has a maximal effect on diseases such as measles, pertussis, and most respiratory infections, and a minimal impact on the outcome of smallpox, typhoid, and others. Yet all infections influence nutrition by reducing appetite, increasing metabolic needs and metabolic losses of nutrients, and decreasing absorption when the gastrointestinal tract is involved. The impact in virgin-soil measles and other epidemics can be severe; on several occasions in the north, disease disabled so many adults, including hunters, that mortality was related as much to extreme hunger and actual starvation as to the disease organisms themselves.[29]

From anecdotal information alone, it is tempting to conclude that the population in the Mackenzie River region went into a free fall. Disease arrived almost annually, in some years affecting one or two groups trading at a single post, and in other years affecting people and places over a wide area. Individuals died in agony and the survivors were adversely affected in numerous ways. Prior to the late 1820s, however, not only is the identity of many contagions unknown, but there was no census of the population from which to calculate a decline. In 1829, the first census allows for a base for population trends over the next several decades. And until 1858, when another census occurred, the population of Mackenzie River was apparently virtually unchanged at between two thousand and three thousand people.

Why the population did not decline sharply from 1829 to 1858 is a puzzle. Neither migration nor underenumeration in the census played any apparent significant role in the census figures. Diseases continued to arrive and kill but the mortality might well have been offset by the decline of female infanticide, which had been widely practiced, and the survival of females to reproductive age.[30]

Moreover, the diseases that arrived spread spottily, were less lethal than indicated by their symptoms alone, affected a population that contained a greater proportion of immune people able to recover more fully from sickness than before, and were more often "influenza" (or something related) than any other affliction. Spread rapidly, its survival enhanced by low humidity and temperature, influenza presents complicated problems because the viral group comprises antigenically distinct groups traditionally known as types A, B, and C. Its impact varies with virus type, how many people are susceptible, and complications including pneumonias and bronchitis. In pandemics, attack rates range from 7 to 70 percent and often increase in distinct waves of infection—20 percent attacked in the first wave, and 50 to 70 percent more in succeeding waves.

Influenza A is deadly. It can develop new strains every several years, and its antigenic profile can change, thus circumventing immunity. It comes on suddenly, with major symptoms like chill, high fever, malaise, anorexia, cough, severe headache, nausea, vomiting, diarrhea, and convulsions. The symptoms last from five days to two weeks or longer and, as a rule, affect children more than adults. This type of influenza can cross species boundaries—as along the Mackenzie River in the 1830s, when a fatal sustained outbreak killed both caribou and people. The other types of influenza are less virulent, causing small localized epidemics and upper respiratory infections similar to a cold. They are often misdiagnosed. Nineteenth-century infections that were "something like influenza" or "influenza" might not have been, and others identified as a cough, sore throat, cold, or "severe cold" might actually have been influenza.[31]

Beyond the problem of identification, "influenza" spread unevenly in the nineteenth-century Subarctic. It tended to spread rapidly to reach people in many bands, even those distant from the trading posts. But it did not travel to all of the posts nor did it affect all bands equally. Because of variations like these, "it is not easy to predict what is likely to happen in small groups before the virus dies out."[32]

These data from three widely separated regions of North America undermine the assumptions behind Dobyns's estimate that eighteen million people inhabited North America on the eve of European arrival. To accept this high figure means agreeing that mere contact with Europeans involved the transmission of a deadly disease; that the earliest diseases inexorably became full-blown pandemics, spreading far beyond their documented source; that diseases always killed large numbers of people; that recorded deaths represent the tip of an iceberg underneath which lay thousands of unreported deaths; and that populations never recovered following epidemics: in sum, that the most poorly documented epidemics invariably had widely devastating impacts.

But we often do not know for certain what the diseases were (much less the precise viral agents in something like influenza), if they arrived, how far they spread, or how many they killed. Seldom do we possess an adequate understanding of epidemiology, a population's beliefs about and responses to disease, or consequent spatial variations in transmission and infectiousness. Devastating in anecdote, vague in mortality, neither the course nor demographic impact of many specific epidemics is sure. As in the Subarctic, there are widespread contradictions between many suspicioned deaths and census data indicating no great population loss.

Critics of Dobyns's analysis have challenged his historiography—his literal reading of documents, selective use of data, unreliable visual or textual sources, and faulty translations—as well as his faith in accurately gauging the number of people a region can "carry" or support.[33] They have disputed the statistical methodology of those on whom his work rests,[34] as well as his own.[35] They have criticized his assumption that between epidemic events, populations grow little if at all. Outside North America (where data are better), populations have recovered following severe epidemics, and recent simulations for population trends following smallpox epidemics in North America suggest that no-growth assumptions are hazardous at best.[36] Yet despite this fundamental critique, most scholars agree that after the point that documentation for the actual arrival of disease in a community or region exists, there is ample evidence for population declines of 80 percent or more—and occasionally of 95 percent—down to late-nineteenth-century population nadirs.

Eliminating eighteen million as an estimate for the aboriginal population of North America leaves us with a range of two to twelve million. Given all the problems, the most sensible figures are four to seven million—the two estimates in the middle. Most people lived in the Southwest, Northeast, California, and Southeast, and the fewest, in the Great Basin, Arctic, and Plateau. The most densely settled regions were California and the Northwest Coast; the least densely settled, the Subarctic, Arctic, and Great Basin (Table 3.2).[37]

These average densities are based on approximately two million inhabitants (the only estimate for which there is substantial detail for all parts of the continent). With a population of four to seven million (the preferred range), the densities were from two to over three times greater—and the impact of the people on land and resources of potentially greater significance. If the regional pattern held, then

TABLE 3.2: *North America, 1500: Population Density by Culture Area Based on 1,894,000 Population*

	POPULATION SIZE	PEOPLE/100 SQUARE MILES
California	221,000	194
Northwest Coast	175,000	140
Southwest	454,000	73
Southeast	204,000	57
Northeast	358,000	49
Plateau	78,000	39
Plains	189,000	16
Great Basin	38,000	10
Arctic	74,000	8
Subarctic	103,000	5
North America	1,894,000	28

densities by culture area would have ranged upward to a possible 386 people per 100 square miles (with four million inhabitants) or 689 people per 100 square miles (with seven million). No doubt there were further variations within regions, sharp differences between riverine and upland populations, or coastal and interior ones, as in New England, where the imprint of man in cleared fields and burned lands was clearly stamped on the densely settled coast but not the sparsely inhabited, thickly wooded northern interior.[38]

These estimates for North America contrasted sharply with those for Europe—the comparative backdrop for those who came to America, some to discover Eden—and even more so as North America's native population declined from epidemic diseases. Europe was far more heavily and densely peopled in the sixteenth, seventeenth, and eighteenth centuries than was North America. In 1700, 92 million people lived in Europe and only 2 million in North America, and one century later, the figures were 145 million and only 5 million.[39]

In England and France, the population surged dramatically from 1600 to 1850—a steady rise for the first century and one-half, followed by an explosive climb. Some thought sixteenth-century England overcrowded and pushed for emigration to alleviate population pressure. By 1750, the density had increased in France and England by some 30 to 40 percent, and certain regions revealed clear signs of what the historian Fernand Braudel called demographic tension resulting from overpopulation. In seventeenth-century England, some continued to advocate emigration from an overcrowded land, yet others thought that ample space remained. Needless to say, each country and region had its own demographic profile, and there were especially sharp differences in population density between rural and urban areas.[40]

The difference between Europe's crowded urban settings and almost all North American locales was vast. In 1600 alone, the population density in France and England was on average from fifteen to nine hundred times that of North America with four to seven million aboriginal inhabitants. The gulf was greater for those who came to North America from dense urban settings in Europe. And when disease struck down native North Americans, it magnified for all this already vast difference.[41]

The Old World environment compared to the New World one was also obviously far more heavily changed and depleted of resources, and it was Europe's transformed landscapes that formed (with attendant demographic pressures) a comparative backdrop for the North American paradise. From the fifteenth through seventeenth centuries, powered by demands, designs, and technology, Europeans profoundly altered their landscapes. They transformed entire sections of the countryside. Woodcutters in search of fuel and farmers after arable land assaulted forests on a broad front. Prior to the mid–seventeenth century, they cleared from sixty-eight thousand to seventy-nine thousand square miles of forest for agricultural and other purposes and, in the next hundred years, put another twenty-one thousand to twenty-five thousand square miles under the ax. In their consumption of forests, farmers were abetted by iron and other mineral smelters, who required charcoal, as well as by naval and merchant interests, which could never get enough timber for ships. The environment changed in myriad ways. Miners sunk shafts for coal, which, when burned, filled the skies with soot. Hunters systematically killed wolves and other animals competing with or predators of red deer, boars, and birds reserved for sport for the wealthy. Poverty was as rife in the countryside as in expanding urban areas. In England, people drained marshes for conversion to arable land, and mined and burned sulfur-laden coal, which darkened urban skies. They engaged in brewing, brick, dyeing, and other industries yet thought it unimportant to control the wastes that fouled waters and air. Increasingly, the English countryside took on new appeal as a place of escape, and some even yearned for wild areas rather than the relentless ploughing of cultivation.[42]

This, then, was the European context for travelers and emigrants to America: a far more heavily and densely populated and urbanized continent, and one whose landscapes had been greatly altered and resources depleted.

In the North American Eden, the immigrant population grew explosively owing to successful reproduction and a constant stream of new immigrants. In only ninety years the numbers went from 275,000 in 1700 to roughly four million, and one century later (in 1900) the total was some seventy-five to ninety million. In the seventeenth century, most lived in the East—more than eight of every ten in Virginia, Massachusetts, Maryland, and Connecticut—and were concentrated further—in Virginia, for example, four of every five blacks and whites lived on the coast. The decline of the indigenous population was as pronounced as the rise in immigrant numbers and the replacement swift: In the South, for example, a population that was 80 percent native in 1685 remained only 3 percent native in 1790.[43]

With rapidly expanding numbers, different technologies, extractive and commodifying economies, and few ideas restraining their relationship to the land or other living beings getting in the way, European immigrants soon made their presence felt. They occupied lands vacant from disease or obtained from Indians by force or in every conceivable kind of transaction. Their effect on the landscape depended on the region and time. Powered by consumer-based needs and wants—by commodification—and soon by industrialism, Europeans and European-Americans converted forests into fuel and timber for ship building and other industries, as well as into arable land.

As their populations grew, so did their demand for land, trees, deer, passenger pigeons, waterfowl, and so on. Reproducing patterns etched into European landscapes, the new immigrants hoed prairies, drained marshes, and cleared forests, leaving stumps behind to define and symbolize deforested landscapes. Abetted by indigenous people participating in new markets, the rapidly growing population of new immigrants from Europe provided the impetus for the extermination of turkeys and beavers in the East (and eventually in many other parts of the continent), the extirpation of deer in the East and South and elk except in the West, and the extinction of passenger pigeons and near extinction of buffalo. Increasingly, colonial and then state legislatures pressed for and passed numerous laws governing the hunting of birds and other animals.[44]

That the relationship between population and the environment might have been important (even if not the entire story) is hardly a novel proposition. Many have argued that there is a crudely intuitive and direct relationship between demography and resources; specifically, the higher a population's size and the greater its density, the more significant the impact on resources. Following one recent "stocktaking of a transformed earth," Robert Kates and his colleagues remarked that population is a "prime transforming agent" for the simple reason that "our species demands basic levels of food, water, fuel, clothing, and shelter for subsistence. Therefore, as population size increases, so does basic biological demand." For this reason they find it "difficult not to conclude that population growth has been the first-tier driving force of environmental change throughout the history of humankind."[45]

Yet the relationship between people and the environment cannot be reduced to demography alone—or, for that matter, to a mechanical combination of population size or density, technology, and per-capita consumption of resources. Christine Padoch, an anthropologist working in tropical forests in Amazonia and Indonesia, suggested that population density alone can be a "poor predictor" of transformations in today's ecosystems, and other social scientists would agree. Today especially, as many argue, the social, political-economic, and cultural causes of environmental change are incredibly complex. The impact of people on the environment is complicated by resource abundance, climatic and environmental changes, acquisitive intentions, productive technology, animal and plant domestication, relations of production, political economy, and global pressures and interdependencies. Human actions (individually often subtle and unintended), beliefs, values, and attitudes are all part of a picture that varies at both community and individual levels, and that is quick to change.[46]

Nevertheless, as men and women have captured greater amounts of energy in the major transitions from foraging to farming to industrial and information ages, human populations have grown, exploited foods more intensively, commodified more resources and products, and had a more systemic impact on the environment. The industrial revolution far outpaced what came before and left unprecedented demographic, technological, and environmental changes in its wake. In recent years, that pace has sped up so greatly and the impacts have become so extensive that we tend to forget that preindustrial societies also had environmental effects, and their success in living within a region's capacity might have had more to do with accident than design. As David Lowenthal, a cultural geographer, remarked, "the acceleration of environmental transformations blinds us to their antiquity."[47]

Yet in many parts of the world, demand for various resources pressured or outstripped supply long before the industrial revolution. For example, in preindustrial Europe the demand for wood exceeded the supply and the record is riddled with examples of deforested lands: northwest Scotland 3,700 years ago, Attica 2,500 years ago, Wales 2,100 years ago, central and western Europe 1,200 years ago. The stark landscape in Greece, later greatly admired, ironically, for its aesthetic quality, was just one erosive product of "extreme" degradation. Medieval forest clearances altered habitats in Spain, Portugal, Italy, and other Mediterranean regions. People first cut trees for fuel, charcoal, and ship construction, and they finished the job by converting forests to pasture for sheep grazing and farming. But Europe was not an isolated example. Even tropical-forest Amazonians "brought about notable transformations in the regional landscape," as one anthropologist said—even if these transformations are modest compared to the wholesale destruction of the rain forest in recent years (about which there is no debate).[48]

The impact of the industrial revolution traveled globally with Europeans as they transformed landscapes changed long before by preindustrial indigenous people (in much the same way as industrial-era Europeans altered already changed landscapes in Europe). As in Europe, prior to this revolutionary expansion, indigenous people had a lasting impact on their surroundings, especially on the local and regional levels. This does not mean that they did not know their environment intimately, with knowledge and insight that a botanist, zoologist, or ecologist might envy today. It simply means that we cannot assume that they always walked lightly on the earth. We need not look far for evidence of their impact on any continent, beginning with fire, the domestication of animals, and farming.[49]

This is the broader context in which North America prior to the arrival of Europeans must be placed—not so that one must conclude that the same had to happen in North America, only that if it did, one should not be surprised in the least. Where they were thickly settled, American Indians pressured land and resources because they placed demands on the forests for fuel, building materials, and domesticated crops. Regardless of their numbers, they resorted frequently (as we shall see) to the widespread practice of burning. Everywhere, their numbers helped determine their relationship to the environment.

With the single possible exception that they were all preindustrial in their technological and economic systems, the fact that indigenous people were rarely thickly settled is probably more important than anything else in understanding why Europeans described Eden in North America. As difficult as it may be for us to imagine how few people there were, just contemplate how often one would see another human in North America if the 1990 population of Alabama or New Jersey, which equal the low and high of the four to seven million range, were spread across the continent. In 1990, population densities comparable to the average estimated for North America in 1500 existed only in Alaska or sparsely inhabited census areas in Utah and other western states.[50]

The native people who molded North America were fully capable of transformative action in ecosystems they knew intimately, but in almost all instances their populations were too small to have made much of a difference. And when people few in number quickly became fewer from disease, the lands they had burned, cleared, and planted—lands transformed and exploited for purposes relating to agriculture, fuel, hunting, gathering, construction, and other ends—rested and recovered from whatever human pressures they had been under.

As Europeans occupied widowed—not virgin—lands, some fell to their knees and thanked God. Many described a new Eden. Even if the imagery and metaphors were framed by their experiences in a vastly more heavily peopled and transformed continent, this paradise, this Eden, was mainly an artifact of demography and epidemiology.

Chapter Four

FIRE

IN 1632, somewhere off the mid-Atlantic coast, a Dutch mariner and merchant named David Pietersz. de Vries wrote about land "smelt before it is seen." An entire continent to the west lay beyond sensation except for the smell of smoke in the air. On arrival, Europeans would find thick clouds of hazy smoke enveloping the land, grasslands reduced to charred stubble, and park-like forests clear of undergrowth. Fire had clearly modified this landscape, and sometimes scarred it deeply—not lightning-caused fire (although some was), but fire ignited by Indians.

Yet when Europeans depicted America in literary texts or on canvas, they often imagined a pristine, primeval land in which an unbroken, vast, tangled, and impenetrable forest figured prominently. Predisposed to find wilderness, as well as savagery romanticized or brutalized, they discovered both. Over centuries, the image of the forest has been consistent, from "infinite thick woods" in the seventeenth century, to the Hudson River School's canvases of deep twisted woods in the nineteenth, to "the shadows and the gloom of mighty forests" in the early twentieth. None immortalized the forest more lastingly than Henry Wadsworth Longfellow in *The Song of Hiawatha*, but as he implored all who "Love the shadow of the forest" to listen to the wild traditions of the native Hiawatha, his imagery was overwhelmingly of an interminable, tangled, solitary, wailing, darksome, moaning, gloomy forest primeval.[1]

This contradiction between the evidence of fires set by man and the literary and artistic image of a primeval forest left the role of Indians misunderstood.[2] Through the years, Indians have been damned either because they could not set fires with significant consequences or because they could and did. In the second half of the nineteenth century, when evolutionary schemes were everywhere on the air, many argued that Indian fires—the fires of "primitive" or "savage" men—could not possibly have had much impact compared to the fires of civilized men. They castigated Indians for technological incompetence. But by the early twentieth century, when historical evidence for Indians' having used fire on a continental scale had emerged (and for European settlers following suit until controlled by local jurisdictions concerned for the safety of agriculture and settlement), critics developed a new appreciation for the power of Indian fires. At this very time, however, forest ecologists branded fires as always destructive and for virtually three-quarters of a century made every effort to halt them in national forests and parks. Even John Muir, the great preservationist, regarded fire as "the great master-scourge of forests." In this context, Indians were damned again, this time for being careless and profligate and more "destructive" than white men. Forest ecologists concerned with forest conservation defined by regulated timber harvest said that Indians could not possibly have cared about "the fall of some score millions of feet of prime timber in a forest conflagration." They thought that Indians were inherently incendiaries, uncontrollable pyromaniacs, and arsonists, and they likened their burning to sin.

The view that Indian burning was benign never, however, completely disappeared. It reemerged in the 1940s when Indians were depicted as conservationists whose campfires never spread. According to the U.S. Department of Agriculture, there was no proof that Indians regularly set large-scale fires; lacking matches, they set "small campfires that they tended carefully." Another forest resident, Smokey the Bear, was beginning his long reign as icon of fire prevention and forest protection. Smokey's slogan, "Remember, Only You Can Prevent Forest Fires," was soon on everyone's lips, and real live Smokeys in Washington's National Zoo warned generations of children and their parents about the incompatibility of fire and forest, and the importance of conservation. Some Indians adopted Smokey's philosophy—one going so far as to say that fighting fires is "the one thing the white man does that makes sense." These ideas later resonated with the unequivocal post-1970 positioning of Indians as Noble Indians at one with nature. Not only were Indians regarded as benign burners, but also they were seen as ecologically prescient:

their fires were based on ecological (systemic) knowledge, and they were conservation-minded.[3]

Forest ecologists, chastened dramatically by the Yellowstone fires of 1988, now tell us that fire prevention often does not make much ecological sense. But what about Indians and fire? How extensively did they burn? Why did they burn? Did they set small and innocuous fires or large and destructive ones? Did they manage carefully the size and intensity of their fires or were their burns uncontrolled? Did they understand the ecological consequences of fire? In fact, North American Indians burned often and for myriad ends, many of which were practical, like keeping voracious mosquitoes and flies at bay. The most important related to subsistence, aggression, communication, and travel.[4]

Indians used fire to improve subsistence more than for any other end. Across the continent, they deployed fire to improve their access to animals, to improve or eliminate forage for the animals they depended on for food, and to drive and encircle animals. In early-seventeenth-century Massachusetts Bay Colony, William Wood reported that Indians burned each November, "when the grass is withered and leaves dried." Fire, he said, "consumes all the underwood and rubbish which otherwise would overgrow the country, making it unpassable, and spoil their much affected hunting." Others agreed, like the Puritan Edward Johnson who said that Indians in Massachusetts burned the woods so that "they may not be hindered in hunting Venson, and Bears, in the winter season." Wood saw understory growth only "in swamps and low grounds that are wet," and on land that Indians "hath not . . . burned" because they had died from epidemic disease. As in Massachusetts, this occurred in much of the East (and elsewhere on the continent), where Indians burned forest in order to eliminate understory and promote the growth of grasses and other forage favored by large animals. The practice was not universal but many burned the woods once a year or twice annually, often in spring and fall. It was the "frequent fiering of the woods," as Johnson remarked, that led so many Europeans to remark on the regular spacing and open grassy ground between oak, walnut, beech, and other trees: They were "thin of Timber in many places, like our Parkes in England."

Others linked burning specifically to hunting large animals like deer—by using fire to create favorable ecological niches. In New England, Virginia, and elsewhere in the East, burning undeniably created extensive meadows bordering open forest, with "edge" habitats ideal for the growth of berry bushes and grasses, where deer browsed and other animals fed. The fire history of landscapes could be seen in "oak openings," hundreds or thousands of acres of cleared meadowlands with oaks, poplars, and other trees scattered throughout, and with strawberry vines growing among charred stumps.[5]

Throughout the continent, especially in the fall, Indians hunted animals by surrounding them with fire. In California, the Shasta encircled mule deer; in the East, the Delaware surrounded white-tailed deer; and on the Plains, many did the same with the buffalo. The hunts demanded cooperation—in the East, dozens and perhaps hundreds of hunters cooperated in lighting fires around a herd of deer and then killing all that were trapped. At times the fire surround was deliberately broken in places, and at times it was totally enclosed. The seventeenth-century Illinois used both techniques. Sometimes Indians set grasslands on fire around a buffalo herd, except for several places through which animals were encouraged to pass to escape the flames, where they would wait and kill some "six score in a day." Sometimes, as Nicolas Perrot described for the seventeenth-century Illinois as well as the Iowa, Pawnee, and perhaps Omaha, people of "an entire village" enclosed buffaloes inside a summer grass fire. Hundreds of men surrounded a herd, evidently at night, and once day broke they set fire to the dry grass on all sides, and a circle of flames and smoke gradually took form. Men ran at animals attempting to escape, keeping them inside the flames. "This produces the same effect to the sight as four ranks of palisades, in which the buffaloes are enclosed. When the savages see that the animals are trying to get outside of it, in order to escape the fires which surround them on all sides . . . they run at them and compel them to re-enter the enclosure; and they avail themselves of this method to kill all the beasts." On some hunts they evidently killed as many as fifteen hundred buffaloes. The Sioux, according to Henry R. Schoolcraft, used an identical technique, first encircling animals and then setting grass on fire. Buffaloes, "having a great dread of fire, retire towards the centre of the grasslands as they see it approach, and here being pressed together in great numbers, many are trampled under foot, and the Indians rushing in with their arrows and musketry, slaughter immense numbers in a short period."[6]

Indians often set fires designed to move animals from one place to another. "Hundreds of *Indians*," Mark Catesby, the naturalist, wrote in the early-eighteenth-century Southeast, "[spread] themselves in Length thro' a great Extent of Country," then "set the Woods on Fire" in order to drive and hunt deer in October. On the Plains they used fire to drive animals toward pounds. On the northern Plains in the fall of 1808, Alexander Henry described how three men set grass or dung ablaze upwind of a herd of several hundred buffaloes, and slowly drove the herd before them, until in sight of a man covered with a robe, who, disguised as a buffalo, piqued the animals' curiosity and led them onward into a pound to their deaths. At times the objective was not a pound but woods or grasslands—wherever animals could more easily be killed. They burned grasslands to force animals from them into river bottoms below, and they fired thick underbrush along river bottoms to drive them out. In the Southwest, Indians used fire to drive deer from ponderosa pine forests into canyons.[7]

Indians routinely burned lands so that animals could not use them. On the Plains, Indians set fires to ruin forage and force animals to find grasses in areas where they were more easily hunted. This was common in late fall, when Indians evidently burned large sections of grasslands and subsequently easily found buffalo, elk, and deer in timbered river bottoms where grasses remained unburned. When buffaloes were scarce, several "sagacious" men once set grass afire "so as to denude the grasslands, except within an area of fifteen or twenty miles contiguous to the camp," which "reduc[ed] greatly," as stated, "the labor of the hunt." Fire may also have attracted some animals: In California, hunters evidently set fires in meadows, then waited to ambush the deer lured to the flames, it was said, from curiosity.[8]

Indians also burned regularly to set the stage for new plant growth and for the return of animals and men when conditions were right. After burning, animals left until another season when they might return for new palatable growth. Again, this was common on the Plains. In the spring or fall, Indians often set fire to grasslands to improve grazing conditions. They ignited spring fires to improve the forage for buffalo in the summer, and fall fires for better pasturage the following spring. The fires, which were sometimes hundreds of miles across, worked. In September 1804, Meriwether Lewis saw recently burnt grassland with three-inch-high grass being consumed by "vast herds of buffalo, deer, elk, and antelope . . . feeding in every direction as far as the eye of the observer could reach."[9] In California, Indians regularly burned small grasslands or meadows of grasses and ferns embedded in forests, so that seed-producing grasses would be productive and enticing to deer, elk, and bears.[10]

Thus, almost everywhere Indians burned the land to surround, drive, frighten, or scorch the animals and reptiles they sought to eat, and to create proper foraging conditions, either in the same or in the following year, for small and large mammals and the predators (including themselves) that sought them.

Indians throughout North America also used fire to increase the production of berries, seeds, nuts, and other gathered foods. Whether or not this end was deliberate or a by-product of others for which fire was deployed, Indians who set fires in eastern woods created not just foraging ground for deer and other large animals and woods free of understory, but niches on the fringes of meadows, and between and under trees free of competition for strawberries, blackberries, and raspberries, all of which flourished, often in profusion. "In its season," one seventeenth-century observer near the Potomac River remarked, "your foot can hardly direct itself where it will not be dyed in the blood of large and delicious strawberries."[11] In the West, a large number of Indians, including three dozen groups in California alone, burned to increase seed and grass yields. The Yurok and Karok burned to improve growth, production, or harvest of huckleberry bushes, hazel sticks (for basket making), "bear grass" (a lily), "wild rice" (grass seed) plants, acorns, and tobacco. Indians burned Oregon's Willamette Valley in late fall prior to collecting "wild wheat," which was probably tarweed. Through regular fires, Indians in western Washington encouraged camas and bracken, which were important sources of carbohydrates, as well as nettles, to grow in profusion, and their fires perpetuated the grasslands where these plants grew.[12]

Indians also used fire in herding and farming. As William Clark remarked in 1805 of upper Missouri River Indians who burned near their villages every spring "for the benefit of their horses," Indians on the Plains and elsewhere set fires regularly to improve pasture for horse herds.[13] Where they farmed maize, beans, squash, melons, pumpkins, and other crops, Indians used fire extensively to clear land, destroy plants competing with crops, and deposit ash on soil. Throughout the East, Indians cleared hundreds and, at times, thousands of acres of ground for their crops. From New England came many reports of fields several hundred acres in extent. In Virginia, mention was made of thousands of acres of cleared land under cultivation. When Europeans arrived on the East Coast, they discovered massive quantities of maize, calculated later in hundreds of thousands of bushels, thousands of barrels, or of sufficient quantity to fill the holds of several ships or to keep people alive for months. East and west, fields and meadows in which burning ceased when they were abandoned by Indians dead from disease or driven away by their enemies again soon became forest.[14]

Indians across North America may have used fire most often in contexts relating to subsistence, but they also collectively employed fire as a weapon, as a means of communication, and to improve travel. As men and women of European descent soon discovered, many Indians unhesitatingly used fire as an offensive and defensive weapon. They employed tactical fires effectively to drive unwanted strangers or enemies from cover or away altogether. Fires lit for these purposes were especially common on the eighteenth- and nineteenth-century Plains where, for example, the Sioux lit the grassy plains to the windward of traders like David Thompson, hoping to drive him and his men into low-lying woods and a waiting ambush. The Blackfeet ignited thickets in which Kit Carson and other trappers had taken refuge. The Blood took similar action against other trappers. One nineteenth-century governmental agent, finding fires lit to his windward several nights in succession, countered the threat by burning all the grass surrounding his camp. Indians used fire against each other as well as against Europeans: A Sioux war party set fire to grass to the windward of two Omaha men with a Sioux captive that they had come across hidden in a ravine, hoping to drive them from cover. Indians set the woods and grasslands ablaze so often in Iowa in the 1830s for these and other reasons, said C. A. Murray, that "the whole country around" was "completely burnt up and devastated" and he and his party had to go elsewhere to find forage and game.

Economic and political motives often propelled Indians to use fire aggressively, as against traders and trappers like David Thompson and Kit Carson, who trespassed and poached, threatening the new Indian economic livelihood. The Cree set fire to their own territory against trespassing Assiniboine hunters, hoping to drive them back to their own territory. Indians near Fort Garry, angry at the implications of a merger of fur trading companies for the favorable exchange rates they had been receiving in a period of competition, burned grasslands to keep buffaloes at a distance and starve the traders. In other instances, Indians burned other native people's hunting territory to force them farther away, or burned near a post to prevent hunting and enhance the value of their own provisions. The strategy sometimes backfired: In 1781, the Cree and Assiniboine set fires so that they alone would have provisions to trade, but drove buffaloes so far away that they were compelled to beg for food. Plains Indians set fire to grasslands to destroy the forage of the horses and mules belonging to their enemies and pursuers, who consequently were more vulnerable or compelled to give up the chase. In addition, Indians burned for the smoke that masked offensive movements or obscured retreat from danger—or that agitated horses and concealed men bent on stampeding and stealing them. Throughout North America, American Indians burned the land pragmatically to confuse, hinder, maim, or kill their enemies, Indian or white, to drive them from or into cover, or to mask their own actions.[15]

Indians also ignited fires to signal each other in a variety of habitats—even Subarctic boreal forest and taiga, where Northern Athapaskan people announced their presence or communicated prearranged messages with moss and lichen fires or by burning an entire spruce. But these types of fires were especially prevalent on the prairies and plains during the summer season. Explorers, trappers, missionaries, soldiers, and others, some no doubt apprehensive about what the flames meant, attributed as many as four of every ten fires to signaling. "Firing the prairie" many called it. The blazes were quick and effective, propelling messages from one group to the next, and could be "read" as far as one hundred miles from their source in as short a time as one-half hour. Indians sometimes arranged signals in advance, lighting a grass fire when they decamped, for example. They ignited fires to alert others to the presence of buffaloes and call them together for hunting. Or, as reported by a prisoner of the Sioux in the late seventeenth century and by many others on the Plains in the centuries that followed, they lit blazes to announce the return of war parties.

Communication was evidently the predominant cause of summer burns in the central portions of the Plains. Here (and elsewhere) Indians used fire to communicate with each other almost endless possible matters including success in war, arrival of white people, sightings of buffaloes, and so on. Often large fires, ignited either on ridges (perhaps diminishing the damage they might do) or on the open plain or grasslands, could and did rage out of control. The soldier and author Bacqueville de la Potherie, who was on the upper Mississippi River in the late seventeenth century, remarked that Indians lit fires in the spring and fall so that different bands knew where others were, but that any single fire became "so strong, especially when the wind rises, and when the nights are dark, that it is visible forty leagues away." Still others spoke of the loss of hundreds of acres from the most "trivial signal"; Captain John Palliser, who was on the Canadian prairies in the late 1850s, remarked that Indians "frequently fire the prairie for the most trivial reasons," especially "signals to telegraph to one another concerning a successful horse-stealing exploit, or in order to proclaim the safe return of a war party." He thought them "very careless about the consequences of such an occurrence," and spoke of "disastrous effects" including "denuding the land of all useful trees" as well as "cut[ting] off the buffalo sometimes from a whole district of country," thereby causing "great privation and distress." There are numerous similar examples. After the Flathead lit one fire in the 1830s to announce their arrival with trappers, "the flames ran over the neighboring hills with great violence, sweeping all before them, above the surface of the ground." Indians also lit fires to warn members of their own tribe of danger. Some Sioux, for example, attacked by the Ojibwa in July 1840, lit three fires to alert other Sioux nearby, and they in turn did the same until all had "set the grasslands on fire in various directions."[16]

In some parts of North America, Indians lit fires to ease travel. In the East, Europeans often remarked that Indians burned the woods to make travel through them easier. According to Thomas Morton, if Indians in seventeenth-century Massachusetts did not set fire to the forest in the spring and fall, then it "would otherwise be so overgrown with underweed, that it would be all a coppice wood, and the people would not be able in any wise to pass through the country out of a beaten path." Fires burned until extinguished by rain in this "custom of firing the country," but despite any ill effects the fires provided "the means to make it passable"—as well as "very beautiful, and commodious." Elsewhere, John Smith spoke of being able to "gallop a horse among these woods any way except when the creeks or rivers shall hinder," and other Europeans, of driving carts and coaches through eastern woods.[17]

Some have argued that Indian burning "was almost universal." It may indeed have been the most prevalent tool employed by Indians to manipulate their environment, but there is no need for hyperbole for a practice that, while widespread, varied from one tribe to the next—as did the ecological effects from one vegetation zone to the next.[18]

Anecdotal historical evidence often suggests that while most Indians used fire, some did not; they burned some areas annually but others less frequently and a few, like California redwood forests and tundra, not at all. Moreover, even those ecosystems burned frequently, like ponderosa pine and chaparral, were not torched totally or with absolute regularity, for Europeans were occasionally stymied by the brush or undergrowth in them. Unfortunately, information on the extent, intensity, and duration of the fires is often poorly known, and while observers might note grasslands or forests burning in every direction, they do not know whether they were set alight by man or lightning.

It is clear that when lit at optimum times of the year, fires had a positive impact on the growth of grasses and animal forage, but in their pragmatism, Indians were not always concerned with how far, fast, or hot each and every fire burned. Objectives such as delivering signals, or killing, discomforting, or hindering one's enemies (the most commonly reported uses of fire in the Plains) were not always compatible with control. And accounts of campsite fires burning thousands of acres are legion. Whether this was "careless" behavior, as many disapprovingly labeled it, depends on what, precisely, must be taken care of and in what way. All this does not mean that Indians were not ecologically or systemically aware, only that they did not always think of the ecological consequences of all the fires they lit. The fires used aggressively or to communicate were not kindled with identical considerations in mind as the fires lit to enhance the productivity of econiches.

To bring tree-ring, historical, and ethnographic evidence to bear on specific burns is seldom possible. In some regions where Indians set fires frequently, like eastern prairies, there are few or no trees to provide corroborating evidence from fire scars. And extrapolating from current fires to ones in the past is inadvisable: Today's burns like the 1988 Yellowstone conflagration can be exacerbated by decades or a century of fuel buildup and are poor analogs for Indian fires in forests burned with regularity. Ethnographic information must also be used with caution, in part because some Indians have clearly adopted the opinion, common until recently among forest ecologists, that fires were uniformly destructive, and that they did not set destructive fires; and in part because by the twentieth century some Indians have forgotten the details of aboriginal burning. The latter is certainly the case with the coastal southern California Chumash, who have no memory of burning. Yet written historical sources make clear that they once burned grasslands extensively in the summer, probably following seed collecting, in order to promote new seed growth and hunt rabbits, and that their burning practices were changed first by friars who gathered the people in mission compounds and later, in the late eighteenth century, by regulations suppressing burning. One hundred years after the regulations, the Chumash had cultural amnesia with respect to fire.[19]

For these reasons, determining the ecological consequences of fire, and the precise Indian role, is a more daunting task than unearthing the widespread anecdotal evidence for burning. Yet even where the relationship between fire and forest is relatively inaccessible, there is much about which one can speculate. The East is one such region that is difficult to approach, in large measure because at a very early date the Indians succumbed to epidemics and the Europeans altered landscapes, and the earliest written historical sources are frequently anecdotal or ambiguous. It is nevertheless clear that Indians in this region used fire to drive or surround white-tailed deer, clear the forest of underbrush, produce forage that deer found "alluring" (as one nineteenth-century writer put it), improve travel, and prepare ground for crops and trees for fuel.

Yet it is difficult to discern how often Indians actually ignited fires for subsistence and other ends. In fact there was most likely considerable variation linked to population size and density, with the greatest frequency of fires (and greatest ecological impact) found where the population was highest and the land most densely settled. Except for its northernmost portions, the East was not one solid forest but a mosaic of forest and grasslands, the latter ranging in size from small meadows to the vast one-thousand-square-mile Shenandoah Valley. The grasslands especially were produced and maintained by fire. They were manipulated and managed habitats whose history could be read in their scattered charred stumps and stunted trees. Their high vegetation attracted buffalo, turkey, and many other mammals and birds. Deer browsed them and their edges. Indians planted corn in some meadows. So important was fire to the maintenance of grasslands that after Indians died from disease or abandoned them, these clearings quickly reverted to forest. Animals that had been at home there went elsewhere or their populations dwindled. One vanished entirely: The heath hen became extinct when fire was eliminated from eastern scrub oak grasslands. Eliminate fire and the change from a mixed grassland-forest habitat to forest alone could be rapid: After only two decades in Virginia, the results included trees with "very good board timber," as Robert Beverley, the early-eighteenth-century historian put it.[20]

Fire (or its absence) affects plants and animals in ecosystems in predictable ways. Without fire, jack pine cones are kept closed by a resinous material and cannot release their seeds; only the heat of fire destroys the volatile resin and opens the cones for propagation. Black spruce is similar. The impact on animals is often beneficial. More often than not, fires burn unevenly and animals small and large survive in safe areas, or what are known as *refugia*. In many cases birds and mammals repopulate burn areas within one or two breeding seasons, and plants increase in vigor due to the ash. While some birds and mammals like the spruce grouse, marten, caribou, wolverine, grizzly bear, and fisher fare poorly during fires, most species notably hold their numbers or increase following the initial aftereffects of fire. Fire also predictably affects succession in ecosystems. In the absence of fire, mesquite, jumping cholla, prickly pear, and other shrubs and trees take over grasslands in the Southwest; following fire, trembling aspen and paper birch become far more abundant in many regions.[21]

Prior to the suppression of fires in the nineteenth century, many of North America's forest and grassland ecosystems were fire-succession ecosystems; that is, fires produced and maintained them. Forest and fire ecologists appreciate the association between regular fire and ecological types and successions in ponderosa pine, chaparral, longleaf pine, and grassland habitats. Native people, keen observers of the environment, surely understood the associations long before. Not only were these ecosystems pyrogenic (produced by fire) but also they were anthropogenic (produced by man) to the degree that the fires which ran through them were also. Through their fires, North American Indians probably played some role in the creation of, and more certainly maintained, a number of fire-succession ecosystems.

Ponderosa pine forest, widespread in the West, is a classic example. From the seventeenth through nineteenth centuries, either lightning or man-caused fires periodically burned forests of ponderosa pine and other conifers in the California Sierras, Sierra Madre, and northern Coast Ranges, and on the eastern slope of Oregon's Cascades. Fires eliminated dense competing understory plants and trees, kept the fire hazard low, and maintained the forest as ponderosa pine. Farther south, in Arizona's twelve thousand square miles of ponderosa pine, fires produced forests that elicited mid-nineteenth-century praise for "gigantic pines, intersected frequently with open glades, sprinkled all over with mountains, meadows, and wide savannas, and covered with the richest grasses." The burns were spaced at intervals of two to twenty years in California, eleven to seventeen years in Oregon's Cascades, and five to twelve years in Arizona.

But most white people misunderstood how those forests came into being. John Wesley Powell, for example, the explorer, geologist, and ethnologist, remarked from the Southwest in 1879 that forest protection "is reduced to one single problem—Can the forests be saved from fire?" He could not have been more misguided. After European settlers arrived, the grasses underneath and between the pines, which had fed deer, produced tons of hay for domesticated animals. But once sheep, increasing numbers of which belonged to Navajo herders, cropped the piney slopes, and people no longer lit fires, ponderosa pine forests changed radically. Then and now, in the absence of fire, ponderosa pine trees grow so thickly that the forest stagnates or (as has happened farther north in Oregon) Douglas fir and other shade-tolerant species quickly develop in dense clumps. In other words, ponderosa pine forests "saved" from fire are forests transformed—and because of the accumulation of surplus fuel, they become even more combustible and susceptible to explosive, destructive fire.[22]

Like ponderosa pine, chaparral, a scrub- or brushland community widespread in California, is also fire-induced. Chamise, manzanitas, oaks, and ceanothus are prominent species in chaparral. Chamise, a remarkable bush that is simultaneously flammable and fire-tolerant, dominates this ecological community. Its dead branches and resinous leaves readily catch fire, but following fire, shrubs sprout and grow rapidly on blackened chamise stumps. Chamise seeds are also very resistant to fire. They lie dormant in soil until after fire has passed, when seedlings erupt in profusion within a matter of weeks or months. Most species in chaparral produce seeds within five years after a fire, but if chaparral is burned again too soon, many seedlings that had sprouted and been browsed can die, with an increased chance of erosion from rains.

Many Indians, it seems, actively managed chaparral with fire, for reasons that are familiar by now: to produce better forage for deer, increase yields of berries, ease the collection of seeds and bulbs, and suppress the destructive consequences of lightning-caused fires. They placed a priority especially on maintaining optimum forage for deer in the winter and spring. Most burns took place in the fall and favored the growth of species browsed by deer in the spring, which was a difficult season for subsistence. Indians lit some spring fires evidently to reduce brushiness and induce sprouting species. Within a matter of months after a fire, mule deer, jackrabbits, quail, other birds, and mice and voles recover their numbers in burned-over, resprouted chaparral. Sometimes they become more numerous. Deer are healthier. Overall, chaparral endures as a robust ecological community only if fires persist.[23]

Like chaparral and ponderosa pine, longleaf pine forests of the Southeast are also intimately associated with fire. After germination, each longleaf pine seedling concentrates energy in its root system, which grows prodigiously, and is protected from fire by thick resistant bark. In its next growth phase, which sometimes comes on the heels of fire, it shoots up rapidly above ground so that its needles are above the level of the next fire. In this way longleaf pines survive fire, but that is only half the story: Regular fires actually perpetuate longleaf pine forests. Fires remove competing trees and shrubs, and destroy a fungal disease that attacks needles. In the absence of fire, longleaf pines fail to reproduce or survive, and within one to seven decades, depending on the soil, drainage, and location, forests of oak, gum, beech-maple, and other pines succeed longleaf pine forests.[24]

Some assert that with their fires, Indians were responsible for the formation of the vast grassland ecosystem of the Great Plains; others, that they did not form it but probably helped maintain it; and still others, that they did neither because their technology could not possibly have played such a formative role in an ecosystem so large. Whatever the influence of Indian fires, there are strong climatic and environmental reasons for doubting that fires were the only or even the major formative one. In the central and western Plains, compared to eastern portions, there is less moisture from rain and snow, lower humidity, higher winds, and more periodic drought. Singly or in combination, these conditions prevent forest formation and growth and would lead to extensive grasslands without help from fires. Yet the increased precipitation found as one moves east makes tree growth far more a reality in the eastern and northern high-grass portions of the Plains, where fire played a greater role maintaining grasslands: For centuries observers remarked on the charred stumps or extensive root systems of mature trees ravaged by regular fires, their remnants enhancing deep grassland soils. In the east and north, fires—some lightning-caused, others anthropogenic—were important in checking the natural succession of grassland by forest. When fires were checked, aspens, oaks, and willows proliferated. In the north, aspen groves expanded, and in the east, oak openings closed as groves of trees broke up the grasslands and in places, forest eventually consumed them.[25]

The effect of grassland fires depends on the same factors as elsewhere: the season of the burn, time of the last burn, heat of the fire, wind, temperature, terrain, soil, moisture, and so on. Grassland fires move with extraordinary speed when grasses are dry and the wind is up, but they also move irregularly over uneven terrain, sometimes skip over areas, and rarely consume plants so completely that their roots are burned. After the fires pass, burned areas cool quickly. Productivity often increases following grassland fires because surface litter is removed. Tall-grass prairie needs at least three years to return to its preburn state, though grazing animals like buffaloes return immediately to tender young plants growing after the burn. But not all grassland fires are benign and restorative. When they are too frequent or hot, when moisture is low, or when heavy rains follow fires and cause erosion, plants may not easily recover.[26]

In Oregon's Willamette Valley, as on the Great Plains, Indian fires shocked many white men. Settlers were horrified by the "long lines of fire and smoke," and by "ravages" of fire, "dense volumes" of smoke, and "sheets of flame." They were unable to make the connection between the valley's extensive grasslands and regular fires. And they rarely saw the use of fire as indicative of ecosystemic knowledge.

White settlers quickly discovered that the Kalapuya Indians torched Willamette Valley grasslands regularly each year between July and November, preferably in the fall. They burned for several reasons related to hunting white-tailed deer, their most important source of animal protein, using fire both to encircle deer and to induce them to browse in the unburned thickets or in the fresh grass that appeared in weeks. These Indians also used fire to harvest tarweed seeds, a staple they stored for winter and later consumed as meal. At maturity, tarweed is covered by a sticky resin that makes harvest exceedingly awkward. Fires both burned off this substance along with any interfering grasses, and dried the pods in which seeds would be collected. Through burning, the Kalapuya also killed grasshoppers, which they gathered up and ate with relish, and safely harvested wild honey. They also probably lit fires to clear underbrush from beneath oak trees, easing acorn collection, enhancing the growth of berry and hazel bushes, both of which grow following fire, and favoring the growth of camas, lupine, and other wild roots.

The Kalapuya maintained the Willamette Valley as an ecosystem consisting, when people of European descent arrived, of grasslands broken by "orchard"-like groves of oaks regularly spaced on hillsides.

But when horrified settlers stopped the burning, which they regarded as incompatible with their settlements, they doomed the grasslands. Trees invaded, oak openings became dense woods, and Douglas firs descended from the Coast Range and from the Cascades to overrun everything before them.[27]

As with the Kalapuya, the burning practices of the Cree, Denesóline, Dene Th'a, and Dunne-za of northern Alberta lend support to the idea that Indians drew on a vast storehouse of knowledge about ecosystems and fire ecology before kindling a fire. These Indians understood that if controlled, burns promoted diversity, mosaic-like habitats, and renewal of growth. They knew that through fire they could create "edge" or "ecotonal" habitats where resources were concentrated and alluring to game. They burned at times that made sense for the production of grasses, berries, bulbs, shrubs, and other early fire-succession species attractive to small and large animals—including the moose, bears, snowshoe hares, muskrats, beavers, lynx, and foxes they sought especially. They recognized that berry bushes would grow in burned areas and attract bears, and that moose came to roll in the ashes of a fire. They understood that fire favored the growth of certain grasses and the mice that grazed on them, and that foxes and martens would come to prey on the mice. They knew that muskrats needed the fresh growth of reeds that fire produces, and that when aspens and poplars returned some four or five years following a burn, so also would beavers that fed on and used them in their construction projects.

In spring, these people burned sloughs and streamsides, meadows and large grasslands, and deadfall areas that were unproductive for game and represented a dangerous accumulation of fuel. They were knowledgeable of the ways that fires could escape their control, and before they burned they weighed their objectives against the season of year, time of day, slope of land, wind and other weather conditions, and the presence or absence of natural firebreaks. Sometimes, in the containing wet of spring, they left fires to smolder in logs; sometimes, when they left their trapping territories until the next year, they ignited fires behind them.

The knowledge of these peoples was "ecological"—that is, systemic, relational, and interactional. One-half century after fire-suppression policies put an end to these and other practices, a Dunne-za woman reflected on the knowledge of those who burned, which she had known only as a child, "They must be very wise, eh? Those people? That time?"[28]

Most people of European descent failed to appreciate not only the Indian ecosystemic knowledge affecting the deployment of fire but especially the myriad indigenous understandings of the natural world. As a rule, Indians animated trees and animals affected by burning and considered fire as a powerful force or being. This affected how Indians interacted with plants and animals. For example, for Indians in the Plateau and elsewhere, conifers and other trees were of symbolic importance and at times were placed or burned at the center of ritual enclosures. Before picking the harvest from berry bushes in anticipation of burning the slopes in order to enhance production the next season, a Northwest Coast Kwakwaka'wakw woman might say to berries, as Franz Boas reported, "I have come, Supernatural Ones, you, Long-Life-Makers, that I may take you, for that is the reason why you have come, brought by your creator, that you may come and satisfy me; you, Supernatural Ones; and this, that you do not blame me for what I do to you when I set fire to you the way it is done by my root (ancestor) who set fire to you in his manner when you get old on the ground that you may bear much fruit. Look! I come now dressed with my large basket and my small basket that you may go into it, Healing Woman; you, Supernatural Ones. I mean this, that you may not be evilly disposed towards me, friends. That you may only treat me well."[29]

Of course, depicting the Kalapuya or the people of northern Alberta as ecologically aware burners, or the Kwakwaka'wakw as respectful toward the berries whose habitats they burn is not the complete story. Their ecological awareness or respect did not stop them or other people from lighting fires at times that, while convenient for itinerant burners, were inopportune from other standpoints. It did not stop them from converting plants and animals into various useful products (indeed they may have equated the health of the environment, and their relationship with it, as contingent on such conversion). Moreover, drawing on the earlier mention of the Chumash, a note of caution must be introduced to our understanding of the burning practices of the native people in northern Alberta. These people had stopped burning some fifty to seventy-five years before reconstructing fire use for late-twentieth-century ethnographers. Had they forgotten those long-ago practices that might have had adverse results? Were memories compromised by the contemporary ideology that Indians were ecologically minded conservationists? After all, some fires lit by these people unintentionally escaped their control to ravage marten and fisher habitat. The anthropologist Henry Lewis remarked that one man "set a fire along his trapline because he happened to be there at that particular time (which wasn't the best time to do it) but he understood what would follow in the days, weeks, and months" to come. From the nineteenth and twentieth centuries comes evidence that Subarctic Indians lit, but did not always extinguish, smoky fires against voracious insects when they rested during summer travels. These, together with fires lit for purposes of communication and subsistence, may account for the extensive stretches of burned ground that traders and others often encountered on their travels through the Subarctic.[30]

A similar case involves the Flathead, Pend d'Oreille, and Kootenai of western Montana, whose territory embraced different ecological zones, including ponderosa pine and Douglas fir forests. Today, these native people deny that their forebears set fires during summers or droughts when they might rage destructively. In arguing that the fires lit by their ancestors did not burn out of control, they sound like the Indians of northern Alberta. They emphasize that they set fires annually to protect the forest against disease and conflagration, to improve hunting through better browse for mule deer and elk, to destroy browse and force deer to places convenient for hunting, to increase the production of berries and licorice-root (a medicine), to improve grazing for horses (after 1730), to clear campsites, and to communicate.

Written historical sources confirm that these Indians burned lowland forests and grasslands where they spent most of their time, and support the idea that they ignited fires for subsistence reasons and understood their ecosystemic consequences. Documentary and fire-scar data suggest that Indians burned with enough regularity to maintain econiches in different stages of succession and ages. They kindled fairly low- or moderate-intensity fires in the spring or fall, which in theory prevented catastrophic hot "crown" fires, promoted the growth of grasses under trees, and produced an open landscape.

But the written sources also suggest, contrary to oral sources, that these Indians did not control fires systematically, that they left fires to burn themselves out, that they did not kindle fires in the same place year after year (which would have greatly damaged browse), that burning varied between and within groups, and that some people did not burn at all. Finally, here as elsewhere—and again in contrast to generally silent oral testimony—when Indians ignited fires for purposes like communication (such as the one lit in August 1833 to announce the arrival of trappers that roared beyond control into a vast, violent conflagration), or neglected or did not extinguish campfires, these Indians sometimes produced hot summer fires with the clear potential to run away.

Most of what the Flathead, Pend d'Oreille, and Kootenai say their ancestors did is confirmed by historical and fire-scar data, but not all is. Nor does oral testimony reveal the entire story of burning in the past. In their remarks on past practices, people in general tend to emphasize the beneficial results of their actions and to elide destructive consequences. Perhaps, like the Chumash, the Flathead and others simply lack a full memory of former burning practices.[31]

But the harmful consequences of fire simply cannot be ignored. The evidence that Indians lit fires that then were allowed to burn destructively and without regard to ecological consequences is abundant. In 1796, David Thompson remarked that Indians were "frequently very careless" when it came to extinguishing fires set in northern forests. These fires, he said, could take off in flammable coniferous trees and burned "until stopped by some large swamp or lake." They killed spruce grouse and other animals and left vast areas "unsightly." Thompson speculated that "this devastation is nothing to the Indian," for the simple reason that "his country is large."

Others confirmed Thompson's impressions, detailing fires that Indians ignited inadvertently, became far larger than intended, burned until rains quenched them, and consumed tens and hundreds of thousands of acres in grasslands and forest. Farther north, Thompson's contemporary Andrew Graham spoke of extensive fires lit "every summer" and "not a track of a living thing" the following winter. In eastern forests and on grasslands, many Indian-lit fires raged until extinguished by rain. Peter Fidler, for example, a Hudson's Bay Company surveyor who was on the northern Plains in the 1790s, spoke of a fire left unextinguished by the Piegan: "They did not put out their fire when they left it, which spread amongst the dry grass & ran with great velocity & burnt with very great fury, which enlightened the night like day, and appeared awfully grand." Some Piegans disapproved of that fire because it might alert hostile Indians to their presence at a season when fires that appeared were what "Inds. make accidentally." Six days later, the fire still raged "very furiously" and grasslands continued to burn for another four days.

These examples could be multiplied. Observers depicted many Indians including the Ojibwa, Cree, Mandan, Arapahoe, Gros Ventres, Shoshone, Blackfeet, Assiniboine, and various Northern Athapaskan people as "careless" burners, by which they meant that Indian fires accidentally blew up into vast conflagrations or burned until rain fell (which may have been what the Indians intended).[32]

At times, as in Saskatchewan in 1789 when a blaze was so hot that the following year "scarcely a blade was seen," fires destroyed plant life. When they roared into huge, hot infernos, burning several hundred thousand square miles and lasting for weeks, they "destroyed," as the trader Daniel Harmon remarked, "great numbers of buffaloes" in the late eighteenth and early nineteenth centuries. Other traders concurred. Charles McKenzie saw "whole herds of Buffaloes with their hair singed—some were blind; and half roasted carcasses strewed our way." Alexander Henry remarked on "blind buffalo . . . seen every moment wandering off" following late-fall grassland fires on the northern Plains. "The poor beasts," Henry said, "have all the hair singed off; even skin in many places is shrivelled up and terribly burned, and their eyes are swollen and closed fast. It was really pitiful to see them staggering about, sometimes running afoul of a large stone, at other times tumbling downhill and falling into creeks not yet frozen over. In one spot we found a whole herd lying dead."

Others spoke of deer, elk, buffaloes, and wolves dead from fires, of herds of up to one thousand animals killed, and of thousands of beavers immolated. Little wonder that smoke made animals nervous and sometimes drove them away. Fires also sometimes destroyed horses and other property and even occasionally torched men and women—as in Saskatchewan in 1812, a very dry year, when "dreadful" fires burned eleven Blackfeet Indians to death.[33]

In recent years, the debate over Indian fire has continued in the context of discussions of the Wilderness Act of 1964. It is basically a dispute over whether or not Indian fires were a "natural" form of fire management and, if they were not, whether fires should be set in wilderness areas. Wildlife biologists, foresters, fire ecologists, and others in the Forest Service, Bureau of Land Management, National Park Service, Fish and Wildlife Service, and other agencies are involved. Beginning in the 1960s, fire-suppression policies in place for over a half-century began to change, and today forest managers burn with greater regularity than at any previous time. Their prescribed and controlled burns implicitly acknowledge the role that fires once played in ecosystems. But the Wilderness Act defines wilderness as "untrammeled by man," as "primeval" in character, and as "affected primarily by the forces of nature, with the imprint of man's work substantially unnoticed." The debate reveals the persistent gap between those who argue that Indians (unlike humans in general) lived in harmony with nature, that their fires had an impact equal to or less than lightning fires, and that they had set fires for hundreds if not thousands of years and therefore qualified as a natural force; and those who disagree, arguing in contrast that Indian fires were not all benign, that thousands of years is not significant in ecosystem evolution, and that "natural" means nonhuman.

The tension is between those who think that Indians were somehow nontechnological or pretechnological, had no impact on the environment, and were therefore "natural," and those who disagree. It recalls the earlier day when many questioned the ability of Indians to light fires of evolutionary consequence. But wilderness, as others have emphasized, is an artifact of a time and place—the twentieth-century United States—and untrammeled wilderness "is a state of mind." By the time Europeans arrived, North America was a manipulated continent. Indians had long since altered the landscape by burning or clearing woodland for farming and fuel. Despite European images of an untouched Eden, this nature was cultural not virgin, anthropogenic not primeval, and nowhere is this more evident than in the Indian uses of fire.[34]

Chapter Five

BUFFALO

IN THE ROLLING PRAIRIE in southern Alberta is a cliff whose edge is so cleverly disguised by a slight rise that an animal running toward it might not be aware of being on the edge of a precipice until it was too late. The Piegan and their predecessors used this cliff for a buffalo jump for thousands of years. Today the precipice has an abrupt drop of thirty-five to forty feet, but that is merely to the top of thirty-foot-thick deposits of bone and soil. The Piegan named this cliff Head-Smashed-In Buffalo Jump (where-he-got-his-head-smashed-in), because one day when they were driving buffaloes over it, a boy too curious for his own good crawled against the cliff to watch buffaloes toppling over the edge, but the drive was so successful that the mounting carcasses finally crushed his head against the face of the cliff. He was not discovered until the animals covering him had been butchered.

In 1981, UNESCO selected Head-Smashed-In Buffalo Jump as a World Heritage Site. An interpretive center was built with the stated aim to present a native rather than an anthropological or archaeological perspective. The interpretive center offers "much to ponder," the *New York Times* reported, including "the skills" of native people who cooperated to drive buffaloes toward a precipice and death and "the wastefulness" of white hunters who caused the extermination of sixty million bison. Others agree. In *American History Illustrated*, one can read that Head-Smashed-In Buffalo Jump is "representative of the North Americans' ingenuity, of their understanding of ecological balances, and of their economical use of the land and its bounty." This is the rhetoric of buffalo hunting on the Plains: White people wasted and caused the extermination of the buffalo, whereas Indians were skillful, ecologically aware conservationists. Since 1987, well over half a million visitors have heard this message at Head-Smashed-In Buffalo Jump and even more have been exposed to it through the wide publicity this site has garnered. Yet this story about conservation and waste is more complicated, as most stories are.[1]

No one really knows how many buffaloes there once were. Asked in the late nineteenth century how many there had been, an Indian signed, "The country was one robe." By then it was too late to count—the buffalo hunt was over—and anyway the magnitude had been too difficult to grasp, although that Native American framed his attempt revealingly in the metaphor of economy not natural history. Today it is even more impossible to know what the numbers must have been like, although historical accounts provide some guidance. At the outset of the seventeenth century, a Spaniard encountered a "multitude so great that it might be considered a falsehood by one who had not seen them."[2]

Some two hundred years later, at the close of the eighteenth century and turn of the nineteenth, the numbers still defied counting. At this time Peter Fidler, a Hudson's Bay Company surveyor, was in the middle of vast herds for over ten days in what is now Alberta, and at one point remarked that "from the N to S the ground is entirely covered by them & appears quite black. I never saw such amazing numbers together before. I am sure there was some millions in sight as no ground could be seen for them in that compleat semicircle & extending at least 10 miles." About the same time, a North West Company trader named Charles McKenzie said that near the Missouri River he had gone "through plains or meadows so thickly covered with Buffaloes that we were often under the necessity of frightening them out of our way by means of Gunpowder;—and we were in constant dread of being overrun and crushed by them at night in our Encampments." In his attempt to speak to the numbers of bison, which he called cattle, McKenzie wrote, "If small things can be compared with great, the herds of Cattle coming to quanch their thirst at these Rivers could be compared to an only Ale-house in a market Place, where the busy crowd go to moisten their palates in the heat of the day—So were the Cattle in the heat of the day Kno[c]king down one another in the passes of the rivers." In 1794 Duncan M'Gillivray, another trader, reached for biblical metaphor when he spoke of bison "as numerous as the locusts of Egypt."[3]

One-half century later, destruction of the buffalo was well under way, but John James Audubon—even as he predicted that this animal would follow the great auk to extinction—wrote that "it is *impossible to describe or even conceive* the vast multitudes of these animals that exist even now." Some twenty-five years later, it was still possible to travel through "an immense herd" for twenty-five miles, as did Colonel Richard Dodge, or "an almost unbroken herd" for over one hundred miles, as William Blackmore did on the Kansas Pacific Railroad.[4]

From 1600 to the 1870s, the language of buffalo herds was cast in phrases like immense numbers, countless numbers, countless thousands, dense masses, one great mass, herds that blackened the plains, bulls roaring like distant thunder or like a river's rapids, and bison in such numbers that they drink a river dry or the ground trembles with vibration when they move. The annual cycle of motion, oscillations across the oceans of the prairies, seemed constant, and awed all who experienced them, perhaps to have their wagon overturned or train halted by the herds. There were bellowing masses, animals grazing all fall to put on fat or crowding and scraping at grasses through winter ice and snow, cows calving in late spring, and bulls at the rut in summer. Because there were so many, natural disasters were magnified: Thousands, if not tens of thousands, froze to death in the snow drifts of heavy blizzards, drowned crossing rotten ice or rivers in spate, or mired in the bogs of muddy streams.

Estimates of the numbers range widely. Flabbergasted by what they witnessed, some observers were awed into wild, unsubstantiatable (and clearly wrong) figures of from one billion to ten billion buffaloes in a herd or one hundred million animals in a 250-square-mile region. According to one of their contemporaries, witnesses of these masses of animals were reportedly "afraid to give out these figures" because they "didn't think anyone would believe them. Nevertheless, *they* believed them."[5]

Over the last century, estimates have been lower—in the thirty to one hundred million range for the total population in AD 1500. Ernest Thompson Seton, the naturalist, was the first to estimate population on the basis of what was called "range allowance" (or carrying capacity). Using different estimates he suggested that in 1500 there had been fifty to seventy-five million bison (he favored "not less than" sixty million), and some forty million at the outset of the nineteenth century.[6] Since Seton's day the tendency has been to lower, not raise, the estimates. One reason is greater appreciation for the uneven distribution of bison over the range regardless of the allowance. Late-eighteenth- and nineteenth-century travelers could go for days without seeing a single animal and then would encounter thousands, sometimes in no-man's-lands between hostile tribes, which acted as refuge areas for animals large and small. Because of the uneven distribution, extrapolation from the largest herds at that time to preceding centuries is quite uncertain. Another reason is drought, which struck the Plains not just at twenty-year intervals in the nineteenth century, but periodically in centuries preceding. These also affected carrying capacity. Dan Flores, a historian who has scrutinized the demise of the buffalo on the southern Plains, suggests that the Plains as a whole carried no more than thirty million bison in days prior to the arrival of the horse.[7]

The range of buffaloes in the sixteenth and seventeenth centuries is more certain than its numbers. At that time they could be found throughout much of the continent, roaming north to Canada's Northwest Territories, south to Mexico, southeast to the Atlantic coast of Georgia and South Carolina, northeast to the east end of Lake Erie, and west to Washington, Oregon, and Nevada. The center of population was always the great western grasslands, where they massed in countless numbers in innumerable herds that moved back and forth from month to month and season to season. It is difficult to know precisely how regular migrations were from one season or year to the next, although in northern parts of its range the bison went from parkland in the winter to prairie in the summer; in any event, movements depended on larger cycles of wet and drought as well as on fire. By the nineteenth century, eradicated in many parts of its range, the bison was even more an animal of the western plains and prairies. That herds once ranged the East to the southeastern Atlantic lowlands is easily forgotten, perhaps because by 1833 the buffalo was extinct east of the Mississippi.[8]

Today there is almost universal agreement that the near extinction of the bison is one of the grimmest narratives in the history of wildlife. At the end, the decline west of the Mississippi was rapid and extravagant to an extreme, because hunters only stripped the robe from each buffalo they killed, leaving carcasses to bloat under the sun. Indians uniformly mourned the passing of the bison. But not whites; some spoke of the buffalo as noble and majestic, but others were unconcerned, and others actively promoted extermination as inevitable in the wake of the westward course of the empire and as a progressive impetus in bringing civilization to native people.

In the last one hundred years, debate over the causes has occasionally reached polemical proportions. Some have blamed Indians for the eradication. Others have asserted that even if people of European descent must share in the blame, Indians probably would have exterminated the animal because their demands were greater than buffalo populations could withstand. Following a winter in the late 1880s—after the bison had disappeared—when native people starved, William Hornaday wrote, "If ever thoughtless people were punished for their reckless improvidence, the Indians and half-breeds of the Northwest Terrritory are now paying the penalty for the wasteful slaughter of the buffalo a few short years ago. The buffalo is his own avenger, to an extent his remorseless slayers little dreamed he could ever be." Others argued in contrast that white people, greedy for a resource that roamed the commons and urged on by governmental spokesmen who proclaimed that each buffalo killed meant fewer Indians, were entirely responsible for the animal's demise.[9]

Unquestionably, the buffalo was the mainstay of Plains Indians, who killed them in large numbers both for domestic use and for trade with other Indians who supplied corn in exchange. It was of paramount importance in the economy and subsistence of tens of thousands of native people on the Plains. "Principal" or "real" food, the bison was lauded while most other foods, especially fish, no matter how plentiful, were denigrated and scorned (the major exception was corn, grown and valued by agricultural people as well as by their trading partners). Native people ate an incredible variety of bison parts with great relish: meat, fat, most organs, testicles, nose gristle, nipples, blood, milk, marrow, and fetus. They dried, roasted, boiled, and ate meat raw; pounded bones to make bone grease; and mixed dry, pounded meat with fat to make pemmican. There were decided preferences, to which we return, for humps, tongues, and fetuses, and for meat from cows.[10]

For people like the Blackfeet, the buffalo provided over one hundred specific items of material culture. They include robes (hair on) for bedding, gloves, winter clothing, and ceremonial and decoy costumes; hides (hair off) for tipi covers and linings, cups, parfleches, moccasins, leggings and other clothing, kettles, shields, and maul covers; hair for stuffing, yarn, and ropes, and sinew for thread, bowstrings, and snowshoe webbing; ribs for arrow straighteners; the paunch and large intestine as containers; the gallstones for yellow pigment; hoofs as rattles or for glue; the tibia and other bones for fleshers, brushes, awls, and other tools; horns for arrow points, bow parts, ladles, cups, spoons, and containers for tobacco and medicines; the brains to soften skins; fat as a paint base or to polish stone; the penis for glue; dung as fuel; and teeth as ornaments. From a purely material standpoint, it would have been virtually impossible to be out of sight, touch, or smell of a product fabricated from bison at any time of day or night. The bison was "a tribal department store," as Tom McHugh, a zoologist, remarked, a "builder's emporium, furniture mart, drugstore, and supermarket rolled into one."[11]

Given the buffalo's importance, it should come as no surprise that Plains Indians developed highly efficient hunting techniques. Some were solitary and others communal. Despite the variation, all people knew some form of solitary hunting, sometimes with snowshoes or other equipment appropriate to the season, perhaps with the hunter disguised by a buffalo or wolf skin to pique the curiosity of the animal and get within range. Getting close to the buffalo was probably not difficult until the press of constant hunting made herds skittish. Many Europeans and European-Americans thought bison to be "stupid"; they might have said that buffaloes in general relied on the herd for security, and that bulls often seemed fearless and stolid in their strength relative to all save man. Buffaloes possess an acute sense of smell and sharp hearing (their sight has been described by some as weak, by others as quite keen), and are spooked easily by a dangerous scent upwind. Sioux evidently thought that foreign smells like coffee and bacon scared bison, but Indians and whites alike discovered that so long as wind direction was taken into account, buffaloes were rather easily killed. At times they were virtually unmoveable. On his voyage across the continent in 1804–6, Meriwether

Lewis remarked that buffaloes were "extremely gentle the bull buffaloe particularly will scarcely give way to you," and on one stretch, "the men frequently throw sticks and stones at them in order to drive them out of the way."[12]

Communal methods involved running bison onto soft ice or into deep snow, a ravine, a box canyon, or an enclosure (also called a pound), and, as the Crow Indians termed it, "driving buffalo over embankments." Some people encircled herds they encountered, sometimes surrounding them on foot, keeping them circling within by waving robes, and at other times using fire to encircle the animals. These techniques resulted in resources shared throughout the community. When possible, the hunts were tightly controlled to prevent individual hunters from premature action spoiling the chances of a massive kill that would be communally shared.[13]

Ritual was often important for the success of the planned hunt, and marked the entire effort from beginning to end. The Mandan and others danced to call the bison near. The Blood and Blackfeet used sacred buffalo stones kept in beaver bundles. Powerful medicine bundles, sweetgrass offerings, tobacco pipes, stones with the power to charm in zoomorphic or other shapes, esoteric knowledge, and songs sung to buffaloes—each nation had its own way, but collectively all were brought to bear to bring buffaloes to people and ensure success; "Help me to fall the buffalo," the Blackfeet buffalo caller said. Smoking tobacco and offering the pipe to propitiate whomever had power to ensure success were common. Failure in the hunt, if not due to an impetuous hunter spoiling it for others, was easily ascribed to an improperly performed ritual.

For the Assiniboine and others, the center of the circular enclosure was ritual space where they erected a sacrificial pole or placed nearby red-painted, feather-bedecked buffalo skulls; they suspended from the pole or placed facing the skulls scarlet cloth, kettles, and other goods as offerings for buffalo spirits. According to John McDonnell, a North West Company trader, in the 1790s the Assiniboine offered a pipe of tobacco to an old bull or all the buffaloes in a pen and said something like, "My grandfather we are glad to see you, & happy to find that you are not come in a shameful manner for you have brought plenty of your young men with you; be not angry at us; tho' we are obliged to destroy you to make ourselves live." After this speech and smoking tobacco, hunters killed the animals and placed vermilion-colored swansdown on the head of each, after which each person could "take what he thinks proper."[14]

Certain men were imbued with special power or knowledge, perhaps because they knew how to lure bison into the trap by imitating their call or, camouflaged under the skin and head of a bison, by taking advantage of their curiosity and poor sight. The elder Alexander Henry remarked that the gestures of Assiniboines dressed in buffalo robes with horns attached and faces covered "so closely resembled those of the animals themselves that had I not been in the secret I should have been as much deceived as" were buffaloes. The "chaser" or "runner"—"He-Who-Brings-Them-In," the Assiniboine called him—trolled buffaloes toward their demise, funneling them inward into a narrowing V-shaped lane whose lines were defined by stacked bison chips, stone piles, or implanted trees. Men and women crouched behind these brakes, ready to jump up, wave robes, and yell and startle the animals into a panicked run toward the trap or cliff edge. The runner's task was demanding and dangerous, and he might have to jump into a cliff-edge hole at the last moment to avoid being trampled or swept over. No wonder he enjoyed respect.[15]

After buffaloes tumbled off a precipice or ran into a pound, men and women alike set about killing them. White men who witnessed this final stage of the hunt reacted strongly. For those who considered themselves sportsmen, this was hardly the "proper" or "sporting" way to hunt and kill buffaloes—"if it can be called hunting," one remarked. For them, the buffalo, easily led compared to wilder animals, was "scarcely considered game." Europeans who came to America for sport were a remarkably varied lot, some bemoaning the decline of the "noble" buffalo and others shooting hundreds merely for the killing. Yet it was not uncommon for them to declare that killing bison for their meat was "legitimate" but for their hides was "illegitimate"; that the "indiscriminate slaughter of cows" was wrong; and that the only "legitimate" way to hunt buffaloes was "by running them down and killing them at close quarters by a rifle or revolver-shot."[16]

In a pound, many white men discovered their sensibilities assaulted by their first experience of a slaughterhouse. The artist Paul Kane spoke of killings "more painful than pleasing"; John James Audubon, of "poor" buffaloes destroyed; and others, of "maimed" or "mangled" carcasses. Catlin's sensitivities were rudely shocked by a surround in which, as he wrote, the "noble" buffaloes "were doomed, like every beast and living thing else, to fall before the destroying hands of mighty man." The explorer Henry Hind thought the slaughter "revolting and terrible" and "a scene of diabolical butchery," in a word, thoroughly "heathen." Others revolted against "savage" behavior: "To look at them without disgust," warned Father Pierre De Smet, "one must have been a little habituated to their customs." For a missionary whose goals were to convert and civilize native people, the sight of men slashing at bison and of women and children "devour[ing] the meat still warm with life" and smearing their faces with blood was a "picturesque and savage scene, a very pandemonium."[17]

Buffaloes driven over grassy bluffs seventy feet high, as many were, would be stunned if not killed in the fall, and likely to break their legs or backs. They and others driven into enclosures that were still alive were shot with bows and arrows (and later, with guns), stabbed with lances, or smacked on the heads with stone mauls. Duncan M'Gillivray, a North West Company trader, was at an Assiniboine pound in the 1790s where many buffaloes "were cut to pieces before the last remainder of life had forsook them." Peter Fidler, a Hudson's Bay Company surveyor, described the scene in a Piegan enclosure in 1792, after a chief killed the first animal: "The young Men kill the rest with arrows, Bayonets tyed upon the end of a Pole, &c. The Hatchet is frequently used & it is shocking to see the poor animals thus pent up without any way of escaping, butchered in this shocking manner, some with the stroke of an axe will open nearly the whole side of a Buffalo & the poor animal runs some times a considerable while all thro' the Pound with all its internals dragging on the ground & trod out by the others, before they dye."[18]

Communal hunts sometimes produced fantastic quantities of meat. The Blackfeet called the enclosure at the base of a cliff "piskun," which has been translated as "deep blood kettle." Hunts surrounded or drove not merely dozens but hundreds of animals: 30, 60, 100, and even 600, 800, 1,000, and 1,400 buffaloes were reported killed. The weights from even modest kills were prodigious. The average mature cow weighed from 700 to 800 pounds, and some cows were as heavy as 1,200 pounds. Butchered heavily (except for a section of the vertebral column with the ribs still attached, which was commonly left in kills found at archaeological sites), the average cow yielded from 225 to 400 pounds of meat, depending on its condition. The hump alone weighed up to 40 pounds, depending on the animal's sex and condition, and on the season. Bulls were much larger, weighing up to 3,000 pounds and averaging 1,800 pounds, from which 550 pounds of meat could be obtained. Thus, fifty cows produced from 11,000 to 20,000 pounds of usable meat; 600 bison (as in the example above), if all cows, yielded from 135,000 to 240,000 pounds of meat—or, if dried, roughly one-fifth of those weights. The amount of food a person consumed each day varied greatly, but all agree that the quantities, when people were feasting or food was plentiful, were prodigious. Estimates of consumption, like estimates of numbers of bison, vary from the conservative to the fantastic, from three to thirty-five pounds per day. But from six to twelve pounds was not uncommon, and the Hudson's Bay Company ration was seven to eight pounds per man daily. The quantities of meat allowed for gourmandizing first, then preparing and drying meat for future consumption, but European observers were struck most by the first and made many remarks about the "profligacy," "improvidence," and "indolence" of successful hunters.[19]

People shared meat widely except for tongues, which were often reserved for the leader responsible for the pound or hunt, the "caller" who lured the animals toward the enclosure or cliff, or respected elders. The decision on how heavily to butcher animals depended on how much meat one had or expected, distance to the camp, means of transportation, and so on. Indians sometimes used all the meat from animals they killed, and they sometimes did not. Given the quantities and weights that could be involved, it may not be surprising that they sometimes butchered animals "lightly," perhaps taking tongues and humps only. At times, they cached meat under skins or snow or left it on the ice of a river, to be consumed days or weeks later.[20]

When it came to the buffalo, Indians had far broader canons of edibility than the white people who observed them. As Audubon said, and others confirmed, Indians ate drowned buffaloes "no matter how putrid their flesh may be." That buffaloes drowned in great numbers cannot be doubted; John McDonnell, a North West Company trader, counted over 7,000 one day in 1795 on the Qu'Appelle River. Charles McKenzie wrote that the Mandan drove "large herds" onto the weakest sections of winter ice on the Missouri, where they fell through, drowned, and were subsequently recovered downstream and left to "take flavor." Some Indians preferred drowned buffaloes over all other types of food. McKenzie wrote, "When the skin is raised you will see the flesh of a greenish hue, and ready to become alive at the least exposure to the sun; and is so ripe, so tender, that very little boiling is required." Bottle-green soup made from it was "reckoned delicious," and the Mandan were so fond of "putrid meat" that they buried animals all winter and ate them in spring.[21]

At times, Indians carried "every eatable part of the animal" to camp where all was "preserved." According to Nicolas Perrot, the Illinois were evidently "careful to gnaw the bones of the animals so clean that no meat whatever is left on them." In the early 1850s, Father Pierre De Smet witnessed an Assiniboine hunt that surrounded six hundred bison; the hunters came from lodges where there were from two thousand to three thousand people, and two days after the hunt "not a vestige of the carnage remained."[22]

But on other occasions, people did not use all the meat from the buffaloes they killed. In 1793, Fidler left one Piegan pound "quite full laying 5 or 6 deep one upon the other, all thro which in the whole was above 250 Buffalo." He added that "when the Wind happened to blow from the Pound in the direction of the Tents, there was an intollerable stench of the great number of putrified carcasses." In 1804, Meriwether Lewis saw "the remains of a vast many mangled carcases of Buffalow which had been driven over a precipice of 120 feet by the Indians and perished; the water appeared to have washed away a part of this immence pile of slaughter and still there remained the fragments of at least a hundred carcases." The following year, the Mandan killed "whole droves" of buffaloes and took only "the best parts of the meat," leaving the rest "to rot in the field." The trader Alexander Henry saw "mangled carcasses strewn about" in a Blackfeet pound in December 1809. The "bulls were mostly entire," Henry reported, "none but the good cows having been cut up," and the stench "was great."

Decades later the descriptions are similar. In 1840, a Cree pound "was strewn with half-devoured carcasses of the animals, the spoils of previous captures," and at another in September 1846, the artist Paul Kane remarked after three herds had been driven into it within twelve days, "the putrefying carcases tainted the air all round." Kane thought that Indians "destroy innumerable buffaloes, apparently for the mere pleasure of the thing. I have myself seen a pound so filled up with their dead carcases that I could scarcely imagine how the enclosure could have contained them while living." He speculated that only "one in twenty is used in any way by the Indians," and that "thousands are left to rot where they fall." In July 1857, Henry Hind first came across the remains of bison, each of which had been "deprived of its tongue and hump only," and then described the Cree building a new pound because they had "literally filled the present one with buffalo" but then abandoned it "on account of the stench which arose from the putrifying bodies." Hind saw the abandoned pound in which more than two hundred bison of all ages were "huddled together in all the forced attitudes of violent death." The Cree had stripped the cows of their flesh, and hung it on stages to dry in the sun, but had not butchered any bulls, which struck Hind as "reckless and wasteful."[23]

As the descriptions make clear, Indians preferred cows over bulls: Cow meat was far more palatable at all seasons (and bulls in rut were virtually inedible), women could more easily work the hides of cows than of thick-hided bulls, and cow robes (with the hair on) were lusher than those made from thinner-haired bulls. They also indulged a taste for parts of the bison considered delicacies, and left behind what they did not need or want. In 1805, the North West Company trader Francois-Antoine Larocque remarked that Crow Indians "are most improvident with regard of Provision." He found it "amazing" how many bison and other animals they killed, how often they "take but the fattest" parts, and thought it "no wonder" that "their love of good eating should expose them to the danger of a temporary fast." Many Indians desired especially the hump, tongue, marrow, and fetus. As Hind and many others remarked, the tongue was greatly desired, especially when there was no fear of shortage. In 1804–5, McKenzie wrote that "large parties" of Gros Ventres daily killed "whole herds" only for the tongues, and took only "the best parts" home, leaving the rest "to rot in the field." "We lived like Kings," McKenzie remarked. On another occasion, McKenzie was with some Cheyennes who killed "250 fat Cows which they left on the field as they fell; excepting the Tongues which they dried for a general feast they were to make for the Missurie Indians, whom they expected all in a Band when we should get home." The Piegan, Peter Fidler commented in February 1793, hunted buffaloes for the fetus, of which they were "remarkably fond." At that season, the "Calves in the Womb are now all well covered with hair," and the "greater part of the Cows the Indians now kill is merely for nothing else but for the calf."[24]

The Indian impact on buffalo herds depended mainly on how they defined their demand for meat and other products, and how they met that demand, through technology and hunting and processing techniques. The preference for cows surely had a damping effect on bison populations, but was it too great for buffalo populations to bear? To answer this question we must know how many bison and people there were, how many bison people required, and bison reproduction rates. As Flores suggested, this is a complicated business and the analysis will always be crude.[25] It is impossible to quantify the kill in 1500 because of uncertainty about the size of human and bison populations. One author, for example, placed the Plains Indians population at that time at 404,000, but after a decade of reflection revised it downward to 189,000. Some critics consider the continental estimate of which the higher figure is part as low by a factor of two or three, but are mute on what an upward continental revision might mean for the Plains.[26]

It makes far more sense to attempt to quantify the kill three centuries later, in 1800, when more than twenty-five separate nations belonging to seven separate major language groups exerted sovereignty in the Plains.[27] They were all equestrian. Formerly dependent on dogs to transport property from one location to another where they hunted and gathered, or from river-bottom horticultural villages to hunting grounds, they had all acquired horses by the last decades of the eighteenth century. The Spanish had introduced horses to the Southwest, and Indian trading and raiding brought them north and east in large numbers after the 1680s. Almost everywhere the horse became a valuable commodity, and by 1800 this animal, in combination with guns and the pursuit of the buffalo, had profoundly affected Plains Indians. Previously they had shown striking variations in language, culture, and adaptations. But from their common historical experience, and especially from their adoption of a way of life dependent on the mounted pursuit of buffaloes, they came superficially to resemble one another.

The impact of the horse on Indians' lives can be measured in terms of increases: in possessions, because four times more could be transported; in raiding and warfare, because horses others owned became intensely desired; in economic and social stratification, because horses were private property unequally possessed; and in the emphasis on values like individualism. Consider, for example, what happened to the need for buffalo hides in domestic use alone: When dogs packed possessions, six to seven hides were used for a tipi cover. After the horse era began, many Indians constructed larger tipis requiring twelve to twenty hides.[28]

In 1800, approximately 120,000 Plains Indians were drawing on approximately thirty million buffaloes. To meet total consumption demands in meat (possibly five pounds a day) and hides, each required six or seven buffaloes a year; the entire population, a total of 720,000 to 840,000 bison annually. If there were more Indians at that time, then the need for bison was correspondingly greater. For example, a human population twice as high (an arbitrary figure) required 1,440,000 to 1,680,000 bison annually. For the sake of argument, we can carry forward the extremes as minimal demand (720,000) and maximal demand (1,680,000). There is so much uncertainty in these calculations that it seems wise to err on the side of caution, with a bison population on the low side, human population on the high side, heavy predation, and maximal consumption estimates.[29]

Could 30 million animals sustain such demand? The keys are clearly mortality, especially of breeding females, and fertility. According to Flores, ungulate populations decline when breeding females representing 7 percent of the total number of animals are killed; 7 percent of 30 million bison is 2.1 million. Little specific is known about mortality or fertility in the nineteenth century, but buffaloes seemed to die in almost incredible numbers by drowning and in blizzards. In confined populations in a predation-free twentieth century, mortality in bison herds in Yellowstone National Park and elsewhere has ranged up to 9 percent and fertility rates around 18 percent. If comparable figures held in the early nineteenth century for all factors but human and wolf predation, then over the course of a year, 30 million buffaloes would lose 2.7 million of their number and gain 5.4 million young. The net gain of 2.7 million was available for people and wolves; some estimate that wolves numbering in the hundreds of thousands killed 30 percent of the increase each year.

One hundred twenty thousand early-nineteenth-century Plains Indians could safely remove 720,000 buffaloes (as 482,000 cows and another 238,000 bulls—the preference for cows being expressed here as two-thirds of the total), the minimum estimated need, from a population of 30 million annually, leaving almost 2 million buffaloes for wolves, without a decrease in the total population of 30 million. And all else being equal, 240,000 Indians could kill 1,680,000 buffaloes (as 1,125,000 cows and 555,000 bulls), the maximum estimated need, leaving 1 million for wolves.[30]

The problem, however, is that all else was not equal then, and perhaps never was. If the buffalo population was less (which some think it was), the number of breeding females that could be removed without detriment to the herds would also be less: for 15 million, 1.05 million; for 8 million, 560,000. The margins were quickly thinner. And in the late eighteenth and nineteenth centuries, bison, human populations, and the land were in dramatic flux. Affecting the health and survival of bison and the size of the herds were not just human predation but also disease, fires, and climate. Human predation was affected by diseases, which were periodically destructive, especially smallpox in 1780–82, 1801–2, 1831–32, and 1837–40. Disease also affected bison (and other animals), as in mid-nineteenth-century Saskatchewan. Fires often swept the grasslands, sometimes maiming and killing buffaloes. Drought, which affected grassland ecosystems broadly, may have been most significant of all. Severe drought hammered the Plains prior to the fifteenth century, episodically in the eighteenth, and especially in the second half of the nineteenth century. One drying cycle began in the early 1840s, resumed, after a wet 1849, in the early 1850s, and became extreme in the early 1860s and early 1870s—at the very moments bison herds were under severe pressure on all other fronts. In fact, the nineteenth-century bison population might have been somewhat lower than 30 million because drought severely crimped the carrying capacity of the grasslands.[31]

Moreover, the human impact on buffalo cannot be measured in predation for domestic consumption alone. Horses that competed for virtually the same grazing niche conceivably affected the massive bison herds even more. In 1800, Indians on the northern Plains had to find forage for thousands of horses when they moved from one camp to another, and through time herds of wild horses increased in size throughout the Plains. In a Mandan village in 1804, Charles McKenzie remarked, "Wood is scarce here, which is the cause that villages are often removed. A great quantity of dry and green wood is required every winter, the dry for fuel, the green for provender; a certain portion of poplar branches is provided for each horse, and the bark, which the horse clears off, is reckoned little inferior to oats." Each million of horses—Flores estimated as many as 2.5 million on the southern Plains alone—meant a million fewer bison that could be supported.[32]

However, native demand, drought, the competition from horses, disease, and fires did not ultimately doom the buffalo. What did were new markets and means of transportation: the rapidly expanding population of European-Americans whose appetite for meat was boundless; expansive new commodity markets for tongues, skins, and robes; and finally railroads that pushed into the heart of buffalo territory in the Plains, with the means to transport buffalo meat and hides to populations elsewhere. By the time of the final rush of the buffalo toward oblivion, many Indians in the southwestern and northern Plains had known of the European demand for bison products literally for two centuries. In the mid–seventeenth century, for example, the Assiniboine and Cree acted as middlemen to the Gros Ventres, Sarcee, Blackfeet, Blood, and others farther south and west, in a pemmican and robe exchange that reached to York Factory, the English post on Hudson Bay, or to French sources inland.[33]

But the demand probably did not significantly affect the lives of these and other Plains Indians until after 1700, after which, for approximately 180 years until the 1880s, the buffalo was increasingly exploited for nonnative markets. The first stage (1700–1800) was fueled by developing European-American appetites for a number of products including buffalo meat, tongues, and hides; the second

(1800–1867) was powered especially by demand for meat and tongues, and for robes useful for coverings during winter travel and clothing and hides for the leather industry; and the final stage (1867–84), which lasted only seventeen years, was marked by intensified killings for essentially the same products and spelled the end of the buffalo.[34]

The details of the exchange are far less well known for the eighteenth century than for the nineteenth. By 1800 almost all Plains people were affected by the exchange of buffalo hides, robes, and tongues for European goods and horses, often through Indian middlemen. Some had a large stake in maintaining these relations; others did not, and even the trading companies themselves did not uniformly encourage a trade in buffalo products against the more lucrative beaver. Some tribes felt the impact before the eighteenth century, when more powerful Indians armed with guns obtained from European traders pushed them from their lands onto the Plains; in this way they came to occupy specific territories on the Plains where Europeans found them.[35]

In the period from 1800 to 1867, the exchange of bison products for European manufactured goods was intense, and the political and military scene fluid, opportunistic, and violent. Plains Indians jockeyed for power against each other as they determined the best course of action in the face of greater numbers of white people and eastern Indians pouring into and through their lands to trade, trap, and live, and of U.S. governmental demands for economic concessions and territory. Influenza, measles, and other diseases periodically swept the region; smallpox ravaged the Omaha and others in 1801 and may have cut the Plains Indian population in half in the late 1830s.

Buffalo tongues and pemmican were universally commodified during this period. By mid-century, the increased intensity of the hunt had taken a toll especially on northern herds near Red River, the settlement that became Winnipeg. In the teens, the major trading companies in this region had warred over control of provisions and encouraged a trade in tons of buffalo products like grease, humps and tongues, and pemmican. After 1821, the year that marked the amalgamation of the North West and Hudson's Bay companies, the Métis descendants of native women and fur trade company trappers and other employees hunted the herds twice a year and became major provisioners of Red River. By 1840, a "modern city," in Alexander

Ross's eyes, of more than fifteen hundred people lived near the herds and Métis carts hauled back to Red River over a million pounds of meat. But they became victims of their success. Each decade they had to travel farther afield to find herds, and by 1850 they had killed all bison in what became Manitoba.

The buffalo robe also became an important commodity, but except in the northern Plains, it was far less significant than the beaver pelt at least until the 1840s, when the successful substitution of silk in hat manufacturing severely undercut the lucrative beaver trade. Nevertheless, as many as one million robes may have been traded in the ten years before 1843. In the 1830s, travelers like Prince Maximilian of Wied were struck not merely by the abundance of animals they encountered but by the "immense destruction" of buffaloes: In the upper Missouri River region, forty thousand to fifty thousand cow buffalo skins were traded each year; in the 1850s twice that number of skins flowed into St. Louis. And after the beaver trade collapsed, traders and Indians paid closer attention to buffalo robes and even more reached market in each of the next two decades. Given that each robe traded probably represented two to three buffaloes—even five—killed, and that the robes generally came from cows not bulls, the demand had an increasing impact on the size of the herds. In some areas the Métis killed large numbers. In others, Indian hunters invaded former no-man's-lands and hunted out the buffalo. And as the century progressed and killings increased and the bison numbers declined, Indian complaints about the trespass and waste of outsiders also increased.[36]

The final stage, from 1867 to 1884, was remarkable for its fury. In 1867, the first of five railroads punched into and through the heart of buffalo range to split forever the population into northern and southern herds, and to splinter these herds again and again. Pressure on the bison increased both during construction, when Buffalo Bill Cody and others made their reputation as provisioners, and afterward when trains brought sportsmen west. In Kansas, Texas, and elsewhere, tension of a different sort came from farmers and ranchers who craved the prairies for crops and cattle. But these pressures paled beside that generated by railroads that made transportation of buffalo hides easy and cheap, and therefore an attractive alternative to cowhides. The subsequent demand for skins to tan for leather products of many kinds, including belting for machinery, was international. Hunters flooded in; unskilled, they wasted three to five times the numbers they killed. The carnage defied description: four to five million killed in three years alone. Hunters went farther afield. Indian complaints of white hunters fell on deaf ears; their "guardians" in the Department of the Interior linked the disappearance of the bison to the civilization and eventual assimilation of Indian tribes. From 1871 to 1878 the hunters shot the southern herd to extinction and then moved north, thousands strong, to exterminate the northern herd by 1883. From 1871 to 1883, they may have taken four million hides. At the beginning of the end, each hide traded may well have represented five buffalo dead, but that ratio plunged as numbers went into a free fall. The commercial hunt was finished by the fall of 1883. Indians, confined to reservations and distressed from hunger, took part until the bitter end—the Piegan until "the tail of the last buffalo" disappeared. The final shipment of hides took place in 1884. With very few exceptions, the buffalo was gone.[37]

Their bones were left. Buffalo bones littered the prairies so thickly that in places it was impossible to walk without rattling against their skeletons. But buffalo bones were a useful carbon-filtering agent in sugar refining as well as (crushed) a valuable phosphate fertilizer, and over the course of several years, hundreds of entrepreneurial "bone pickers" took them all away. They vacuumed the prairies and lined the tracks with enormous rectangular mounds of bones that in turn formed mountainous piles at carbon works where they were processed. In 1872, railroads shipped over a million pounds east, the next year almost three million, and the year following that, seven million pounds. In 1890 the bones of 200,000 bison left Saskatoon by boxcar, and that marked the end of most traces of the wild buffalo. A few farsighted individuals prevented its total extinction; their early efforts at conservation in Yellowstone and elsewhere have led, in this century, to a success story. Remnant herds sought refuge in Yellowstone National Park, were nurtured for travel with Buffalo Bill Cody, or were privatized and crossed with cattle for a domestic meat market. Buffaloes survived. But that does not change the fact that in 1890, the Buffalo Era had come to an end.[38]

In this story, the role of market hunters is undisputed. If Red Cloud, the nineteenth-century Sioux leader, actually said what has been attributed to him, he may well have been correct: "Where the Indian killed one buffalo, the hide and tongue hunters killed fifty." In Canadian territory, the hunters were mainly of joint European and native extraction; in U.S. territory they were mostly of European origin. They exploited the commons for new, hungry markets. They killed a useful game resource that was free to all comers, owned by no one sufficiently powerful or interested to stop them. In the United States, there was neither will on the part of a government whose intent was ambiguous at best, nor might on the part of Indians or whites appalled at a slaughter that grew and grew. Territorial and federal game laws were too few and too late.[39]

To conserve a resource, in its most widespread definition, means not to waste it. Indians who ate only the buffalo's tongue, only the fetus, or only the hump, or who abandoned bulls because they preferred cows, were not by definition conservationists—unless the definition is altered.

Had they somehow been corrupted by an irresistible and insatiable European-American marketplace? Assigning blame to market forces has been a popular pastime for decades; in his fictional account of a Piegan buffalo caller written after the end of the Buffalo Era, James Willard Schultz put the following words into the mouth of the protagonist Apauk, "Then came the building of Fort Benton and the demand of the traders for robes, robes, and still more robes. That kept our hunters busy. They began killing buffalo in great numbers; hunting them daily in the season of prime hides. The camp was always red with meat, and out on the plains thousands and thousands of carcasses rotted or were eaten by the wolves." In this story the demand was insatiable and the Indians had no choice but to feed it.[40]

Historical descriptions of communal hunting (many penned by traders) postdate the onset of the trade. But participation in the trade in buffalo products that formed in the seventeenth century was uneven, and the process whereby buffalo products became commodities was slow to gather momentum. In the 1790s, the Piegan paid little attention to the trade until just before their annual trip to the post. Then they focused "industrious[ly]" on it, killing animals for their skins at the last instant. Native people elsewhere were more interested in the robe trade, but robes were not important commodities until the 1830s, when a fifteen-year-old market to St. Louis matured. In the following decade, Audubon remarked that buffaloes were impounded in the fall months "when the hides are good and salable," and Edwin Denig, an American Fur Company bookkeeper at Fort Union, noted that production always depended on the labor of women, who needed two days to prepare a robe for the market and produced an average of eighteen to twenty and a maximum of thirty-five robes per winter.

By Denig's and Audubon's time, the trade in robes was well oiled, and waste was taking place in an exchange context not just in the American West but farther north, where, in one chase, Métis hunters killed 2,500 bison but took the meat of only 750, and in other parts of the West, where Indians killed large numbers of buffaloes for tongues exchanged for whiskey. Yet the body of evidence suggests that Indians also wasted animals killed at communal hunting sites and used in domestic consumption only, well before the mature commercialization of the buffalo trade.[41]

The archaeological record provides abundant evidence for the antiquity of communal hunting and helps determine how ancient waste might be. Communal hunting archaeological sites are scattered throughout the Plains. Luring or driving bison into shifting sand dunes or bogs, against arroyo cutbanks, into rivers, or over cliffs is an ancient technique used to kill buffaloes for well over eleven thousand years.[42] At different seasons but especially in winter, people used sites repeatedly over hundreds or thousands of years: several hundred years at the Vore Buffalo Jump in northeastern Wyoming; five hundred years at the Wardwell enclosure in Wyoming; over sixteen hundred years at Gull Lake in southwestern Saskatchewan; over fifteen hundred years of intensive and continuous use at Old Women's Buffalo Jump in southern Alberta; and over fifty-five hundred years of discontinuous use at Head-Smashed-In Buffalo Jump. At one site there is even evidence for the antiquity of ritual: the remains of a post centrally placed in a butchering area, and perhaps of a flute and dog.[43]

The antiquity and repeated use of pound and jump sites produce certain interpretive problems; deposits of bone dozens of feet thick are sometimes so confused and intermingled that little can be said about any single episode. Adding to the difficulty was the commercial exploitation of sites in the twentieth century, when deep bone deposits were ransacked and stripped for use in sugar refining and as fertilizer.[44]

Olsen-Chubbuck is one of the rare sites that does not have one of these problems; its excavation controlled, the site offers compelling evidence of the antiquity of butchering techniques. Located in southern Colorado, Olsen-Chubbuck records a single episode that took place eight millennia ago, when hunters drove a herd of bison (of a species one-third larger than today's) over the bank of a dry gulch where almost two hundred, a mixed group of adults and juveniles, cows and bulls, perished. Archaeologists who excavated the site found skeletons massed on twisted skeletons, wedged in massive piles against piles and against the steep banks of the narrow gulch. The event probably happened in a flash. The bison in advance plunged headfirst into the bottom of the arroyo, and others behind crashed into and over them. The butchering began, and piles of segments grew: forelegs, pelvic girdles, spinal columns, skulls missing jawbones. As people butchered the animals, they ate the tongues, scattering the bones throughout the site. When it was over, they had completely butchered the buffaloes on top, but they cut the ones beneath them less thoroughly, and hardly (if at all) touched the ones on the bottom, especially in the deepest parts of the arroyo. In all, they completely butchered three of every four bison, and either butchered partly or left untouched one of every four. They left at least forty bison whole or nearly whole; inaccessible because of the narrowness of the arroyo and others on top of them, and perhaps not needed, they rotted unused. The kill produced over 50,000 pounds of meat.[45]

Waste is ancient—if we can draw on this analysis of Olsen-Chubbuck. Indians who hunted buffaloes at Olsen-Chubbuck evidently had as little interest in conservation as did the many Indians using communal hunting sites in the eighteenth and nineteenth centuries. Yet late-nineteenth- and twentieth-century native accounts—memories of the communal hunt, or accounts of others' memories—tend to omit mention of waste while simultaneously stressing the sacrality of the hunt. Blackfeet Indians, for example, told George Bird Grinnell at the end of the nineteenth century that after butchering, an enclosure "was cleaned out, the heads, feet, and least perishable offal being removed," leaving only scraps for small scavenging animals and birds (and enabling the pound to be reused). In 1948, an Assiniboine said that pounds were "sacred" not commercial, used only when necessary, and cleaned up after buffaloes had been butchered. In the 1950s, a Blood Indian remarked that his mother and others told him that "everything was taken and the surplus meat was either dried or made into pemmican." And Joseph Epes Brown, whose work with Black Elk is well known, wrote recently that "considering how efficiently the Indians used the total animal [buffalo] in their diet and daily needs, it is understandable that they were so repulsed by the wasteful non-Indian hide hunters who often took no more than the tongue and hide."[46]

These accounts might not be "wrong"—in some instances people did indeed use thoroughly the animals they killed—only ungeneralizable. The most recent sources lack direct knowledge of the days when people drove buffaloes over cliffs. In their blanket denials of indigenous waste and quickness to contrast presumed native with nonnative behavior, they reflect genuine horror at the excesses of the final stages of the demise of the buffalo. But they must be used with caution, for embedded in them may well be understandings of conservation and ecology co-opted from a discourse in which native people are used as icons of harmonious existence with nature.

In days when people drove buffaloes into enclosures and over jumps, obtaining and preserving edible meat (as culturally defined) was far more important, as a practical matter, than avoiding wasting what one killed. A first priority of Plains Indian people was to ensure that they had an adequate supply of the animal on which they were totally dependent. With tens (or hundreds) of thousands of buffaloes within sight each year, there may have been no compelling reason to curb waste. Moreover, while efficient, the communal hunt in general, and the numbers of buffaloes killed at a jump in particular, could not easily be controlled; Alexander Henry said of Blackfeet drives that "no effort of man suffices to arrest a herd in full career after the cow that leads them."[47]

Yet it would be a mistake to assume that Plains Indians acted purely from broadly sensible practical premises. In order to "see" with their eyes, we must also consider their belief systems on the basis of which their rationality formed.[48] For them, religion and the economy were not entirely separate, and important as the buffalo was to daily existence, it also figured significantly in mythology and religious expression. The degree to which religious belief permeated the hunt has already been mentioned, from the extensive ritual considered necessary to "call" buffaloes successfully, and the decorated pole and skulls at the center of the enclosure, to the prayer to buffaloes before the final killing, when they were addressed as sentient beings. Plains Indians were concerned above all to do what was necessary to ensure a successful hunt. When the Arikara placed fourteen buffalo skulls with artemisia in the eye sockets and nostril vents in a row on bluffs, it was (according to John Bradbury) as an "honour" to the bison killed "in order to appease their spirits, and prevent them from apprising the living buffaloes of the danger they run in approaching the neighbourhood."[49]

Among the Plains Indians' most widespread beliefs were, first, that a force or power pervaded the universe and came to reside in certain geophysical features, meteorological phenomena, spiritual essences, natural beings, and artifacts, making them sacred or holy; and second, that one's relations with other-than-human beings like buffalo, bear, other animals, plants, and so on were regulated by expectations and obligations similar to those that governed relations between kin or allies. People gave different labels to the diffuse power, whose existence was more important than its source (or monotheistic personalization, which became important after Christian missionaries presented alternative models and metaphors on which to draw). The Sioux called it, in its totality, *wakan tanka*, which has been translated as "great spirits" or "great incomprehensibility." Diverse people differed as to which beings or essences were most important in the origin of the world, humanity, and culture.[50]

Plains Indians animated buffaloes in ways that were fundamentally unfamiliar to their alien observers. Buffaloes were among the most important of all the beings in which power was distributed—the most sacred of all the animals for the Blackfeet, according to Grinnell. For some Indian people, a day long past existed when buffaloes had ascendancy over man, a state reversed by a culture hero (man or woman) who taught men how to use bows and arrows, or how to lure buffaloes over cliffs. Particular culture heroes, or dextrous figures who have received names like creators, transformers, and tricksters, entered into relationships with various nonhuman animals. They also transformed themselves into animals—so did ordinary men and women—or were animals themselves. Plains Indians believed there was a time when men and women conversed with, fought, killed, had sexual intercourse with, shared food with, and were kin to buffaloes and other animals; as with other humans, those relations varied from beneficial to harmful. The buffalo had its place in both private and public rites. Formal societies used buffalo imagery or parts of the buffalo to call the buffalo near or to cure the sick. The most public ceremony was the Sun Dance, the annual world-renewal ceremony held in early summer at the same time as important communal buffalo hunting. In many of its performances, buffalo tongues, meat, skulls, and myths were important sources of food, ritual paraphernalia, and metaphor and imagery, as ritual specialists invoked the relationship between man and buffalo, and between buffalo and various sources of power.[51]

Understanding that buffaloes were animated other-than-human persons helps make sense of two beliefs with implications for conservation and ecology. The first is that buffaloes that escaped from an enclosure or jump would warn others away. In 1792, Peter Fidler remarked that the same Piegan who wasted meat were also "always very anxious never to let a single buffalo escape that has been in a Pound" and were quick to hunt down buffaloes that stumbled off from a jump.

It may seem contradictory to kill even more when all is not used to start with, but according to Fidler, the Piegan said that should animals that escape "at any future time be in the Band of Buffalo that they might be bringing to the Pond, by their once being caught in the Trap they would evade going into it again, for in general when ever a single one breaks out of the Dead Men, all the rest will follow." John McDougall, a missionary, reporting from his experiences with the Cree in the 1860s, was even more explicit about this attitude: "Not one buffalo is allowed to escape. The young and the poor must die with the strong and fat, for it is believed that if these were spared they would tell the rest, and so make it impossible to bring any more bufalo into a pound."[52]

The "telling" (McDougall's word) opens a window on the Plains

Indians' beliefs about buffaloes. No doubt people who depended so utterly on the buffalo studied and discussed thoroughly its anatomy, life cycle, and ethology or behavior. Ethology, of course, is cultural and Plains Indian ethology encoded beliefs about buffaloes as other-than-human persons. Buffaloes, it was believed, not only profited from experience and avoided similar dangers presenting themselves in the future; they also warned other buffaloes away just as human beings might do. (Perhaps they were not so easily fooled a second time by the so-called "Dead Men"—knee-high piles of buffalo dung or branches marking the funnel leading toward a trap or cliff edge; sensing danger, they were perhaps more likely to veer away from the trap.) While buffaloes no doubt managed to escape, this was less important than a belief whose consequence was to try to kill as many as possible whether they were used or not. How many other Indians were like the Algonquian Piegan and Cree in holding to this belief, and how long this belief persisted, are uncertain. According to Colonel Richard Dodge, whose information is secondhand (and whose main interest was in settling and civilizing Indians), when buffaloes escaped from surrounds in the 1870s, mounted Indians let them go if pursuit risked alarming other herds; and the early-twentieth-century Plains Ojibwa said that they always let the leader escape (although how they managed to do so is unspecified).[53]

A second Plains Indian belief affecting the hunt is that when buffaloes disappeared for the season, they went to lake-bottom grasslands, and that when they reappeared they came from those habitats. Many Plains Indians believed that buffaloes came originally from beneath lakes and that they emerged from underground through certain cave mouths, springs, or other egresses. Again according to Dodge, the Cheyenne, Arapahoe, and other Indians "firmly believed that the buffalo were produced in countless numbers in a country under the ground; that every spring the surplus swarmed, like bees from a hive, out of great cave-like openings to this country." Some had seen buffaloes coming "in countless throngs" from certain caves, or knew of others who had witnessed this. Stone Calf, a Southern Cheyenne, told Dodge (before, apparently, losing faith) that "the Good God had provided this means for the constant supply of food for the Indian, and that however recklessly the white men might slaughter, they could never exterminate them."[54] Farther north, Indians thought that buffaloes went to and came from a certain lake in Canada "whose waters never rested: 'See, it is from under our lake that our buffalo comes. You say they are all gone; but look, they come again and again to us. We cannot kill them all—they are there under that lake. Do you hear the noise which never ceases? It is the buffalo fighting with each other far down under the ground, and striving to get out on the prairie—where else can they come from?' "[55]

Such a belief would have fundamental consequences for how an ecological "system" is conceptualized. Plains Indian ecological spaces would not be within the parameters of a Western ecologist's ecosystem. It is easy to see how a belief of this nature would not encourage conservation or management of a declining resource under conditions like those obtaining increasingly on the nineteenth-century Plains. If buffaloes did not return when they were expected or in the numbers anticipated, it was not because too many were being killed but because they had not yet left their lake-bottom prairies. If buffaloes returned each year from the earth because they were of the earth, how could they possibly go extinct? How could one kill too many if one held to this belief?[56]

Perhaps conservation and waste should be construed in other than narrowly utilitarian terms. It may be that wasting one's total relationship with buffaloes—a relationship expressed in religious and kinship idiom as well as in other ways—was far more risky than wasting a hide or an entire herd. But especially given the incomplete and fragmentary nature of historical evidence, this is a point that can easily be exaggerated. Indians surely did not always react to the buffalo only in sacred idiom just because it figured significantly in myth and ritual. Nor did they all show "respect" to the animated world in exactly the same way everywhere.

Were these Indians ecologists or conservationists? To call them ecologists, one must allow for the presence, in some of their ecological systems, of lakes under which buffaloes disappeared. And to brand them conservationists is to accept that what might have been most important to conserve was not a herd, or an entire buffalo, or even buffalo parts, but one's economically vital, culturally defined, historically contingent, and ritually expressed relationship with the buffalo.

Chapter Six

DEER

IN THE SIXTEENTH CENTURY, Thomas Harriot, an optimist urging Englishmen onward to the New World, predicted that through "trafficke for trifles" his countrymen could obtain thousands of deerskins yearly from Virginia's "naturall inhabitants." In one sense Harriot was right: English traders in North America could exchange goods costing a pittance to manufacture and transport for furs and skins fetching tempting sums in fashion and industrial markets at home. Profit awaited those with backing, industry, and luck. But this was only half the picture, and from Harriot and others in later centuries, a common misconception about the trade for animal pelts and skins gradually emerged. It was that Europeans alone understood the true value of merchandise and pelts, and that Indians, the "natural" residents, neither understood nor profited.

The problem with this conventional wisdom, as many have remarked, is that what were trifles to Harriot and other Europeans were assuredly not to Indians, who also leapt at the chance to exchange what was mundane and common (furs and skins) for what was not (goods of new technological and symbolic value). Some North American Indians greeted Europeans by waving pelts in their hands, signaling unambiguously the familiarity of exchange as well as their keenness to obtain the rare and useful objects Europeans possessed. Many were familiar with exchange from trading with other native people long before Europeans arrived; some had had previous (but unrecorded) encounters with Europeans. Regardless, many knew what they wanted. In Carolina in 1670, Sewee Indians greeted an English boat by "[running] up to ye middle in mire and watter to carry us a shoare where when we came they gaue us ye stroaking Complimt of ye country and brought deare skins some raw some drest to trade with us for which we gaue them kniues beads and tobacco and glad they were of ye Market."[1]

Some scholars argue that Indians who participated eagerly in the exchange were seduced by new technology and alcohol. Corrupted, these Indians were left at the mercy of the boundless greed of European merchant-capitalists, stripped of free will and agency, transformed into a monolithic forest proletariat dependent on European traders for the goods essential for survival. However, a more rounded picture of Indians after the arrival of European merchants is of people who in the short term actively created choices for themselves, defined new roles, found paths in the new order in myriad and sometimes contradictory ways, and did not become dependent either rapidly or predictably—even if, over the course of centuries, diseases and new markets ultimately spelled profound demographic and structural changes in their lives.[2]

Similarly, it has become conventional wisdom that Indians who exterminated deer, beaver, and other animals whose pelts were sought by Europeans did so because they had been corrupted by Europeans into abandoning the traditional conservation measures based in intricate taboo systems. At the heart was the belief that sentient, animated animals would punish hunters who flouted the rules for proper behavior. In the South, the regional focus of this chapter, one anthropologist argued that "an ethos in which hunter and prey were both members of a family" existed prior to the arrival of Europeans, and in this context, "it was unthinkable for a hunter to kill more game than needed." But after Europeans arrived, this "relationship to the natural world" deteriorated, and "it became increasingly difficult for the tribes to perceive themselves as partners in any sort of harmonious relationship with the world around them." The historian James Axtell added that Indians "omitted their religious obligations" and killed more white-tailed deer than needed.[3]

In a word, received wisdom has it that Indians sacrificed harmony, balance, and conservation on the altar of chaos, commodities, and accumulation. Formerly restrained by traditional ideas from overexploiting animals, they abandoned tradition in the face of consumer temptations.

Of the many trades in which Indians participated, the most famous centered on white-tailed deer and beaver, whose skins and pelts Europeans coveted and commodified. The deerskin trade consumed relations in the South for over a century. There were literally millions of deer in North America when Europeans arrived; perhaps as many as forty million, as Ernest Thompson Seton, the naturalist, proposed. Europeans found solitary deer, small groups of deer, and herds numbering in the hundreds of animals, depending on ecological circumstances. They encountered one hundred white-tails in the space of a mile in seventeenth-century New England, five hundred in a herd on the prairies, or thousands in the course of a day in the West. They found deer in habitats ranging from full canopy hardwood and conifer forests to grasslands; in the South, in every conceivable habitat. White-tails used prairies in large numbers. They gathered in large herds in winter in protected woods in swamps. But their favorite habitat was clearly the forest or swamp edge, a mosaic-like habitat that ecologists call an *ecotone*, as well as burn-induced grasses and shrubs and acorn-producing bottomland hardwood habitat. Largely sedentary and nonmigratory, and most active at dawn and dusk, white-tailed deer went about actively grazing and browsing, and then processing in their four-chambered stomachs an eclectic mix of foods including grasses, leaves, buds and twigs of shrubs and trees, berries, acorns, chestnuts, beechnuts, mushrooms, grapes, sumac, rhododendron leaves, flowers, domesticated crops, and so on.[4]

The deerskin trade took place over a wide area, but it is above all a story of the South, where Indians participated with relish in the exchange. At the dawn of their contact with Europeans, Indians who lived in the South were greatly varied, especially in language. Muskogean, Iroquoian, Siouan, Algonquian, and Timucuan—all major language families—were spoken in the region. The numerous ethnonyms (the names people used for themselves as ethnic groups) signaled clearly the separate identities of the many distinct groups. Many Indians lived in populous societies whose leaders were capable of organizing labor for monumental building projects, limiting access to basic resources, controlling trade and tributary villages, and coordinating ritual expressions. Trade linked communities and sent both exotic and ordinary objects, including deerskins, over networks of long-established trails.

The arrival of Europeans in the sixteenth century was a watershed event, introducing both epidemic diseases and a new kind of turmoil, and many of the South's indigenous people died. Some reorganized themselves socially and politically, no doubt building on extant understandings and surviving power to forge new ethnic identities. The most widely known names today of people who survived the epidemiological nightmare and reorganization include the Catawba, Cherokee, Creek, Chickasaw, and Choctaw.[5]

Despite linguistic diversity, the South's native people shared certain cultural and adaptive features. Most, for example, were farmers for whom maize, beans, squash, and other cultivated domesticated plants were a vital part of the diet. All gathered nuts and other wild foods and shellfish. All hunted numerous animals, where they were available, including deer, turkeys, bison, passenger pigeons, migratory waterfowl, and fish.

Throughout the South, white-tailed deer were arguably the most important animals hunted, and venison, whose consumption some men believed made them "swifter and more sagacious," the most important meat. People used a variety of techniques to hunt whitetails, including stalking solitary animals while wearing a wooden decoy mask or the skin and head of a deer. Collectively, they drove or surrounded deer with and without fire, and also used fire to produce habitat attractive to deer.

Everywhere, the autumn and winter hunt, when deerskins were in prime condition and the chase interfered least with the agricultural tasks of planting and harvest, was crucial. It was also the time of the rut. Often shy and timid, possessed of sharp hearing and an acute sense of smell, white-tailed bucks were distracted during the rut. With their necks swollen and antlers sharpened, and their noses to the ground, they followed, in mounting desperation, trails of urine-sprayed musk produced by does from glands between the toes of their feet and on the inside of their hocks. In this condition, dangerous but also oblivious to man, bucks were readily killed. For up to eight weeks between September and February, bucks, "blind and mad with desire," as Seton phrased it, devoted all of their energies to trailing and copulating with does, which when healthy produced from one to three fawns some six and one-half to seven months later.[6]

For Indians of this region, white-tails were never far from sight, taste, or mind. The meat (venison), tongues, and skins of deer were important not just in daily subsistence but in numerous rituals and major feasts. Deerskins were of practical importance in the production of breechcloths, leggings, moccasins, fringe, dresses, bedding, and other products. For domestic use, a Creek family needed at least twenty-five to thirty deerskins each year. Meat and skins circulated as objects of practical or symbolic significance in a number of social contexts. At marriage, a Cherokee groom presented venison to the bride, which she prepared and in turn re-presented to him. Each signaled thereby their willingness to work with the other, he by hunting, she by preparing what he killed. Cherokee and other ritual specialists used deer tongues in divination, by throwing them onto a fire using the manner in which they burned or popped to forecast sickness or health, success or failure, drought or rainfall; and they used deerskins to protect crystals used for divining and to hold ritual paraphernalia. Deer were also salient in numerous nontactile ways for all Indians of this region. They entered social configurations in the names of descent groups important in marriage, rights in land, ceremonies, and other contexts. They became personal names when the Chickasaw called their daughters doe or pretty fawn. Finally, deer figured in narratives about the origin of the known world and its inhabitants. According to the Cherokee, deer led all animals from the darkness of the underground, out of the mouth of a cave onto the surface of the earth, and generally bested animals in contests—even rabbit, a notorious trickster, but not before rabbit had filed deer's teeth so short that he was ever after confined to the foods he could browse or graze.[7]

Europeans complicated forever how native people thought about, had relations with, and used deer. Despite their almost continuous presence in Florida from the early sixteenth century on, Europeans came into the heart of the South haltingly. The intrusion began in the 1530s, at the end of which Hernando de Soto traveled through the South, discovering evidence of villages emptied by epidemics some two years before, and leaving in his wake social displacement.

When Europeans arrived in greater numbers in the heart of the

South a century later, they encountered societies greatly altered from their pre-Soto state. This second coming involved the Spanish, British, French, and in time, Americans. Their motivations for possession of the South were complex but centered on political and economic fortune, on empire and on hegemony, at the heart of which was the control of trade. Exchange fueled relationships. Europeans brought with them a range of manufactured goods and quickly discovered that they did not have to go to extremes to interest indigenous people in these goods, or to convert desire into necessity. Native people needed little convincing that metal tools, guns, ammunition, and textiles improved their lives, and were only too eager to supply in exchange what they could readily gain access to: deerskins, which Europeans craved above all else save land and slaves.[8]

The deerskin trade began in earnest in sixteenth-century Spanish Florida. Over the next century an active trade—both direct and through middlemen—developed not only on the Gulf and southern Atlantic coasts but in the interior where Creeks and other Indians lived. Farther north, sixteenth-century English colonists in Roanoke, Virginia, spoke of the potential of the trade as they exchanged goods for the skins that native people eagerly supplied. In the 1670s the exchange intensified. The demands of Europeans for skins and of Indians for firearms, brass effigies, and other goods escalated. By this time the deerskin trade was familiar throughout the South or would be soon. Although many other objects, such as pelts and skins of beaver and other animals, trees for ship masts and lumber, fish, rare metals, human slaves, and so on, had secure status as commodities in the European marketplace, deerskins and slaves were the supreme commodities in the eighteenth-century South. As John Lawson, the traveler and natural historian, remarked shortly after 1700, "Deer-Skins are one of the best Commodities *Carolina* affords, to ship off for *England*, provided they be large."[9]

Europeans turned deerskins into breeches, gloves, harnesses, saddles, and bindings for books. European cattle supplied this market until the beginning of the eighteenth century. Then in 1710–14 and at several later times during the eighteenth century, diseases hammered cattle herds in France, causing a precipitous decline. England, a center for leather working, banned the importation of diseased cattle or their skins from the continent, at which point leather workers substituted American deerskins for cattle hides, and the dictates of industry and fashion determined their use. In France, tanners made a Moroccan grain leather from heavy deerskins scraped on one side, and parchment or book bindings from lighter skins scraped of both hair and flesh. Fashion heightened the demand: Yellow "buckskin," or depilated, suede breeches became the rage. Everywhere, the best deerskins were turned into fine, soft gloves.[10]

In America, merchants conducted important export trades from Virginia, Charleston, Savannah, Pensacola, Mobile, and New Orleans; the town of Augusta and American posts inland figured significantly in the networks along which skins and manufactured products flowed. Competition over trade in both deerskins and Indian slaves was typical—among both Europeans and Indians. Traders vied with each other, as did colonial powers. Virginia traders, for example, established a direct link with Cherokees by 1673, but Charleston traders, who were engaged with the Catawba, Cherokee, and other Indians in their exchange, almost immediately opposed them. After the turn of the century, a brief but fiery war engulfed Carolina and the Yamasee.

As for Indians, all seem to have participated in the trade. Some, like the Creek, put almost all other activities aside in order to take part with gusto. All showed an intense desire for guns, not just to hunt deer but because they enhanced success in war and the capture of enemy men and women for the slave trade.[11]

In exchange for deerskins, native war captives destined for enslavement, and horses, Indians desired a range of manufactured goods. Guns and ammunition were near the top of their list, and the quantities traded guaranteed that the assault on white-tails would continue unabated. Many Indians in Virginia and Carolina possessed flintlocks in the late seventeenth and early eighteenth centuries, and well before the end of the eighteenth century Indians throughout the South were armed with smooth-bore muskets. They also appreciated the technological advances represented by metal kettles, and iron hoes, axes, and knives. And they demanded dry goods: Stroud, duffel, flannel, linen, cotton, and silk all found a ready market in this region. All Indians prized heavy duffel blankets and overcoats for winter wear, and also eagerly sought broadcloth, garters, shirts, and so on. The trade revolutionized the dress of Creeks and others, and more than one eighteenth-century observer remarked that fringe, lace, ruffled shirts, and embroidery brought a Scottish look to fashion in the South.

In the South, Indians were not passive consumers but—to use the historian James Merrell's phrase—"discriminating shoppers." The Choctaw, Creek, and others unhesitatingly refused to trade when they thought goods were inferior or not to their taste. The drive for European consumer goods developed quickly, over the space of a generation, and here as elsewhere, the older generation sometimes complained of the change. In the early eighteenth century, an ancient Natchez was reported to have wondered, rhetorically, "what use" are European goods, and to have answered, "To seduce our women, to corrupt our nation, to lead our daughters astray, to make them proud and lazy." Now, he said, "Young married men must work themselves to death to keep their wives in luxury." His vision of the past was paradisiacal and of the future was pessimistic: "Before the French came into our lands, we were men, we were happy with what we had, we walked boldly upon all our paths, because we were our own master. But today we tread gropingly, fearing thorns. We walk like the slaves which we will soon be, since they already treat us as though we were." But not everyone agreed. "We old men see it," this Natchez elder said, "but the young men do not. The supplies from Europe please them."

So pleased were they that throughout the South, Indians played traders against each other to maximize their own return and avoided paying debts to particular traders. Through time, their deerskins increased in value. In 1718, for example, a Creek hunter needed 25 heavy dressed skins for a gun, 20 for a stroud coat, 18 for a laced hat, 12 for a pistol, 6 for a striped duffel blanket or double-striped cloth shirt, 4 for an ax or hoe, and 1 skin for a pound of powder, 40 bullets, or 20 flints. Five decades later, the number of deer required for the coveted gun had dropped from 25 to 16 and in some cases only 10. And at one point in the mid–eighteenth century, the Creek obliged traders to accept undressed skins in place of dressed ones. Some Creeks were so interested in the market that they killed not the twenty-five to one hundred deer required for a family's annual domestic needs in goods each year, but two hundred to four hundred to meet their expanding needs.[12]

Indians' needs changed through time. It has often been remarked that prior to the arrival of Europeans, Indians hunted only what they "needed," presumably for domestic consumption. In aboriginal times, however, deerskins flowed along trails of tribute in the South as a principal commodity to exchange for important social and political considerations or for exotic goods; just as after Europeans came, skins traveled along the trade routes to European markets as a commodity to exchange for manufactured goods.

In no other area did needs change as significantly as in the escalating spirits trade during the eighteenth century. At first, Indians demanded brandy in the form of a gift to lubricate the rest of the exchange. Then, fueled by West Indian rum and an influx of small traders, the trade in alcohol itself developed, reaching fiercely destructive proportions among the Choctaw, Creek, Chickasaw, and others in the 1760s and 1770s. All eagerly sought rum. But every trader in the South, needing no convincing that watered rum contained the secret of unlimited profit, pushed the exchange. As it overwhelmed, or threatened to overwhelm, the exchange in durable goods, rum solved any problem of "inelasticity" in the Indians' demand for European or American products. For rum, the Creek would even part with their horses. As Charles Stuart, an Indian Affairs agent, remarked in 1770, "it is certain there is nothing the Indians like better, and nothing the traders had rather give."

Near the end of the century, four-fifths of the trade to the Choctaw might have consisted of liquor. Not without controversy: Some Choctaws asked that a stop be put to the exchange, and one leader called for regulation to prevent the "profuse Importation" of liquor, to which he attributed "all disorder and Quarreling." But regulation was impossible. Too many Choctaws were too willing to do what they had to in order to obtain rum, and there is no doubt that demand for spirits heightened the pressure on deer populations. In the end, rum chained hunters to traders, ensuring an endless supply of deerskins.[13]

Indians and whites were both so eager to engage in the exchange that after expanding sharply in the last decade of the seventeenth century, the deerskin trade reached fabulous proportions during the eighteenth century. In the late 1690s and early 1700s, as many as 85,000 skins were exported each year from Charleston and Virginia combined. In 1707, 120,000 skins left Charleston. The Carolina-Yamasee war damped the trade but annual exports from Charleston bounced back to 80,000 skins in the 1730s, and then kept increasing in the 1740s to 1750s to as high as 178,000 skins. In the 1750s to 1760s, Savannah became a major export point for 100,000 to 153,000 skins annually. Midway through the 1760s, a British administrator estimated that approximately 400,000 deerskins were traded in the area under their control each year. In the meantime, the yearly trade in French and Spanish Louisiana paralleled Charleston in growth, although it was less in volume. It grew from relatively low numbers in the teens to 15,000 deerskins in 1720 and 50,000 skins in 1739. These numbers later fell back to 30,000 from 1756 to 1760 as a result of disease and political unrest, but grew again to 85,000 raw and dressed skins exported yearly from Mobile and Pensacola in the 1770s. In the 1780s, the Choctaw traded 100,000 deerskins annually, and for most of this and the next decade (1783–99), Panton, Leslie and Company, an English firm granted monopoly over trade in the Spanish Gulf Coast territory, exported a total of at least 124,000 deerskins each year. After the turn of the nineteenth century, under pressure of competition from an American government store that collected roughly 25,000 skins each year, that firm's export total (from Pensacola) fell to 80,000 skins annually.

In sum, then, an annual trade that numbered up to 85,000 deerskins in the last years of the seventeenth century grew to hundreds of thousands of skins in the first half, and to over 500,000 skins in the middle decades, of the eighteenth century, before easing off to the low 100,000s in the beginning of the nineteenth century. The ultimate numbers are of course incompletely known, but when the trade was at its height in the eighteenth century, Indians were conceivably killing, as Kathryn Holland Braund, a historian of the trade, suggested, up to one million deer annually to supply both domestic and exchange needs.[14]

The deerskin trade was as good as over after 1800. A decline in value began in the preceding decade and never reversed itself. Conspiring against the trade were skins from newly healthy cattle and a shift in commerce toward commodities like tobacco, indigo, cotton, and sugar cane as the way to an agrarian future embracing both

Indians and European immigrants to the South. Despite the invidious policy of encouraging Indians to amass trading debts at government stores only to erase them through cessions of land, by the early nineteenth century American policy makers thought that Indians should be civilized through agriculture and animal husbandry rather than a skin-and-pelt trade. By this time, deer were terribly scarce. Hard pressed to find remaining white-tails, the Choctaw and others agreed that their future was as farmers and stockraisers, not deer hunters.[15]

On arrival in the South, some Europeans found many white-tails near the coast, while others, hinting at the existing pressure on deer populations, remarked that the largest herds were the farthest removed from the centers of the indigenous population. Perhaps some deer populations increased where epidemics meant fewer hunters and more improved habitat in the form of fallowed lands. There were still many white-tailed deer in the late seventeenth century; in Virginia in the 1680s, Thomas Ashe spoke of "infinite Herds."

But these great numbers soon showed the effects of escalating consumer demand, and concentrated market hunting from winter skin-processing camps. The heavy toll of market hunting was noticeable by the end of the seventeenth century. In Virginia, the colonists closed the season on white-tails—so ominously had deer populations plunged. Deer were so scarce among the Tuscarora in 1701 that they poached on others' lands. Then the Yamasee declared war against Carolina colonists, in part from the destruction of white-tails along the coast. Each year, it seemed, Indians had to go farther afield to find deer. In the early eighteenth century, the Choctaw apparently killed most deer near their towns and consequently poached on Chickasaw territory, with war as a result. In the 1730s, the Choctaw established winter hunting camps just several miles away from their towns, but twenty years later some traveled three hundred miles in order to make a successful hunt. Catawba hunting parties also roamed widely.

The pressure on herds mounted steadily. To try to stem the decline, colonial governments passed statutes prohibiting killing fawns, does in the season when they gave birth, and bucks during the rut—except for subsistence purposes. But in the middle decades of the century,

Indians "destroyed" white-tails, Mark Catesby, the naturalist, thought, "chiefly for the Sake of their Skins," and Creek and other hunters stripped the skins from the animals they killed in order to obtain rum, leaving the rest behind. Shortages occurred in the 1760s among the Creek, when an Upper Creek headman remarked that deerskins "are becoming scarce" and that hunters went to Cherokee territory to find animals. Deer were scarce in the 1780s among the Choctaw and in the 1790s among the Creek. To find white-tails at the end of the century, the Creek and Chickasaw trespassed on Cherokee lands and the Choctaw spent increasing amounts of time west of the Mississippi. Benjamin Hawkins, who traveled through Creek territory at the time, described a disturbed and deteriorated landscape showing signs of soil exhaustion and frequent burning, and lacking not only old-growth forests and bears but deer, in theory favored by the new mosaic of habitats. Hawkins said that there was "no game of any kind" on Yuchi lands and that Creek hunters had a difficult time finding enough game to support themselves. In 1801, Mad Dog, a Creek chief, complained that "our deer and game is almost gone."[16]

Colonial governments took action not just because Indians were killing large numbers of deer but because Europeans and Africans pouring into the South in large numbers placed additional pressure on deer populations. Throughout the eighteenth century, the new immigrants (who numbered over 1,500,000 people by 1790) placed broadening strains on southern habitats. European immigrants considered woodlands in general and bottomlands in particular as transformable commodities. Their demands for firewood, venison, and arable land for crops and domestic cattle and pigs escalated to affect adversely both forest and deer. But in the region as a whole the pressures were variable; they were most concentrated east of the mountains in Virginia and the Carolinas, where over 90 percent of the new immigrants lived, and less intense elsewhere. In many areas, European immigrants demanded and usurped river bottomlands and unhesitatingly hunted deer for skins alone. Indians responded by intensifying their exploitation of the uplands and consequently struggled increasingly with immigrant neighbors craving their lands, or with Indians whose territories held more deer than their own.

The thriving trade in indigenous slaves and the conflicts feeding it also greatly complicated relations between different Indian groups.

When they were at peace in the eighteenth century, Indians tried to remain focused on the deerskin hunt and exchange, but the hunt often embroiled them with their neighbors. As hunters stayed in deer-hunting camps longer or traveled farther to kill the animals needed to obtain goods they had come to rely on, they increasingly encountered their neighbors in lands that held deer but also served as buffer zones. When conflict escalated as a result (or for other reasons), men waged war on each other, not on deer, and white-tails were conserved as an unintended consequence of war. But when peace reigned, warriors again became hunters and renewed their assault on deer, at times in valuable hunting lands that had changed hands as a condition for peace.[17]

Periodically, then, white-tailed deer virtually disappeared from parts of the South. But this did not spell their end. Some local populations apparently went into a linear decline but others did not. For example, despite the steady pace of their eighteenth-century trade, the Creek still managed to supply over 100,000 deerskins for trade after the turn of the nineteenth century, which was testament either to the remarkable recuperative abilities of local white-tail populations or to the successful hunt of a refuge population farther afield. Gregory Waselkov, an anthropologist who has scrutinized the trade among the Creek, argued that despite local overhunting there are "no documented instances of extirpated white-tailed deer populations until the nineteenth century." And Timothy Silver, an environmental historian, concluded that white-tailed deer did not become extinct as a species in the colonial South. Yet there is no doubt that overhunting had a marked impact on local deer populations. The demand for white-tails for domestic consumption and exchange in the Atlantic economy took a cumulative toll of up to one million deer annually and resulted in local exterminations.[18]

If Indians hunted white-tailed deer to extreme scarcity and even to local extinction, the question then arises whether they first abandoned, in the face of consumer temptations, traditional ideas about conserving the natural world. In a region of such linguistic and cultural diversity, generalization is perilous. Even though Indians did share belief in an animated natural world and in a bygone era when men and animals interacted with each other as humans, for the most part little is known about their conservation beliefs. For the Cherokee, however, the historical and ethnographic evidence is especially rich.

In the very old days (one Cherokee narrative goes), men and women spoke with, understood, and lived peacefully with animals, birds, fish, insects, and plants. But as the human population increased, friction developed both because of their greater numbers and because men invented weapons with which they killed animals large and small for meat and skins. Thoughtlessly, carelessly, and contemptuously (from the animals' standpoint), greater numbers of human beings also trod on greater numbers of smaller animals than ever before. As a result, the animals agitated for action to protect themselves against the pressure of human population and man's cavalier attitudes.

First, the Cherokee say, bears met in a council over which their leader, Old White Bear, presided. After complaining that man killed too many of them for their meat and skins used for clothing and adornment, the bears decided to use man's bows and arrows against him. One bear sacrificed himself so that his guts might be used to make bowstrings. Another gave up his claws after discovering that they interfered with the arrow's flight. Old White Bear decided at this point that the cost was too great. Bears needed their claws for climbing more than they needed to declare war on man. As a result, his council ended inconclusively and indecisively.

Organized by their chief, Little Deer, the deer convened the second council. After discussion they decided to send crippling rheumatism to hunters who failed to ask forgiveness of the deer they killed. Afterward, smaller animals, fish, reptiles, birds, and insects all came together in their own councils and decided that they would follow the example set by the deer, and make thoughtless men sick with diseases. As the list of plagues that would afflict man became longer and longer, grubworm, who was especially vulnerable because he was underfoot, was pleased, and when someone suggested that menstruation be occasionally fatal he cried out "Thanks!" and shook so hard that he fell over on his back where he remained forever. Given the animals' attitudes, man would have been in a bad way if not for the plants, who determined in their own council to provide a cure for every ailment sent by the others, and to let men use them for medicine.[19]

In this mythic narrative, the emphasis is on man increasing in numbers and becoming more demanding, contemptuous, or thoughtless until animals felt sufficiently wronged to organize to send disease in their defense. In this effort, deer played a prominent role. One anthropologist sees in this myth "the Cherokee concept of natural balance," and realization on the part of the Cherokee "that man is inconsiderate of nature, abusing it, and that nature is capable of striking back." But if balance or harmony prevailed at some primordial time, it was upset by an increasing human population as much as by man's loutish behavior, which included certain "wrongs" like killing an animal without subsequently asking its pardon. The narrative is silent on whether killing too many deer, killing deer in order to use skins in a market exchange, and using only part of what one killed were offensive to deer and their chief, Little Deer.[20]

In theory, the Cherokee needed to approach and treat deer properly when they hunted them. The Cherokee believed that animals, like humans, acted on emotions such as desire for vengeance against those who contravened the rules of behavior. And when animals acted, they could make people sick. When they became sick, the Cherokee said it was because spirits, ghosts, or gods were angry at them for violating taboos, or because of the malevolence of sorcerers. They consulted a medicine man or "curer of them" who based his divination and healing on charms, physical procedures, and knowledge of sometimes hundreds of species of plants. A curer used particular plants because of their presumed medicinal properties or their evocation of processes or symptoms involved in specific instances of sickness and recovery. Medicine men also drew on *idi:gawé:sdi*—the singular form, *i:gawé:sdi*, means "something that one says (or merely thinks) or sings"—which were various magical formulas, songs, and incantations designed to influence the course of love, hunting, illness, and other human affairs. After 1821, using the syllabary invented by Sequoyah that made the Cherokee literate in their language, they recorded *idi:gawé:sdi* in small "medicine books" that today offer great insight on traditional Cherokee culture.[21]

The Cherokee used *idi:gawé:sdi* to ensure optimum conditions and results in hunting and many other endeavors. Most Cherokee men probably knew several *idi:gawé:sdi* designed specifically to influence the chase, and what they did not know they could purchase from specialists who might know many. Before leaving for the hunt or after arriving near where they expected to find deer, hunters might sing "repeatedly," perhaps four times, a song to influence deer, such as,

O Deer, you stand close by the tree,
You sweeten your saliva with acorns,
Now you are standing near,
You have come where your food rests on the ground.[22]

Creek Indians also emphasized the need to prepare themselves thoroughly when setting off on a hunt. They cleansed themselves, rubbed medicine on their bodies and guns, and carried charms attractive to deer. They were also reported to exhort and implore deer to "Awake, arise, stand up!" to their fate:

Somewhere (the deer) lies on the ground, I think; I walk about.
Somewhere (the deer) lies on the ground, I think; I walk about.
Somewhere (the deer) lies on the ground, I think; I walk about.
Awake, arise, stand up!

It is raising up its head, I believe; I walk about.
It is raising up its head, I believe; I walk about.
It is raising up its head, I believe; I walk about.
Awake, arise, stand up!

It attempts to rise, I believe; I walk about.
It attempts to rise, I believe; I walk about.
It attempts to rise, I believe; I walk about.
Awake, arise, stand up!

Slowly it raises its body, I think; I walk about.
Slowly it raises its body, I think; I walk about.
Slowly it raises its body, I think; I walk about.
Awake, arise, stand up!

It has now risen on its feet, I presume; I walk about.
It has now risen on its feet, I presume; I walk about.
It has now risen on its feet, I presume; I walk about.
Awake, arise, stand up!

Startling the deer into revealing itself by kicking a log after every second line, a hunter's thoughts, words, and actions were all aimed at ensuring success, albeit against a sentient animal that surrendered itself to him if his requests were proper.[23]

Before and during the chase, a Cherokee hunter also might have prayed to the powerful spirits of fire and water. In his important collections and translations of nineteenth-century Cherokee myths and *idi:gawé:sdi*, the anthropologist James Mooney recorded the following prayer to fire and water:

> Give me the wind. Give me the breeze. Yû! O Great Terrestrial Hunter, I come to the edge of your spittle where you repose. Let your stomach cover itself; let it be covered with leaves. Let it cover itself at a single bend, and may you never be satisfied. And you, O Ancient Red, may you hover above my breast while I sleep. Now let good (dreams?) develop; let my experiences be propitious. Ha! Now let my little trails be directed, as they lie down in various directions(?). Let the leaves be covered with the clotted blood, and may it never cease to be so. You two (the Water and the Fire) shall bury it in your stomachs. Yû!

In this prayer, the hunter's imagery evoked the powers of fire, wind, and water as he propitiated river water and, through a metaphorical link, a great mythical hunter identified with the river. Thus the hunter came to the frothy river edge, to its "spittle" (saliva being a powerful life force or "vital fluid"), and called for leaves to be covered always with the blood of mortally wounded deer. The hunter was focused. He asked for a successful chase. He hoped that game would be plentiful. He prayed that the hunt would be easy. He hoped that spirits would never be sated with enough blood or meat. When, concealed beneath the skin of a deer and behind a wooden decoy mask possessing the power to affect deer magically, he finally took aim at a deer—with bow and arrow or gun—he asked for a quick death, commanding his reed arrow or bullet "instantly" to "strike you in the very center of your soul—instantly." With a final "Yû!," he released the arrow or pulled the trigger.[24]

In annotated translations of *idi:gawé:sdi*, Jack and Anna Kilpatrick remarked on certain texts that reflect "the intensity with which [the Cherokee] observed natural phenomena." If we can extrapolate from these *idi:gawé:sdi*, there can be little doubt that the Cherokee possessed extensive knowledge of white-tailed deer anatomy, biology, ethology, and ecology. The Kilpatricks remarked that the Cherokee "went to school to Nature with a spirit that can best be defined as scientific." But their knowledge—their science—was cultural. One

Cherokee medicine man, for example, said that a hunter needed to neutralize the special senses of a buck, which possessed a channel from its foot to its ear through which the buck could hear him four miles away. To counter a buck's magic, the twentieth-century Oklahoma Cherokee used a number of deer-hunting songs of Muskogean origin; in one *i:gawé:sdi* of two parts, a buck sang the first part to affect the hunter adversely and the hunter responded (four times) in the second to combat the buck.[25]

The Cherokee believed that if they failed to ask forgiveness of the deer they killed, then the deer could cause rheumatism. Little Deer, the chief of the deer and the animal spirit who took vengeance on unthinking hunters, ran as swiftly as the wind to a deer just killed. Bending over the blood spots on the ground, Little Deer asked the spirit of the deer if it had heard the hunter make amends, the proper prayer. If the answer was yes, then Little Deer left. If no, then Little Deer followed the trail of blood left by the hunter who carried the deer to the hunter's door, where he "[put] into his body the spirit of rheumatism that shall rack him with aches and pains from that time henceforth."[26]

There were various ways to combat rheumatism depending on whether deer or another spirit was responsible (for avenging the hunter's improper behavior)—not always a straightforward diagnosis. A medicine man might treat an inflamed joint (a rheumatic or arthritic symptom) by invoking blue, yellow, black, and white squirrel spirits four times to scratch the skin of the painful joint, or by words mentioning the spirits of watermelons, pumpkins, corn, and beans. As the colors progressed from blue-yellow-black with their associated meanings of weakness-failure-defeat-death to white and its principal meanings of peace and happiness, and (using a natural analogy) as the water content of the vegetables lessened, the hope was that joint pain would ease and swelling decrease. If the Cherokee determined that a vengeful Little Deer was the cause of an affliction, they sometimes used an *i:gawé:sdi* invoking dog, a more powerful spirit than deer, in the hope of driving it away:

> Listen! Ha! In the Frigid Land you repose, O Blue Dog. O now you have swiftly drawn near to hearken. O great adawhi [spirit], you never

> fail in anything. O appear and draw near running, for your prey never escapes. You are now come to remove the intruder. Ha! You have settled a very small part of it far off there at the end of the earth.[27]

Even if deer and disease figured differently in their mythologies than in those of the Cherokee, other Indians in the South were surely articulate about the rules of behavior, which, if broken, could explain the lack of hunting success, affect the course of future hunts, or cause sickness. At the same time as he belittled such rules, Lawson, the naturalist, confirmed that Indians in early-eighteenth-century Carolina both possessed and adhered to them: "They have thousands of these foolish Ceremonies and Beliefs," Lawson said, of which "they are strict Observers." One rule kept a hunter from eating from the first buck he shot; a second apparently led Indians to keep track of and burn the bones of animals they had eaten, else animals would "leave the Country." A third rule pertained to the skins of diseased animals, which, according to James Adair, a trader resident among many southeastern Indian tribes from 1735 to 1746, Creek Indians were not supposed to touch. One hunter who did "soon paid dear," Adair said, "by a sharp splintered root of a cane running almost through his foot." Other Indians interpreted this as his punishment. Many Indians followed a rule involving a sinew—possibly in the hamstring—which they cut from the thigh and discarded, evidently believing that if they ate it they would develop cramps in their own thighs when running. The Chickasaw, Creek, and others were careful to propitiate spirits with small offerings of venison, or with the first buck of the year or season; they pulled a deer's carcass through the fire, or threw a piece of meat or fat into the fire either in thanks that their health was good or in the hope that it would continue to be.[28]

We will never know what all the rules were. Nor will we know how many Indians actually observed the rules either before or after Europeans arrived. Centuries ago, cultural knowledge atrophied as the victim of epidemics that took such a toll of human lives. The changes might have been abrupt. Only several decades after Lawson's remark that Carolina Indians strictly observed thousands of beliefs, Adair spoke of a "religious oeconomy" formerly observed identically by "every hunter" now being "practiced only by those who are the most retentive of their old religious mysteries." For some the cultural loss was rapid but could not have been even everywhere. Nineteenth-century Cherokee hunters, for example, evidently built fires behind them in the paths they took home so that Little Deer could not follow them all the way to their cabins and camps. The very action—the lighting of fires—suggests that they did not always follow Little Deer's advice on how to avoid rheumatic retaliation, but that they continued to believe that Little Deer could make them ill.[29]

Regardless of their other forms of hunting advice (like asking forgiveness of deer just killed), spirits were silent about killing too many animals or about killing animals for their skins only. If Indians were focused on any single thing when it came to the hunt for white-tails, it was on how to kill as many deer as they needed. In early-seventeenth-century Virginia, Ralph Hamor reported, Indians killed deer as "doe wee Beefes in England," by which he meant "all the year long, neither sparing young nor olde, no not the Does readie to fawn, not the yong fawnes, if but two daies old." William Strachey said virtually the same about the Powhatan killing deer, turkeys, and other animals "at all times and seasons" without regard to age, sex, or breeding state, "at no time sparing any that they can katch in their power."[30]

The Cherokee might not have listed killing too many deer among offenses because they believed in the reanimation, or reincarnation, of their prey. Medicine men, according to James Mooney, said that "there is assigned to *every* animal a definite life term which can not be curtailed by violent means." Each animal had an allotted time to be alive. If it was killed before its time was up, "the death," as Mooney said, "is only temporary and the body is immediately resurrected in its proper shape from the blood drops, and the animal continues its existence until the end of the predestined period, when the body is finally dissolved and the liberated spirit goes to join its kindred spirits in the Darkening land." The animal ghosts of the reincarnations were more powerful than the ghost of the original incarnation.

Some Cherokees thought that the reanimations following death totaled either four or, their "supremely sacrosanct numeral," seven. In work addressing Cherokee beliefs about reincarnation and other matters—and confirming Mooney's earlier suggestions—two anthropologists, Frank G. Speck and Leonard Broom, and a Cherokee collaborator named Will West Long noted the belief that "animals called out and killed by hunters who employ the formulistic magic come back to life again," and that there was therefore "no diminution in the supply of game through hunting." One killing begat potentially at least three and as many as six additional lives, and set the stage for three to six future killings. This belief in reincarnation or reanimation provides speculative ground for why conservation would have been foreign to the Cherokee, even senseless, as a check on killing deer to satisfy evolving consumer needs.[31]

Was conservation as senseless for other Indians who participated in the deerskin trade in the South as it appears to have been for the Cherokee? That would depend on how widely shared their belief in reanimation was, as well as on how other Indians actually behaved. Even if we knew the answers to these questions for the South, we would be left wondering about the rest of North America.

As white-tailed deer numbers plunged in the South, states (as colonies before them) signaled their concern in game laws whose aim was to protect does, fawns, or bucks, or sometimes entire populations of white-tails. Despite their intentions, legislators never adequately enforced the restrictions on hunting. As a consequence, white-tailed deer depletions so evident in the seventeenth and eighteenth centuries continued in the nineteenth. By 1900, deer were extremely scarce in the South and two decades later few were left.

However, white-tails can rapidly repopulate regions given the chance, as they have throughout the East since the 1920s. In six years, one population of six white-tails (four does and two bucks) in a controlled area multiplied into 160! In the South, restocking programs were instituted in the 1930s to 1940s, and as a result a population that numbered in the tens of thousands in the 1920s increased to 300,000 by 1950 and approximately two and one-half million by 1970. Today, well over twenty-five million white-tails again browse throughout North America, their recovery a success story in the annals of big-game animals. But without predators—including man—deer herds ironically now suffer from overpopulation, while many regard them as suburban menaces who graze gardens, transport ticks, and annihilate automobiles, and as badly in need of control by methods ranging from bow hunting to immunocontraception.[32]

Chapter Seven
BEAVER

IN 1637, Thomas Morton, the merchant, lawyer, and libertine, looked about Massachusetts Bay and described a "Catalogue of commodities"—trees, herbs, fruits, birds, stones, minerals, fish, and beasts. It is striking how often he and other Europeans construed North America's natural resources as commodities, giving them meaning as useful market products. Noteworthy objects were chief, rich, profitable, or potential commodities, valuable precisely because they could be exchanged for other products. Many objects lacking exchange value were ignored unless they were exotic or peculiar.[1]

Beaver appeared prominently on Morton's list. Their pelts, he proclaimed, were "the best marchantable commodity that can be found to cause ready money to be brought into the land."[2] In fact, the beaver pelt was arguably the most famous commodity in North America.

Like the white-tailed deer and buffalo, the beaver, *Castor canadensis*, was amazingly abundant in North America. The naturalist Ernest Thompson Seton speculated that in 1600 as many as fifty million swam in waters across the continent. Today, their traces can be read in the countless banks, creeks, runs, brooks, rivers, ponds, meadows, mountains, valleys, and towns bearing their name. Anthropomorphized and occasionally domesticated, beavers have attracted intense scrutiny over the centuries. Many authors have commented on the architecture and engineering of their dams and lodges, and on their character and mentality, enshrining them in a cloak of cleanliness, monogamous family values, and—as "eager beavers"—industriousness. Indeed, beavers are monogamous, local, and sedentary—the basic winter social group lives in a lodge and consists of a mated pair and their young from two years—and like all rodents must chew, else their continuously growing incisors would curve fatally into their skulls.

If beavers did not construct dams, lodges, canals, dens, and escape tunnels, they would not have a suitable, secure living habitat near their food sources. Herbivores, they prefer aquatic plants and the leafy parts and bark of trees like aspen and poplar. They can fell six-inch-diameter trees in an hour; larger ones are sometimes collaborative projects. When they exhaust the food resources bordering their pond, they often excavate fifty-foot-long canals to nearby tree-lined ponds. Their lodges are free-standing or located in dams; some have multiple chambers and hunters have killed more than thirty-five beavers in such apartment complexes.

Beavers construct wood, stone, and mud dams over several nights, and given enough beaver power, a colony, which consists of the beavers associated with one dam, can erect impressively large dams—from twelve to eighteen feet high and from four hundred to eight hundred feet long. One dam reportedly was four thousand feet long! These are products of larger beaver colonies. Not surprisingly, beavers alter their habitat profoundly through all their activity, forming pond ecosystems when dams are built, and meadow ecosystems when dams are destroyed due to fast streamflow, flood, or abandonment.[3]

European explorers and fishermen became involved in a trade for beaver pelts the instant they put to shore in North America. The exchange started in the Northeast in the late fifteenth and early sixteenth centuries, grew to tens of thousands of beaver pelts annually by the early seventeenth century, and eventually became almost continental. Since the items exchanged for them cost little to manufacture and transport and the pelts brought handsome profits at home, it is easy to understand why Europeans pushed the trade. But Indians relished it also, eager to exchange common pelts, worth a trifling amount to them, for novel foods like bread, peas, beans, and prunes and for rare and useful manufactured goods like copper kettles, axes and knives, and cloth. In seventeenth-century New France, a Montagnais leader, knife in hand, jested to a Jesuit missionary, "'The English have no sense; they give us twenty knives like this for one Beaver skin.'" Some Indians might have been wary of the Europeans, some neutral, and others aggressive from knowing that these foreigners were dangerous—but few were reluctant to trade. In this atmosphere, can it be coincidental that complaints of a dearth of beavers poured in as early as the late seventeenth century?[4]

Europe, where otter, beaver, marten, and other furs were in popular demand, provided the predominant market for North American pelts. For centuries the beaver pelt was paramount in that market. It appeared as the emblem of the famed Hudson's Bay Company (HBC), which obtained a Royal Charter over a vast territory in North America in 1670, and became the standard of exchange as the Made Beaver, which was an average-size male pelt in prime condition. Merchants found beavers attractive not for their lustrous pelt, however, but for the underhairs held together by interlocking barbs when pressed together, a quality making them without parallel in felt hat production. The significance of the underhairs was reflected in the HBC's motto, *pro pelle cutem*, meaning "the skin for the fur or wool." For years traders literally traded furs known as coat beaver (*castor gras*) from Indians' backs. Worn for months as clothing, hair inside, coat beaver was primed for felting: friction from the wearer's body loosened the coarse guard hair roots and thinned the pelts, while sweat—a natural fulling agent in felting—and oils penetrated downy and absorbent underhairs.

The French defined the fashion for felt hats or *castors* until the mid–sixteenth century, when the English and others adopted it. Felt hats became an essential part of the male wardrobe throughout Europe for three hundred years. Once European beaver populations were decimated, hatters cast their eyes toward America. As imperial and colonial powers jockeyed for power and economic control, hunters killed millions of beavers. Hats went through many styles, and as fashion changed, so did the trade. A preference for smaller brims in the late seventeenth century, together with an influx of low-grade dry (*sec*) and summer pelts damaged the trade. In the 1840s, consumers accepted silk as a substitute for beaver felt in their hats, and the market for beavers shifted to fur coats and fancy furs, where they vied with martens and minks. From that time on, beaver trapping was never again as intense, yet merchants shipped millions of beaver pelts to London in the second half of the nineteenth century.[5]

As it moved inland, the beaver trade repeatedly obliterated beaver populations. A number of scholars proposed that hunters devastated fur bearers and other resources in most places where the fur trade was carried on more or less permanently. Ultimately, this may have been the case but it did not happen in the same way everywhere. As Toby Morantz, an anthropologist, and others suggested, the trade was complicated by local circumstances; by migration, warfare, disease, middlemen, trespassers, and poachers; as well as by culturally determined and historically contingent attitudes toward animals, exchange, and accumulation.[6]

Thus there were many beaver trades, not one; and the narrative of the trade must account for both local variations and regional or continental patterns. Each region had its own history. In New England, for example (where beavers were not overly numerous to start with), the acquisitiveness was strong on both sides—for beaver pelts and for manufactured goods—and hunters all but exterminated beavers (and other animals) by the end of the seventeenth century.[7]

Beavers were scarce in the greater Northeast by this date. The Huron and Iroquois pressured these animals intensely; Gabriel Sagard, a Récollet missionary, was prophetic when he wrote after a visit to the country of the Huron in the 1620s that "I cannot think but that the end is in sight." By the mid-1630s beavers were almost gone in southern Ontario, and the Huron spent even more time as traders.[8] Over the next four decades, the five tribes that formed the Iroquois Confederacy killed most beavers nearby, "absolutely exhaust[ing]" their lands, and in trapping parties of hundreds of men, trespassed aggressively and successfully on the territories of their neighbors. As in the South, politics and warfare often affected both animals and the trade. In general, when hostilities raged, hunters left beavers alone and when peace reigned, they made war on beavers.[9]

Farther west the beaver trade took on a different narrative, as competing interests made some Indians desultory trappers, and religious reasons (perhaps stemming from the importance of medicines relating to beaver in prosecuting buffalo hunts) precluded trapping for others. This left the field open to the few foreigners daring enough to trespass and poach, and into the breach stepped trappers of European extraction, so-called "mountain men" who killed formidable quantities in the Rocky Mountains and elsewhere in the West, as well as Iroquois, hired by fur trade companies or on their own and the most renowned Indians for roaming far afield for beavers.[10] They and many others used steel traps baited with castoreum, the powerful attractant from the glands of the beaver. Algonquian Indians had used castoreum since at least the seventeenth century, and merchants distributed steel traps widely after the mid–eighteenth century; in the nineteenth century, as mass production put millions of traps into circulation, both were commonplace. Lethal in combination, they hastened the decimation of beavers: Nineteenth-century trapping records of mountain men show tallies of 250 beavers in a season, and even 150 in a day.[11]

By the late nineteenth century, the beaver harvest was 10 percent of its level one century before, and beavers were scarce or locally extinct in North America. They disappeared from New Jersey by 1820 and New Hampshire by 1865. By 1890, they were rare or absent in Pennsylvania, Wisconsin, Minnesota, most of New York, many parts of Quebec and Ontario, and elsewhere.

Concerned legislators passed laws designed to halt the destruction of beavers as they had with deer. Men and women active in the conservation movement that formed in the last three decades of the nineteenth century were appalled by the eradication of buffaloes, passenger pigeons, and other wildlife including beavers. New conservationists spoke of a "mad rush at the counter for fur and pseudo-fur" and the fashion for fur as a "craze." In the twentieth century, conservation sentiments and regulations had taken stronger hold and for beavers, the tide turned. Many understood with Roderick MacFarlane, long employed by the HBC, that "if let alone, or not much disturbed by hunting, the beaver will rapidly increase in numbers." In the first two decades of the twentieth century, restocking programs were instituted widely in the United States and Canada. Together with stringent laws restricting trapping, the programs succeeded—to the extent that within just a few years in the Adirondacks, where beavers had been extinct, New York's Conservation Commission called them "interesting but destructive," responsible for flooding highways and railroads. This success brought renewed trapping during fur booms in the 1920s and 1940s. Soon most states again allowed beaver trapping and the annual harvest in North America climbed to hundreds of thousands of pelts.[12]

Like white-tailed deer, beavers survived to recover much of their former range. Deer regained their place as a result of restricted seasons, lowered hunting pressures, and greatly expanded edge habitats between grain fields and new forests. Beavers recovered as a consequence of trapping restrictions, restocking, changes in fashion, and conservation. In the 1990s, antifur lobbies and changing fashions have cast trapping as a pariah profession, leaving beaver populations unchecked. Anthropomorphized, beavers are loved in the abstract—until like deer their unbridled populations explode into suburban cultural landscapes as pests, attracting headlines like "Busy Beavers Gnaw on Suburban Nerves" and "Besieged by Beavers in Rural New York." As the millennium approaches, these "annoying overachievers" once again busily and eagerly are altering every conceivable habitat in North America.[13]

In Canada, the fur trade figures significantly in national identity and national history, and *Castor canadensis* has often been proposed for the nation's coat of arms. The trade was paramount in the eastern half of Canada. This is a vast region, containing hundreds of thousands of square miles of prime beaver habitat in lakes, ponds, and rivers in boreal and deciduous forests. Complex culturally, this region has been home for centuries to tens of thousands of people speaking Iroquoian and Northern Algonquian languages. Our interest here is in the latter, whom linguists classify as speakers of Ojibwa (in the south and west) and Cree and Montagnais (in the north). Through time these Northern Algonquians have used different names for themselves. Their group or band names came originally from natural features or territories. Then outsiders gave them names associated with trading posts, regions, or labels applied by their neighbors. With naming so clearly linked to identity and power, some today prefer the names with origins in traditional self-designations—for example, Innu ("human being"), not Montagnais (applied by seventeenth-century French to the people living in the mountains north of the St. Lawrence River); or Anishinaabe ("Indian, human being, ordinary man") rather than Ojibwa/Chippewa ("puckered up"—from the toe of a moccasin), which white people generalized widely beyond one specific group using the label for themselves.

The Montagnais and Cree speakers include the Montagnais/Innu, Naskapi, Attikamek, and various Cree groups; their lands extend from the Labrador Sea and Gulf of St. Lawrence to central Alberta over two thousand miles west. To their south, Ojibwa speakers have a history of expansion, often at the expense of the Cree. Pushed by their neighbors the Iroquois, who threatened or initiated trade-related wars, and pulled by lands ripe for exploitation and middleman trade, Ojibwa speakers spread north and south of Lake Superior in the late seventeenth century from north of Lake Huron and Superior's east end, and Michigan's Upper Peninsula. By 1800 Ojibwa speakers occupied lands across Ontario and Manitoba and in northern Michigan, Wisconsin, and Minnesota; in these places they were known as the Algonquin, Nipissing, Ottawa, Saulteaux, Ojibwa, and Chippewa.[14]

Before Europeans appeared, Northern Algonquians found beavers a vital source of food and clothing, and also used their prominent orange-enameled incisors as cutting, gouging, and sharpening tools, and their scapulas (stripped of their flesh) as instruments of divination. After the arrival of Europeans, beavers continued to be valuable in the domestic economy but they also obviously became commodities in the European marketplace, which altered through time their use in domestic contexts. Not surprisingly, against animals so important, Northern Algonquians have marshaled an impressive and changing battery of weapons including traps, deadfalls, snares, nets, clubs, spears, bows and arrows, axes, ice chisels, and guns.

They also have controlled the hunting of beavers (and other animals) in defined areas known as family hunting territories. The territory is a bounded piece of land, and the "family" in question is a group of people united by kinship, marriage, and other ties of social solidarity and led by someone in whom authority and management rights are vested. Both territory and authority descend from one generation to the next—often, but not always, from a man to his son. The family is especially likely to use the territory (and to exercise control over or manage renewable and nonrenewable, and sedentary and mobile, resources) from late fall through spring.

There is considerable variation in an institution so widespread—variation in the size, ecology, and resources of a territory, in the size and composition of the family, in the definition of trespass and sanctioning of intruders, in the nature of "ownership" or management, in which resources are reserved to the family and which are not, and in what happens to the territory from one generation to the next. Despite differences, many Northern Algonquians distinguish the use of mobile animals important for subsistence from sedentary animals significant as commodities. Anyone can kill the former (caribou, for example) without consequence, especially when needy; but the latter (beavers, for example) are usually reserved for the territory's managing partners—unless a person is starving, in which case he can kill a beaver for its lifesaving flesh as long as he delivers the pelt to the rightful owners. Clearly, without territories, management—including efficient hunting or conservation—of sedentary animals is difficult, and with territories, management is possible; the animal most often managed is the beaver.

One question is whether territories resulted from the fur trade or were aboriginal. They do seem to have become increasingly prominent through time. Debate has raged for eighty years. Almost always cast as a choice between alternatives, the prevailing argument was initially that the territories were ancient. Then scholars identified the fur trade as the cause. This disagreement entered general debates in sociological and historical theory, because Marxist theorists denied that precapitalist hunting and gathering people could have private property, and if these Northern Algonquians did, through their family hunting territories, then where did that leave the general theory?

Today, that row seems esoteric, and most will agree that an institution so widespread and varying surely had multiple beginnings under specific historical and ecological circumstances.[15]

Although the decline of beavers in eastern and central Canada was widespread, we cannot assume that it is explained in the same way everywhere. Not all Northern Algonquians were equally enthusiastic participants in the trade, especially when it conflicted with traditional subsistence activities. Here, a series of single snapshots or frames of specific people, times, and places, each depending entirely on the existence of adequate historical evidence, will provide a range of opportunities to understand the history, culture, and behavior in specific locales as we seek answers to the question, Did Indians possess conservation ideals and family hunting territories prior to the onset of the trade only to abandon them in the face of a seductive array of novel goods, or did they develop both as a result of outside influences?

The first snapshot is of the Montagnais in the 1630s. These people had probably been drawn into the transatlantic trade in the preceding century when European mariners put to shore to dry and process fish, but the near absence of documentation leaves the period hazy. In the seventeenth century, record-keeping Jesuit proselytizers arrived in New France and set down the first comments about the exchange and its impact on beavers. Like Europeans, these Montagnais seem to have relished the trade, one "jokingly" telling Father Paul Le Jeune, head of the Jesuit mission in Quebec, one day that "the Beaver does everything perfectly well, it makes kettles, hatchets, swords, knives, bread; in short, it makes everything."[16]

There was more than banter in these remarks. Montagnais and many other native people were indeed fond of items like copper kettles, clothing, metal tools, guns, and many other goods that rapidly took the place of bark containers, stone tools, and a host of traditional artifacts. They eagerly exchanged beavers for these objects, which may have had a rapid impact on beaver populations, for there is evidence for an immediate decline. By 1635, for instance, beavers were very scarce near Three Rivers and elsewhere along the St. Lawrence, evidently because of overtrapping.[17] The year before, Le Jeune spent the winter with a Montagnais band. He alluded vaguely to this group's "boundaries" and spoke of Indians who came "to hunt upon our very grounds, taking away our game and our lives at the same time" during a time of extreme hardship. This band (and others later in the century), it seems, lived in lands that band members considered theirs to exploit and perhaps manage. But when Le Jeune remarked that one goal of his mission was to settle Montagnais near Three Rivers so that they would hunt in specific territories—or cultivate the soil—he gave the impression that the families possessed no such territories.[18]

Le Jeune's remarks relating to conservation were emphatically negative. When the Montagnais he knew found a beaver lodge, they "kill all, great and small, male and female." Le Jeune prophesied that they "will finally exterminate the species in this Region, as has happened among the Hurons, who have not a single Beaver." The nearby

Mi'kmaq, similarly intent on trade, also possessed a "disposition," according to Nicolas Denys, a trader and governor of Acadia in the years following 1635, to "take all" beavers in a lodge, and "not to spare the little ones any more than the big ones." Involved in an exchange with Europeans for several generations, they treated all animals the same, killing "all of each kind" they captured; before Europeans arrived, Denys speculated, they took meat they needed and left skins on the ground.[19]

To prevent these Montagnais from following the example of the Huron, Le Jeune proposed "locating" specific families so that each would take "its own territory for hunting, without following in the tracks of its neighbors." He also thought of "counseling" them "not to kill any but the males and of those only such as are large." This way, Le Jeune thought, "they will have Beaver meat and skins in the greatest abundance." This not only represents one of the earliest recorded European designs to promote conservation and family-managed hunting territories in North America but implies that both were novel ideas.[20]

The second frame is of the seventeenth- and eighteenth-century Cree who lived on the East Main—a large area east and southeast of James Bay. The Cree in this region were initially associated with specific bands identified with inland or coastal regions, rivers, or individual leaders. They later drew a group identity from trading posts and their regional geographical location on the East Main or east of James Bay.

While the East Main Cree took part in the fur trade in the seventeenth century, little is known of the central issues of conservation and control over beaver populations prior to the eighteenth. The evidence is simply too thin. It does seem, however, that in the southern parts of the region in south-central Quebec, the Cree used beavers extensively for food and clothing and pursued them with bows, arrows, deadfalls, and nets, and by breaking into lodges or burrows located with the help of dogs, and that native people in the northern parts of this region considered caribou more important than beaver for food and clothing. The Cree who traded at Rupert House in the southernmost part of James Bay evidently possessed hunting territories in the 1670s: Each spring they were said to decide how to adjust the boundaries of hunting grounds and allocate them to "families" in the coming year. Even though this is a secondhand account written forty years after the fact, it does open the possibility that men negotiated hunting territories anew each year, with the entire band in mind.[21]

As for what form that management took, we are in the dark except for an enigmatic note from the 1650s to 1660s, in which Pierre Esprit Radisson remarked that some Crees who came south to the Great Lakes to trade were unlike other Indians in not killing young beavers. We know neither who these Crees were nor whether they left young beavers so that they might mature and reproduce the colony or acquire larger, more valuable prime winter pelts.[22]

From Eastmain, a HBC post on the southeast coast of James Bay, where beaver was by far the most valuable fur exchanged in the eighteenth century, comes evidence of lands hunted out. Probably as a result of French competition and Iroquois and other poachers, the number of pelts traded at this post declined sharply in the 1730s (and again in the 1760s). By 1730, lands in the southern parts of this region were "Drained of animals" and "ruined." One Jesuit wrote that beaver populations might rebound only if lands were abandoned, but that "would be asking The Impossible from the savages. They would travel ten leagues to kill a beaver a year old, summer or winter, if they could find it." In the following decades, trespass and poaching by outside Indians and the East Main Cree themselves continued to be an issue. In 1745, one East Main Cree reported restrictions on killing fur bearers "in one anothers Leiberty." Another Cree on whose lands he was hunting told him that he could kill and keep rabbits or caribou but not martens—thus distinguishing animals consumed from those destined for exchange (which is a sign of commodification) and signaling the existence of hunting territories (evidently also possessed by the Cree who traded at Fort Albany to the west), for which evidence becomes more marked in the second half of the eighteenth century.[23] Were hunting territories born in events like these? Did trespassers from outside the band or tribe initially cause resentment when they stripped the lands of resources newly transformed into commodities; and embittered, did people subsequently clamor for hunting territories over which they could exercise control when members of their own band emulated the outsiders?

For the next snapshot we move west to York Factory, the HBC post on the southwest side of Hudson Bay, in the period 1738–75.[24] Competition for the Cree trade was keen throughout the eighteenth century. Before 1763, the value of beaver, expressed as a percent of the total return, declined steadily and at times sharply at York Factory. The decline was due in part to gift giving and French competition but also to faunal cycles, disease, and a static demand for trade goods.

These Crees had a fairly inelastic need for goods. For each hunter each year the demand amounted to a gun (if the hunter's gun was broken beyond repair) plus powder and shot, a powder horn, two hatchets, an ice chisel, four knives, a fishing net, a file, six awls, one brass kettle, four yards of cloth, and over seven pounds of tobacco. To purchase these goods, a hunter required seventy beaver pelts or the equivalent in other furs. Andrew Graham, resident at York Factory for two decades in the second half of the eighteenth century, commented that a standard of trade adjusted "in favour of the natives, would ruin it all; for I am certain if the natives were to get any more for their furs, they would catch fewer." Graham thought this was because "one canoe brings down yearly to the Fort one hundred made beaver in different kinds of furs, and trades with me seventy of the said beaver for real necessaries. The other thirty beaver shall so puzzle him to trade, that he often asks me what he shall buy, and when I make an answer, Trade some more powder, shot, tobacco and hatchets etc., his answer is, I have traded sufficient to serve me and my family until I see you next summer; so he will drink one half, and trade the other with me for baubles."

The trade in brandy, as well as in other goods requiring measures that the traders might leave "short," resulted in tidy profits for the traders. But even when traders signaled a greater demand for furs in the prices (in goods) they were willing to pay, Indians did not respond by increasing the supply. Instead they brought the same number or sometimes less (producing what is known as a backward-sloping supply curve, contradicting the idea that "economic man" invariably responds "rationally" to heightened demand with a greater supply). Working against an increased supply were the limited capacity of canoes and human bodies, a mobile life, a greater interest in being generous by giving away than in accumulation for its own sake, and lavish gift giving on the part of European traders to offset temptation to trade with their competitors.[25]

According to Graham and his predecessor James Isham, the York Factory Cree hunted beavers during all seasons, and Isham thought it "a Little strange" that the animals did not "Diminish greatly considering the many thousands that is Killd. of a Year." Like the East Main Cree, the York Factory Cree distinguished the domestic from the commodity value of beavers. In Isham's words, "When Severall Indians is togeather, they have sett Rules to the Right of the Beaver skin, which is;—if one finds a beaver house, all the Rest goes with and assists him to Kill them, he that found the house having all the skins, and the flesh Equaly Divided, otherwise some wou'd gett all and other's none."

On measures designed to conserve beavers, neither trader is very helpful despite their combined five decades of residence. Isham remarked equivocally that "in some houses an Indian will Kill 15 or 20 beaver, and in other's not above 2 or 3"—surely inconclusive on whether beavers were deliberately left alive in a lodge. On the one hunt he witnessed, Graham reported that the Cree killed all the beavers they found in a lodge, which amounted to two. Following a single winter in residence at York Factory, T. F. Drage said in contrast that when the Cree "take a house" of beavers, "they generally leave two to breed." His comment is intriguing and perhaps linked to Radisson's report a century earlier on the Cree leaving young beavers to mature, perhaps to control multiple "harvests" of beavers from the same lodge. Yet in 1700, the soldier and author Bacqueville de la Potherie remarked that Indians who traded at Fort Nelson/York Factory marked beaver lodges, claiming the pelts within for themselves, but then went about their business destroying beaver lodges and dams and netting or killing beavers with spears and arrows seemingly without regard for the morrow.

In contrast to sedentary beavers, the hunting of which could be controlled in theory, caribou migrated rapidly through territories and across major rivers. Their numbers, as well as the carnage and waste hunting them, astounded the traders at York Factory. Isham remarked that the Cree "frequently" killed "scores" of caribou, taking "only the tongues or heads" and letting "the body or carcass go a Drift with the tide." Over a three-week period, they "Kill'd upwards of 1,000 Deer [caribou] by the Quantity of tongues I have Rec'd from them." Drage linked the assault on pregnant cows in spring for their tongues to a recent decline in numbers of caribou and remarked that HBC traders "reproved" some Crees who "uselessly destroy'd" these caribou.

The great destruction and waste struck Graham also. He used almost identical language as Isham had in talking about the hunt for migrating caribou in May and September: The Cree killed "several score" at once and took only "the tongues, heads, hearts and feet, according as they choose; letting the carcasses go adrift in the river." Graham branded the coastal-dwelling Cree as indolent gourmands, yet argued that behavior "unaccountable to Englishmen" made sense to people who were mobile and carried their belongings. They killed the animals for their own use, and for tongues, fat, and other choice products to exchange for brandy and other trade goods. They then set the carcasses adrift. They killed more than they needed, and more than they used. Graham thought that they believed they could not kill too many. "They kill animals out of wantonness," he said, "alleging the more they destroy the more plentiful they grow."[26]

Graham's observations were largely for the years 1753–74. The period between roughly 1750 and 1830 was a watershed era for the development of conservation and family hunting territories. Before, their traces were fleeting, local, or absent. After, the evidence for both was widespread. There were two important reasons for the change: the great decline in the numbers of beavers and other mammals, and the active promotion of conservation and territories by the HBC.

During this eighty-year era, the assault on beavers was continuous and the decline in beaver populations ubiquitous. Competition for furs was stiff throughout the eighteenth century. The French and English vied with each other on Hudson Bay and inland, with especially keen competition in the two decades before mid-century. In 1763, the English emerged victorious but in the Northern Algonquian trade, free market conditions ruled widely. Trading companies, with the HBC and North West Company as the main antagonists from the 1780s onward, and the XY and other short-lived companies in supporting roles, intensified the struggle for pelts. They waged bitter contests for fur in the final decades of the eighteenth century, and after the end of the first decade of the nineteenth, traders voiced sharp complaints about the "great scarcity of Beaver" everywhere east of the Rocky Mountains. Beavers were decimated in most productive boreal forest, deciduous forest, parkland, and river-bottom tall grass prairie habitats. Few remained in southwestern Ontario, southern and central Manitoba, or central Saskatchewan; these and other regions were "nearly exhausted in Fur bearing Animals," and to find beavers Indians had to go farther afield every year. There is no doubt that persistent and aggressive trapping, fueled by competition and an influx of new trappers who were mainly Indian but also of European descent, were principally responsible for the decline. Abetting them were drought, lodge-destroying fires, mismanagement, and—twice—disease, which one time left beavers "red and bloody about the heart" and caused great mortality.

In the last decade of this period, traders urged that conservation measures and a territorial system be developed in order to curb the carnage of beavers. The pivotal moment occurred in 1821 with the merger of the HBC and North West Company, which marked the end, for the time being, of fierce competition in lands that drained into Hudson Bay. With George Simpson at the helm of the newly amalgamated firm, the victorious HBC faced lands over which it asserted monopoly control but which with rare exception were depleted of furs. Beginning with Simpson, few doubted that action was needed if beaver were ever again to be traded. Determined to reverse the course, he called upon traders to conserve the severely depleted populations. His twin priorities were to "nurse the country," that is, not to hunt it and allow beavers and other depleted fur-bearing animals to "recruit" or recover; and to encourage native people to develop hunting territories in which they could conserve beavers. "Nursing" included halting the trade in pelts from young and summer-killed beavers, whose pelts were small or inferior in quality; dissuading the use of steel traps, "the scourge of the Country"; and installing a quota system in districts where animals were especially depleted. The policy was reiterated in formal resolutions at HBC council meetings in the 1820s to 1830s. Hunting territories were also seen as part of the solution. By "alloting certain tracts of the country to the different bands," Simpson thought it possible to control hunting and allow animal populations to recover.

The results were admittedly uneven. Simpson did report later that the attempt "to confine the natives throughout the country now by families to separate and distinct hunting grounds" seemed "to take among them by degrees." But, skeptical of the reach of his authority, he also confessed that "it is a difficult matter to change the habits of Indians" even when they "may see the ultimate benefit" of action. Two problems linked to subsistence intervened: Some Indians depended on beaver flesh and others had to search widely for food of any kind. Given this, Simpson realized that it was not entirely practical to expect all people to confine themselves to certain localities or to refrain from killing summer or small beavers. Success in curtailing the summer hunt was sometimes impermanent. "By entreaties and threats," Simpson reported that he succeeded in curbing some destructive summer hunts of roaming Indians but that in the winter they returned to kill beavers in lodges they discovered the previous summer. Even if one could persuade hunters to leave beavers to breed or mature, an adverse season would undo that success. But the results were not entirely bleak. In some instances, where muskrats were an acceptable substitute for trade and subsistence, beavers recovered, and when trading posts closed, all fur-bearer populations rebounded.

Despite its monopoly, the HBC did not conduct the trade in identical fashion everywhere, nor was its control absolute. Traders varied in their willingness to enforce policies. They could not prevent Indians from dealing with competing American and Métis traders on the border with the United States, nor could they control the inroads of "free traders" not in their employ, who filtered north as the nineteenth century wore on. Neither native people nor traders seemed able to develop a renewable harvest of beavers, and the decline in these animals continued until the 1840s, when the HBC introduced more stringent measures against trapping, as well as premium prices for other furs. In combination, they relieved pressure on the beaver populations, which rebounded. Then almost immediately silk hats replaced felt hats, and the most intense action shifted away from beavers to other furs. Thus, market forces in combination with HBC policies and perhaps other factors led to the eventual recovery of beaver populations.[27]

The next three snapshots in quick succession are of the Cree near Lake Winnipegosis from the 1790s through the 1820s, the Cree on the East Main in the period 1820–50, and the Northern Ojibwa in northern Ontario from the 1790s through the 1840s.

Like some other regions, Lake Winnipegosis was the scene of fierce and escalating competition involving the HBC and North West and XY companies in the late eighteenth and early nineteenth centuries. David Thompson, the HBC surveyor who was among the Western Woods Cree in the 1790s, spoke generally about the destructive consequences of the era of intense rivalry, and especially of the lethal combination of castoreum (the product of a set of paired glands near the beaver's anus), whose seductive properties had been known to some Algonquian-speaking Indians since the seventeenth century, and steel traps, which became available in the eighteenth. By the late eighteenth century, trappers combined both in the beaver hunt, and here, as elsewhere, beavers disappeared rapidly.

According to Thompson, one old Cree linked the decline to his tribesmen's desire for manufactured goods, to the lack of control over hunting, and to the attitude of a Cree creator. That old man said that for some reason, the "Great Spirit"—probably Kihcimanitōw, the benevolent creator—twice became "angry" with beavers. The first time was long ago when beavers lived on land as ancient people and were wise and powerful until Kihcimanitōw ordered Wīsahkēcāhk, a trickster-transformer being, to "drive them all into the water and there let them live, still to be wise, but without power; to be food and clothing for man, and the prey of other animals. . . ." The second time, Kihcimanitōw determined that beavers "are now all to be destroyed" and Wīsahkēcāhk subsequently showed the Algonquin and Nipissing the "secret of the destruction"—castoreum—of which beavers were "more fond . . . than we are of fire water." The old man concluded, "We are now killing the Beaver without any labor, we are now rich, but [shall] soon be poor, for when the Beaver are destroyed we have nothing to depend on to purchase what we want for our families, strangers now run over our country with their iron traps, and we, and they will soon be poor." Thompson remarked, "For several years all these Indians were rich, the Women and Children, as well as the Men, were covered with silver brooches, Ear Rings, Wampum, Beads and other trinkets. Their mantles were of fine scarlet cloth, and all was finery and dress." But predicated on an endless supply of beaver, this consumption could not last. "Every intelligent man saw the poverty that would follow the destruction of the Beaver, but there were no Chiefs to controul it; all ways perfect liberty and equality.

Four years afterwards (1797) almost the whole of these extensive countries were denuded of Beaver, the Natives became poor, and with difficulty procured the first necessaries of life. . . ."[28]

These Crees obligingly hunted beavers. If they possessed territories, they resisted complaining about or taking action against trespass. Others surely trespassed and poached during this period. Outsiders like Mohawk trappers and "Freemen," who were former employees of Canadian fur companies, poured into Cree territory. They and the Cree reaped the benefits of steel and castoreum. One trader complained that Iroquois had "dispersed all over where ever a beaver was known to be which will finish the Destruction of the Country as they leave nothing wherever they come."

After 1821, HBC traders pushed conservation policies at Cumberland House northwest of Lake Winnipegosis. While some Crees did evidently lay off the summer muskrat hunt so that these animals might raise their young, most Crees continued to bring in summer beaver pelts, against HBC policy. When one trader said five years later that he was willing to cut the price for beaver by 50 percent in order to "allow" them "to increase," the Cree responded "very coolly" by stating that "Beaver meat was too good to let Pass when there was any chance of killing it." With great ambiguity, this trader remarked that "Sacrificing" beavers "is the preservation of the Lives of the Indians." Did he mean merely that the flesh was a food on which the Cree depended? Or that the pelts were sacrificed? Or that in sacrifice they somehow assured a continuing supply?[29]

Some distance away from Cumberland House, the Cree who lived on the east side of James Bay and traded at Rupert House had a different history of development of territories and conservation. As Toby Morantz showed, the development of hunting territories among the James Bay Cree could not have originated with George Simpson's policies. These Crees had restricted hunting in one another's areas as far back as the mid–eighteenth century. They possessed loosely organized territories one decade before the amalgamation of the HBC and North West Company, and the Rupert House Cree were said to be "tenacious of their Property in their Lands and are not pleased when other Indians encroach on them" only two years after the HBC monopoly began. For this reason, perhaps, when traders asked them the next year to spare "Cub Beaver," they responded that it was "perfectly accordant with their own Ideas on the subject and their Desires of not impoverishing their Lands."

But because beaver continued to be important for subsistence, it had been necessary to ask. To help the Cree resist the temptation, the traders lowered the tariff on fishing tackle and ammunition—but not uniformly. In the southern parts of the region where competition lingered, the HBC did not discourage the use of steel traps or killing young and summer beavers, but developed a scorched-earth policy to encourage the trade to them, not to their competitors, even if it meant killing all animals.

The potential for conservation in family hunting territories was clear. In "alternate years" in the early 1840s, the Rupert House Cree hunted "different sections of their lands, leaving such to recruit two or even three years"—a rotational practice that would have conserved beavers. If they had not done so, one trader speculated, "Long ago their lands (particularly the Coast Indians whose beaver grounds are so limited) would have been exhausted." The HBC nevertheless felt the need to curtail further the beaver pelt trade in that decade. The Rupert House Cree complained that Indians from other posts trespassed on lands they had deliberately left idle and, to the east, the Mistassini Cree had identical complaints about poachers who killed beavers during the summer and other seasons. That decade the HBC also established beaver preserves on two islands in James Bay to go along with the rules against hunting young or summer animals. When restrictions were lifted, the total value of beavers traded at Rupert House almost doubled within a decade, a visible sign of newly robust populations.[30]

The story of the Northern Ojibwa who moved into northwestern Ontario in the eighteenth century is familiar: Indians unhesitatingly exchanged mundane beaver pelts for rare and useful European technology, competition fueled exchange, and beavers became scarce. At the start, beavers were up to the pressure, by one report "so plentiful" between Lakes Superior and Winnipeg that Indians "place little value on it and only collect the large skins which they send to the

English." At first, many Northern Ojibwas threw smaller pelts away and folded the quest for furs into their primary hunt for moose and caribou. But later in the century, the fierce competition between the HBC and North West Company left a lasting impact on beavers, and after the turn of the nineteenth century, the trade deteriorated rapidly. Over the next two decades, traders on both sides reported "impoverished," "barren and poor," or "exhausted" country; scarce, few, or absent beavers; and plummeting profits. At Osnaburgh House, an HBC post, the number of large pelts dropped by 50 percent in one year and by 90 percent in a decade. Caribou also declined greatly and moose disappeared entirely, and starving Indians increasingly turned to fish for subsistence, and rabbits for food and clothing.[31]

Prior to the nineteenth century there was no sign of conservation or territoriality among the Northern Ojibwa of Osnaburgh House-Lac Seul, as Charles Bishop, an anthropologist, showed. In the 1790s, beavers were still so plentiful that Indians continued to throw small pelts away. Then, moose, caribou, and beaver (in the wake of competition) declined in numbers. In these conditions, an indigenous system to control the hunt for beaver was born. Previously, lands were allotted to specific individuals by consensus or group leaders. Now, Ojibwa hunters, more focused on sedentary resources than ever before, started to mark beaver lodges as their own. HBC traders might have influenced this effort to claim lodges and territories because it coincided with developing HBC policy to get the Osnaburgh House-Lac Seul Ojibwa and other Indians to conserve beavers and exert firmer control over where they hunted. In the 1820s traders alerted the Northern Ojibwa to beaver-hunting restrictions, refused cub or summer-killed beaver pelts at some posts, and attempted to outlaw the lethal steel traps.

Lodge marking notwithstanding, trespass loomed as a major impediment to conservation in the 1820s. One trader complained, "One tribe pays no attention to the mark of another." Indians commonly trapped territories considered by other bands as their own; they killed beavers "when they see them." Territoriality was not firmly institutionalized everywhere; "it is very hard if not impossible to prevent the Natives from killing every little animal they see as well as the larger," one trader remarked, "so long as the ground is common among them." The Northern Ojibwa roamed and poached and with familiar results, "[flew] upon everything they can catch even beavers of a span long," and "destroyed all the Furred animals."

The Northern Ojibwa sometimes stepped up their own kill as a management strategy as well as to combat poachers. In the late 1830s one Ojibwa "almost ruined his lands," evidently by overtrapping, but then moved to a different area "to let his Beaver recover." Some eight years later, he was using the same strategy but this time when he returned to a river he had deliberately not hunted for three years in order to let beavers recover, he discovered that "Strange Indians" armed with steel traps had trapped it out. He was determined not to let poachers gain advantage over him again—but the only option he had was to trap out the lands himself.

The Northern Ojibwa adopted territories and conservation haltingly. For two decades, HBC traders pushed the conservation policy but did not enforce it in the same way everywhere. Ignoring traders, some Indians continued to eat beavers and bring summer and cub beaver pelts to posts. If these pelts were refused, they simply traded them to other Indians who in turn took them to less discriminating traders whose regions held more beavers. Trespassers were uninterested in conservation, and Indians who preemptively stripped their own lands ahead of poachers apparently could not afford to be interested themselves. In the 1830s, the evidence for family hunting territories becomes clearer and finally abundant, and by mid-century, complaints against trespass declined, perhaps signaling a general acceptance of territorial boundaries and rights. In the ensuing decades, family hunting territories with sanctions against trespass were common among the Osnaburgh House Ojibwa.[32]

From having been rare in the teens, beavers recovered in the 1830s, and for the rest of the century, their populations fluctuated from scarcity (1840s) to abundance (1870s to 1880s) to scarcity again (1890s), a pattern produced mainly by alternating conservation and overtrapping and by the mid-1840s substitution of silk in the manufacturing of hats. In the final decade of the century, Indians once again "exterminated" beavers; "annually driven further back by the encroachment of hunters from other places," they evidently "no longer spare a few animals for breeding, even on their own lands, as has hitherto been their custom." The trader who reported this was right: Beavers were again being hunted out. But if by "hitherto" he meant at some primordial pre-European time, he produced no evidence (and we have none); the origins of that custom, an artifact of historical circumstances that began some seventy years before, were already obscure.[33]

Thus far we have six frames of Northern Algonquians from the seventeenth through nineteenth centuries. In the first three—the Montagnais in the 1630s, the East Main Cree in the period from 1650 to 1745, and the York Factory Cree from 1738 to 1775—the concept of conservation seems to have been largely absent; most Indians—but not all—had no interest whatsoever in it. These Indians killed as many beavers as they needed to satisfy their desire for trade goods and domestic consumption. And while some staked claims to beaver lodges or hunting territories, others evidently did not honor those rights. Perhaps family hunting territories emerged where people wished to repel trespassers and manage their own beaver lodges to produce renewable commodities; perhaps outsiders like Le Jeune had some sway over conservation attitudes; perhaps Northern Algonquians felt toward beavers, as the York Factory Cree did toward caribou, that "the more they destroy the more plentiful they grow."

The last three frames—the Cree near Lake Winnipegosis in the 1790s to 1820s, the Cree on the East Main in the 1820s to 1840s, and the Northern Ojibwa in northern Ontario in the 1790s to 1840s—took place during a period of intense fur-trade company competition followed by monopoly; of dedicated trapping and consumerism; of steady destructive pressure on the beaver populations; and of stated interest on the part of traders in the conservation of beavers and territorial behavior. The Cumberland House Cree, needing beavers for food, paid no attention to the calls for conservation. The Rupert House Cree, in contrast, appear to have had a tradition of both conservation and hunting territories. And while some Northern Ojibwas developed both conservation and territorial systems at the same time as, and seemingly in response to, new HBC regulations, others lived by trespassing and poaching.

Conservation and territoriality in this vast region clearly were affected by local variations in ecological, demographic, social, cultural, and historical circumstances.[34] As among Ojibwa speakers[35] and other Algonquian speakers[36] farther south, population pressure, fur-trade company competition, game depletions, and fur traders concerned that destroyed commodities would erode their profits hastened the moment that conservation and territoriality became concrete for the nineteenth-century Northern Ojibwa, and perhaps for the eighteenth-century East Main Cree and others.

Twentieth-century Northern Algonquians have shown an abiding concern for conservation, preventing waste, and managing hunting in family territories. In the first two decades of the century the signs came from all directions. Montagnais who lived at Lac St. Jean "regulated" the hunt in territories that descended from fathers to their children in order to consume "only the increase" and leave enough animals "to insure a supply for the following year." Timiskaming Algonquin hunting territory leaders made beavers "the object of the most careful 'farming,' " keeping careful track of the numbers and ages in each lodge in order not to "deplete the stock." The Temagami Ojibwa had similar concerns. To promote conservation, they ideally hunted just one-quarter of their territory each year and left the center entirely alone until needed. Trespass could undermine these practices, especially among the Mistassini Cree and Lac St. Jean Montagnais, who did nothing against a trespasser because they believed that he would sicken, have an accident, or starve; in contrast, trespass was a serious crime for the Timiskaming Algonquin, who once were said to punish it with death.[37]

In the late nineteenth and early twentieth centuries, white trappers, loggers, and others placed Northern Algonquian lands under increasingly relentless pressure. Like the HBC earlier in the nineteenth century, several outsiders demonstrated a heightened interest in helping relieve the pressure. Filling a similar role taken by HBC traders in the 1820s to 1830s was Frank Speck, an anthropologist. In 1908, Speck began three decades of ethnographic observations among the Cree, Montagnais, Naskapi, Ojibwa, and other Algonquian people. From the 1910s through the 1930s, he was the single most influential proponent of the primordial nature of conservation and hunting territories. An anthropologist-activist dedicated as much to helping native people articulate their political causes as to the analysis of culture, Speck helped native people develop strategies to protect themselves from outsiders who wanted their lands. As Harvey Feit, an anthropologist, revealed, Speck, drawing liberally on a letter by Armand Tessier, an Indian Affairs governmental employee, claimed that Indians possessed "instinctive" understandings of nature and that conservation was a "natural law" among them. In opposition—here was the relevant context for his remarks—hypocritical white intruders "often accused" native people "of being improvident as regards the killing of game," and of being wasteful and thinking only about the present, and sought restrictions on Indian hunting and control over Indian lands.[38]

Northern Algonquians had discovered their own political voice some time before. In 1915, in reaction to accusations that they were "improvident," the Lac St. Jean Montagnais issued a conservation manifesto in which they argued that from a dietary perspective, the beaver was to them as "the bison to the Plains Indians, or the reindeer to the Arctic tribes"—or as pork was to white people. The Montagnais hunter, they maintained, "instinctively . . . understands how to operate with a natural law, which no game commission can improve upon, and to maintain the beaver there for his subsistence. He understands, moreover, that he cannot abuse his opportunity. Thus it is that the Indian, obeying a natural law of conservation, which is worth more than any written law to him, never destroys all the members of a beaver family. He knows enough to spare a sufficient number for the continuation of the family and the propagation of the colony."

Adding that Indians owned the land and that families used their individual territories "in the beginning of time," Chief Aleck Paul of the Temagami Ojibwa confirmed this conservationist sentiment: "So these families would never think of damaging the abundance or the source of supply of the game, because that had come to them from their fathers and grandfathers and those behind them. . . . We would only kill the small beaver and leave the old ones to keep breeding. Then when they got too old they too would be killed, just as a farmer kills his pigs, preserving the stock for his supply of young." In contrast, Chief Paul noted, was the white man "who needs to be watched. He makes the forest fires, he goes through the woods and kills everything he can find, whether he needs the flesh or not, and then when all the animals in one section are killed he takes the train and goes to another where he can do the same." Except for the ending, the imagery and language were largely Speck's (and Tessier's). Chief Paul showed that he could co-opt the language and imagery of private property and conservation to score points against outsiders who threatened. To achieve their goal—control over the exploitation of resources—all three mounted an argument based on primordial possession of private property and conservation principles. The Cree and Montagnais co-opted a similar imagery. That their land "ownership" might have been more in the form of a stewardship shared with others who possessed collective-use rights, or that they trapped beavers so as to prevent white trappers from hunting them was far less important than countering the external political threat against their lands, which was simply too dire to bother with ambiguous or conflicting details.[39]

Faced once again with depleted beaver populations and with low fur prices and an influx of aggressive white trappers in the 1930s, the HBC, Quebec, and later, Ontario and the federal government joined forces to institute beaver preserves. Before they were finished, the preserves had grown to over 100,000 acres in northern Quebec and Ontario.

A trading post manager and his wife, James and Maud Watt, pushed the design to restock depleted areas and institute conservation measures; to restrict the annual take to the estimated population increase; and to reserve beavers for native people. Small booklets printed and distributed at Rupert House showed graphically with small images of beavers and a text in Cree syllabics how these animals, left alone, would increase naturally, and how many could then safely be harvested. In the Rupert House preserve, the number of beavers increased from 25 to over 15,000 in fourteen years.

Yet while many Indians emphasized throughout this period that they were not supposed to, and did not, waste, there seemed no unanimity on how to perpetuate beaver populations. In the 1930s, the Attikamek "systematically conserved" beavers on family hunting territories by leaving younger beavers alive to breed (for other fur bearers, they left a central portion of their territories untouched as a reserve). They considered poaching beavers as "the supreme crime" yet (as explained below) left sanctions to so-called animal bosses who punished hunters for improper behavior. At mid-century, Western

Montagnais left two beavers in each lodge in sharply defined territories, but in contrast, the Natashquan Montagnais killed all the beavers they found, reasoning that since both hunters and beavers moved around (and beavers would eventually return to repopulate the habitat), there was no point in leaving any animals behind in a lodge. Even in the context of increasing suggestions from all sides that beaver conservation was a good thing, there were local variations.[40]

Northern Algonquians have continued to hunt beavers to the present day, and over the last three decades the story of conservation has been inseparable from the all-embracing political and economic movement to control Northern Algonquian lands and energy. Since 1970, the Cree, Ojibwa, Innu, and other First Nations people—the collective ethnonym used today by Canada's native people—have struggled to reaffirm their political and economic rights, settle outstanding land claims and treaty issues, and keep at bay or control the large-scale exploitation of timber and energy resources.

For the Cree (and Inuit) in northern Quebec, the paramount defining event was the decision in 1971 to dam and harness their rivers for hydroelectric power. Facing one of the largest construction projects of all time, these native people demanded recognition of their aboriginal rights and compensation. In 1975 they signed under extreme pressure the James Bay and Northern Quebec Agreement (JBNQA or the Agreement), in which the Cree (who are the focus here) agreed to relinquish aboriginal title and allow Hydro-Quebec, the power company, to proceed, in exchange for $137 million, lands reserved for exclusive subsistence rights, and other privileges. None of these benefits has relieved the Cree of the feeling that from that time forward, they have been under monstrous assault. In short order, Hydro-Quebec built two hundred dams and dikes, moved and poured two hundred million cubic yards of fill, and flooded forty-five hundred square miles of land. The ecological and social effects of these and related projects are demonstrable: At least one massive drowning of caribou, mercury poisoning of fish, deforestation, and community relocation. Moreover, a planned second phase—James Bay II—has loomed threateningly periodically during the 1980s and 1990s.[41]

The JBNQA gave the Cree great authority and control over issues that were paramount to them: hunting, trapping, and fishing rights.

Increasingly, the Cree and other First Nations people stressed that they should have control over the management of beavers and other animals. Many have argued that they, not outsiders, have a historical and cultural right to decide resource and conservation issues. In the 1970s, Billy Diamond, Chief of the Grand Council of the Crees and an indisputably successful political leader at a critical moment in the history of his people, remarked that the Agreement "guarantees that we can continue to live in harmony with nature."

Diamond's view has prevailed in published reports on the James Bay Cree. Today, almost one-quarter century after the Agreement, the Cree take care to assert that "nothing is wasted" and that nothing ever was. Matthew Coon-Come, the current Grand Chief, proclaimed that "we have hunted and fished, in balance with nature, for more than 300 generations." Remarks like these do not stand alone. In northern Quebec, the comments are aimed against massive energy development projects and the culture of waste associated with industrialism and a consumer society. They are linked to charges of environmental racism levied against Quebec and to the charge that "the Whiteman," in contrast to the Cree, "has no feeling of love for all life on the earth."[42]

Several anthropologists and natural scientists who have written extensively on the impact of the JBNQA on renewable resources like Cree fisheries, goose hunting, and beaver and caribou hunting have echoed the rhetoric of harmony, balance, respect, and conservation used by Billy Diamond and Matthew Coon-Come. The most prolific is Harvey Feit, who started to collect extensive information on Waswanipi Cree hunting and conservation ideology in the late 1960s and has been a strong advocate of helping native people articulate policy goals and implement change. Over the last twenty years, the separate interests have often fused in his work, when, for example, he proposed that hydroelectric engineers emulate the Cree or framed Cree management of natural resources—so-called "self-management"—in the context of global environmental problems.

In the 1960s to 1970s, the Waswanipi Cree hunted in territories managed by bosses with extensive practical and cultural knowledge of the land and its resources. According to Feit, senior hunters possessed detailed understandings of animal behavior, population dynamics, and long- and short-term ecological trends, which were filtered culturally: Hunters who showed respect in how they "hunt, butcher, consume, and use" animals were given more animals by God, the north wind (as the helper of Jesus), or other spirits. Hunters showed respect especially by ensuring that animals did not suffer and by "not over exploiting" animals. A hunter should not kill "more than he is given"—knowledge difficult to divine but arrived at by interpreting dreams, closely observing environmental and animal signs, and possessing profound knowledge of ecological relationships and systems (in which animals may be understood as persons). This knowledge, Feit argued, promoted conservation—as did built-in practical flexibility and a propensity to hunt different sections of one's territory from one year to the next, thereby resting sections and allowing animals to recover.

Since the JBNQA was signed in 1975, the Cree have been guided by its provisions for game management and conservation. The Agreement defined conservation as pursuit of "optimum natural productivity" and protection of "ecological resources" in order to "protect endangered species." According to Feit, this definition converged with Waswanipi Cree historical practice. It was "consistent with present Cree practises which include a wide range of cultural rules for hunting in ways that maintain ecological systems, and cultural rules for limiting harvests when species populations decline or are endangered." These practices—including family hunting territories, percipient managers, and conservation—he asserted, "extend back several centuries," that is, into the 1600s, and "plausibl[y]" even "before contact with Europeans."

In this view, history legitimates the Cree authority, rather than provincial or federal authority, to manage natural resources. Yet the historical evidence is lacking for conservation until long after the arrival of Europeans, and is quite equivocal and mixed for a family territorial system. At times, the Cree and other Northern Algonquians seemed eager to kill as many animals as they could find. Even today, conservation is problematic despite its asserted importance in the Agreement. At the time of the Agreement, most James Bay Crees lived in towns and depended on welfare and summer labor for income; since signing, almost half have taken advantage of an income security program subventing hunting, fishing, and trapping in bush camps—a program that newly energized bush life despite real uncertainties about the development of new dependencies. In the 1970s to 1980s, discussions focused on the need to set quotas and bag limits and to educate young hunters who have mainly known town-based life on how to behave properly. More recently, a "steady flow" of conservation problems, including overhunting, has been reported in Cree communities. According to Feit, however, these problems are minor, local, and—given the resources for enforcement—solvable.[43]

The emphasis placed by the contemporary Waswanipi Cree on showing respect to animals as a requisite to hunting success is a reminder of the importance of the meanings given by Northern Algonquians to beavers and other animals. They often parallel those associated with white-tailed deer in the South: Beavers and other animals figured in people's narratives of long-ago times when distinctions between animals and men were often blurred; they participated then and now in social relations with human persons; and they were sentient and animate. This explains why the elder Alexander Henry could record in the 1760s that following the death of a bear, Ojibwa hunters took its head "in their hands, stroking and kissing it several times; begging a thousand pardons for taking away her life; calling her their relation and grandmother. . . ." This exact behavior might not have extended to less powerful animals than bears but the personal, affective relations capture broader understandings of animals and "nature" that set Northern Algonquians apart from many (but not all) people of European descent for whom there were sharp differences between animals and men.[44]

Northern Algonquians said that animals made themselves available to hunters who treated them properly but did not give themselves up to hunters who treated them poorly by breaking, knowingly or unawares, certain rules. The rules were expressed as both dictates to follow and taboos to avoid, and have been widely described among Northern Algonquians for over four hundred years. For example, a seventeenth-century Montagnais whose dogs found and ate the bones of beavers, or who spilled a beaver's blood on the ground, might no longer have success killing beavers. But if he burned beaver bones carefully or returned them to water, or cut the tips of tails from beavers and strung them together, then his success would continue. Montagnais told the missionary Le Jeune that beavers knew what men did because "before the Beaver was entirely dead . . . its soul comes to make the round of the Cabin of him who has killed it, and looks very carefully to see what is done with its bones; if they are given to the dogs, the other Beavers would be apprised of it and therefore they would make themselves hard to capture. But they are very glad to have their bones thrown into the fire, or into a river; especially the trap which has caught them is very glad of this." At the same time that they recorded this treatment of beaver bones, Jesuits also registered "astonishment" at the "waste of meat."[45]

Three hundred years later (in the 1920s), the Parry Island Ojibwa admonished, "Do not throw beaver and bear bones to the dogs, but place them in water or hang them to trees; for the beaver and bear will use these bones again when they are reincarnated. If you violate this taboo," they said, drawing their imagery from the logging camps where many of them worked, "the boss beaver and the boss bear will be offended." What they called (in English) "boss," others have referred to commonly as a species "master" or "owner." According to the anthropologist A. Irving Hallowell, the Ojibwa sometimes called the species masters, sun, moon, four winds, Thunderbirds, and High God, some stones, animals, and trees, and other "other-than-human persons" collectively "our grandfathers." The Parry Island Ojibwa thought that a species master was larger and whiter than ordinary members of the species, and that its mastery consisted of the power to regulate local population numbers and to punish human persons who broke taboos.

Punishment generally took the form of hunting failure. As Hallowell remarked, a grandfather offended because a hunter has not treated an animal in the right manner "will not allow those animals to be caught." The Parry Island Ojibwa believed that a person who tortured an animal will "surely meet with misfortune," such as his "child will fall sick." The hunter who happened to "kill a porcupine idly and throw away its meat" ran the risk that "its shadow will harm [his] children." Both cruelty to wild animals and waste of porcupine meat could be punished by disease. The Ojibwa understood that it was "necessary . . . for men to kill animals in order to live" but felt that it was "wrong . . . to cause them unnecessary suffering." Ideally, as their ceremonies have reflected, their lives were marked by moderation, sharing, and balance in relations between human persons and other-than-human persons.[46]

Social relations involving humans and beavers were ideally marked by mutual affection and good thoughts. In the late nineteenth century, the Southwestern Ojibwa related a story about a long-ago time when a woman married a beaver and then returned to human society and told people, "Never speak you ill of a beaver!" If they did, she warned, they would never kill another one. The storyteller remarked, "Therefore such was what the people always did; they never spoke ill of the beavers, especially when they intended hunting them. Such was what the people truly know. If any one regards a beaver with too much contempt, speaking ill of it, one simply (will) not (be able to) kill it. Just the same as the feelings of one who is disliked, so is the feeling of the beaver. And he who never speaks ill of a beaver is very much loved by it; in the same way as people often love one another, so is one held in the mind of the beaver; particularly lucky then is one at killing beavers." Through narratives like this, the Southwestern Ojibwa confirmed their emotional and social relationship with beavers. They knew that beavers were willing to give themselves to those who loved them. Waste or conservation did not affect the willingness of beavers one way or another. Although it is not obvious in this story, they also understood that death was not final but a prelude to rebirth.[47]

Throughout the twentieth century, many Crees and Innus have continued to place a special emphasis on treatment of the beaver carcass after death, carefully placing, for example, beaver skulls in trees or on poles. Earlier in the century, Lac St. Jean Montagnais reserved shoulder and pelvic bones and forelegs for purposes of divination, and teeth for cutting and sharpening tools, but threw the rest of a beaver's bones and its eyes into the water, and the Mistassini Cree spoke about the "proper disposal of animal remains" as "obligatory" else hunting might fail.[48] In recent years, the Mistassini Cree have continued to believe that animals give themselves generously to hunters who respect them. Respect, according to the anthropologist Adrian Tanner, is the most important general injunction and is demonstrated by not making fun of animals; by wearing charms and decorating one's clothing; and especially by treating bones, intestines, blood, and other parts of animals killed in a prescribed manner. They should display land-animal antlers, scapulas, and skulls in trees and carefully place the bones of beavers and other water animals in water. Animals treated well in this manner will come to hunters who have demonstrated their friendship. But if a hunter breaks a rule or taboo, the species master (whose relationship to the species is conceived by the Mistassini Cree today as an owner's to his "pet") causes starvation by withholding game.[49]

Thus there is abundant evidence that beliefs about animals, taboos prescribing behavior, and a system linking events with their causes (a hunter fails to kill animals because he has behaved improperly) existed from the sixteenth up to the twentieth century. But that does not mean that the rules making up the system have remained unchanged or that new ones have not emerged. Neither the system nor the rules exist outside of history.

In fact, what is striking about the taboos—especially for those who accept Feit's conclusion about their several-century time depth or the historian James Axtell's assessment that Indians abandoned "ancient taboos," one of which was a "conservation ethic that preserved a minimal breeding population for the next year's hunt"[50]—is that they apparently had nothing to do with waste and the conservation of animal populations until recently. The seventeenth-century Montagnais and Mi'kmaq did not have rules about waste or exterminating beavers in a lodge or region; one need only recall the Jesuit "astonishment" at the Montagnais' "waste of meat," or the lack of taboos or beliefs concerning killing too many beavers among the nearby Mi'kmaq. These Indians were only supposed to heed the typical regulations about treatment of bones to prevent beavers from deserting a region.

Twelve hundred miles west and one century later, the York Factory Cree voiced similar taboos as crucial to success in the hunt. If the taboos were followed, animals would make themselves available to be killed; if not, animals would not. While the evidence on beaver hunting is ambiguous, there was no check on killing too many caribou, as James Isham, Andrew Graham, and others reported of the eighteenth-century Cree who believed they could not kill too many.[51]

One can only speculate on the consequences of such beliefs for conservation. If caribou or other animals made themselves available to be killed no matter how many had been killed, then why stop killing them? For the Rock Cree of northern Manitoba at this time—Robert Brightman, an anthropologist, argued from ethnographic and historical evidence—failure to kill animals who offered themselves to the hunter might have constituted an offense. If beavers disappeared from a region, the disappearance had nothing to do with hunting too many and everything to do with a deliberate or inadvertent taboo infraction. The reappearance of beavers was contingent not on adjusting how many animals one killed in the future but on exercising far greater care obeying the taboos. One reason to change tactics and, say, leave two beavers per lodge to produce the next generation, is if one started to doubt the wisdom of killing all beavers in the destructive synergy of competition and commodification (and if one was not starving). If a hunter could protect his ground from trespassers and poachers, then this new "rationality"—leaving a breeding core undisturbed—might influence how he managed beaver populations on his territory. Perhaps this is what was happening at York Factory at Drage's time in the mid–eighteenth century.[52]

Why would the York Factory Cree allege that "the more they destroy the more plentiful they grow"? As in the South, belief in reincarnation is ancient among Northern Algonquians, and has continued to exist in the twentieth century alongside alternative beliefs. "Everything," a Parry Island Ojibwa remarked in the 1920s, "trees, birds, animals, fish (and in earlier times human beings also) return to life; while they are dead their souls are merely awaiting reincarnation." As long as hunters placed beaver bones in water, beavers could use them "when they are reincarnated." The Parry Island Ojibwa debated (perhaps always) precisely how this happened. One man thought that a beaver's soul used any beaver bones it came across and was thus reborn, and another that a beaver's soul used its former bones: "When I was young old hunters would sometimes cut a cross in the leg-bone of a beaver and place it in a creek or somewhere away from the dogs. Later they would kill a beaver with exactly the same mark on its leg-bone. Plainly it was the same beaver that had come to life again, and reassumed the same bones."[53]

Most Northern Algonquians possessed ideas about reincarnation and like the Parry Island Ojibwa, many probably have debated the particulars. The twentieth-century Cree, Naskapi, and Montagnais

> have all treated bones with respect so that reincarnation might occur. In recent years the Chisasibi Cree seem not to have a concept of reincarnation of animals, but the Waswanipi Cree who show respect to animals are "appreciated by the animals, whose souls survive to be reborn again." And Mistassini Cree hunters who respectfully and properly place beaver bones in water find more beavers who give themselves up to be killed because they have disposed of the carcass in a proper manner. This "assures the continued appearance of animals," according to Adrian Tanner, either because new animals take form as flesh grows onto discarded bones, as stated in myth, or because—the "more commonly-held belief"—the bones are returned to a species "bank," and animal masters are pleased.[54]

Apparently, today's conservation ethic and practices were largely absent among Northern Algonquians until certain historical conditions emerged in the wake of the arrival of European outsiders mainly interested in controlling Indians economically and spiritually. Before the nineteenth century the conditions were local and nascent, as was the interest in conservation. During the nineteenth century they became widespread, as did the interest in conservation.

Conservation ultimately became of such obvious practical importance that it was widely incorporated into native systems of thought, including taboos, and action. By the time Frank Speck worked among Northern Algonquians, conservation of caribou was a recurrent motif among the Naskapi and conservation of fish of signal importance to the Naskapi and Innu. For native people at Speck's time, conservation found expression mainly in new prohibitions against waste. The Naskapi, for example, said that they could kill caribou only if they used the entire carcass—meat, bones, and skins—in domestic consumption. Caribou were then scarce and almost impossible to kill, the Naskapi believed, because hunters had slaughtered great numbers and the caribou master, informed by caribou offended by the stench of the bones of the dead, took umbrage and would not let caribou make themselves available to hunters. The Innu believed that moosefly punished fishermen who wasted fish by withholding fish from those men. South of the St. Lawrence, the Mi'kmaq and Maliseet linked their failure to kill caribou to earlier waste of meat. These taboos against waste were important expressions of a growing and changing conservationist sentiment; one hundred years earlier, the Naskapi in northern Quebec took only the skins and choice parts of meat from the caribou they killed, but thought that if they wasted a skin and a particular spirit found out, he would refuse out of anger to release the caribou from their winter abode.[55]

But it is one matter to sanction waste, and another to be attentive to population dynamics and take measures to prevent or correct the decline of animal populations. To ensure reincarnation, it was necessary only to follow the rules that Western ecologists would argue are unrelated to breeding success and conservation. A tension emerged between this ancient system of belief and behavior rooted in reincarnation and taboos, and the new one expressed in Western principles of biology and animal behavior. To judge from evidence for the belief in reincarnation as well as for leaving beavers in lodges in order that they might breed, separate understandings about the perpetuation of beavers have coexisted for a long time among Northern Algonquians. The ones linked to Western game management practices seem to have emerged as a result of thoughts about beavers and family hunting territories traceable to the Western commodification and historical decline of beavers and the initiation—by Jesuits, the HBC, the Watts, anthropologists like Speck, and native people themselves—of new measures designed to allow beaver populations to recover.

In some communities this tension persists. In the 1960s, the Northern Ojibwa argued that trappers should leave two beavers in each lodge so they could reproduce, but some maintained this was unnecessary because God gave beavers to man whenever he needed them. The contemporary Manitoba Rock Cree, in Robert Brightman's careful estimation, hold a similar range of beliefs. Some hunters do not conserve, arguing that conservation "is unnecessary because animals will be reborn." Others do conserve, giving reasons identical to those that Western game managers might give. Still others show what Brightman calls a "creative synthesis" of Cree and Western beliefs in defining lack of conservation as equal to the infraction of a taboo.[56]

The Cree and other First Nations people who claim the right to decide resource and conservation issues often base their claim on a natural right stemming from their relationship to the environment, which, in opposition to large-scale development projects, they present as balanced and harmonious. For Quebec's Innu, a literal translation of the verb they use when speaking to their posture toward the natural world is "attending" to it mentally or "paying attention" to it in order to match or fit it to their thinking—in order to have control over it, as a parent has over a child, a band chief over band members, a master spirit over animal species, or God over man. Matching or fitting the environment to one's thinking involves keeping watch over, taking care of, conserving, preserving, and looking after it. The relationship is conceived as reciprocal: The land supports them and they in return, as guardians, "must look after it and be careful not to deplete or destroy it." They therefore reason that they, rather than governmental or private interests, should be responsible for environmental management.[57]

The Wemindji Cree use similar imagery. In their spring goose hunt in the 1980s, hunters emphasized the importance of avoiding waste, resting and rotating among hunting sites, and stopping the kill when they sensed they possessed as many geese as they should, all by way of showing respect to geese. It mattered not at all that the hunt contravened international Migratory Bird Conventions (MBC), as well as the JBNQA, which allowed the Cree and Inuit to hunt at any time and place if allowed by the MBC and conservation regulations. In the 1980s, Chisasibi Cree elders blamed the failure of caribou to appear on some hunters who, the year before, shot more than they could use and did not conceal (by burning or burying) what they wasted; these hunters had not "taken care of the caribou."[58]

Some might be tempted to argue that if conservation is a recent phenomenon, then native people have no right to manage their natural resources today and nonnative resource managers should have that right by default. But there is no logical basis for this argument. In the Canadian and Alaskan North, there is great emphasis today on "co-management" of natural resources, which means management directed jointly by indigenous organizations with strong community support, on the one hand, and nonindigenous state agencies, on the other. The old way of management amounted to control imposed by government agencies alone, usually uninfluenced by indigenous opinion. Agreements like the one forged on James Bay have cast the old way onto the dust heap and opened the door for new arrangements informed and determined by native knowledge of animals and habitats.

For no one doubts that native people who spend their lives hunting, fishing, and trapping possess the ability to understand animal behavior and population dynamics. No one disputes that senior hunters have gained a detailed and sophisticated understanding (albeit cultural) of their surroundings and the animals they have pursued during their lives. When beaver hunters read population health and breeding success in minute signs like incisor marks on trees and uterine placental scars, their knowledge parallels if not exceeds that possessed by many wildlife biologists. Moreover, an ideology permeated by the hope of reciprocity deeply embedded in native social and natural relations also parallels the ideological predispositions of many Western ecologists and wildlife biologists. Although neither community is single-minded in outlook or behavior, each can usefully complement the other.[59]

Epilogue

NATIVE NORTH AMERICANS were close to the environment in ways that seem foreign today to urban dwellers and nonindigenous Westerners. Their origin stories and histories tell about long-ago eras when significant boundaries between humans and animals were absent. Animal-human beings like raven, coyote, and rabbit created them and other things, and then tricked them. People modeled relationships with sentient other-than-human beings on human relationships, and toward many acted with respect (culturally defined) and in expectation of reciprocity; or expressed kinship or alliance with them in narratives, songs, poems, parables, performances, rituals, and material objects.

While native people formerly held widely to such ideas, and some believed that for the world as they knew it to continue, they were required to maintain balance with other living things, all aspects of their lives have changed greatly over the centuries. If they express traditional closeness to "nature" today—and many do—they are likely to emphasize a generalized reverence for sacred lands and sites where important historical events unfolded, a special "sense of place," and respect for other living beings.

American Indians were also close to the land in a physical sense, befitting dependence on it. To guarantee sustenance, shelter, and security, they killed animals, cut trees, and cleared and farmed lands to support populations that grew with the domestication of crops. They deployed fire to render seeds palatable, make habitats attractive to animals on which they liked to dine, ready lands for domesticated seeds, or for ends related to communication or their enemies. To obtain desired products, they "managed" resources, whether seeds, nuts, rabbits, deer, buffalo, water, farmlands, or entire habitats like ponderosa pine or chaparral. Even though their populations were low relative to populations in Europe and elsewhere, and disease damped them further, their demands for wood, water, and other basic resources were evidently at times too great to sustain. Like preindustrial people on other continents, some of them deforested landscapes, and might have brought too many salts onto arable but arid lands or helped place animal populations on the brink of extinction. Not fully understanding the long-term systemic consequences of their actions, or unable or unwilling to take corrective action in time to forestall environmental degradation, people moved where resources were more promising, or disappeared.

One major purpose of this book is to determine the extent to which Indians were ecologists and conservationists (as is commonly understood today). Native people clearly possessed vast knowledge of their environment. They understood relationships among living things in the environment, and to this extent their knowledge was "ecological." But knowledge is cultural, and each group in its own way made the environment and its relationships cultural. Their ecologies were premised on theories of animal behavior and animal population dynamics unfamiliar to Western science, beginning, for some, with the belief in reincarnation. And their ecological systems embraced components like underground prairies, which were absent from the ecological systems of Western scientists. Their actions, while perfectly reasonable in light of their beliefs and larger goals, were not necessarily rational according to the premises of Western ecological conservation.

Prior to the twentieth century, the evidence for Western-style conservation in the absence of Western influence is mixed. On one hand, native people understood full well that certain actions would have certain results; for example, if they set fire to grasslands at certain times, they would produce excellent habitat for buffaloes one season or one year later. Acting on their knowledge, they knowingly promoted the perpetuation of plant and animal species favored in the diet. Inasmuch as they left available, through these actions, species of plants and animals, habitats, or ecosystems for others who came after them, Indians were "conservationists."

On the other hand, at the buffalo jump, in the many uses of fire, in the commodity hunt for beaver pelts and deerskins, and in other ways, many indigenous people were not conservationists. Yet their actions probably made little difference for the perpetuation of species (the Pleistocene extinctions being too distant and contingent on climate to implicate Indians alone) until Europeans, with their far greater numbers, commodified skins, pelts, and other animal and plant products.

The Indians whose lives were examined here were motivated to obtain the necessary resources and desired goods in proper ways. Many believed that animals returned to be killed, sometimes in virtually infinite numbers, as long as hunters demonstrated proper respect. Waste and overkill (as defined by Western conservationists) were apparently largely foreign concepts based in Western science and practice. Indians embraced them as alternative ways of explaining the decline of deer, beaver, and other animals as a result of Western commodification. And by avoiding waste and overkill, they adopted alternative ways of righting depleted animal populations.

Evidently conservation was largely an artifact of Western ideology and practice for other native people also. The Yupiit of southwestern Alaska, for example, thought that the more meat they consumed and shared, the more they would have; that animals would regenerate infinitely as long as they received proper respect from men; and that animal populations declined from lack of respect not overhunting. Beliefs about human rebirth were widespread in North America; perhaps those of animal reincarnation were also.[1]

What are the implications of this analysis for contemporary resource issues in Indian Country? Since 1970, Indians themselves have set expectations for their behavior consistent with, and helping to enforce, the image of the Ecological Indian thriving in public culture. Many write of Indians as ecologists and conservationists who have never wasted and have always led harmonious lives in balance with nature.[2] Important to their identity as Indians, the Ecological Indian finds reinforcement in popular books flooding the mass market, like *Earth Prayers*, in which indigenous people timelessly chant, pray, and sing for the earth.[3] Writers and poets speak of an animistic natural world and—as Chief Dan George, widely known to the public through his movie and television roles, said—of "deep respect" for nature and of having "always done all things in a gentle manner."[4] In *Native Wisdom*, Ed McGaa (Eagle Man), a Lakota, writes with feeling about a "Natural Way" of balance and harmony to which indigenous people have privileged access. Sun Bear, a White Earth Chippewa, speaks of spirits that work "to keep the Earth in harmony and balance" and of wisdom flowing from that state. Entire Indian tribes or nations may feel, as the Iroquois stated, that "our philosophy teaches us to treat the natural world with great care. Our institutions, practices, and technologies were developed with a careful eye to their potential for disturbing the delicate balance we live in."[5] The image is resilient even in texts whose authenticity is in question—the paramount example being Chief Seattle's speech, a version of which has been a best-selling text for the environmental movement over the last 30 years. However, that version was written in 1970 by a freelance speechwriter for the American Baptist Convention and its anachronisms and pointed contrasts between Indian and white attitudes toward the environment were his words, not Seattle's.[6]

Yet throughout the five-hundred-year history of imagery of indigenous nobility is a rich tradition whereby the Noble Indian—including today's Ecological Indian—is a foil for critiques of European or American society. As Vine Deloria, Jr., the Lakota activist, remarked, white people "*destroyed planet earth.*" Writing as heatedly, many since 1970 have excoriated American society for all the environmental damage in Indian Country, and pointedly charged white people of environmental racism and "radioactive colonialism."[7]

At first glance, native people have in recent years acted in ways befitting their image as respectful stewards of the earth and its resources—as Ecological Indians. In Minnesota, they have improved common tern nesting sites, counted breeding birds, restored wetlands, and developed programs to teach young people about caring for the land. In Nevada and Idaho, they have joined with conservation organizations or governmental agencies to bring back trout and wolves. In Rhode Island, they rejected a hazardous-waste incinerator as inappropriate for Indian enterprise. In California, native people purchased land that had been heavily logged and plan to remove logging roads, stabilize eroded stream banks, and establish a native-plant nursery. And in the West, Indians plead that buffaloes leaving the boundaries of Yellowstone not be killed (to prevent the spread of the disease brucellosis) but signed over to the Inter-Tribal Bison Cooperative.[8]

Moreover, in several infamous cases, native people and their lands have indeed suffered terribly at the hands both of industry exploiting their resources and lacking environmental controls, and of inept and paternalistic governmental caretakers. In one of the most notorious cases that unfolded in the 1960s, a New York-based Reynolds Aluminum plant and General Motors industrial landfill (that later became a Superfund site) almost destroyed Akwesasne, the St. Regis Mohawk reserve straddling the St. Lawrence River, with mercury, polychlorinated biphenyls (PCBs), and other pollutants. Dairy cattle, white pines, birds, bees, and fish died and a toxic cocktail of effluents imperiled Mohawk health. A quarter-century of regulation and decontamination has been necessary for fish again to be free of deformities and sores—although still unfit to eat—and for eagles, minks, and other animals to return to the land.[9]

Another even more notorious case unfolded after Navajo and Hopi tribal councils agreed in the 1960s to allow Peabody Coal Company to strip-mine coal from their lands, with which utility companies generated approximately 2 percent of the nation's electricity—for American cities, not native people. Pollution cut sunlight by 15 percent downwind in Flagstaff, Arizona. At the source—the arid reservations—deeply scarred, stripped lands will take centuries to recover. Uranium mining simultaneously affected the Navajo with active tailings, one large spill, ground and animal contamination, and irradiated workers. For years these huge projects have roiled Navajo and Hopi politics, exacerbating splits between antidevelopment traditionalists (to whom environmentalist outsiders have been drawn) and prodevelopment progressives; they also led to demands for indigenous control over—if not a halt to—the extraction of resources.[10]

But what should be made of the differences of opinion among the Navajo? Of Hopi Indians who favor strip-mining, arguing that the most important part of their guiding philosophy and prophecy is to know "how to use the gifts of Mother Earth"? Of Miccosukee Indians, who proposed building sixty-five houses in Everglades National Park against the objections of the Park Service and environmentalists whispering that they are poor stewards of the land and therefore undeserving of special rights as Indians? Of the Alaskan Inupiat, who killed hundreds of caribou in the 1970s, used only part of the kill, left bloated carcasses behind, and were accused by white hunters (who had acted in virtually identical fashion themselves) of placing the herds in jeopardy? Of the Wisconsin Chippewa, who reportedly let thousands of fish spoil in warm weather? Of Rosebud Sioux activists, who wanted to stop use of the reservation for off-reservation trash out of concern—as the tribal chairman remarked facetiously—for Mother Earth, yet had never protested Rosebud's existing open dumps? Of Crow Indians and Indians from Wind River, the joint Shoshone-Arapahoe reservation in Wyoming, who, in separate incidents, killed many elk and, to the horror of big-game hunters and biologists, reputedly took only choice cuts for themselves, or only meat or antlers for sale, leaving many animals to rot? Or of the Ute who want a dam and reservoir—over strong objections from the Sierra Club Legal Defense Fund—probably to transport low-sulfur coal through a coal slurry pipeline to power plants at some future time?[11]

For the sake of a simple narrative, critics who excoriate the larger society as they absolve Indians of all blame sacrifice evidence that in recent years, Indian people have had a mixed relationship to the environment. They victimize Indians when they strip them of all agency in their lives except when their actions fit the image of the Ecological Indian. Frozen in this image, native people should take only what they need and use all that they take, and if they must participate in larger markets, far better it be to profit from hydroponic vegetables, fish, or other "traditional" products than from oil, coal, trash, and like commodities. As one journalist remarked, "native people are supposed to be keepers of the earth, not protectors of its poisons."[12]

The connections between Indians and nature have been so tightly drawn over five hundred years, and especially in the last quarter of the twentieth century, that many non-Indians expect indigenous people to walk softly in their moccasins as conservationists and even (in Muir's sense) preservationists. When they have not, they have at times eagerly been condemned, accused of not acting as Indians should, and held to standards that they and their accusers have seldom met.

Resource use issues in Indian Country have historically been complicated by the tribal status of Indians and by their relationship with the federal government, especially the Bureau of Indian Affairs

(BIA). Over the last twenty-five years, many Indians have heatedly debated the legitimacy of tribal governments and the BIA, both of which decide natural resource policy. Many have accused the BIA of cutting deals on water, air, coal, uranium, and timber, favoring industry over tribes. Some have accused tribal leaders of making decisions of which many tribal members—in particular those who choose not to participate in tribal governments—are unaware and from which leaders often benefit. Others blame outside agitators of all stripes, including environmentalists, of unduly influencing tribal members. The scene does not yield readily to generalizations.

Native people have indeed often fought economic development when it is controlled by others and threatens their livelihood, and have taken firm stands for conservation. For example, since 1975, the Sokaogon Chippewa have fought Exxon's attempt to extract large copper-zinc deposits in northern Wisconsin. The Sokaogon fear that sulfuric acid, acid rain, wastes, and tailings will destroy the lakes they depend on for fish and wild rice, resources at the core of their identity as well as important for their subsistence. They reason that once Exxon gets a toehold, other companies will seek to mine uranium deposits. Despite great pressure from industry and the state, the Sokaogon, backed by environmentalists and sport fishermen, refuse to grant Exxon the right to mine. Local opposition to Exxon is growing but the company has powerful allies in the governor's office; this issue is far from settled.[13]

Today's alliance between the Sokaogon and sport fishermen is astounding, because in ugly scenes just a few years ago, sport fishermen violently confronted the Wisconsin Chippewa, who were asserting treaty rights to spear spawning walleyes and muskellunge. As "Save a Walleye, Spear an Indian" bumper stickers proliferated, sport fishermen branded Chippewas abortionists because they speared females swollen with eggs. Ultimately, however, the Chippewa prevailed. As the number of fish speared increased tenfold, Wisconsin's Department of Natural Resources predicted that sport bag limits would be introduced, but the Chippewa took only part of their allowable harvest (and a small fraction of the total harvest), and placed eggs from speared females in hatcheries. They themselves were also divided over how many fish they should spear—some Chippewas accused others of being overly greedy—but on balance have been interested in maintaining a healthy population of fish.[14]

In the 1990s many American Indians have taken action usually associated with environmentalists—protesting timber cutting, for example, as the Navajo and others have done. The actions have often stemmed from the desire to protect animals and the land. For example, from the late 1970s through the mid-1980s, the Confederated Salish and Kootenai of western Montana decided that they would rather protect the environment than grow as an industrial force. The tribe derived revenues from fifty-year-old dam and timber deals, as well as a new contract with Montana Power Company for a 180-megawatt power plant on reservation lands. But it resisted other projects that might threaten the environment after sewage, fertilizer algal blooms, and wood stove and automobile emission pollution became pressing contemporary problems. Instead the tribe began a concerted effort to protect grizzly bears and other wildlife, minimize air pollution, and ensure that undeveloped lands remained undeveloped. It also refused to allow the transportation of radioactive materials through the reservation. One tribal leader, who described himself as "a no-growth advocate," clearly privileged an environmental ethic converging with that held by many non-Indian environmentalists. Other leaders have followed suit. "Progress," one tribal environmental advocate said to tribal members interested in economic development, "is your death."[15]

At times, native people have based their opposition to land and resource projects on religious grounds. When the BIA planned to place a high-voltage power line through New Mexico's Jemez Mountains in the late 1980s, four Pueblo governments and the All Indian Pueblo Council objected on First Amendment grounds that it would intrude on sacred lands and infringe on their right to practice their religion. Environmental groups concerned about a loss of habitat for endangered species, including the bald eagle and peregrine falcon, joined them. Around the same time, the Blackfeet argued that the Forest Service's plans to allow Chevron and Petrofina to drill exploratory wells in a 100,000-acre roadless area of Montana south of Glacier National Park amounted to a violation of First Amendment religious rights. Traditionalists argued that it would "cut out the heart" of their religion, and that the land "is our church." And Salish Indians, one of whose traditional leaders echoed John Muir when he said that "the forest is our temple," joined with the Sierra Club and others to block construction of a logging road on lands of continuing importance to the exercise of their traditional religion.[16]

Yet native people have often favored the extraction of resources, storage of waste, and other development projects—even those with a serious potential environmental impact—if they can gain control over them. They have debated these issues heatedly. In the 1970s to 1980s, the arguments unfolded many times in the context of coal and energy development. For example, Crow Indians sought to gain control over the lease of their lands for strip-mining—not because they were opposed to stripping coal but because the leases negotiated for them by the BIA shortchanged them.[17] The Northern Cheyenne sued to break BIA-negotiated leases. Like the Crow, they wanted to develop coal reserves themselves—but they were also interested in controlling the ravages of strip-mining and energy production on their lands.[18] Their strong interest in halting environmental degradation put them on a collision course with the Crow. When the Northern Cheyenne tried to use recently established Environmental Protection Agency (EPA) rules on air quality to block coal gasification plants, Patrick Stands Over Bull, the Crow tribal chairman, asked the EPA to delay the ruling for fear it might imperil coal development on the Crow reservation. The Northern Cheyenne retorted that they preferred development in renewable resources like timber and agriculture, which represented "the cores of our value systems as people," rather than extraction of nonrenewable resources like coal, which did not.[19]

Other Indians have behaved more like the Crow than the Northern Cheyenne, favoring development over alternatives. In 1980 the chief of the Osage Indians of Oklahoma tried to kill outright a bill to create a Tallgrass Prairie National Park on oil- and gas-producing Osage lands. Having endured several boom-and-bust cycles since the turn of the century, the Osage were not about to jeopardize the revenues from almost ten thousand pumping wells making them (at the dawn of the casino era) the wealthiest Indians in the United States.[20] Two years later, the Oklahoma Cherokee, fed up with BIA mismanagement—including market lease bids discounted by over 90 percent—took oil and gas development into their own hands. They founded their own Energy Resource Company, attracted Japanese investors interested in tax breaks due Indian-owned enterprises, and sought lease bids themselves.[21] Sometimes Indians have sought to reconcile development with greater environmental protection than had existed before. In the 1980s, the Passamaquoddy Indians of Maine (with land claims settled) purchased a cement plant that had been a money-losing polluter and in seven years both turned it into a profitable enterprise and patented a pollution-control system lowering the acidic content of emissions.[22]

In recent years the debate over resource issues has shifted from oil and gas development to dumps for the disposal of over three hundred billion pounds of garbage that Americans produce annually and other forms of trash and waste—including nuclear. In the late 1980s and early 1990s, waste companies have increasingly approached Indian tribes to store trash and toxic waste.[23]

Some tribes responded positively. Several even took the initiative, offering their lands to waste-disposal companies for dumps. Seventy miles from San Diego, the Campo Band of Mission Indians invited San Diego County to use their small reservation for a dump for the next two decades. Their non-Indian neighbors were livid over potential groundwater pollution and urged the state authorities to intervene (states lack jurisdiction over reservations but traditionally attempt to ensnarl action in the courts and legislature at all levels). The Campo Indians argued that managing the dump could help solve high unemployment problems and that their solid waste codes would be stronger than California's. Indians have even been willing to store radioactive waste. Over the objections of all their neighbors and other Indians, for instance, the Tonkawa Indian tribe of Oklahoma expressed strong interest in storing radioactive waste on its reservation. The Yakima in Washington, Mescalero Apache in New Mexico, and Chickasaw and the Sac and Fox Nation in Oklahoma also expressed interest.[24]

But voices opposed to landfills and nuclear waste have risen strongly. Aided by environmentalists, tribes have fought landfills and the transportation and storage of spent nuclear fuel and other wastes. In

1991, with monetary support from Greenpeace, five hundred activists from almost fifty tribes assembled in the Protecting Mother Earth Conference determined to fight the storage of all types of trash and what a Greenpeace organizer called the "dirty industry" of nuclear power. The Council of Energy Resources Tribes, an Indian consortium promoting energy development, thought that tribes could strike resource deals preserving tribal control and sovereignty and bringing needed income. But the Conference resolved to combat what it (and others) saw clearly as environmental racism and never to strike deals with polluters.[25]

Landfill and waste storage issues have split Indian communities. Both the Mississippi Choctaw and the Rosebud Lakota of South Dakota argued heatedly over landfills favored by tribal councils but opposed by tribal members skeptical of the economic benefits and concerned about the environmental impact. In the Choctaw case, tribal opponents of a hazardous-waste dump persevered against all odds over their prodevelopment, highly successful, and powerful chief, Phillip Martin.[26]

Many tribes have rebuffed nuclear waste. In the early 1990s, the Cherokee helped close a nuclear processing plant in Oklahoma, and the Yankton Sioux formally resolved to ban all waste storage on their reservation in South Dakota. The Yakima protested potential environmental contamination at the federal nuclear weapons plant at Hanford, Washington. In Minnesota, the Mdewakanton Sioux joined forces with environmentalists to combat Northern States Power's plan to store nuclear waste at a nuclear power plant it had constructed just off their Prairie Island reservation. A number of groups have threatened action against nuclear waste transportation and fought companies eyeing new uranium mines; in Idaho, the Shoshone-Bannock halted a truck carrying spent nuclear fuel attempting to cross their reservation lands.[27]

The most visible case involving spent nuclear fuel has concerned the Mescalero Apache of New Mexico. In the early 1990s, the Mescalero expressed strong interest in storing nuclear waste from some thirty utility companies on their reservation for up to forty years. This tribe has had a strong prodevelopment record and successfully built a casino, ski and hotel resort, and artificial lake. The Mescalero saw nuclear storage as a way to solve continuing unemployment problems and a housing shortage. But the issue has split them internally, as several votes have made clear. As in other tribes, opinion ranges from a prodevelopment tribal council to a silent minority emphasizing the importance and sacrality of tribal lands yet participating little in tribal affairs. Swayed by arguments about the sacred nature of their lands and by apocalyptic dreams of iridescent leaks, and upon the urging of environmentalists and New Mexico's governor, legislature, and senators and congressmen, tribal members voted in 1995 against nuclear waste storage. Within two months, following an intense lobbying effort reputedly by people who controlled access to reservation housing and jobs, and after contemplating as much as $1 billion over 40 years, the voters reversed themselves. Some descendants of Geronimo and Cochise, the nineteenth-century warriors, were angry with environmentalists and other outsiders who accused them of selling out their tribe. One said, "These outsiders are ignorant. . . . How dare they tell us how to live and what is good for us?"[28]

American Indians and environmentalists have opposed each other not just on waste, energy, and water but on hunting and trapping. Debates over whaling have embroiled conservation and native organizations struggling to find acceptable exceptions for indigenous people to international bans on hunting endangered whales. The Alaskan Inupiat, for example, traditionally hunted bowhead whales not merely for subsistence but to fulfill a range of spiritual and cultural desires; in many ways the bowhead was—and is, they argue—at the center of Inupiat identity and culture. In the late 1970s, the Inupiat put to sea with more boats than ever before, and struck and lost many endangered bowheads. The International Whaling Commission (IWC), swayed perhaps by the argument that the Inupiat, who participate in today's modern world with modern technology, are no different from other people, and hence deserve no special status, banned the hunt. Angered deeply, the Inupiat took court action and struck a deal wherein they were allowed to kill one and one-half dozen bowheads annually. In years since, local whaling captains and scientific and governmental entities have together determined the yearly limit, which has increased gradually.[29]

When three gray whales were trapped in the ice of the Bering Strait in the fall of 1988, animal rights advocates for whom whales (or trees) have the same ethical rights or legal "standing" due human beings were surprised to find that the Inupiat did not seem to share their concern. Greenpeace was involved almost from the start in the rescue effort, the whales were humanized with names (ironically, Inupiat ones), President Reagan called out the Alaska National Guard, and governments spent more than $1 million freeing the two whales that made it, thanks to a Soviet icebreaker. Meanwhile, some Inupiats with gustatory thoughts wanted to kill the whales, except that gray whales were far less esteemed than bowheads as food—and under the circumstances, shooting them would not have been popular. Others wondered why the Guard was called out to free whales but not hunters lost on ice the year before (who died). Still others saw irony in, as one resident said, "making a big deal out of nature's way of feeding other animals."[30]

In 1997, the IWC gave the Makah Indians of Washington's Olympic Peninsula permission to revive the hunt for gray whales for subsistence, spiritual, and cultural reasons. The tribe's head of natural resources argued that overfishing had depleted salmon stocks, the Makah had clear-cut their heavily forested lands, and El Niño had completed what was not already devastated. The Makah, he said, needed the whales. He also guaranteed that they would use harpoons that explode on impact, which was the most humane way of killing whales (but they have settled on a .50-caliber rifle that will kill quickly and safely). Makah elders complained that the hunt wasn't necessary and no one really knew how to conduct it since the last one had taken place more than seventy years ago—in 1926! It was clear that no one knew how to butcher a whale and that its meat would have to become an acquired taste. Greenpeace took no stand on this indigenous hunt. But Humane Society International threatened a lawsuit. And Paul Watson, head of the Sea Shepherd Conservation Society, complained that the Makah were clearly not dependent on whales for subsistence but thoroughly involved with marina, retail, and other modern operations; that they had no idea how to hunt; and that he would put the Society's ninety-five-foot boat between them and their prey or seek to keep whales beyond their range.[31]

The Pacific Northwest has been an environmental battleground on land as well as sea. This region boasts the last remaining significant old-growth forests in North America, including the celebrated seventeen-million-acre Tongass National Forest in southeast Alaska's panhandle. With its two-hundred-foot-tall spruce and hemlock and eagles, bears, salmon, and nesting marbled murrelets, this temperate rain forest, environmentalists agree, is one of the most important North American ecosystems to preserve in the face of relentless exploitation by timber and paper interests.

All Northwest Coast forests are gravely threatened. In British Columbia, native people have been steadfastly opposed to logging, especially where it threatens the traditional harvest and marketing of salmon, herring, and kelp. In Alaska, the Alaska Native Claims Settlement Act of 1971 (ANCSA) established native corporations to manage resources including forty-four million acres of land. Under its provisions, native people could swap development rights on their own lands for development rights elsewhere. They have pursued this strategy in southeast Alaska, where some Indians might not have wanted to cut timber in their backyards but were not at all averse to profiting from timber cutting on other lands. With the help of a three-year congressional legislation rewarding them for losing money, native corporations encouraged clear-cutting and environmental destruction.

Environmentalists have fought hard to preserve the Tongass National Forest over the last thirty years, and in the process have faced off against native corporations, which hold rights to over 500,000 acres of timber. Sealaska, the regional native corporation whose membership is predominantly Tlingit, has developed substantial investments not just in canneries, construction, and oil and gas but in timber, and with local native corporations has clear-cut forests to beach edges and stream banks. The resultant environmental damage angered some Sealaska shareholders who branded the corporation's annual per capita distributions "hush money." "Compared to the native corporations," one resident of southeast Alaska remarked, "the Forest Service are saints."

This was not an isolated incident. In the mid-1980s, Klukwan Inc., the village of Klukwan's corporation, logged twenty-three thousand acres and was reluctant to sign on to a pact to protect eagles if it jeopardized its claim on millions of acres in the Chilkat Valley. Native corporations in Sitka and Juneau wanting to log the west side of

Admiralty Island angered the Angoon Tlingit living nearby—yet these Tlingit saw nothing wrong in wanting to exchange their own timber rights close to home for logging rights somewhere else in southeastern Alaska. Driven by not-in-my-backyard sentiment, Alaska's native corporations were no different from many other communities. When Chugach Alaska Corporation clear-cut spruce and hemlock along Icy Bay in the northeastern Gulf of Alaska in the mid-1990s, it emulated not just other native corporations but the state, which had clear-cut lands west of the bay in the previous decades. Chugach also intended to leave nesting trees for eagles and buffer zones protecting rivers—to follow new laws, which, critics argue, are inadequate—but did not promise to go further. One official with the state's Department of Fish and Game commented ruefully that "people have a right to make money on" private lands, that "This is America."[32]

Native people have thus often been at loggerheads with environmentalists, whose pursuit of preservation in the spirit of John Muir has pitted them on innumerable occasions against Indians whose everyday realities do not afford them the same luxuries. Like people in communities elsewhere, they are also at odds with each other. In some parts of the country they squabble over federal recognition because of the implications for casino revenues. In others they fight over environmental and resource-related issues.

For example, the Aleut of King Cove, Alaska, who have the misfortune of living in a town where the winds are so fierce that they close the airport two-thirds of the year and make travel to the open airport across Cold Bay perilous, have proposed building a road to connect them with secure services across the bay. The Audubon Society and twenty other national environmental groups (and Bruce Babbitt, Secretary of the Interior) oppose them, arguing that the road would cross a National Wildlife Refuge and Wilderness area and do untold damage to sensitive nesting and migrating birds and other animals. Native Alaskans from over fifty villages in western Alaska are against the plan for monetary reasons; they claim that the King Cove Aleut just want to transport fish by truck and gain an economic advantage over them.[33]

But perhaps the most famous case over the last decade has pitted the Inupiat against the Gwich'in, environmentalists, and the U.S.

Fish and Wildlife Service. The issue is whether or not to drill for oil in the Arctic National Wildlife Refuge (ANWR), which is the second largest wildlife refuge in the nation, the calving and summer grazing ground for 180,000 caribou—and the site of possibly significant petroleum reserves. The Gwich'in, for whom caribou represent a significant source of protein and identity, and whose chiefs proclaimed in a gathering that the herd "is essential to meet the nutritional, cultural, and spiritual needs of our people," are staunchly anti-oil. The residents of Arctic Village (the nearest Gwich'in town) have not been totally averse to development—in fact, they invited Exxon and other companies to prospect for oil and gas on their 1.7 million acres of land where caribou wintered—but they steadfastly remained against development in the Refuge where caribou calved. In 1991, they mounted an intensive advertising campaign with full-page ads in the *New York Times* and elsewhere asking, "Must we now die for six months of oil," after enduring for thousands of years?

Allied with the Gwich'in were the Wilderness Society, Natural Resources Defense Council, Audubon Society, and other environmental and conservation organizations. But opposed to them were the Inupiat who live in the small coastal village of Kaktovik, are oriented to the sea, and are dependent on revenues from ANCSA and oil development. They argue that when the Gwich'in chose not to be part of ANCSA they gave up rights over territory outside their own. Proclaiming "thumbs up for development" and "oil is the future," Inupiats say that they do not want to and cannot return to the past. Some are admittedly ambivalent and others outright opposed to further drilling—especially in the ocean where it might affect seals and bowhead whales—but most do not want to lose health, education, and other benefits from North Slope oil and feel that they should get something from what they sense is inevitable.

But in 1991, the U.S. Senate voted against an energy bill that would have opened the coastal plain to oil exploration. In 1995 Alaska's senators inserted a line item in the budget bill to open up the Refuge, but this and other attempts to open ANWR for drilling were vetoed, and the attention of the oil industry shifted to a parcel of land to the west, in the National Petroleum Reserve. This round has gone to the Gwich'in, the caribou, and their allies.[34]

By now it should be clear that in recent years native people have not been of one mind on resource issues. They probably never have been. Some people are self-proclaimed traditionalists and others are progressives, some are antidevelopment and others are prodevelopment, some favor the old ways and others are eager for new jobs. Some wish to preserve the environment at all costs and to take actions premised on a religious relationship with an animated natural world, and on landscape as a repository of sacredness and history. In contrast, others want to develop land and resources, which represent jobs, household income, and economic security; they have a more narrowly utilitarian relationship with resources as commodities. Few like the impact of strip-mining on landscapes, the contamination of groundwater, and air pollution, but many would like to be employed. For every story about Indians being at the receiving end of environmental racism or taking actions usually associated with conservation or environmentalism is a conflicting story about them exploiting resources or endangering lands—and inevitably disappointing non-Indian environmentalists and conservationists. In Indian Country as in the larger society, conservation is often sacrificed for economic security.

The issues surrounding the Ecological Indian have attracted uncompromising and sweeping statements on both sides. Those who despair at the pace and extent of environmental change at the end of the millennium, are blind to the environmental impacts of preindustrial societies, and adhere to the notion that native or indigenous people have always represented a kinder, gentler way of relating to the environment will no doubt be disturbed by this book's conclusions—despite the pains taken to acknowledge their ambiguities and limitations. Since 1970, many have looked for less destructive ways of relating to nature than the often shortsighted pursuits of convenience and economic gain; many are themselves American Indians. Some look toward an alternative "ecological" Christianity that would reconcile this religion with environmental care. Others believe that Taoism or Buddhism provides a better model for ideal attitudes toward nature. Still others turn to Native America and to indigenous thought about the world and living beings. Many native people themselves draw on a tradition of texts promulgating noble imagery that has generally had deeper roots in European self-criticism than in indigenous realities.

Given the appropriation of Indian lands and the vast changes wrought by people of European descent, one can understand and be sympathetic with the reasons for the emergence and persistence of the "purified" image of native people used as a counterweight.

In the winter of 1996, Dennis Martinez, who is of O'odham and Chicano heritage, wrote in a special issue of *Sierra* devoted to Native Americans and the environment of the need to listen to native people who have "taken care of the landscape for thousands of years." They are "wise environmental managers," Martinez remarked, who understand "ecology and land stewardship." Several years before, Winona LaDuke, an Anishinaabe from White Earth Reservation in Minnesota, contrasted what she called the industrial way of thinking from the indigenous way. There is no question what she values: the indigenous way, characterized by ecological thinking and "natural law" in which conservation, sustainability, cyclicity, respect, and balance all figure. In 1995, *Time,* citing LaDuke for her work on environmental issues selected her as one of fifty promising national leaders under the age of forty.[35]

Voices like LaDuke's and Martinez's will undoubtedly remain undiminished in future land and natural resource issues in Indian Country. But (as should now be obvious) they will not be the only ones. In the late 1980s, David Lester, executive director of the Council of Energy Resources Tribes—a forty-three member tribal consortium—remarked that "the debate" over significant natural resource holdings "is pretty much over as to whether we should engage in economic development." As far as he and many others are concerned, such development is the only course for the future.[36]

Yet most underscore the complexities involved in the decisions on natural resource and land issues. Many people in Indian Country desire the trappings of middle-class American life—cars, televisions, stereos, jobs, money—but do not want to lose their Indianness or sense of belonging to place. As one Choctaw (who reminded his non-Indian interviewer that he did not want "to be you") remarked, "I like living in this community, and I like being Choctaw, but that's all there is to it. Just because I don't want to be a white man doesn't mean I want to be some kind of mystical Indian either. Just a real human being."[37]

In 1997, *Entertainment Weekly* named the Crying Indian one of the fifty "greatest commercials of all time" and in April 1998, Keep America Beautiful brought it back "by popular neglect" as an advertisement about an advertisement. At first the pro bono agency helping Keep America Beautiful was wary. An agency copywriter remarked, "You're sure you want to do that? It's an incredibly different world; people are a lot more cynical and savvy." It was decided in the end to produce a spot for local and national broadcast on cable and network television, showing a poster of the original Iron Eyes, iconic tear on iconic cheek, at a bus shelter. People wait for the bus and litter the ground, the bus arrives and they board, and a living, flowing, wet tear tumbles down Iron Eyes's cheek.[38]

Endnotes

Introduction

1. "Equal Time," *New Yorker* 49 (January 7, 1974): 21–22; Philip W. Quigg, "Keep America Beautiful, With No Deposit, No Return," World Environment Newsletter, *Saturday Review/World* (June 4, 1974): 35; John G. Mitchell, "Keeping America Bottled (and Canned)," *Audubon* 78 (March 1976): 106–13; Ted Williams, "The Metamorphosis of Keep America Beautiful," *Audubon* 92 (March 1990): 124–34; "Biographical Sketch: Iron Eyes Cody, the 'Crying Indian,'" Keep America Beautiful, Inc., Stamford, Connecticut, January 1993.
2. The literature on representations of American Indians and on the Noble (and Ignoble) Savage/Indian is vast. Begin with Benjamin Bissell, *The American Indian in English Literature of the Eighteenth Century* (New Haven: Yale University Press, 1925); Hoxie Neale Fairchild, *The Noble Savage: A Study in Romantic Naturalism* (New York: Columbia University Press, 1928); Lois Whitney, *Primitivism and the Idea of Progress in English Popular Literature of the Eighteenth Century* (Baltimore: Johns Hopkins Press, 1934); Gilbert Chinard, *L'Amérique Et Le Reve Exotique* (Paris: Librairie E. Droz, 1934); Arthur O. Lovejoy and George Boas, *Primitivism and Related Ideas in Antiquity* (New York: Octagon Books, 1965 [1935]); George Boas, *Essays on Primitivism and Related Ideas in the Middle Ages* (New York: Octagon Books, 1966 [1948]); Gilbert Chinard, *L'Homme Contre La Nature: Essais D'Histoire De L'Amérique* (Paris: Hermann & Cie, 1949); Roy Harvey Pearce, *Savagism and Civilization: A Study of the Indian and the American Mind* (Berkeley: University of California Press, 1988 [orig. 1953]); Maurice Marc Wasserman, *The American Indian as Seen by the Seventeenth Century Chroniclers*, Ph.D. dissertation (Department of English, University of Pennsylvania, 1954); Harry Levin, *The Myth of the Golden Age in the Renaissance* (Bloomington: Indiana University Press, 1961); Percy G. Adams, *Travelers and Travel Liars, 1660–1800* (Berkeley and Los Angeles: University of California Press, 1962); Howard Mumford Jones, *O Strange New World: American Culture: The Formative Years* (London: Chatto & Windus, 1965); Henri Baudet, *Paradise on Earth: Some Thoughts on European Images of Non-European Man*, trans. Elizabeth Wentholt (New Haven: Yale University Press, 1965); Donald B. Smith, *Le Sauvage: The Native People in Quebec Historical Writing on the Heroic Period (1534–1663) of New France*. National Museum of Man, Mercury Series, History Division Paper No. 6 (Ottawa: National Museums of Canada, 1974); Louise K. Barnett, *The Ignoble Savage: American Literary Racism, 1790–1890* (Westport, CT: Greenwood Press, 1975); Nancy B. Black and Bette S. Weidman, eds., *White on Red: Images of the American Indian* (Port Washington, NY: Kennikat Press, 1976); Robert F. Berkhofer,

Jr., *The White Man's Indian: Images of the American Indian from Columbus to the Present* (New York: Alfred A. Knopf, 1978); Laura Schrager Fishman, *How Noble the Savage? The Image of the American Indian in French and English Travel Accounts, ca. 1550–1680*, Ph.D. dissertation (Department of History, City University of New York, 1979); Ray Allen Billington, *Land of Savagery/Land of Promise: The European Image of the American Frontier* (New York: W. W. Norton & Company, 1981); Anthony Pagden, *The Fall of Natural Man: The American Indian and the Origins of Comparative Ethnology* (Cambridge: Cambridge University Press, 1982); Olive Patricia Dickason, *The Myth of the Savage and the Beginnings of French Colonialism in the Americas* (Edmonton: University of Alberta Press, 1984); William Brandon, *New Worlds for Old* (Athens: University of Ohio Press, 1986); James A. Clifton, ed., *The Invented Indian: Cultural Fictions and Government Policies* (New Brunswick, NJ: Transaction Publishers, 1990); Don D. Fowler, "Images of American Indians, 1492–1892," *Halcyon 90. A Journal of the Humanities* 11 (1991): 75–100; Daniel Francis, *The Imaginary Indian: The Image of the Indian in Canadian Culture* (Vancouver, B.C.: Arsenal Pulp Press, 1992); Anthony Pagden, *European Encounters with the New World: From Renaissance to Romanticism* (New Haven: Yale University Press, 1993).

3. *The Compact Edition of the Oxford English Dictionary*, Complete text reproduced micrographically, Volume II, P–Z (Oxford: Oxford University Press, 1971), 2646. *Savage* also connotes an uncultivated or uncivilized state. Yet many people in the New World cultivated the land. Moreover, the Aztec, Mayan, and Inca all lived in cities, possessed writing, and had monumental architecture—all attributes that scholars interested in societal classification commonly ascribed to the state (*civilization* is sometimes considered a synonym), not to the band or tribe.
4. Another problem with *savage* is that American Indians did not live in a state of nature. The primary meaning of *indigenous* is originating naturally in a place or region, and of *aboriginal* is first or earliest or "inhabiting or existing in a land from the earliest times or from before the arrival of colonists." The term *indigenous* is in wider use than *aboriginal* in North America (the latter is largely confined to Canada), even though strictly speaking it presumes a "natural" origin for people in a particular place that would deny the history of migrations. *The Compact Edition of the Oxford English Dictionary*, Complete text reproduced micrographically, Volume I, A–O, 7, 1417; R. E. Allen, ed., *The Concise Oxford Dictionary of Current English*, eighth edition (Oxford: Clarendon Press, 1990), 3, 602.
5. Shepard Krech III, "Noble Indians and Ecological Indians," unpublished manuscript, 112 pages. The information in this and the next several sections (also see notes 6 to 14) is drawn from this manuscript.
6. Arthur Barlow, in late-16th-century Virginia, in a tract intended as a promotion for settlement. See Levin, *The Myth of The Golden Age*, 66; Gary B. Nash, "The Image of the Indian in the Southern Colonial Mind," *William and Mary Quarterly* 29 (1972): 197–320, p. 207; Bissell, *The American Indian in English Literature*, 3; see also Fairchild, *The Noble Savage*, 13; A. L. Rowse, *The Elizabethans and America* (New York: Harper & Brothers, 1959), 199–215; Jones, *O Strange New World*, 18–19; Robert Daiutolo, Jr., "The Early Quaker Perception of the Indian," *Quaker History* 72, No. 2 (1983): 103–19; Wasserman, *The American Indian as Seen by the Seventeenth Century Chroniclers*, 137–68.
7. Brandon, *New Worlds for Old*, 86.
8. Charles Alexander Eastman (Ohiyesa), *The Soul of the Indian: An Interpretation* (Lincoln: University of Nebraska Press, 1980 [orig. Boston, 1911]). The role of his

wife in Eastman's many books is debated; after they separated he never published again.

9. Charles A. Eastman, *Indian Scout Craft and Lore* (New York: Dover Books, 1971 [orig. *Indian Scout Talks: A Guide for Boy Scouts and Camp Fire Girls*, 1914]), 1–6, 188–90, and passim.
10. Lynn White, Jr., "The Historical Roots of Our Ecological Crisis," *Science* 155 (1967): 1203–7.
11. John G. Neihardt, *Black Elk Speaks: Being the Life of a Holy Man of the Oglala Sioux* (Lincoln: University of Nebraska Press, 1961 [orig. 1932]); Lucile Aly, "John G. Neihardt," in *A Literary History of the American West* (Fort Worth: Texas Christian University Press, sponsored by The Western Literature Association, 1987), 739–53, p. 748.
12. For humanitarians and ecologists of all stripes, see Thomas Berry, *The Dream of the Earth* (San Francisco: Sierra Club Books, 1988); A. Vittachi, *Earth Conference One* (Boston: Shambhala Publications, 1989); Bill Devall and George Sessions, *Deep Ecology* (Salt Lake City: Gibbs Smith, 1985); J. Nollman, *Spiritual Ecology* (New York: Bantam Books, 1990); Gary Snyder, *The Practice of the Wild* (San Francisco: North Point Press, 1990); Judith Plant, *Healing the Wounds* (Philadelphia and Santa Cruz: New Society Publishers, 1989); Ed McGaa, *Mother Earth Spirituality* (New York: Harper & Row, 1990); Sun Bear, Wabun, and Nimimosha, *The Bear Tribe's Self-reliance Book* (New York: Prentice Hall, 1988).
13. Wilbur Jacobs, "The Great Despoliation: Environmental Themes in American Frontier History," *Pacific Historical Review* 47 (1978): 1–26; Jacobs, "Indians as Ecologists and Other Environmental Themes in American Frontier History," in *American Indian Environments*, ed. Christopher Vecsey and R. W. Venables (Syracuse: Syracuse University Press, 1980), 46–65 ("conservators"; "America's first ecologists"; "preserved a wilderness ecological balance wheel"); J. Donald Hughes, *American Indian Ecology* (El Paso: Texas Western Press, 1987), 1 ("the secret of how to live in harmony with Mother Earth, to use what she offers without hurting her; the secret of receiving gratefully the gifts of the Great Spirit"); Roderick Frazer Nash, ed., *American Environmentalism: Readings in Conservation History*, third edition (New York: McGraw-Hill, 1990), 13 ("the first American environmentalists" who "understood nature as a community to which humans as well as every other living thing belonged and on which they depended"). Frank Speck, an anthropologist, remarked that Indians of the northeastern woodlands prohibited "wasteful or arbitrary destruction of life in any form" (Frank Speck, "Aboriginal Conservators," *Bird-Lore* 40 [1938]: 258–61); see Chapter 7, "Beaver."
14. Vine Deloria, Jr., *We Talk, You Listen: New Tribes, New Turf* (New York: Macmillan, 1970), 186 (italics in original). See "Epilogue" for discussion about Indian Country today.
15. George Perkins Marsh, *Man and Nature; Or, Physical Geography as Modified by Human Action*, ed. David Lowenthal (Cambridge: Belknap Press of Harvard University Press, 1965 [orig. 1864]), xxiii; Clarence J. Glacken, *Traces on the Rhodian Shore: Nature and Culture in Western Thought from Ancient Times to the End of the Eighteenth Century* (Berkeley: University of California Press, 1967); Frank N. Egerton, "Changing Concepts of the Balance of Nature," *Quarterly Review of Biology* 48 (1973): 322–50; Frank N. Egerton, "Ecological Studies and Observations before 1900," in *Issues and Ideas in America*, ed. Benjamin J. Taylor and Thurman J. White (Norman: University of Oklahoma Press, 1976), 311–51, p. 311 (definition of ecology); Robert P. McIntosh, "Ecology since 1900," in *ibid.*,

353–72; Eugene Odum, "The Emergence of Ecology as a New Integrative Discipline," *Science* 195 (1977): 1289–93; Donald Worster, *Nature's Economy: The Roots of Ecology* (San Francisco: Sierra Club, 1977); Keith Thomas, *Man and the Natural World: A History of the Modern Sensibility* (New York: Pantheon Books, 1983), 278; Robert P. McIntosh, *The Background of Ecology: Concept and Theory* (Cambridge: Cambridge University Press, 1985); Anna Bramwell, *Ecology in the Twentieth Century: A History* (New Haven: Yale University Press, 1989); Frank N. Egerton, "The History and Present Entanglements of Some General Ecological Perspectives," in *Humans as Components of Ecosystems: The Ecology of Subtle Human Effects and Populated Areas*, ed. Mark J. McDonnell and Steward T. A. Pickett (New York: Springer-Verlag, 1993), 9–23.

16. Daniel Botkin, *Discordant Harmonies: A New Ecology for the Twenty-first Century* (New York: Oxford University Press, 1990), 9; Daniel Botkin, "A New Balance of Nature," *Wilson Quarterly* (Spring 1991): 61–72; William K. Stevens, "New Eye on Nature: The Real Constant Is Eternal Turmoil," *New York Times*, July 31, 1990, C1–2; William K. Stevens, "Balance of Nature? What Balance Is That?," *New York Times*, October 22, 1991, C4; Steward T. A. Pickett and Mark J. McDonnell, "Humans as Components of Ecosystems: A Synthesis," in *Humans as Components of Ecosystems*, 310–16; Emily W. B. Russell, "Discovery of the Subtle," in *ibid.*, 81–90; Donald Worster, *The Wealth of Nature: Environmental History and the Ecological Imagination* (New York: Oxford University Press, 1993).

17. David Pepper, *The Roots of Modern Environmentalism* (New York and London: Routledge, 1986), 13–36.

18. Michael Pollan, *Second Nature: A Gardener's Education* (New York: Atlantic Monthly Press, 1991), 183.

19. For meanings of *conservation*, see *The Compact Edition of the Oxford English Dictionary*, Volume I, 524–25 ("preservation from . . ."); Robyn Eckersley, "Exploring the Environmental Spectrum: From Anthropocentrism to Ecocentrism," in *An Overcrowded World?*, ed. Philip Sarre and John Blunden (New York: Oxford University Press, 1995), 49–57; David W. Ehrenfeld, *Conserving Life on Earth* (New York: Oxford University Press, 1972), 3 ("By conservation I mean not just the preservation . . . but the conservation . . . of the world's natural communities"); Jean Dorst, *Before Nature Dies* (Boston: Houghton Mifflin Company, 1970).

20. For Muir and Pinchot, see, for example, Stephen Fox, *John Muir and His Legacy* (Boston: Little, Brown and Company, 1981), 144; Roderick Nash, *Wilderness and the American Mind* (New Haven: Yale University Press, 1982), 161; Bryan G. Norton, "Conservation and Preservation: A Conceptual Rehabilitation," *Environmental Ethics* 8 (1986): 195–220; Ehrenfeld, *Conserving Life on Earth*, 14–18.

21. Ehrenfeld, *Conserving Life on Earth*, 14 ("first principle"); Dorst, *Before Nature Dies*, 164–70.

22. Max Nicholson, *The Environmental Revolution: A Guide for the New Masters of the World* (London: Hodder and Stoughton, 1970), 170–72.

23. P. J. LeRoux, "Environment Conservation: Why and How?," in *Are We Killing God's Earth*, ed. W. S. Vorster (Pretoria: University of South Africa, 1987), 29–44 ("of human use to the biosphere . . ." International Union for the Conservation of Nature and Natural Resources); Nicholson, *The Environmental Revolution*, 240 ("all that man thinks and does").

24. Norton, "Conservation and Preservation," 200; John Passmore, *Man's Responsibility for Nature* (New York: Charles Scribner's Sons, 1974), 73. Pinchot's conservation (use) of trees probably rattled the arch-preservationist Muir, who said, perhaps with

Pinchot in mind, "Any fool can destroy trees. They cannot run away; and if they could they would still be destroyed" (Ehrenfeld, *Conserving Life on Earth*, 15).

25. Carl F. Jordan, *Conservation: Replacing Quantity with Quality as a Goal for Global Management* (New York: John Wiley and Sons, 1995), 3 ("despoil, exhaust, or extinguish").

26. On historiography and the narratives we use to represent ourselves or others, which structure, in a cultural sense, the past, see Hayden White, *Metahistory* (Baltimore: Johns Hopkins University Press, 1973); Eric Hobsbawm and Terence Ranger, eds., *The Invention of Tradition* (Cambridge: Cambridge University Press, 1983); Edward M. Bruner, "Ethnography as Narrative," in *The Ethnography of Experience*, ed. Victor Turner and Edward M. Bruner (Urbana: University of Illinois Press, 1986), 135–55; Greg Dening, *History's Anthropology: The Death of William Gooch* (New York: University Press of America, 1988), 2; T. H. Breen, *Imagining the Past* (Reading, MA: Addison-Wesley, 1989); A. Hanson, "The Making of the Maori," *American Anthropologist* 91 (1989): 890–902; Gyan Prakash, "Writing Post-orientalist Histories of the Third World," *Comparative Studies in Society and History* 32 (1990): 383–408; Shepard Krech III, "The State of Ethnohistory," *Annual Review of Anthropology* 20 (1991): 345–75.

27. White's voice is guarded or openly skeptical. So is historian William Cronon's. With others, they raise questions about the authenticity of Seattle's speech, the universality and historical depth of the idea of Mother Earth, and human impact like deforestation and erosion. They caution avoiding the idea that "Indians passively 'adapted' to their regional environments." They have influenced the direction taken in this book. On Cronon's, White's, and related essays, see Lynn Hirschkind, "The Native American as Noble Savage," *Humanist* 43, No. 1 (March–April 1983): 16–18, 38; William Cronon and Richard White, "Indians in the Land," *American Heritage* 37 (August 1986), 18–25, p. 20 ("demeans . . ."); Sam D. Gill, *Mother Earth: An American Story* (Chicago: University of Chicago Press, 1987); Richard White and William Cronon, "Ecological Change and Indian-White Relations," in *Handbook of North American Indians, Volume 4, History of Indian-White Relations*, ed. Wilcomb Washburn (Washington, DC: Smithsonian Institution, 1988), 417–29, p. 417 ("passively 'adapted' "); Jared Diamond, "The Golden Age That Never Was," *Discover* 9 (December 1988): 71–79; William M. Denevan, "The Pristine Myth: The Landscape of the Americas in 1492," *Annals of the Association of American Geographers* 82, No. 3 (1992): 369–85; Karl W. Butzer, "No Eden in the New World," *Nature* 362 (March 4, 1993): 15–17. *The Ecological Indian* is also related to an old argument with the historian Calvin Martin, author of *Keepers of the Game: Indian-Animal Relationships and the Fur Trade* (Berkeley: University of California Press, 1978), who deals at length with the decimation of beaver and touches briefly on Pleistocene extinctions, fire, and buffalo hunting. Martin concluded that Indians played a full role in rushing animals to their demise, but his explanations are very different from mine. See Shepard Krech III, ed., *Indians, Animals, and the Fur Trade: A Critique of "Keepers of the Game"* (Athens: University of Georgia Press, 1981), and notes 19 and 56 in Chapter 7, "Beaver."

28. Brackenridge's talk of "refinement" reflects his station and day. H. M. Brackenridge, *Journal of a Voyage up the Missouri Performed in Eighteen Hundred and Eleven*, second edition, in *Early Western Travels 1748–1846*, ed. Reuben Gold Thwaites (Cleveland: Arthur H. Clark Company, 1904), 128–29.

29. Another way of stating this is to say that the image is hegemonic. T. J. Jackson Lears, "The Concept of Cultural Hegemony: Problems and Possibilities," *American*

Historical Review 90 (1985): 567–93; Roger Keesing, "Creating the Past: Custom and Identity in the Contemporary Pacific," *Contemporary Pacific* 1 (Spring/Fall 1989): 19–42; Marshall Sahlins, "Goodbye to *Tristes Tropes*: Ethnography in the Context of Modern World History," *Journal of Modern History* 65 (March 1993): 1–25.

30. Raymond Williams, *Keywords: A Vocabulary of Culture and Society* (New York: Oxford University Press, 1976), 117–18.

Chapter One: Pleistocene Extinctions

1. Paul S. Martin, "Pleistocene Overkill," *Natural History* 76 (December 1967): 32–38, p. 36; Paul S. Martin, "The Discovery of America," *Science* 179 (1973): 969–74. *Blitzkrieg*, which means "lightning war," was used initially to refer to the German onslaught against Poland in 1939. To quote from *War Illustrated* of that year, "In the opening stage of the war all eyes were turned on Poland, where the German military machine was engaged in *Blitz-Krieg*—lightning war—with a view to ending as soon as possible" (R. W. Burchfield, ed., *The Compact Edition of the Oxford English Dictionary. Volume III: A Supplement* [Oxford: Clarendon Press, 1987], 292).
2. "Slaughter of Mastodons Caused Their Extinction," *Geo* 6 (June 1984): 110; Jared Diamond, "The American Blitzkrieg: A Mammoth Undertaking," *Discover* 8 (June 1987): 82–88; Bernard W. Powell, "Were These America's First Ecologists?," *Journal of the West* 26 (July 1987): 17–25; "Talking about Earth: Did Early North Americans Mount a Mammoth 'Blitzkrieg'?," *Earth Science* 40, No. 4 (Winter 1987): 6–7; Rick Gore, "Extinctions," *National Geographic* 175, No. 6 (June 1989): 664–98, p. 695; cf., Bruce Bower, "Extinctions on Ice," *Science News* 132 (October 31, 1987): 284–85.
3. Martin, "Pleistocene Overkill," 38; Paul S. Martin, "Prehistoric Overkill," in *Pleistocene Extinctions: The Search for a Cause*, ed. P. S. Martin and H. E. Wright, Jr. (New Haven: Yale University Press, 1967), 75–120, p. 115; Paul S. Martin, "Prehistoric Overkill: The Global Model," in *Quaternary Extinctions: A Prehistoric Revolution*, ed. Paul S. Martin and Richard G. Klein (Tucson: University of Arizona Press, 1984), 354–403.
4. Thomas S. Kuhn, *The Structure of Scientific Revolutions* (Chicago: University of Chicago Press, 1962); William Glen, ed., *The Mass-Extinction Debates: How Science Works in a Crisis* (Stanford: Stanford University Press, 1994); Donald K. Grayson, "Perspectives on the Archaeology of the First Americans," in *Americans before Columbus: Ice-Age Origins*, ed. Ronald C. Carlisle (Pittsburgh: Department of Anthropology, University of Pittsburgh, 1988), 107–23; David J. Meltzer, "On 'Paradigms' and 'Paradigm Bias' in Controversies over Human Antiquity in America," in *The First Americans: Search and Research*, ed. Tom D. Dillehay and David J. Meltzer (Boca Raton, FL: CRC Press, 1991), 13–49.
5. David M. Hopkins, "Aspects of the Paleogeography of Beringia during the Late Pleistocene," in *Paleoecology of Beringia*, ed. David M. Hopkins et al. (New York: Academic Press, 1982), 3–28; Stephen C. Porter, "Landscapes of the Last Ice Age in North America," in *Americans before Columbus*, 1–24; H. E. Wright, Jr., "Environmental Conditions for Paleoindian Immigration," in *The First Americans*, 113–35; John Hoffecker et al., "The Colonization of Beringia and the Peopling of the New World," *Science* 259 (1993): 46–53; Constance Holden, "Tooling Around: Dates Show Early Siberian Settlement," *Science* 275 (February 28, 1997): 1268; cf.,

Ann Gibbons, "Doubts over Spectacular Dates," *Science* 278 (October 10, 1997): 220–22.

6. Hopkins et al., eds., *Paleoecology of Beringia;* Hopkins, "Aspects of the Paleogeography of Beringia during the Late Pleistocene," in *ibid.*, 3–28; Dennis Hibbert, "History of the Steppe-Tundra Concept," in *ibid.*, 153–56; Steven B. Young, "The Vegetation of Land-Bridge Beringia," in *ibid.*, 179–91; R. Dale Guthrie, "Mammals of the Mammoth Steppe as Paleoenvironmental Indicators," in *ibid.*, 307–26; and C. E. Schweger et al., "Paleoecology of Beringia—A Synthesis," in *ibid.*, 425–44.
7. Larry D. Martin and A. M. Neuner, "The End of the Pleistocene in North America," *Transactions of the Nebraska Academy of Sciences* 6 (1978): 117–26; Larry D. Martin, R. A. Rogers, and A. M. Neuner, "The Effect of the End of the Pleistocene on Man in North America," in *Environments and Extinctions: Man in Late Glacial North America*, ed. Jim I. Mead and David J. Meltzer (Orono, ME: Center for the Study of Early Man, 1985), 15–30; C. V. Haynes, "Clovis Origin Update," *Kiva* 52, No. 2 (1987): 83–93; Wright, "Environmental Conditions for Paleoindian Immigration"; Roy L. Carlson, "Clovis from the Perspective of the Ice-Free Corridor," in *Clovis: Origins and Adaptations*, ed. Robson Bonnichsen and Karen L. Turnmire (Corvallis: Oregon State University, 1991), 81–90; E. C. Pielou, *After the Ice Age* (Chicago: University of Chicago Press, 1991); Karen Freeman, "9,700-Year-Old Bones Back Theory of a Coastal Migration," *New York Times*, October 6, 1996, 32; David Sandweiss et al., "Quebrada Jaguay: Early South American Maritime Adaptations," *Science* 281 (1998): 1830–35; Heather Pringle, "Traces of Ancient Mariners Found in Peru," *Science* 281 (1998): 1775–77.
8. The genus (pl., genera) is the biological category more inclusive than the species. For descriptions, see Björn Kurtén, *Before the Indians* (New York: Columbia University Press, 1988), 45–46, 71–72, 77–82, 88–93, 98–101, 104–11, 118–25, and passim; Martin, "Prehistoric Overkill," 75–120; Paul S. Martin and John E. Guilday, "A Bestiary for Pleistocene Biologists," in *Pleistocene Extinctions*, 1–62; Björn Kurtén and Elaine Anderson, *Pleistocene Mammals of North America* (New York: Columbia University Press, 1980); Elaine Anderson, "Who's Who in the Pleistocene: A Mammalian Bestiary," in *Quaternary Extinctions*, 40–89; Jim I. Mead and David J. Meltzer, "North American Late Quaternary Extinctions and the Radiocarbon Record," in *ibid.*, 440–50; Paul S. Martin, "Catastrophic Extinctions and Late Pleistocene Blitzkrieg: Two Radiocarbon Tests," in *Extinctions*, ed. Matthew H. Nitecki (Chicago: University of Chicago Press, 1984), 153–89; David J. Meltzer and Jim I. Mead, "Dating Late Pleistocene Extinctions: Theoretical Issues, Analytical Bias, and Substantive Results," in *Environments and Extinctions*, 145–73.
9. Martin, "The Discovery of America"; James E. Mosimann and Paul S. Martin, "Simulating Overkill by Paleoindians," *American Scientist* 63 (1975): 304–13; Paul S. Martin, "The Pattern and Meaning of Holarctic Mammoth Extinction," in *Paleoecology of Beringia*, 399–408.
10. David Webster, "Late Pleistocene Extinction and Human Predation: A Critical Overview," in *Omnivorous Primates: Gathering and Hunting in Human Evolution*, ed. Robert S. O. Harding and Geza Teleki (New York: Columbia University Press, 1981), 556–94; Stephen L. Whittington and Bennett Dyke, "Simulating Overkill: Experiments with the Mosimann and Martin Model," in *Quaternary Extinctions*, 451–65; see Frank Albini, "Simulating Overkill," *American Scientist* 63 (1975): 500; Sylvia Hallam, "The Relevance of Old World Archaeology to the First Entry of Man into New Worlds," *Quaternary Research* 8 (1977): 128–48; C. E. Stauffer,

"Overkill," *American Scientist* 63 (1975): 380–81; Kit Wesler, "Models for Pleistocene Extinction," *North American Archaeologist* 2 (1981): 85–100.

11. Dena Dincauze, "An Archaeo-logical Evaluation of the Case for Pre-Clovis Occupations," in *Advances in World Archaeology*, Volume 3, ed. Fred Wendorf and Angela Close (New York: Academic Press, 1984), 275–323; Roger C. Owen, "The Americas: The Case against an Ice-Age Population," in *The Origins of Modern Humans: A World Survey of the Fossil Evidence*, ed. Fred H. Smith and Frank Spencer (New York: Alan R. Liss, 1984), 517–63; Robert Kirk and Emöke Szathmary, eds., *Out of Asia: Peopling the Americas and the Pacific* (Canberra: The Journal of Pacific History, 1985); Emöke Szathmary, "Peopling of North America: Clues from Genetic Studies," in *ibid.*, 79–104; Stephen Zegura, "The Initial Peopling of the Americas: An Overview," in *ibid.*, 1–18; Christy G. Turner II, "The Dental Search for Native American Origins," in *ibid.*, 31–78; Joseph H. Greenberg, Christy G. Turner II, and Stephen L. Zegura, "The Settlement of the Americas: A Comparison of the Linguistic, Dental, and Genetic Evidence," *Current Anthropology* 27 (1986): 477–97; Christy G. Turner II, "Telltale Teeth," *Natural History* 96 (January 1987): 6–10; Stephen L. Zegura, "Blood Test," *Natural History* 96 (July 1987): 8–11; Paul S. Martin, "Clovisia the Beautiful!," *Natural History* 96 (October 1987): 10–13; Joseph H. Greenberg, "Language in the Americas," *Current Anthropology* 28 (1987): 647–67; J. M. Adovasio, A. T. Boldurian, and R. C. Carlisle, "Who Are Those Guys? Some Biased Thoughts on the Initial Peopling of the New World," in *Americans before Columbus*, 45–61; Lyle Campbell, "Review of *Language in the Americas* by Joseph H. Greenberg," *Language* 64 (1988): 591–615; Warwick Bray, "The Paleoindian Debate," *Nature* 332 (1988): 107; Grayson, "Perspectives on the Archaeology of the First Americans"; Ruth Gruhn, "Linguistic Evidence in Support of the Coastal Route of Earliest Entry into the New World," *Man* 23 (1988): 77–100; Roger Lewin, "American Indian Language Dispute," *Science* 242 (1988): 1632–33; David J. Meltzer, "Why Don't We Know When the First People Came to North America?," *American Antiquity* 54 (1989): 471–90; Johanna Nichols, "Linguistic Diversity and the First Settlement of the New World," *Language* 66 (1990): 475–521; Thomas F. Lynch, "Glacial-Age Man in South America? A Critical Review," *American Antiquity* 55 (1990): 12–36; Eliot Marshall, "Clovis Counterrevolution," *Science* 249 (1990): 738–41; Virginia Morrell, "Confusion in Earliest America," *Science* 248 (1990): 439–41; Dillehay and Meltzer, eds., *The First Americans*; Bonnichsen and Turnmire, eds., *Clovis: Origins and Adaptations*; John Horgan, "Early Arrivals," *Scientific American* 266, No. 2 (1992): 17, 20; John Hoffecker et al., "The Colonization of Beringia and the Peopling of the New World," *Science* 259 (1993): 46–53; Michael Kunz and Richard Reanier, "Paleoindians in Beringia: Evidence from Arctic Alaska," *Science* 263 (1994): 660–62; Lisa Busch, "Alaska Sites Contend as Native Americans' First Stop," *Science* 264 (1994): 347; John Noble Wilford, "Doubts Cast on Report of Earliest Americans," *New York Times*, February 14, 1995, C12; A. C. Roosevelt et al., "Paleoindian Cave Dwellers in the Amazon: The Peopling of the Americas," *Science* 272 (1996): 373–84; Ann Gibbons, "The Peopling of the Americas," *Science* 274 (1996): 31–33; John Noble Wilford, "Human Presence in Americas Is Pushed Back a Millennium," *New York Times*, February 11, 1997, A1; Rick Gore, "The Most Ancient Americans," *National Geographic* 192, No. 4 (October 1997): 93–99; Ann Gibbons, "Monte Verde: Blessed But Not Confirmed," *Science* 275 (1997): 1256–57; David J. Meltzer, "Monte Verde and the Pleistocene Peopling of the Americas," *Science* 276 (1997): 754–55; John Noble Wilford, "Chilean Field Yields

New Clues to Peopling of Americas," *New York Times*, August 25, 1998, F1; Charles W. Petit, "Rediscovering America," *U.S. News and World Report* (October 12, 1998), 56–64.

12. Not only are there few sites, but also intense interest in them has skewed the radiocarbon record, presenting additional difficulty. Cynthia Irwin-Williams, "Associations of Early Man with Horse, Camel, and Mastodon at Hueyatlaco, Valsequillo (Puebla, Mexico)," in *Pleistocene Extinctions*, 337–47; Arthur J. Jelinek, "Man's Role in the Extinction of Pleistocene Faunas," in *ibid.*, 193–200; Martin, "The Discovery of America," 969; Paul S. Martin, Robert S. Thompson, and Austin Long, "Shasta Ground Sloth Extinction: A Test of the Blitzkrieg Model," in *Environments and Extinctions*, 5–14; Meltzer and Mead, "Dating Late Pleistocene Extinctions," 162–65; Larry D. Agenbroad, "Clovis People: The Human Factor in the Extinction Equation," in *Americans before Columbus*, 63–74; Grayson, "Perspectives on the Archaeology of the First Americans"; S. David Webb and Anthony D. Barnosky, "Faunal Dynamics of Pleistocene Mammals," *Annual Review of Earth and Planetary Sciences* 17 (1989): 413–38.
13. David Webster and Gary Webster, "Optimal Hunting and Pleistocene Extinction," *Human Ecology* 12 (1984): 275–89; George C. Frison, "Prehistoric, Plains-Mountain, Large-Mammal, Communal Hunting Strategies," in *The Evolution of Human Hunting*, ed. Matthew H. Nitecki and Doris V. Nitecki (New York: Plenum Press, 1987), 177–223; Grayson, "Perspectives on the Archaeology of the First Americans"; David J. Meltzer, "Late Pleistocene Human Adaptations in Eastern North America," *Journal of World Prehistory* 2 (1988): 1–52; Kenneth B. Tankersley and Barry L. Isaac, eds., *Early Paleoindian Economies of Eastern North America*, Research in Economic Anthropology Supplement 5 (Greenwich, CT: JAI Press, 1990); Robson Bonnichsen, "Clovis Origins," in *Clovis*, 309–29; Alan L. Bryan, "The Fluted-Point Tradition in the Americas—One of Several Adaptations to Late Pleistocene American Environments," in *ibid.*; George C. Frison, "The Goshen Paleoindian Complex: New Data for Paleoindian Research," in *ibid.*, 133–51; Eileen Johnson, "Late Pleistocene Cultural Occupation on the Southern Plains," 215–36; Bradley T. Lepper and David J. Meltzer, "Late Pleistocene Human Occupation of the Eastern United States," in *ibid.*, 175–84; Richard E. Morlan, "Peopling of the New World: A Discussion," in *ibid.*, 303–7; Judith A. Willig, "Clovis Technology and Adaptation in Far Western North America: Regional Pattern and Environmental Context," in *ibid.*, 91–118; Wilford, "Human Presence"; Gibbons, "Monte Verde"; John Noble Wilford, "A 10,000-Year-Old Site Yields Trove of Data in Florida," *New York Times*, November 11, 1996, A10.
14. Estella B. Leopold, "Late-Cenozoic Patterns of Plant Extinction," in *Pleistocene Extinctions*, 203–46; Donald K. Grayson, "Pleistocene Avifaunas and the Overkill Hypothesis," *Science* 195 (1977): 691–93; David W. Steadman and Paul S. Martin, "Extinction of Birds in the Late Pleistocene of North America," in *Quaternary Extinctions*, 466–77; Donald K. Grayson, "Death by Natural Causes," *Natural History* 96 (May 1987): 8–13.
15. James J. Hester, "The Agency of Man in Animal Extinctions," in *Pleistocene Extinctions*, 169–92; John E. Guilday, "Differential Extinction during Late-Pleistocene and Recent Times," in *ibid.*, 121–40; Ernest L. Lundelius, Jr., "Late-Pleistocene and Holocene Faunal History of Central Texas," in *ibid.*, 287–319; Peter J. Mehringer, Jr., "The Environment of Extinction of the Late-Pleistocene Megafauna in the Arid Southwestern United States," in *ibid.*, 247–66; Kurtén and Anderson, *Pleistocene Mammals of North America*, 361; R. Dale Guthrie, "Mosaics,

Allelochemics, and Nutrients: An Ecological Theory of Late Pleistocene Megafaunal Extinctions," in *Quaternary Extinctions,* 259–98; Russell W. Graham and Ernest L. Lundelius, Jr., "Coevolutionary Disequilibrium and Pleistocene Extinctions," in *ibid.,* 223–49 (enzymes); James E. King and Jeffrey Saunders, "Environmental Insularity and the Extinction of the American Mastodont," in *ibid.,* 315–39; Douglas J. Brewer, "Herpetofaunas in the Late Pleistocene: Extinctions and Extralimital Forms," in *Environments and Extinctions,* 31–52; Wright, "Environmental Conditions for Paleoindian Immigration"; John E. Guilday, "Pleistocene Extinction and Environmental Change," in *Quaternary Extinctions,* 250–58; Richard A Kiltie, "Seasonality, Gestation Time, and Large Mammal Extinctions," in *ibid.,* 299–314; Webster, "Late Pleistocene Extinction and Human Predation," 567–69, 590–93; Grayson, "Death by Natural Causes"; Webb and Barnosky, "Faunal Dynamics of Pleistocene Mammals."

16. Guilday, "Differential Extinction"; Bob H. Slaughter, "Animal Ranges as a Clue to Late-Pleistocene Extinction," in *Pleistocene Extinctions,* 155–67; Grover S. Krantz, "Human Activities and Megafaunal Extinctions," *American Scientist* 58 (1970): 164–70; Roger Lewin, "What Killed the Giant Mammals?," *Science* 221 (1983): 1036–37; Bruce D. Patterson, "Mammalian Extinction and Biogeography in the Southern Rocky Mountains," in *Extinctions,* 247–93; Jared M. Diamond, " 'Normal' Extinctions of Isolated Populations," in *ibid.,* 191–246; Norman Owen-Smith, "Pleistocene Extinctions: The Pivotal Role of Megaherbivores," *Paleobiology* 13 (1987): 351–62; Roger Lewin, "Domino Effect Invoked in Ice Age Extinctions," *Science* 238 (1987): 1509–10; Ernest L. Lundelius, Jr., "What Happened to the Mammoth? The Climatic Model," in *Americans before Columbus,* 75–82; FAUNMAP Working Group: Russell W. Graham, Ernest L. Lundelius, Jr., et al., "Spatial Responses of Mammals to Late Quaternary Environmental Fluctuations," *Science* 272 (1996): 1601–6.
17. Peter J. Mehringer, Jr., "The Environment of Extinction of the Late-Pleistocene Megafauna in the Arid Southwestern United States," in *Pleistocene Extinctions,* 247–66; S. David Webb, "A History of Savanna Vertebrates in the New World. Part I: North America," *Annual Review of Ecology and Systematics* 8 (1977): 355–80; S. David Webb, "A History of Savanna Vertebrates in the New World. Part II: South America and the Great Interchange," *Annual Review of Ecology and Systematics* 9 (1978): 393–426; Kurtén and Anderson, *Pleistocene Mammals,* 357; S. David Webb, "Ten Million Years of Mammal Extinctions in North America," in *Quaternary Extinctions,* 189–210. For extinctions in earth's history, see Roger Lewin, "Extinctions and the History of Life," *Science* 221 (1983): 935–37; Walter Alvarez et al., "Impact Theory of Mass Extinctions and the Invertebrate Fossil Record," *Science* 223 (1984): 1135–41; Richard A. Kerr, "Periodic Impacts and Extinctions Reported," *Science* 223 (1984): 1277–79; Roger Lewin, "A Thermal Filter to Extinction," *Science* 223 (1984): 383–85; David M. Raup, "Biological Extinction in Earth History," *Science* 231 (1986): 1528–33; Thomas J. Crowley and Gerald North, "Abrupt Climate Change and Extinction Events in Earth History," *Science* 240 (1988): 996–1002; Stephen K. Donovan, ed., *Mass Extinctions: Processes and Evidence* (New York: Columbia University Press, 1989); Richard A. Kerr, "Dinosaurs and Friends Snuffed Out?," *Science* 251 (1991): 160–62; Richard A. Kerr, "The Greatest Extinction Gets Greater," *Science* 262 (1993): 1370–71; M. J. Benton, "Diversification and Extinction in the History of Life," *Science* 268 (1995): 52–58; Richard Kerr, "Cores Document Ancient Catastrophe," *Science* 275 (1997): 1265.
18. Jelinek, "Man's Role in the Extinction of Pleistocene Faunas"; William Ellis

Edwards, "The Late-Pleistocene Extinction and Diminution in Size of Many Mammalian Species," in *Pleistocene Extinctions*, 141–54; Kurtén and Anderson, *Pleistocene Mammals*, 361; C. Vance Haynes, "Were Clovis Progenitors in Beringia?," in *Paleoecology of Beringia*, 383–98; Anderson, "Who's Who in the Pleistocene," 41; Graham and Lundelius, "Coevolutionary Disequilibrium and Pleistocene Extinctions," 224; Jerry McDonald, "The Reordered North American Selection Regime and Late Quaternary Faunal Extinctions," in *Quaternary Extinctions*, 404–39; David J. Meltzer, "The Cedar Creek Transcripts: A Roundtable Discussion on Pleistocene Extinction," in *Environments and Extinctions*, 175–98; S. David Webb, "A Repopulation," *Science* 252 (1991): 1008.

19. In the Pacific, the Ecological Hawaiian and the Ecological Maori are companion images of the North American Ecological Indian. See notes 20–22. Storrs L. Olson, "Extinction on Islands: Man as a Catastrophe," in *Conservation for the Twenty-first Century*, ed. David Western and Mary Pearl (New York: Oxford, 1989), 50–53; David W. Steadman, "Extinction of Birds in Eastern Polynesia: A Review of the Record, and Comparisons with Other Pacific Island Groups," *Journal of Archaeological Science* 16 (1989): 177–205; Patrick V. Kirch et al., "Ancient Environmental Degradation," *National Geographic Research* 8 (1992): 166–79; David W. Steadman, "Prehistoric Extinctions of Pacific Island Birds: Biodiversity Meets Zooarchaeology," *Science* 267 (1995): 1123–31.
20. Patrick V. Kirch, "The Impact of the Prehistoric Polynesians on the Hawaiian Ecosystem," *Pacific Science* 36 (1982): 1–14; Patrick V. Kirch, "Transported Landscapes," *Natural History* 91 (December 1982): 32–35; Storrs L. Olson and Helen F. James, *Prodromus of the Fossil Avifauna of the Hawaiian Islands* (Washington, DC: Smithsonian Institution Press, 1982); Storrs L. Olson and Helen F. James, "The Role of Polynesians in the Extinction of the Avifauna of the Hawaiian Islands," in *Quaternary Extinctions*, 768–80; Steve Yates, "On the Cutting Edge of Extinction," *Audubon* 86 (1984): 62–84.
21. Kenneth B. Cumberland, "Moas and Men: New Zealand about A.D. 1250," *Geographical Review* 52 (1962): 151–73; C. A. Fleming, "The Extinction of Moas and Other Animals during the Holocene Period," *Notornis* 10 (1962): 113–17; Michael M. Trotter and Beverley McCulloch, "Moas, Men, and Middens," in *Quaternary Extinctions*, 708–27; Atholl Anderson, "The Extinction of Moas in Southern New Zealand," in *ibid.*, 728–40; Richard Cassels, "Faunal Extinction and Prehistoric Man in New Zealand and the Pacific Islands," in *ibid.*, 741–67; J. Golson and P. W. Gathercole, "The Last Decade in New Zealand Archaeology," Part I, *Antiquity* 36 (1962): 168–74.
22. R. Battistini and P. Vérin, "Ecologic Changes in Protohistoric Madagascar," in *Pleistocene Extinctions*, 407–24; Robert E. Dewar, "Extinctions in Madagascar: The Loss of the Subfossil Fauna," in *Quaternary Extinctions*, 574–93; David A. Burney and Ross D. E. MacPhee, "Mysterious Island," *Natural History* 97 (July 1988): 47–54; David A. Burney, "Recent Animal Extinctions: Recipes for Disaster," *American Scientist* 81 (1993): 530–41; Elisabeth Culotta, "Many Suspects to Blame in Madagascar Extinctions," *Science* 268 (1995): 1568–69; cf., Jared Diamond, "The Golden Age That Never Was," *Discover* 9 (1988): 71–79.
23. Vine Deloria, Jr., *Red Earth, White Lies: Native Americans and the Myth of Scientific Fact* (New York: Scribner, 1995), 108ff., 124–25, 207–30, and passim. Deloria scathingly takes on "dreadfully silly scientific scenario[s]" in his critique, unfortunately condemning all science as he wonders (with Paul Martin in mind) if "*anything* that a member of the scientific establishment says receives uncritical accep-

tance by his peers as scientific even if it doesn't make any sense at all?" But Martin's peers have not accepted his theories unanimously or uncritically, and Deloria's bluster is spent on a strawman. My conclusion that Martin's single-cause explanation is lacking converges ironically with Deloria's critique, but we depart in other ways—especially in my idea that Paleoindians probably hunted efficiently and played some role in extinction (as preindustrial indigenous people have in extinctions elsewhere) versus Deloria's idea that earthquakes, volcanoes, and floods of Indian legend account for the Pleistocene extinctions (for which evidence is required). See also Donald K. Grayson, "Explaining Pleistocene Extinctions: Thoughts on the Structure of a Debate," in *Quaternary Extinctions,* 807–23 (an especially valuable searching critique); Larry G. Marshall, "Who Killed Cock Robin? An Investigation of the Extinction Controversy," in *ibid.,* 785–806; Jared M. Diamond, "Historic Extinctions: A Rosetta Stone for Understanding Prehistoric Extinctions," in *ibid.,* 824–62.

Chapter Two: The Hohokam

1. Formerly, the Akimel O'odham (River People) were known as Pima Indians, and the Tohono O'odham (Desert People) as Papago Indians. Phoenix received its name even before it was incorporated as a town in 1881. Early European-American settlers could not miss the extensive Hohokam ruins: monumental architectural features, ceramic pots and figurines, objects of stone and shell, copper bells, and other exotic artifacts. Cremations—ashes—and inhumations were on every side. *Salina, Stonewall,* and other names were suggested for the rising settlement, but the story is that Darrell Duppa, an Englishman with classical knowledge (hence of the tale of the mythical phoenix that burnt itself then arose in the ashes of its pyre), suggested *Phoenix* and it took. Sylvester Baxter, *The Old New World: An Account of the Explorations of the Hemenway Southwestern Archaeological Expedition in 1887–88, under the Direction of Frank Hamilton Cushing* (Salem, MA: Salem Press, 1888), 2; James H. McClintock, *Arizona: Prehistoric-Aboriginal-Pioneer-Modern.* Volumes I–III (Chicago: S. J. Clarke Publishing Company, 1916), Volume II, 565–69; Will H. Robinson, *The Story of Arizona* (Phoenix: The Berryhill Company, 1919), 386–89; Omar A. Turney, "Prehistoric Irrigation," Part I, *Arizona Historical Review* 2, No. 1 (1929): 12–52, p. 16; Harold S. Gladwin et al., *Excavations at Snaketown: Material Culture,* Medallion Papers 25 (Globe, AZ: Gila Pueblo, 1937), 5; Henry C. Shetrone, "A Unique Prehistoric Irrigation Project," in *Annual Report, Smithsonian Institution, 1945* (Washington, DC: Government Printing Office, 1945), 379–86, p. 382; Ruth D. Simpson, "Those Who Have Gone Still Live: The Hohokam since 1400 A.D.," *Masterkey* 20 (1946): 73–80; Odd S. Halseth, "Arizona's 1500 Years of Irrigation History," *Reclamation ERA* 33 (1947): 251–54; Emil W. Haury, "The Hohokam: First Masters of the American Desert," *National Geographic* 131 (May 1967): 670–701, p. 672; Emil W. Haury, *The Hohokam, Desert Farmers & Craftsmen: Excavations at Snaketown, 1964–1965* (Tucson: University of Arizona Press, 1976), 5; Neal W. Ackerly, Jerry B. Howard, and Randall H. McGuire, *La Ciudad Canals: A Study of Hohokam Irrigation Systems at the Community Level,* Ciudad Monograph Series 2 (Tucson: Office of Cultural Resource Management, Department of Anthropology, Arizona State University, 1987), 1; Donald Bahr, Juan Smith, William Smith Allison, and Julian Hayden, *The Short Swift Time of Gods of Earth: The Hohokam Chronicles* (Berkeley: University of California Press, 1994), 1.
2. Bernard Powell, "Were These America's First Ecologists?," *Journal of the West* 26 (September 1987): 17–25, p. 22.

3. Haury, *The Hohokam*, 8–9, 140–41; see notes 36 and 41.
4. Glen Rice, "The Organization of Hohokam Communities during the Pre-Classic Period, in Regional Organization in the American Southwest," *American Archeology* 4 (1984): 162–223, 194–206, p. 194; David Gregory, David Doyel, Randall McGuire, and Glen Rice, "Panel Discussion," in *Proceedings of the 1983 Hohokam Symposium, Parts I and II*, ed. Alfred E. Dittert, Jr., and Donald E. Dove (Phoenix: Arizona Archaeological Society, 1985), Part II, 747–64; Steadman Upham and Fred Plog, "Comments on Hohokam Regional Exchange," in *Proceedings . . . 1983 . . . Part II*, 511–22; David E. Doyel, "A Short History of Hohokam Research," in *Emil W. Haury's Prehistory of the American Southwest*, ed. J. Jefferson Reid and David E. Doyel (Tucson: University of Arizona Press, 1986), 193–210; George J. Gumerman, "Understanding the Hohokam," in *Exploring the Hohokam: Prehistoric Desert Peoples of the American Southwest*, ed. George J. Gumerman (Albuquerque: University of New Mexico Press, 1991), 1–27; Natalie Waugh, "La Ciudad: Unearthing the First Phoenix," *Arizona Highways* 60, No. 2 (1984): 2–11, 14.
5. Phoenix and Tucson also draw on Colorado River waters. Gladwin et al., *Excavations at Snaketown*, 1–3 ("mile-wide scar . . ."); Haury, *The Hohokam*, 8; Amadeo M. Rea, "Resource Utilization and Food Taboos of Sonoran Desert Peoples," *Journal of Ethnobiology* 1, No. 1 (May 1981): 69–83, p. 71; Amadeo M. Rea, "The Ecology of Pima Fields," *Environment Southwest* 484 (1981): 8–15; Amadeo M. Rea, *Once a River: Bird Life and Habitat Changes on the Middle Gila* (Tucson: University of Arizona Press, 1983); Charles H. Miksicek, "Historic Desertification, Prehistoric Vegetation Change, and Hohokam Subsistence in the Salt-Gila Basin," in *Hohokam Archaeology along the Salt-Gila Aqueduct, Central Arizona Project, Volume VII: Environment and Subsistence*, Archaeological Series No. 150, ed. Lynn S. Teague and Patricia L. Crown (Tucson: Cultural Resource Management Division, Arizona State Museum, University of Arizona, 1984), 53–80, pp. 57–61; W. Bruce Masse, "The Quest for Subsistence Sufficiency and Civilization in the Sonoran Desert," in *Chaco & Hohokam: Prehistoric Regional Systems in the American Southwest*, ed. Patricia L. Crown and W. James Judge (Santa Fe: School of American Research Press, 1991), 193–223, pp. 196–97; Suzanne K. Fish and Gary P. Nabhan, "Desert as Context: The Hohokam Environment," in *Exploring the Hohokam*, 29–60.
6. Mark D. Elson, David E. Doyel, and Teresa L. Hoffman, "Hohokam Settlement and Economic Systems in the Northern Periphery: A Comparative Analysis," in *Proceedings . . . 1983 . . . Part I*, 45–64; James B. Rodgers, "Prehistoric Agricultural Variability in the Hohokam Northern Periphery," in *Hohokam Settlement and Economic Systems in the Central New River Drainage, Arizona*, Volume I, Soil Systems Publications in Archaeology Number 4, ed. David E. Doyel and Mark D. Elson (Los Angeles: U.S. Army Corps of Engineers, 1985), 249–96; David Doyel, "The Hohokam Village," in *The Hohokam Village: Site Structure and Organization*, ed. David E. Doyel (Colorado Springs: Southwestern and Rocky Mountain Division of the American Association for the Advancement of Science, 1987), 1–20; Patricia L. Crown, "Prehistoric Agricultural Technology in the Salt-Gila Basin," in *Hohokam Archaeology . . . VII*, 207–60; David E. Doyel, "Hohokam Cultural Evolution in the Phoenix Basin," in *Exploring the Hohokam*, 231–78.
7. Jeffrey S. Dean, "Thoughts on Hohokam Chronology," in *Exploring the Hohokam*, 61–99; Paul R. Fish, "The Hohokam: 1,000 Years of Prehistory in the Sonoran Desert," in *Dynamics of Southwest Prehistory*, ed. Linda S. Cordell and George J. Gumerman (Washington, DC: Smithsonian Institution Press, 1989), 19–63, pp. 24–34.

8. Charles C. Di Peso, *The Upper Pima of San Cayetano del Tumacacori: An Archaeohistorical Reconstruction of the Ootam of Pimeria Alta* (Dragoon, AZ: The Amerind Foundation, Inc., 1956); J. Charles Kelley, "Mesoamerica and the Southwestern United States," in *Handbook of Middle American Indians, Volume Four, Archaeological Frontiers and External Connections*, ed. Gordon F. Ekholm and Gordon R. Willey (Austin: University of Texas Press, 1966), 95–110; Haury, *The Hohokam*, 149–51, 193, 343–53, and passim; Carl O. Sauer, "Comment," *American Anthropologist* 56 (1954): 553–56; Richard B. Woodbury, "A Reappraisal of Hohokam Irrigation," *American Anthropologist* 63 (1961): 550–60; Richard B. Woodbury and John Q. Ressler, "Effects of Environmental and Cultural Limitations upon Hohokam Agriculture, Southern Arizona," *University of Utah Anthropological Papers* 62 (1962): 41–55; Doyel, "The Hohokam Village," 7; Edwin N. Ferdon, Jr., "The Hohokam 'Ball Court': An Alternate View of Its Function," *Kiva* 33 (1967): 1–14; David E. Doyel, "From Foraging to Farming: An Overview of the Preclassic in the Tucson Basin," *Kiva* 49 (1984): 147–65, p. 158; William W. Wasley, "Classic Period Hohokam," ed. and introduced by David E. Doyel, *Kiva* 45 (1980): 337–52; Carroll L. Riley, "Mesoamerica and the Hohokam," in *Current Issues in Hohokam Prehistory: Proceedings of a Symposium*, Anthropological Research Papers No. 23, ed. David Doyel and Fred Plog (Tempe: Arizona State University, 1980), 41–48; J. Charles Kelley, "Discussion of Papers by Plog, Doyel and Riley," in *ibid.*, 49–66; Charles C. Di Peso, "The Hohokam and the O'otam," in *ibid.*, 224–30; William H. Doelle, "Comments on Papers by Di Peso and Masse," in *ibid.*, 231–35; Doyel, *Late Hohokam Prehistory in Southern Arizona*, 47–56, 72–74; Paul E. Minnis, "Peeking under the Tortilla Curtain: Regional Interaction and Integration on the Northeastern Periphery of Casas Grandes," *American Archeology* 4 (1984): 181–93; Jill E. Neitzel, "The Organization of the Hohokam Regional System," *American Archeology* 4 (1984): 207–16; Patricia L. Crown, "Intrusive Ceramics and the Identification of Hohokam Exchange Networks," in *Proceedings . . . 1983 . . . Part II*, 439–58; David E. Doyel, "Hohokam Exchange and Interaction," in *Chaco & Hohokam*, 225–52; David R. Wilcox, "Hohokam Social Complexity," in *ibid.*, 253–75; David E. Doyel, "Classic Period Hohokam in the Gila River Basin, Arizona," *Kiva* 42, No. 1 (1976): 27–37; David E. Doyel, "The Prehistoric Hohokam of the Arizona Desert," *American Scientist* 67 (1979): 544–54.
9. J. Walter Fewkes, "Excavations at Casa Grande, Arizona, in 1906–07," *Smithsonian Miscellaneous Collections* 50 (1907): 289–329; Walter Hough, *Culture of the Ancient Pueblos of the Upper Gila River Region, New Mexico and Arizona*, Smithsonian Institution, United States National Museum Bulletin No. 87 (Washington, DC: Government Printing Office, 1914); Gladwin et al., *Excavations at Snaketown*; Emil W. Haury, *The Excavation of Los Muertos and Neighboring Ruins in the Salt River Valley, Southern Arizona*, Papers of the Peabody Museum of American Archaeology and Ethnology, 24, No. 1 (Cambridge, MA: Harvard University, 1945), 49ff., 205ff.; Harold Sterling Gladwin, *A History of the Ancient Southwest* (Portland, ME: The Bond Wheelwright Company, 1957), passim; Haury, *The Hohokam*, passim; Fred Plog, "Explaining Culture Change in the Hohokam Preclassic," in *Current Issues*, 4–22, pp. 4–14; W. Bruce Masse, "The Hohokam of the Lower San Pedro Valley and the Northern Papagueria: Continuity and Variability in Two Regional Populations," in *ibid.*, 205–23; David E. Doyel, *Late Hohokam Prehistory in Southern Arizona* (Scottsdale, AZ: Gila Press, 1981); John S. Cable and David E. Doyel, "Hohokam Land-Use Patterns along the Terraces of the Lower Salt River Valley: The Central Phoenix Project," in *Proceedings . . . 1983 . . . Part I*, 263–310; Doyel, "The Hohokam

Village," 5–7, 10–17; Jeffrey S. Dean, "Thoughts on Hohokam Settlement Behavior: Comments on 'The Hohokam Village,' " in *Hohokam Village*, 253–62, pp. 254–55; Glen Rice, "La Ciudad: A Perspective on Hohokam Community Systems," in *ibid.*, 127–58; Earl W. Sires, Jr., "Hohokam Architectural Variability and Site Structure during the Sedentary-Classic Transition," in *ibid.*, 171–82; Alfred E. Johnson, "Archaeological Excavations in Hohokam Sites of Southern Arizona," *American Antiquity* 30 (1964): 145–61; Haury, "The Hohokam," 674; Donald H. Morris, "Red Mountain: An Early Pioneer Period Hohokam Site in the Salt River Valley of Central Arizona," *American Antiquity* 34, No. 1 (1969): 40–53; Doyel, "Classic Period Hohokam"; Doyel, "The Prehistoric Hohokam"; Patricia L. Crown, "The Hohokam: Current Views of Prehistory and the Regional System," in *Chaco & Hohokam*, 135–57; David A. Gregory, "Form and Variation in Hohokam Settlement Patterns," in *ibid.*, 158–93; Jill Neitzel, "Hohokam Material Culture and Behavior: The Dimensions of Organizational Change," in *Exploring the Hohokam*, 177–230; Patricia L. Crown, "The Roles of Exchange and Interaction in Salt-Gila Basin Hohokam Prehistory," in *ibid.*, 383–415.

10. Gary P. Nabhan, *The Desert Smells Like Rain: A Naturalist in Papago Indian Country* (San Francisco: North Point Press, 1982); Robert E. Gasser and Scott M. Kwiatkowski, "Food for Thought: Recognizing Patterns in Hohokam Subsistence," in *Exploring the Hohokam*, 417–59; Fish, "The Hohokam: 1,000 Years of Prehistory," 21–22.
11. Lawrence Kaplan, "The Cultivated Beans of the Historic Southwest," *Annals of the Missouri Botanical Garden* 43 (1956): 189–251; Haury, *The Hohokam*, 113–20; Woodbury and Ressler, "Effects of Environmental and Cultural Limitations," 42–43, 47–48; Vorsila L. Bohrer, "Ethnobotanical Aspects of Snaketown, A Hohokam Village in Southern Arizona," *American Antiquity* 35 (1970): 413–30; Doyel, *Late Hohokam Prehistory in Southern Arizona*, 41–46; David E. Doyel, "Summary and Discussion," in *Hohokam Settlement and Economic Systems in the Central New River Drainage, Arizona, Volume II*, Soil Systems Publications in Archaeology Number 4, ed. David E. Doyel and Mark D. Elson (Los Angeles: U.S. Army Corps of Engineers, 1985), 727–34; Robert E. Gasser, "Prehistoric Subsistence and Settlement in the New River Area: The Flotation Evidence," in *Hohokam Settlement and Economic Systems . . . Volume I*, 317–42; David E. Doyel, "Current Directions in Hohokam Research," in *Proceedings . . . 1983 . . . Part I*, 3–26; *ibid.*, 10–12; Suzanne K. Fish et al., "Prehistoric Agave Cultivation in Southern Arizona," *Desert Plants* 7, No. 2 (1985): 100, 107–12; Robert Gasser and Charles Miksicek, "The Specialists: A Reappraisal of Hohokam Exchange and the Archaeobotanical Record," in *Proceedings . . . 1983 . . . Part II*, 483–98; Jennifer W. Gish, "Pollen from the New River Project, and a Discussion of Pollen Sampling Strategies for Agricultural Systems," in *Hohokam Settlement and Economic Systems . . . Volume I*, 343–403; Frank Bayham and Pamela Hatch, "Archaeofaunal Remains from the New River Area," in *ibid.*, 405–33; Suzanne K. Fish, "Agriculture and Subsistence Implications of the Salt-Gila Aqueduct Project Pollen Analyses," in *Hohokam Archaeology . . . VII*, 111–70; Frank W. Hull, "Archaeological Evidence of Nonagricultural Subsistence," in *ibid.*, 171–206; Allen Dart, "Agricultural Features," Part IV in *Hohokam Archaeology along the Salt-Gila Aqueduct, Central Arizona Project, Volume III: Specialized Activity Sites*, Archaeological Series No. 150, ed. Lynn S. Teague and Patricia L. Crown (Tucson: Cultural Resource Management Division, Arizona State Museum, University of Arizona, 1983), 345–573, pp. 541–47; David A. Gregory et al., *The 1982–1984 Excavations at Las Colinas:*

Research Design, Archaeological Series No. 162, Volume 1 (Tucson: Cultural Resource Management Division, Arizona State Museum, University of Arizona, 1985), 36–38; Masse, "The Quest for Subsistence Sufficiency and Civilization," 204–16; Christine R. Szuter and Frank E. Bayham, "Sedentism and Prehistoric Animal Procurement among Desert Horticulturalists of the North American Southwest," in *Farmers as Hunters: The Implications of Sedentism*, ed. Susan Kent (Cambridge: Cambridge University Press, 1989), 80–95; Fish and Nabhan, "Desert as Context," 51; Robert E. Gasser and Scott M. Kwiatkowski, "Food for Thought: Recognizing Patterns in Hohokam Subsistence," in *Exploring the Hohokam*, 417–59; Paul Fish, personal communication, May 27, 1997 (on beans).

12. Gary Paul Nabhan and Thomas Edward Sheridan, "Living Fencerows of the Rio San Miguel, Sonora, Mexico: Traditional Technology for Floodplain Management," *Human Ecology* 5, No. 2 (1977): 97–111; Gary Paul Nabhan, "The Ecology of Floodwater Farming in Arid Southwestern North America," *Agro-Ecosystems* 5 (1979): 245–55; Patricia L. Crown, "Adaptation through Diversity: An Examination of Population Pressure and Agricultural Technology in the Salt-Gila Basin," in *Prehistoric Agricultural Strategies in the Southwest*, ed. Suzanne K. Fish and Paul R. Fish (Tempe: Arizona State University, 1984), 5–25; Suzanne K. Fish, Paul R. Fish, and Christian Downum, "Hohokam Terraces and Agricultural Production in the Tucson Basin," in *ibid.*, 55–71; William E. Doolittle, "Agricultural Change as an Incremental Process," *Annals of the Association of American Geographers* 74, No. 1 (1984): 124–37; Dart, "Agricultural Features," 439–49; Masse, "The Quest for Subsistence Sufficiency and Civilization," 204–16; Doyel, "The Prehistoric Hohokam," 547; Doyel, "Hohokam Cultural Evolution in the Phoenix Basin," 264–65.

13. F. W. Hodge, "Prehistoric Irrigation in Arizona," *American Anthropologist* 6 (1893): 323–30, p. 323; Omar A. Turney, *The Land of the Stone Hoe* (Phoenix: Arizona Republican Print Shop, 1924), 5 ("engineering triumph"), 9 ("Canal Builders"); Omar A. Turney, "Prehistoric Irrigation," Part II, *Arizona Historical Review* 2, No. 2 (1929): 11–52; Odd S. Halseth, "Prehistoric Irrigation in Central Arizona," *Masterkey* 5 (1932): 165–78; Shetrone, "A Unique Prehistoric Irrigation Project," 381.

14. This composite picture of Hohokam irrigation comes from many sources, mainly (chronologically) F. W. Hodge, "Prehistoric Irrigation in Arizona," *American Anthropologist* 6 (1893): 323–30; H. R. Patrick, *The Ancient Canal Systems and Pueblos of the Salt River Valley, Arizona*, Phoenix Free Museum Bulletin No. 1 (Phoenix: Phoenix Free Museum, 1903), 4, 8; Byron Cummings, "Ancient Canals of the Casa Grande," *Progressive Arizona* 3 (1927): 9–10, 43; Turney, "Prehistoric Irrigation," Part I, 20 (acreage); Turney, "Prehistoric Irrigation," Part II, 11–52; Neil M. Judd, "Arizona Sacrifices Her Prehistoric Canals," in *Explorations and Field-Work of the Smithsonian Institution in 1929* (Washington, DC: Smithsonian Institution, 1930), 177–82; Neil M. Judd, "Arizona's Prehistoric Canals, from the Air," in *Explorations and Field-Work of the Smithsonian Institution in 1930* (Washington, DC: Smithsonian Institution, 1931), 157–66; Kirk Bryan, "Flood-Water Farming," *Geographical Review* 19 (1929): 444–56; Joe Ben Wheat, "Prehistoric Water Sources of the Point of Pines Area," *American Antiquity* 17 (1952): 185–96; Albert H. Schroeder, "Prehistoric Canals in the Salt River Valley, Arizona," *American Antiquity* 8, No. 4 (1943): 380–86; Haury, *The Excavation of Los Muertos*, 8, 41–42; Halseth, "Arizona's 1500 Years of Irrigation History," 252; Shetrone, "A Unique Prehistoric Irrigation Project"; Gladwin, *A History of the Ancient Southwest*, 84 ("outstanding accomplishment"); Richard B. Woodbury, "The

Hohokam Canals at Pueblo Grande, Arizona," *American Antiquity* 26 (1960): 267–70; Richard B. Woodbury, "Systems of Irrigation and Water Control in Arid North America," in *Proceedings of the 34th International Congress of Americanists, Vienna* (Vienna, 1962), 301–5; Frank Midvale, "Prehistoric Irrigation of the Casa Grande Ruins Area," *Kiva* 30, No. 3 (1965): 82–86; Frank Midvale, "Prehistoric Ruins and Irrigation in the Eastern Buckeye Valley," *Arizona Archaeologist* 8 (1974): 37–39; Haury, *The Hohokam*, 120–51; W. Bruce Masse, *The Hohokam Expressway Project: A Study of Prehistoric Irrigation in the Salt River Valley, Arizona* (Tucson: Arizona State Museum, University of Arizona, 1976), 12–43; W. Bruce Masse, "Prehistoric Irrigation Systems in the Salt River Valley, Arizona," *Science* 214 (October 1981): 408–15 (1,000 miles of minor canals); Robert M. Herskovitz, "Arizona U:9:46: A Dual Component Hohokam Site in Tempe, Arizona," *Kiva* 47, Nos. 1–2 (1981): 1–90; William L. Graf, "Channel Instability in a Braided, Sand Bed River," *Water Resources Research* 17 (1981): 1087–94; Linda M. Nicholas, *Irrigation and Sociopolitical Development in the Salt River Valley, Arizona: An Examination of Three Prehistoric Canal Systems,* M.A. thesis (Department of Anthropology, University of Arizona, 1981); Linda Nicholas and Jill Neitzel, "Canal Irrigation and Sociopolitical Organization in the Lower Salt River Valley: A Diachronic Analysis," in *Prehistoric Agricultural Strategies in the Southwest*, 161–78; Dart, "Agricultural Features," 388–89, 399–401, 403–37, 552 ("[turn] the alluvial plains . . . into a virtual garden"), 557; Patricia L. Crown, "Prehistoric Agricultural Technology in the Salt-Gila Basin," in *Hohokam Archaeology . . . VII*, 207–60, pp. 224, 229, and passim ("recent estimate" and estimated 350 miles of main canals and 1,000 miles of minor canals along the Salt River); Patrick, *The Ancient Canal Systems*, 5–6; Fred L. Nials and Suzanne K. Fish, "Canals and Related Features," in *The 1982–1984 Excavations at Las Colinas: The Site and Its Features*, Archaeological Series No. 162, Volume 2, ed. David A. Gregory et al. (Tucson: University of Arizona, 1988), 275–305, pp. 287–305; William E. Doolittle, "The Use of Check Dams for Protecting Downstream Agricultural Lands in the Prehistoric Southwest: A Contextual Analysis," *Journal of Anthropological Research* 41 (1985): 279–305; Patricia L. Crown, "Water Storage in the Prehistoric Southwest," *Kiva* 52, No. 3 (1987): 209–28; Ackerly et al., *La Ciudad Canals*, 8–35, 91–110; Fred L. Nials and David A. Gregory, "Irrigation Systems in the Lower Salt River Valley," in Donald A. Graybill et al., *The 1982–1984 Excavations at Las Colinas: Environment and Subsistence*, Archaeological Series No. 162, Volume 5 (Tucson: Cultural Resource Management Division, Arizona State Museum, University of Arizona, 1989), 39–58, p. 58 ("technologically simple and relatively inefficient"); Nials and Fish, "Canals and Related Features," 275–87; Gregory et al., *The 1982–1984 Excavations . . . Research Design*, 34–36; Fred L. Nials, David A. Gregory, and Donald A. Graybill, "Salt River Streamflow and Hohokam Irrigation Systems," in *The 1982–1984 Excavations . . . Environment and Subsistence*, 59–76, pp. 70–75 (6,960–10,441 acres along the Salt); Gregory, "Form and Variation in Hohokam Settlement Patterns," in *Chaco & Hohokam*, 158–93; Masse, "The Quest for Subsistence Sufficiency and Civilization," 212–14, p. 214 ("prevented the Hohokam from achieving . . ."); Suzanne K. Fish and Paul R. Fish, "Prehistoric Farmers of the American Southwest," *Annual Review of Anthropology* 23 (1994): 83–108, p. 88.

15. Baxter, *The Old New World*, 19–20; A. F. Bandelier, *Final Report of Investigations among the Indians of the Southwestern United States, Carried on Mainly in the Years from 1880 to 1885, Parts I-II,* Papers of the Archaeological Institute of America, American Series, III-IV (Cambridge: University Press, 1890, 1892), Part II, 420;

Hodge, "Prehistoric Irrigation in Arizona," 330; Patrick, *The Ancient Canal Systems*, 8; Turney, "Prehistoric Irrigation," Part I, 28, 34; Schroeder, "Prehistoric Canals in the Salt River Valley," 380–86; Woodbury, "A Reappraisal"; David E. Doyel, "Hohokam Social Organization and the Sedentary to Classic Transition," in *Current Issues*, 23–40; Suzanne K. Fish, Paul R. Fish, and John H. Madsen, "A Preliminary Analysis of Hohokam Settlement and Agriculture in the Northern Tucson Basin," in *Proceedings . . . 1983 . . . Part I*, 75–100; Doyel, *Late Hohokam Prehistory in Southern Arizona*, 69–70; Doyel, "The Hohokam Village," 19; Wilcox, "Hohokam Social Complexity," 261–63; Doyel, "The Prehistoric Hohokam"; Paul R. Fish and Suzanne K. Fish, "Hohokam Social and Political Organization," in *Exploring the Hohokam*, 151–75; David E. Doyel, "Hohokam Cultural Evolution in the Phoenix Basin," 265–66; Fish, personal communication, May 27, 1997.

16. For interplay of irrigation, population, centralized political authority, and other variables, see Julian H. Steward et al., *Irrigation Civilizations: A Comparative Study: A Symposium on Method and Result in Cross-cultural Regularities*, Social Science Monographs I (Washington, DC: Pan American Union, 1955); Theodore E. Downing and McGuire Gibson, eds., *Irrigation's Impact on Society*, Anthropological Papers of the University of Arizona No. 25 (Tucson: University of Arizona Press, 1974). On Hohokam, see Haury, *The Excavation of Los Muertos*, 32 (Fewkes); Emil W. Haury, "Speculations on Prehistoric Settlement Patterns in the Southwest," in *Prehistoric Settlement Patterns in the New World*, Viking Fund Publications in Anthropology No. 23, ed. Gordon R. Willey (New York: Wenner-Gren Foundation for Anthropological Research, 1956), 3–10, p. 8; Richard B. Woodbury, "Social Implications of Prehistoric Arizona Irrigation," *Actes VIe Congrès des Sciences Anthropologiques et Ethnologiques*, Tome II, Volume 1 (1960), 491–93; Woodbury, "Reappraisal," 556–57; Woodbury and Ressler, "Effects of Environmental and Cultural Limitations," 49–50; Martin E. McAllister and J. Scott Wood, "Comments on the Papers by Plog, Doyel and Riley," in *Current Issues*, 67–71; David R. Wilcox, "The Current Status of the Hohokam Concept," in *ibid.*, 236–42; Doyel, "The Hohokam Village," 10–14; David A. Gregory, "The Morphology of Platform Mounds and the Structure of Classic Period Hohokam Sites," in *Hohokam Village*, 183–210; W. Bruce Masse, "Prehistoric Irrigation Systems in the Salt River Valley, Arizona," *Science* 214 (October 1981): 408–15, p. 414; Neal W. Ackerly, "Irrigation, Water Allocation Strategies, and the Hohokam Collapse," *Kiva* 47, No. 3 (1982): 91–106; Jerry B. Howard, "The Lehi Canal System: Organization of a Classic Period Irrigation Community," in *Hohokam Village*, 211–21; Doyel, "From Foraging to Farming," 147–65; Linda Nicholas and Jill Neitzel, "Canal Irrigation and Sociopolitical Organization in the Lower Salt River Valley: A Diachronic Analysis," in *Prehistoric Agricultural Strategies in the Southwest*, 161–78; Lynn S. Teague, "The Organization of Hohokam Exchange," in *Proceedings . . . 1983 . . . Part II*, 397–418; David R. Wilcox, "Preliminary Report on New Data on Hohokam Ballcourts," in *ibid.*, 641–54; William H. Doelle, "The Southern Tucson Basin: Rillito-Rincon Subsistence, Settlement, and Community Structure," in *Proceedings . . . 1983 . . . Part I*, 183–98; David A. Gregory and Fred L. Nials, "Observations Concerning the Distribution of Classic Period Hohokam Platform Mounds," in *ibid.*, 373–88; Randall H. McGuire, "The Boserup Model and Agricultural Intensification in the United States Southwest," in *Prehistoric Agricultural Strategies*, 327–34; Kent G. Lightfoot and Steadman Upham, "Complex Societies in the Prehistoric American Southwest: A Consideration of the Controversy," in *The Sociopolitical Structure of Prehistoric Southwestern Societies*,

ed. Steadman Upham, Kent G. Lightfoot, and Roberta A. Jewett (Boulder: Westview Press, 1989), 3–30; Linda M. Nicholas and Gary M. Feinman, "A Regional Perspective on Hohokam Irrigation in the Lower Salt River Valley, Arizona," in *ibid.*, 199–235; Suzanne K. Fish, Paul R. Fish, and John Madsen, "Differentiation and Integration in a Tucson Basin Classic Period Hohokam Community," in *ibid.*, 237–67; Kent G. Lightfoot and Steadman Upham, "The Sociopolitical Structure of Prehistoric Southwestern Societies: Concluding Thoughts," in *ibid.*, 583–93; Gregory, "Form and Variation in Hohokam Settlement Patterns," 170–76 and passim; Masse, "The Quest for Subsistence Sufficiency and Civilization," 203–4; David R. Wilcox, "Hohokam Social Complexity," in *Chaco & Hohokam*, 253–75, pp. 263–67; Paul R. Fish and Suzanne K. Fish, "Hohokam Social and Political Organization," in *Exploring the Hohokam*, 151–75; Jill Neitzel, "Hohokam Material Culture and Behavior: The Dimensions of Organizational Change," in *ibid.*, 177–230; Gary M. Feinman, "Hohokam Archaeology in the Eighties: An Outside View," in *ibid.*, 461–83.

17. Richard B. Woodbury, "The Hohokam Canals at Pueblo Grande, Arizona," *American Antiquity* 26 (1960): 267–70, p. 267; Haury, *The Hohokam*, 129–30 and passim; Gregory, "Form and Variation in Hohokam Settlement Patterns," 182–83; Masse, "The Quest for Subsistence Sufficiency and Civilization," 219–22; Doyel, *Late Hohokam Prehistory in Southern Arizona*, 75–76.
18. Frank Hamilton Cushing, "Preliminary Notes on the Origin, Working Hypothesis and Primary Researches of the Hemenway Southwestern Archaeological Expedition," *Proceedings, 7th International Congress of Americanists, Berlin, 1885* (Berlin, 1890), 151–94, p. 162; [Frank Hamilton Cushing], "The Ancient Cities of Arizona," *American Antiquarian* 19 (1888): 325–30; Turney, "Prehistoric Irrigation," Part I, 19–25, 33–38; Haury, *The Excavation of Los Muertos*, 12, 210; Gregory et al., *The 1982–1984 Excavations . . . Research Design*, 34.
19. George E. Goodfellow, "The Sonora Earthquake," *Science* 11 (1888): 162–66; E. Fay Bennett, "An Afternoon of Terror: The Sonoran Earthquake of May 3, 1887," *Arizona and the West* 19 (Summer 1977): 107–20; John Randolph Sumner, "The Sonora Earthquake of 1887," *Bulletin of the Seismological Society of America* 67, No. 4 (August 1977): 1219–23; Susan M. DuBois and Ann W. Smith, *The 1887 Earthquake in San Bernardino: Historic Accounts and Intensity Patterns in Arizona*, Special Paper No. 3 (Tucson: State of Arizona Bureau of Geology and Mineral Technology, 1980).
20. Haury, *The Excavation of Los Muertos*, 211; Haury, *The Hohokam*, 151, 355; Gladwin, *A History of the Ancient Southwest*, 295; Shetrone, "A Unique Prehistoric Irrigation Project," 385; Woodbury and Ressler, "Effects of Environmental and Cultural Limitations," 47; Plog, "Explaining Culture Change," 16–17; Dart, "Agricultural Features," 543–44; Patrick, *The Ancient Canal Systems;* Cummings, "Ancient Canals of the Casa Grande," 43; Turney, *The Land of the Stone Hoe*, 2–5, 11 ("forces of nature"); Schroeder, "Prehistoric Canals in the Salt River Valley"; Robert A. Hackenberg, "Economic Alternatives in Arid Lands: A Case Study of the Pima and Papago Indians," *Ethnology* 1 (1962): 186–96, p. 193 (1854 drought); Donald E. Weaver, Jr., "A Cultural-Ecological Model for the Classic Hohokam Period in the Lower Salt River Valley, Arizona," *Kiva* 38, No. 1 (1972): 43–52, p. 49; Doyel, *Late Hohokam Prehistory in Southern Arizona*, 67–69, 74, 77; Nicholas, *Irrigation and Sociopolitical Development;* Jill E. Neitzel, "The Organization of the Hohokam Regional System," *American Archeology* 4 (1984): 207–16; Miksicek, "Historic Desertification," 61–66.

21. Arthur Powell Davis, "Irrigation near Phoenix, Arizona," in *Water-Supply and Irrigation Papers of the United States Geological Survey*, No. 2, House of Representatives, Document No. 342 (Washington, DC: Government Printing Office, 1897), 15–95, p. 44 ("impregnated with alkali"); Frank Russell, "The Pima Indians," in *Twenty-sixth Annual Report of the Bureau of American Ethnology for the Years 1904–1905* (Washington, DC: Government Printing Office, 1908), 3–389, p. 87 ("sterile plains" [Mange]); Turney, *The Land of the Stone Hoe*, 4; Turney, "Prehistoric Irrigation," Part I; Turney, "Prehistoric Irrigation," Part II, 12, 29, and passim; Odd S. Halseth, "Prehistoric Irrigation in the Salt River Valley," *University of New Mexico Bulletin* 296, Anthropological Series 1, No. 5 (1936): 42–47; Halseth, "Prehistoric Irrigation in Central Arizona," 167–68; Halseth, "Arizona's 1500 Years of Irrigation History," 252; Julian D. Hayden, "Salt Erosion," *American Antiquity* 10 (1945): 373–78, p. 377; Julian D. Hayden, *Excavations, 1940 at University Indian Ruin, Tucson, Arizona*, Southwestern Monuments Association Technical Series, Volume 5 (Globe, AZ: Gila Pueblo, 1957), 105–11, 189, 197–98; Schroeder, "Prehistoric Canals in the Salt River Valley," 385; Shetrone, "A Unique Prehistoric Irrigation Project," 385 and passim; Woodbury and Ressler, "Effects of Environmental and Cultural Limitations," 43–46; Haury, *The Hohokam*, 9; Dart, "Agricultural Features," 400–401; Rea, *Once a River*, 22–23 (mid-nineteenth-century [Kearney] expedition); Ackerly et al., *La Ciudad Canals*, 6, 27, 28; Nials and Gregory, "Irrigation Systems," 43–44, 49–50; James E. Ayres, "Man—The Desert Farmer," in *Hydrology and Water Resources in Arizona and the Southwest*, Volume 1, Proceedings of the 1971 Meetings of the Arizona Section, American Water Resources Association, and the Hydrology Section, Arizona Academy of Science, April 22–23, 1971, Tempe, Arizona (Tucson: Water Resources Research Center, 1971), 373–79, p. 378; Waugh, "La Ciudad," 5.
22. Daniel Hillel, *Out of the Earth: Civilization and the Life of the Soil* (Berkeley: University of California Press, 1991), 82–86, 135–58, p. 83 (the quotations). On Mesopotamia, see Michal Artzy and Daniel Hillel, "A Defense of the Theory of Progressive Soil Salinization in Ancient Southern Mesopotamia," *Geoarchaeology: An International Journal* 3, No. 3 (1988): 235–38; H. E. Hayward, "Plant Growth under Saline Conditions," in *Reviews of Research on Problems of Utilization of Saline Water* (Paris: UNESCO, 1954), 37–71; Thorkild Jacobsen and Robert M. Adams, "Salt and Silt in Ancient Mesopotamian Agriculture," *Science* 128 (1958): 1251–58; Adams, "Historic Patterns of Mesopotamian Irrigation Agriculture," in *Irrigation's Impact on Society*, 1–6; Gibson, "Violation of Fallow and Engineered Disaster in Mesopotamian Civilization," in *ibid.*, 7–20; Thorkild Jacobsen, "Salinity and Irrigation Agriculture in Antiquity: Diyala Basin Archaeological Projects: Report on Essential Results, 1957–58," in *Bibliotheca Mesopotamica*, Volume 14, ed. Giorgio Buccellati (Malibu: Undena Publications, 1982).
23. C. H. Southworth, "The History of Irrigation along the Gila River," in *Hearings before Committee on Indians Affairs*, House of Representatives, 66th Congress, 1st Session, Volume 2, 103–223, p. 116 and passim; Russell, "The Pima Indians," 87 (Akimel O'odham leaching); Turney, "Prehistoric Irrigation," Part II, 31–35 and passim; Edward F. Castetter and Willis H. Bell, *Pima and Papago Indian Agriculture*, Inter-Americana Studies 1 (Albuquerque: University of New Mexico Press, 1942), 172–73; Haury, *The Hohokam*, 8, 144 (on Hohokam flushing salts); Hayward, "Plant Growth under Saline Conditions"; Leon Bernstein, *Salt Tolerance of Field Crops*, Agriculture Information Bulletin No. 217, U.S. Department of Agriculture (Washington DC: U.S. Government Printing Office, 1960); Schroeder,

"Prehistoric Canals in the Salt River Valley"; Donald E. Weaver, Jr., "A Cultural-Ecological Model," 43–52; Woodbury and Ressler, "Effects of Environmental and Cultural Limitations," 45; Dart, "Agricultural Features," 546–47; Ackerly et al., *La Ciudad Canals*, 22–35, p. 24 (impermeable and saline soils along the Salt), 53–54.

24. James F. Rusling, *The Great West and Pacific Coast* (New York: Sheldon & Company, 1877), 380–84, 394–96 (1867 flood); Powell quoted in W. Bruce Masse, "Archaeological Sediments of the Hohokam Expressway Canals," Appendix C, in *The 1982–1984 Excavations . . . The Site and Its Features*, 333–53, p. 342; Russell, "The Pima Indians," 38, 52, 62; Hackenberg, "Economic Alternatives," 193; Robert A. Hackenberg, "Changing Patterns of Pima Indian Land Use," in *Indian and Spanish American Adjustments to Arid and Semiarid Environments*, arranged by Clark S. Knowlton (Lubbock: Texas Technological College, 1964), 6–15; Robert A. Hackenberg, *Pima-Maricopa Indians: Aboriginal Land Use and Occupancy of the Pima-Maricopa Indians*, Volumes 1–2 (New York: Garland Publishing Inc., 1974), Volume 1, 155–58.
25. Turney, "Prehistoric Irrigation," Part II, 15, 33–34 and passim; Russell, "The Pima Indians," 62; Hackenberg, *Pima-Maricopa Indians,* Volume 1, 155; Dart, "Agricultural Features," 439; Nials and Gregory, "Irrigation Systems," 48–49.
26. Harold S. Gladwin, "Excavations at Casa Grande, Arizona, February 12–May 1, 1927," *Southwest Museum Papers, Number Two* (Los Angeles: Southwest Museum, 1928), 26–27 ("recurring menace"); Masse, "Prehistoric Irrigation Systems in the Salt River Valley," 409–10, 414 ("monumental," "savage and unpredictable"), an especially influential analysis.
27. There were evidently no floods in the greater Southwest in 2200–400 BC, a moderate number of severe floods in AD 1000–1200, few in AD 1200–1400, and many since AD 1400. Ackerly et al., *La Ciudad Canals*, 9–35; Masse, "Prehistoric Irrigation Systems in the Salt River Valley," 409–10; Donald A. Graybill and Fred L. Nials, "Aspects of Climate, Streamflow and Geomorphology Affecting Irrigation Systems in the Salt River Valley," in *The 1982–1984 Excavations . . . Environment and Subsistence*, 5–23; Donald A. Graybill, "The Reconstruction of Prehistoric Salt River Streamflow," in *ibid.*, 25–38; Fred L. Nials, David A. Gregory, and Donald A. Graybill, "Salt River Streamflow and Hohokam Irrigation Systems," in *ibid.*, 59–76; Masse, "Archaeological Sediments," 333–53; Gregory, "Form and Variation in Hohokam Settlement Patterns," in *Chaco & Hohokam*, 183–88; Masse, "The Quest for Subsistence Sufficiency and Civilization," 215–16; Miksicek, "Historic Desertification," 79; Lisa L. Ely, Yehouda Enzel, Victor R. Baker, and Daniel R. Cayan, "A 5000-Year Record of Extreme Floods and Climate Change in the Southwestern United States," *Science* 262 (1993): 410–12.
28. George J. Gumerman, "Understanding the Hohokam," 3; Fish and Fish, "Prehistoric Farmers of the American Southwest," 89–90.
29. Ayres, "Man—The Desert Farmer," 377.
30. Simpson, "Those Who Have Gone Still Live"; Frank Midvale, "Prehistoric Irrigation in the Salt River Valley, Arizona," *Kiva* 34, No. 1 (1968): 28–32, pp. 28–29; Woodbury and Ressler, "Effects of Environmental and Cultural Limitations," 42; Halseth, "Arizona's 1500 Years of Irrigation History," 252; Haury, "The Hohokam," 695; Doyel, "The Hohokam Village," 7; W. Bruce Masse, "A Reappraisal of the Protohistoric Sobaipuri Indians of Southeastern Arizona," in *The Protohistoric Period in the North American Southwest, AD 1450–1700,* Anthropological Research Papers No. 24, ed. David R. Wilcox and W. Bruce Masse (Tempe: Arizona State University, 1981), 28–56.

31. In Arizona the Spanish discovered Uto-Aztecan Akimel O'odhams, Tohono O'odhams, and Sobaipuris; Athapaskan Western Apaches; and various Yuman speakers including Walapais, Havasupais, lower Colorado River Maricopas, and Mohaves. See essays on Yumans, Maricopas, Pimas and Papagos, and Western Apaches in *Handbook of North American Indians, Volume 10, Southwest*, ed. Alfonso Ortiz (Washington, DC: Smithsonian Institution, 1983), 1–3, 71–85, 125–60, 462–88.
32. Bandelier, *Final Report of Investigations . . . Part I*, 102–17, 251–59; Edward F. Castetter and Willis H. Bell, *Pima and Papago Indian Agriculture*, Inter-Americana Studies 1 (Albuquerque: University of New Mexico Press, 1942); Hackenberg, "Economic Alternatives"; Paul H. Ezell, "Is There a Hohokam-Pima Culture Continuum?," *American Antiquity* 29 (1963): 61–66; Weaver, "A Cultural-Ecological Model," 49–50; Joseph C. Winter, "Cultural Modifications of the Gila Pima: A.D. 1697–A.D. 1846," *Ethnohistory* 20 (1973): 67–77; Hackenberg, *Pima-Maricopa Indians;* Rea, "Resource Utilization"; William H. Doelle, "The Gila Pima in the Late Seventeenth Century," in *The Protohistoric Period in the North American Southwest*, 57–70; Carroll L. Riley, "Sonora and Arizona in the Protohistoric Period: Discussion of Papers by Sheridan, Reff, Masse, and Doelle," in *ibid.*, 123–28; *Handbook of North American Indians, Volume 10, Southwest*, 1–3, 71–85, 125–60, 462–88.
33. A Mr. Walker, whose source might have been Akimel O'odhams, told Bandelier the tale. Bandelier, *Final Report of Investigations . . . Part II*, 434–35, 462–68, p. 464; "Reports by A. F. Bandelier on His Investigations in New Mexico during the Years 1883–84," *Archaeological Institute of America, Fifth Annual Report of the Executive Committee, and Third Annual Report of the Committee on the American School of Classical Studies at Athens, 1883–84* (Cambridge: John Wilson and Son, University Press, 1884), 55–98, pp. 80–81; F. E. Grossman, "The Pima Indians of Arizona," *Annual Report of the Board of Regents of the Smithsonian Institution, 1871* (Washington, DC,: Government Printing Office, 1873), 407–19.
34. Jesse Walter Fewkes, "Excavations at Casa Grande," 315–17, 324–29; Jesse Walter Fewkes, "Prehistoric Ruins of the Gila Valley," *Smithsonian Miscellaneous Collections* 52, Volume 5, Part 4 (1909): 403–36, pp. 434–36; Jesse Walter Fewkes, "Casa Grande, Arizona," in *Twenty-eighth Annual Report of the Bureau of American Ethnology to the Secretary of the Smithsonian Institution, 1906–1907* (Washington, DC: Government Printing Office, 1912), 33–160, pp. 33, 42–72, 153–60; Russell, "The Pima Indians," 23–24; Donald M. Bahr, "Who Were the Hohokam? The Evidence from Pima-Papago Myths," *Ethnohistory* 18 (1971): 245–66; Haury, *The Hohokam*, 8–9; Doyel, *Late Hohokam Prehistory in Southern Arizona*, 75–81; Doyel, "Hohokam Cultural Evolution in the Phoenix Basin," 266–67.
35. Donald Bahr, Juan Smith, William Smith Allison, and Julian Hayden, *The Short Swift Time of Gods of Earth: The Hohokam Chronicles* (Berkeley: University of California Press, 1994), 1–29, 281–84; Halseth, "Prehistoric Irrigation in Central Arizona," 170; Stephen Trimble, *The People: Indians of the American Southwest* (Santa Fe: SAR Press, 1993), 357.
36. Haury, *The Hohokam*, 8–9, 140–41; see notes 3 and 41.
37. Plog, "Explaining Culture Change," 16; Suzanne K. Fish, "The Modified Environment of the Salt-Gila Aqueduct Project Site: A Palynological Analysis," in *Hohokam Archaeology . . . VII*, 39–51; Suzanne K. Fish, "Agriculture and Subsistence Implications of the Salt-Gila Aqueduct Project Pollen Analyses," in *ibid.*, 111–70; see also Gregory et al., *The 1982–1984 Excavations . . . Research*

Design, 33; Ayres, "Man—The Desert Farmer," 373–79; Vorsila L. Bohrer, "Paleoecology of Snaketown," *Kiva* 36, No. 3 (1971): 11–19; Rea, "The Ecology of Pima Fields"; Henry F. Dobyns, "Who Killed the Gila?," *Journal of Arizona History* (Spring 1978): 17–30; Donald E. Dove, "Subsistence Issues and Population Stability in the Northern Hohokam Periphery," in *Proceedings . . . 1983 . . . Part I*, 65–74; Patricia L. Crown, "Comments on Social and Economic Issues," in *ibid.*, 119–24.

38. Robinson, *The Story of Arizona*, 296ff.; Judd, "Arizona's Prehistoric Canals, from the Air," 157–66; Gladwin et al., *Excavations at Snaketown*, 3; Shetrone, "A Unique Prehistoric Irrigation Project," 384–85; Di Peso, *The Upper Pima of San Cayetano del Tumacacori*; Hackenberg, "Changing Patterns"; Charles W. Polzer, "Use and Abuse of Southwestern Rivers: Historical Man—The Spaniard," in *Hydrology and Water Resources*, 387–96; Bert Fireman, "Use and Abuse of Southwestern Rivers: Historic Man—The Anglo," in *ibid.*, 397–403; Charles C. Di Peso, "Use and Abuse of Southwestern Rivers: The Pueblo Dweller," in *ibid.*, 381–85; Bohrer, "Paleoecology," 18; Dobyns, "Who Killed the Gila?"; Henry F. Dobyns, *From Fire to Flood: Historic Human Destruction of Sonoran Desert Riverine Oases* (Socorro, NM: Ballena Press, 1981); Rea, "The Ecology of Pima Fields"; Rea, *Once a River*; Dean A. Hendrickson and W. L. Minckley, "Ciénegas—Vanishing Climax Communities of the American Southwest," *Desert Plants* 6 (1984): 131–75; Miksicek, "Historic Desertification," 53–57; Conrad Joseph Bahre, *A Legacy of Change: Historic Human Impact on Vegetation in the Arizona Borderlands* (Tucson: University of Arizona Press, 1991).
39. Baxter, *The Old New World*, 12–17, 24–27 (he wrote from Camp Hemenway, Cushing's base, in April 1888).
40. Fish, "The Hohokam: 1,000 Years of Prehistory," 162; Fish, personal communication, May 27, 1997.
41. Haury, "The Hohokam," 695; Haury, *The Hohokam*, 354. See also notes 3 and 36, and Charles C. Di Peso, "The Structure of the 11th Century Casas Grandes Agricultural System," in *Prehistoric Agricultural Strategies in the Southwest*, 261–69; Doyel, "Hohokam Cultural Evolution in the Phoenix Basin," 234; Paul R. Fish, Suzanne K. Fish, George J. Gumerman, and J. Jefferson Reid, "Toward an Explanation for Southwestern 'Abandonments,' " in *Themes in Southwest Prehistory*, ed. George J. Gumerman (Santa Fe: School of American Research, 1994), 136–63.

Chapter Three: Eden

1. I use "Eden" throughout for these comingled ideas, despite its highly specific origin and associations (similar difficulties adhere to all possible substitute terms); thanks to David Harris Sacks (personal communication, September 4, 1998) for discussing the pitfalls surrounding the use of these terms. William Cronon (*Changes in the Land: Indians, Colonists, and the Ecology of New England* [New York: Hill and Wang, 1983]) covers the same ground as in the first several pages of this chapter in greater detail. Francis Higginson, *New-England's Plantation. Or, a Short and True Description of the Commodities and Discommodities of That Country*, second edition, London, 1630 (reproduced by The New England Society in the City of New York, 1930), no pagination; [Arthur Barlow or Philip Amadas], "The First Virginia Voyage, 1584," in Richard Hakluyt, *Voyages to the Virginia Colonies* (London: Century, 1986), 75; David B. Quinn and Alison M. Quinn, eds., *The First Colonists*

(Raleigh: North Carolina Department of Cultural Resources, 1982), 2; William Wood, *New England's Prospect*, ed. Alden T. Vaughan (Amherst: University of Massachusetts Press, 1993), 50, 53, 56; John P. Dempsey, *New English Canaan by Thomas Morton of "Merrymount": A Critical Edition*, Ph.D. dissertation (Department of English, Brown University, 1998), 57; Howard S. Russell, *Indian New England before the Mayflower* (Hanover: University Press of New England, 1980), 128–29 (Champlain); Paul Lindholdt, ed., *John Josselyn, Colonial Traveler: A Critical Edition of "Two Voyages of New-England"* (Hanover: University Press of New England, 1988), 33, 71, 77, and passim; John Lawson, *A New Voyage to Carolina*, ed. Hugh Talmage Lefler (Chapel Hill: University of North Carolina Press, 1967), liii, 51; Carl O. Sauer, *Sixteenth Century North America* (Berkeley: University of California Press, 1971), 54 (Verrazzano); Francis Harper, ed., *The Travels of William Bartram* (New Haven: Yale University Press, 1958), 16, 32, 44, 66, 68, 134, 222, 225, and passim; Frank Bergon, ed., *The Journals of Lewis and Clark* (New York: Penguin Books, 1989), 108.

2. William E. Doolittle, "Agriculture in North America on the Eve of Contact: A Reassessment," *Annals of the Association of American Geographers* 82, No. 3 (1992): 386–401; Gordon M. Day, "The Indian as an Ecological Factor in the Northeastern Forest," *Ecology* 34 (1953): 329–46, p. 330; William A. Starna, George R. Hammell, and William L. Butts, "Northern Iroquoian Horticulture and Insect Infestation: A Cause for Village Removal," *Ethnohistory* 31 (1984): 197–207; Michael Williams, "An Exceptionally Powerful Biotic Factor," in *Humans as Components of Ecosystems: The Ecology of Subtle Human Effects and Populated Areas*, ed. Mark J. McDonnell and Steward T. A. Pickett (New York: Springer-Verlag, 1993), 24–39 (2.3 acres/person in cultivation); R. Douglas Hurt, *Indian Agriculture in America* (Lawrence: University Press of Kansas, 1987), 66–67 (0.3 acre/person; 1 acre/person; 2.3 acres/person); on Indians possibly returning after a period, Carolyn Merchant (personal communication, July 1998).
3. Alfonso Ortiz, ed., *Handbook of North American Indians, Volume 10, Southwest* (Washington, DC: Smithsonian Institution Press, 1983); Stephen Plog and Shirley Powell, *Papers on the Archaeology of Black Mesa, Arizona, Volume II* (Carbondale: Southern Illinois University Press, 1984); George J. Gumerman, ed., *The Anasazi in a Changing Environment* (Cambridge: Cambridge University Press, 1988); Steadman Upham, Kent G. Lightfoot, and Robert A. Jewett, eds., *The Sociopolitical Structure of Prehistoric Southwestern Societies* (Boulder: Westview Press, 1989).
4. On Cahokia and Mississippians, James B. Griffin, "Eastern North American Archaeology: A Summary: Prehistoric Cultures Changed from Small Hunting Bands to Well-organized Agricultural Towns and Tribes," *Science* 156 (1967): 175–91; Melvin L. Fowler and Robert L. Hall, *Archaeological Phases at Cahokia*, Papers in Anthropology, No. 1 (Springfield: Illinois State Museum, 1972); Melvin L. Fowler, "A Pre-Columbian Urban Center on the Mississippi," *Scientific American* 233, No. 2 (1975): 93–101; Melvin L. Fowler, ed., *Explorations into Cahokia Archaeology*, Illinois Archaeological Survey, Inc., Bulletin No. 7 (Urbana: University of Illinois, 1977); Bruce D. Smith, ed., *Mississippian Settlement Patterns* (New York: Academic Press, 1978); James B. Stoltman, "Temporal Models in Prehistory: An Example from Eastern North America," *Current Anthropology* 19 (1978): 703–46; Charles J. Bareis and James W. Porter, *Archaeology in the American Bottom: Progress Report of the Illinois FAI-270 Archaeological Mitigation Project, Proceedings of a Symposium Presented at the Midwest Archaeological Conference, Milwaukee, Wisconsin, October 12–14, 1979*, Research Report No. 6 (Urbana-

Champaign: Department of Anthropology, University of Illinois at Urbana-Champaign, 1981); Jon Muller, "The Southeast," in *Ancient North Americans*, ed. Jesse D. Jennings (New York: W. H. Freeman and Company, 1983), 373–420; Charles J. Bareis and James W. Porter, eds., *American Bottom Archaeology: A Summary of the FAI-270 Project Contribution to the Culture History of the Mississippi River Valley* (Urbana: University of Illinois Press, 1984); James B. Stoltman, ed., *Prehistoric Mound Builders of the Mississippi Valley, Proceedings of a Symposium sponsored by the Putnam Museum, Davenport, Iowa, November 15–17, 1985*; James B. Griffin, "Changing Concepts of the Prehistoric Mississippian Cultures of the Eastern United States," in *Alabama and the Borderlands: From Prehistory to Statehood*, ed. R. Reid Badger and Lawrence A. Clayton (Tuscaloosa: University of Alabama Press, 1985), 40–63; Bruce D. Smith, "Mississippian Patterns of Subsistence and Settlement," in *ibid.*, 64–79; Vincas P. Steponaitis, "Prehistoric Archaeology in the Southeastern United States, 1970–1985," *Annual Review of Anthropology* 15 (1986): 363–404; Bruce D. Smith, "The Emergence of Ranked Agricultural Societies, 1500–1000 B.P.," in *Advances in World Archaelogy*, Volume 5, ed. Fred Wendorf and Angela E. Close (Orlando: Academic Press, 1986), 1–92; George R. Milner, "The Late Prehistoric Cahokia Cultural System of the Mississippi River Valley: Foundations, Florescence, and Fragmentation," *Journal of World Prehistory* 4, No. 1 (1990): 1–43; Thomas E. Emerson and R. Barry Lewis, eds., *Cahokia and the Hinterlands: Middle Mississippian Cultures of the Midwest* (Urbana: University of Illinois Press, 1991); Jon Muller and Jeanette E. Stephens, "Mississippian Sociocultural Adaptation," in *ibid.*, 297–310; John E. Kelly, "Cahokia and Its Role as a Gateway Center in Interregional Exchange," in *ibid.*, 61–80. On Monks Mound, which in 1811 Henry Brackenridge called "a stupendous monument of antiquity" (its name is from a nearby monastery run by Trappists in the early 19th century), see Cyrus Thomas, "Cahokia or Monk's Mound," *American Anthropologist* 9 (1907): 362–65; Fowler, ed., *Explorations into Cahokia Archaeology*, 1–30 (Brackenridge), 49–88 (engineers and triangulation system); Melvin L. Fowler, "Cahokia and the American Bottom: Settlement Archeology," in *Mississippian Settlement Patterns*, 455–78; Charles R. McGimsey and Michael D. Wiant, "Limited Archaeological Investigations at Monks Mound: Some Perspectives on its Stability, Structure, and Age," in *Studies in Illinois Archaeology*, No. 1 (Springfield: Illinois State Historic Preservation Office, 1984), 1–50; James M. Collins and Michael L. Chalfant, "A Second-Terrace Perspective on Monks Mound," *American Antiquity* 58 (1993): 319–32; George R. Holley, Rinita A. Dalan, and Philip A. Smith, "Investigations in the Cahokia Site Grand Plaza," *American Antiquity* 58 (1993): 306–19.

5. On the Mississippi floodplain environment, diet, etc., see Bruce D. Smith, "Variation in Mississippian Settlement Patterns," in *Mississippian Settlement Patterns*, 479–503; Neal H. Lopinot, "Analysis of Flotation Sample Materials from the Late Archaic Horizon," in *The 1982 Excavations at the Cahokia Interpretive Center Tract, St. Clair County, Illinois*, Center for Archaeological Investigations Research Paper No. 37, by Michael S. Nassaney, Neal H. Lopinot, Brian M. Butler, and Richard W. Jefferies (Carbondale: Southern Illinois University, 1983), 105–14; George R. Milner, assisted by Joyce A. Williams, with contributions by Paula G. Cross and Lucy Whalley, *The Turner and DeMange Sites (11-S-50) (11-S-447)* (Urbana: University of Illinois Press, 1983); George R. Milner, assisted by Kelly R. Cox and Michael C. Meinkoth, with contributions by Paula G. Cross, Sissel Johannessen, James W. Porter, and Norman Meinholz, *The Robinson's Lake Site (11-Ms-582)*

(Urbana: University of Illinois Press, 1984); Bareis and Porter, eds., *American Bottom Archaeology*, 15–33, 158–86, 197–214, 215–32, 253–61; Thomas J. Riley, "Ridged-field Agriculture and the Mississippian Economic Pattern," in *Emergent Horticultural Economies of the Eastern Woodlands*, Center for Archaeological Investigations, Occasional Paper No. 7, ed. William F. Keegan (Carbondale: Southern Illinois University, 1987), 295–304; William I. Woods, "Maize Agriculture and the Late Prehistoric: A Characterization of Settlement Location Strategies," in *ibid.*, 275–94; Richard W. Yerkes, *Prehistoric Life on the Mississippi Floodplain: Stone Tool Use, Settlement Organization, and Subsistence Practices at the Labras Lake Site, Illinois* (Chicago: University of Chicago Press, 1987); David Rindos and Sissel Johannessen, "Human-Plant Interactions and Cultural Change in the American Bottom," in *Cahokia and the Hinterlands*, 35–45. On society and polity, see Patricia J. O'Brien, "Urbanism, Cahokia and Middle Mississippian," *Archaeology* 25, No. 3 (1972): 188–97; Christopher S. Peebles and Susan M. Kus, "Some Archaeological Correlates of Ranked Societies," *American Antiquity* 42 (1977): 421–48; George R. Milner, "Social and Temporal Implications of Variation among American Bottom Mississippian Cemeteries," *American Antiquity* 49 (1984): 468–88; Thomas E. Emerson, "Middle Mississippian Societies of the American Bottom and the Central Illinois Valley," in *Prehistoric Mound Builders*, 9–16; Robert L. Hall, "Upper Mississippi and Middle Mississippi Relationships," *Wisconsin Archeologist* 67, Nos. 3–4 (1986): 365–69; Steponaitis, "Prehistoric Archaeology."

6. In the century-long debate over the population of Cahokia, estimates have ranged from 3,000 to 5,000 upward. Today, 10,000 and under is favored for what may have been an elite center surrounded by dispersed communities. The population reached its height in AD 1050–1150. Michael L. Gregg, "A Population Estimate for Cahokia," in *Perspectives in Cahokia Archaeology*, Illinois Archaeological Survey, Inc. Bulletin No. 10 (Urbana: University of Illinois, 1975), 126–36; Fowler, "A Pre-Columbian Urban Center on the Mississippi," 100; Melvin L. Fowler, "Cahokia and the American Bottom: Settlement Archeology," in *Mississippian Settlement Patterns*, 455–78; Yerkes, *Prehistoric Life on the Mississippi Floodplain*, 28 (another Brackenridge quote); George R. Milner, "Mississippian Period Population Density in a Segment of the Central Mississippi River Valley," *American Antiquity* 51 (1986): 468–88; Milner, "The Late Prehistoric Cahokia Cultural System"; Muller and Stephens, "Mississippian Sociocultural Adaptation," 306; George R. Milner, "Disease and Sociopolitical Systems in Late Prehistoric Illinois," in *Disease and Demography in the Americas*, ed. John W. Verano and Douglas H. Ubelaker (Washington, DC: Smithsonian Institution Press, 1992), 103–16.
7. Don G. Wyckoff, "Secondary Forest Succession Following Abandonment of Mesa Verde," *Kiva* 42 (1977): 215–31; Robert C. Euler et al., "The Colorado Plateaus: Cultural Dynamics and Paleoenvironment," *Science* 205 (1979): 1089–101; Mark A. Stiger, "Mesa Verde Subsistence Patterns from Basketmaker to Pueblo III," *Kiva* 44 (1979): 133–45; Julio L. Betancourt and Thomas R. Van Devender, "Holocene Vegetation in Chaco Canyon, New Mexico," *Science* 214 (1981): 656–58; Stephen Plog, "Regional Perspectives on the Western Anasazi, in Regional Organization in the American Southwest," *American Archeology* 4 (1984): 162–70; Jeffrey S. Dean et al., "Human Behavior, Demography, and Paleoenvironment on the Colorado Plateaus," *American Antiquity* 50 (1985): 537–54; Michael S. Berry, "Data, Assumptions, and Models: A Reply to Dean," *American Antiquity* 50 (1985): 648–49; Kenneth Lee Petersen and Meredith H. Matthews, "Man's Impact on the Landscape: A Prehistoric Example from the Dolores River Anasazi, Southwestern

Colorado," *Journal of the West* 26 (July 1987): 4–16; Timothy A. Kohler and Meredith H. Matthews, "Long-term Anasazi Land Use and Forest Reduction: A Case Study from Southwest Colorado," *American Antiquity* 53 (1988): 537–64; Stephen H. Lekson et al., "The Chaco Canyon Community," *Scientific American* 259 (1988): 100–109; Jill Neitzel, "The Chacoan Regional System: Interpreting the Evidence for Sociopolitical Complexity," in *The Sociopolitical Structure*, 509–56; Robert D. Leonard, "Resource Specialization, Population Growth, and Agricultural Production in the American Southwest," *American Antiquity* 54 (1989): 491–503; Daniel O. Larson and Joel Michaelsen, "Impacts of Climatic Variability and Population Growth on Virgin Branch Anasazi Cultural Developments," *American Antiquity* 55 (1990): 227–49; "Ancient People and Their Environments," *Earth Science* 43, No. 3 (1990): 9–10; Janet D. Orcutt, "Environmental Variability and Settlement Changes on the Pajarito Plateau, New Mexico," *American Antiquity* 56 (1991): 315–32; George Johnson, "Social Strife May Have Exiled Ancient Indians," *New York Times*, August 20, 1996, C1, 6.

8. For various scenarios, including the overexploitation of trees—and the consequences of deforestation including the loss of tree-associated species of birds and animals and increased erosion, sedimentation, and flooding—and related health issues at Cahokia and Moundville to the south, see Robert L. Hall, "An Interpretation of the Two-Climax Model of Illinois Prehistory," in *Early Native Americans: Prehistoric Demography, Economy, and Technology*, ed. David L. Browman (Paris: Mouton Publishers, 1980), 401–62; James W. Porter, "Concluding Remarks," in *American Bottom Archaeology*, 241–52; Christopher S. Peebles and Glenn A. Black, "Moundville from 1000 to 1500 AD as Seen from 1840 to 1985 AD," in *Chiefdoms in the Americas*, ed. Robert D. Drennan and Carlos A. Uribe (Lanham, MD: University Press of America, 1987), 21–41; George R. Milner, "Health and Cultural Change in the Late Prehistoric American Bottom, Illinois," in *What Mean These Bones?: Studies in Southeastern Bioarchaeology*, ed. Mary Lucas Powell, Patricia S. Bridges, and Ann Marie Wagner Mires (Tuscaloosa: University of Alabama Press, 1991), 52–69; Robert L. Hall, "Cahokia Identity and Interaction Models of Cahokia Mississippian," in *Cahokia and the Hinterlands*, 3–34; David Rindos and Sissel Johannessen, "Human-Plant Interactions and Cultural Change in the American Bottom," in *ibid.*, 35–45; William I. Woods and George R. Holley, "Upland Mississippian Settlement in the American Bottom Region," in *ibid.*, 46–60; C. Margaret Scarry, "Variability in Mississippian Crop Production Strategies," in *Foraging and Farming in the Eastern Woodlands*, ed. C. Margaret Scarry (Gainesville: University Press of Florida, 1993), 78–90; Neal H. Lopinot and William I. Woods, "Wood Overexploitation and the Collapse of Cahokia," in *ibid.*, 206–31; Lee A. Newsom, "Plants and People: Cultural, Biological, and Ecological Responses to Wood Exploitation," in *ibid.*, 115–37.

9. Victor Shelford, *Ecology of North America* (Urbana: University of Illinois Press, 1963); Alice B. Kehoe, *North American Indians: A Comprehensive Account* (Englewood Cliffs, NJ: Prentice Hall, 1992); Molly R. Mignon and Daniel L. Boxberger, eds., *Native North Americans: An Ethnohistorical Approach*, second edition (Dubuque, IA: Kendall Hunt, 1997).

10. Genital or venereal syphilis (over which there has been much debate) is indicated in pre-Columbian North America despite great difficulty interpreting the treponematosis complex (yaws, pinta, and endemic and venereal syphilis) from skeletal remains. On these and other issues, see Virgil J. Vogel, "Indian Health and Disease," *Ecologist* 5, No. 7 (August/September 1975): 254–58; Brenda J. Baker and George J.

Armelagos, "The Origin and Antiquity of Syphilis," *Current Anthropology* 29 (1988): 703–37; Verano and Ubelaker, *Disease and Demography in the Americas*; Donald J. Ortner, "Skeletal Paleopathology," in *ibid.*, 5–13; Mary Lucas Powell, "Health and Disease in the Late Prehistoric Southeast," in *ibid.*, 41–53; Douglas W. Owsley, "Demography of Prehistoric and Early Historic Northern Plains Populations," in *ibid.*, 75–86; Milner, "Disease and Sociopolitical Systems in Late Prehistoric Illinois," 103–16; Shelley S. Saunders, Peter Ramsden, and D. Ann Herring, "Transformation and Disease," in *ibid.*, 117–25; Georgieann Bogdan and David S. Weaver, "Pre-Columbian Treponematosis in Coastal North Carolina," in *ibid.*, 155–63; Douglas H. Ubelaker and John W. Verano, "Conclusion," in *ibid.*, 279–82; John Noble Wilford, "Tuberculosis Found to be Old Disease in New World," *New York Times*, March 15, 1994, B5, 10; Clark Spencer Larsen, "In the Wake of Columbus: Native Population Biology in the Postcontact Americas," *Yearbook of Physical Anthropology* 37 (1994): 109–54.

11. Russell Thornton, *American Indian Holocaust and Survival: A Population History since 1492* (Norman: University of Oklahoma Press, 1987), 42–133 (Harriot, Pilgrims, etc.) and passim; David Henige, *Numbers from Nowhere: The American Indian Contact Population Debate* (Norman: University of Oklahoma Press, 1998), 150–53 (Harriot); Ann F. Ramenofsky, *Vectors of Death: The Archaeology of European Contact* (Albuquerque: University of New Mexico Press, 1987); Henry F. Dobyns, *Their Number Become Thinned: Native American Population Dynamics in Eastern North America* (Knoxville: University of Tennessee Press, 1983), 8–32; Verano and Ubelaker, *Disease and Demography in the Americas*; John D. Daniels, "The Indian Population of North America in 1492," *William and Mary Quarterly* 49 (1992): 298–320; William M. Denevan, ed., *The Native Population of the Americas in 1492*, second edition (Madison: University of Wisconsin Press, 1992); Clark Spencer Larsen and George R. Milner, eds., *In the Wake of Contact: Biological Responses to Conquest* (New York: Wiley-Liss, Inc., 1994). Smallpox, chickenpox, influenza, measles, mumps, rubella, yellow fever, and common cold are viral; pneumonia, scarlet fever, whooping cough, diphtheria, typhus, dysentery, cholera, and bubonic plague are bacterial; malaria and amebic dysentery are protozoal.
12. Alfred W. Crosby, *The Columbian Exchange: Biological and Cultural Consequences of 1492* (Westport, CT: Greenwood Press, 1972); Alfred W. Crosby, "Virgin Soil Epidemics as a Factor in the Aboriginal Depopulation in America," *William and Mary Quarterly* 33 (1976): 289–99.
13. James H. Howard, *The British Museum Winter Count*, Occasional Paper No. 4 (London: British Museum, 1979), 5–8, 46; James Mooney, "Calendar History of the Kiowa Indians," *Seventeenth Annual Report of the Bureau of American Ethnology to the Secretary of the Smithsonian Institution* (Washington, DC: Government Printing Office, 1896), 141–447, pp. 274–75.
14. George Catlin, *Letters and Notes on the Manners, Customs, and Conditions of the North American Indians*, 2 volumes (New York: Dover, 1973), Volume 2, 257–59; John C. Ewers et al., *Views of a Vanishing Frontier* (Omaha: Joselyn Art Museum, 1984); Mooney, "Calendar History of the Kiowa"; Arthur J. Ray, "Smallpox: The Epidemic of 1837–38," *Beaver* 306 (Autumn 1975): 8–13; Clyde D. Dollar, "The High Plains Smallpox Epidemic of 1837–38," *Western Historical Quarterly* 8, No. 1 (January 1977): 15–38; Michael K. Trimble, "The 1832 Inoculation Program on the Missouri River," in *Disease and Demography in the Americas*, 257–64.
15. For historical demography in North America, see James Mooney, "The Aboriginal Population of America North of Mexico," *Smithsonian Miscellaneous Collections* 80,

No. 7 (1928): 1–40; A. L. Kroeber, "Native American Population," *American Anthropologist* 36 (1934): 1–25; Henry F. Dobyns, "Estimating Aboriginal American Population: An Appraisal of Techniques with a New Hemispheric Estimate," *Current Anthropology* 7 (1966): 395–416; Wilbur R. Jacobs, "The Tip of an Iceberg: Pre-Columbian Indian Demography and Some Implications for Revisionism," *William and Mary Quarterly* 31 (1974): 123–32; Douglas H. Ubelaker, "Prehistoric New World Population Size: Historical Review and Current Appraisal of North American Estimates," *American Journal of Physical Anthropology* 45 (1976): 661–65; Henry F. Dobyns, *Native American Historical Demography: A Critical Bibliography* (Bloomington: Indiana University Press, 1976); Russell Thornton and Joan Marsh-Thornton, "Estimating Prehistoric American Indian Population Size for United States Area: Implications of the Nineteenth Century Population Decline and Nadir," *American Journal of Physical Anthropology* 55 (1981): 47–53; S. Ryan Johansson, "The Demographic History of the Native Peoples of North America: A Selective Bibliography," *Yearbook of Physical Anthropology* 25 (1982): 133–52; Dobyns, *Their Number Become Thinned*; Thornton, *American Indian Holocaust and Survival*; Ramenofsky, *Vectors of Death*; Douglas Ubelaker, "North American Indian Population Size, A.D. 1500 to 1985," *American Journal of Physical Anthropology* 77 (1988): 289–94; Leslie Roberts, "Disease and Death in the New World," *Science* 246 (1989): 1245–47; Ezra Zubrow, "The Depopulation of Native America," *Antiquity* 64 (1990): 754–65; William M. Denevan, "Native American Populations in 1492: Recent Research and a Revised Hemispheric Estimate," in *The Native Population of the Americas in 1492*, xvii–xxix; Douglas H. Ubelaker, "The Sources and Methodology for Mooney's Estimates of North American Indian Populations," in *ibid.*, 243–88; Woodrow Borah, "The Historical Demography of Aboriginal and Colonial America: An Attempt at Perspective," in *ibid.*, 13–34; Daniels, "The Indian Population of North America in 1492."

16. The two lowest continental estimates (just over and just under 2 million) are by Douglas Ubelaker, an anthropologist, on the basis of published and unpublished data in the projected 20-volume *Handbook of North American Indians.* Other scholars adjusted Ubelaker's or Dobyns's estimates, defining a middle zone from 4 to 12 million. William Denevan, a geographer, modestly doubled the lower of Ubelaker's two estimates to 3.8 million. Ann Ramenofsky, an archaeologist, lowered Dobyns's 18 million to 12 million on the basis of her appreciation for both the devastation of disease and the variability in the course of disease and in the archaeological record. Russell Thornton, a sociologist, considered Dobyns's nadir flawed but not his idea that populations declined from an aboriginal high to a historical low by a factor of 20 or 25 (the so-called depopulation ratio); following the course from a different low point, he arrived at 7 million for North America. Dobyns, "Estimating Aboriginal American Population"; Ubelaker, "Prehistoric New World Population Size"; Dobyns, *Their Number Become Thinned*; Thornton, *American Indian Holocaust and Survival*, 15–41; Ramenofsky, *Vectors of Death;* Ubelaker, "North American Indian Population Size, A.D. 1500 to 1985"; Denevan, "Native American Populations in 1492: Recent Research and a Revised Hemispheric Estimate," xviii–xxi; Douglas H. Ubelaker, "North American Indian Population Size," in *Disease and Demography in the Americas*, 169–76.
17. Francis Jennings, *Invasion of America: Indians, Colonialism, and the Cant of Conquest* (Chapel Hill: University of North Carolina Press, 1975), 14–31; Wilbur R. Jacobs, "The Tip of an Iceberg: Pre-Columbian Indian Demography and Some Implications for Revisionism," *William and Mary Quarterly* 31 (1974): 123–32;

Dobyns, "Estimating Aboriginal American Population"; David Henige, "If Pigs Could Fly: Timucuan Population and Native American Historical Demography," *Journal of Interdisciplinary History* 16 (1986): 701–20, p. 702 ("ideological morass"); David E. Stannard, *American Holocaust: Columbus and the Conquest of the New World* (New York: Oxford University Press, 1992), 11, 33; Lenore A. Stiffarm with Phil Lane, Jr., "The Demography of Native North America: A Question of American Indian Survival," in *The State of Native America: Genocide, Colonization, and Resistance*, ed. M. Annette Jaimes (Boston: South End Press, 1992), 23–53.

18. Ubelaker and Verano, "Conclusion," 280–81.

19. Dobyns, *Their Number Become Thinned;* William Engelbrecht, "Factors Maintaining Low Population Density among the Prehistoric New York Iroquois," *American Antiquity* 52 (1987): 13–27; Dean R. Snow and Kim M. Lanphear, "European Contact and Indian Depopulation in the Northeast: The Timing of the First Epidemics," *Ethnohistory* 35 (1988): 15–33; Henry F. Dobyns, "More Methodological Perspectives on Historical Demography," *Ethnohistory* 36 (1989): 285–99; Snow and Lanphear " 'More Methodological Perspectives': A Rejoinder to Dobyns," *Ethnohistory* 36 (1989): 299–304; Dean R. Snow and William A. Starna, "Sixteenth-Century Depopulation: A View from the Mohawk Valley," *American Anthropologist* 91 (1989): 142–49; Roberts, "Disease and Death in the New World"; Martha L. Sempowski, Lorraine P. Saunders, and James W. Bradley, "New World Epidemics," *Science* 247 (1990): 788–89; Dean R. Snow, "Disease and Population Decline in the Northeast," in *Disease and Demography in the Americas*, 177–86; Catherine C. Carlson, George J. Armelagos, and Ann L. Magennis, "Impact of Disease on the Precontact and Early Historic Populations of New England and the Maritimes," in *ibid.*, 141–53; Brenda J. Baker, "Pilgrim's Progress and Praying Indians: The Biocultural Consequences of Contact in Southern New England," in *In the Wake of Contact*, 35–45; Dean R. Snow, "Microchronology and Demographic Evidence Relating to the Size of Pre-Columbian North American Indian Populations," *Science* 268 (1995): 1601–4.

20. Dobyns, *Their Number Become Thinned*, 8–32; Ann M. Palkovich, "Historic Population of the Eastern Pueblos: 1540–1910," *Journal of Anthropological Research* 41 (1985): 401–26; Daniel T. Reff, "The Introduction of Smallpox in the Greater Southwest," *American Anthropologist* 89 (1987): 704–8; Reff, "Old World Diseases and the Dynamics of Indian and Jesuit Relations in Northwestern New Spain, 1520–1660," in *Ejidos and Regions of Refuge in Northwestern Mexico*, ed. N. Ross Crumrine and Phil C. Weigand (Tucson: University of Arizona Press, 1987), 85–94; Ramenofsky, *Vectors of Death*; Henry F. Dobyns, "Native Historic Epidemiology in the Greater Southwest," *American Anthropologist* 91 (1989): 171–74; Daniel T. Reff, "Disease Episodes and the Historical Record: A Reply to Dobyns," *American Anthropologist* 91 (1989): 174–75; Thomas L. Pearcy, "The Control of Smallpox in New Spain's Northern Borderlands," *Journal of the West* 29, No. 3 (July 1990): 90–98; Daniel T. Reff, *Disease, Depopulation, and Culture Change in Northwestern New Spain, 1518–1764* (Salt Lake City: University of Utah Press, 1991); Ann L. W. Stodder and Debra L. Martin, "Health and Disease in the Southwest before and after Spanish Contact," in *Disease and Demography in the Americas*, 55–73; Henry F. Dobyns, "Native American Trade Centers as Contagious Disease Foci," in *ibid.*, 215–22; Steadman Upham, "Population and Spanish Contact in the Southwest," in *ibid.*, 223–35; Daniel T. Reff, "Contact Shock in Northwestern New Spain, 1518–1764," in *ibid.*, 265–76; Ann M. Palkovich, "Historic Epidemics of the American Pueblos," in *In the Wake of Contact*, 87–95; Ann L. W. Stodder,

"Bioarchaeological Investigations of Protohistoric Pueblo Health and Demography," in *ibid.*, 97–107.

21. Roy M. Anderson and Robert M. May, "Population Biology of Infectious Diseases: Parts I–II," *Nature* 280 (1979): 361–67, 455–61; Roy M. Anderson and Robert M. May, "Directly Transmitted Infectious Diseases: Control By Vaccination," *Science* 215 (1982): 1053–60; Roy M. Anderson and Robert M. May, *Infectious Diseases of Humans: Dynamics and Control* (Oxford: Oxford University Press, 1992).
22. The native people of this region are the Northern Athapaskan Sahtúot'ine, Denesóline, Tlicho, Dunne-za, Gwich'in, K'áshot'ine, Shíhta Got'ine, Deh Gáh Got'ine, and T'atsaot'ine. The analysis that follows is adapted from Shepard Krech III, "Historic Demography of Native Americans: Some Cautionary Thoughts," Seminar in Atlantic Culture and History, Johns Hopkins University, February 1985; Shepard Krech III, "The Influence of Disease and the Fur Trade on Arctic Drainage Lowlands Dene, 1800–1850," *Journal of Anthropological Research* 39 (1983): 123–46 (Table 3.1 adapted from this article).
23. Hugh Paul, *The Control of Diseases* (Baltimore: The Williams & Wilkins Company, 1964), 159–77ff.; Z. Deutschmann, "The Ecology of Smallpox," in *Studies in Disease Ecology*, ed. Jacques M. May (New York: Hafner Publishing Co., 1961), 1–13; John E. Gordon, *Control of Communicable Diseases in Man* (New York: American Public Health Association, 1965), 215–19; D. A. J. Tyrrell, "Aspects of Infection in Isolated Communities," in *Health and Disease in Tribal Societies* (Amsterdam: Elsevier, 1977), 137–53.
24. Jacques M. May, *The Ecology of Human Disease* (New York: MD Publications, 1958), 152–70, 189–215; Paul, *The Control of Diseases*, 293–301; Gordon, "Amebiasis," in *Control of Communicable Diseases in Man*, 24–26; James V. Neel, "Infectious Disease among Amerindians," *Medical Anthropology* 6 (1982): 47–54.
25. Gordon, *Control of Communicable Diseases in Man*, 87–90, 257–60; Paul, *The Control of Diseases*, 43–60, 269–92; May, *Ecology of Human Diseases*, 171–88; M. Burnet and D. O. White, *The Natural History of Infectious Disease* (Cambridge: Cambridge University Press, 1972), 193–201; Ann Carmichael, "Infection, Hidden Hunger, and History," *Journal of Interdisciplinary History* 14, No. 2 (1983): 249–264.
26. Anna C. Gelman, "The Ecology of Tularemia," in *Studies in Disease Ecology*, 89–112 ("sudden and prostrating . . ."); Gordon, *Control of Communicable Diseases in Man*, 256–57. In an earlier publication (Shepard Krech III, "On the Aboriginal Population of the Kutchin," *Arctic Anthropology* 15, No. 1 [1978]: 89–104), I speculated that the 1825 epidemic was meningococcal meningitis.
27. Paul, *The Control of Diseases*, 104–16; Gordon, *Control of Communicable Diseases in Man*, 264–65.
28. As much as one-fifth of mortality in measles may depend on genetically determined susceptibility. Fatality rates in specific measles epidemics were 9 percent in lowland South America villages receiving medical care (or not) and 27 percent in Fiji in 1875. See B. G. Corney, "The Behavior of Certain Epidemic Diseases in Natives of Polynesia, with Especial Reference to the Fiji Islands," *Epidemiological Society of London* 3 (1884): 76–95; J. F. Marchand, "Tribal Epidemics in the Yukon," *American Medical Association Journal* 123 (1943): 1019–20; A. F. W. Peart and F. P. Nagler, "Measles in the Canadian Arctic, 1952," *Canadian Journal of Public Health* 54 (1954): 146–56; J. A. Hildes, "Health Problems in the Arctic," *Canadian Medical Association Journal* 83 (1960): 1255–56; Paul, *The Control of Diseases*, 92–103; Gordon, *Control of Communicable Diseases in Man*, 147–49; James V. Neel et al., "Notes on the Effect of Measles and Measles Vaccine in a Virgin-Soil Population of

South American Indians," *American Journal of Epidemiology* 91 (1970): 418–29; Francis Black et al., "Evidence for Persistence of Infectious Agents in Isolated Human Populations," *American Journal of Epidemiology* 100 (1974): 230–50; Francis Black, "Measles," in *Viral Infections of Humans: Epidemiology and Control*, ed. Alfred S. Evans (New York: Plenum Press, 1976), 297–316; Francis Black et al., "Epidemiology of Infectious Disease: The Example of Measles," in *Health and Disease in Tribal Societies*, 115–35; David Morley, "Severe Measles," in *Changing Disease Patterns and Human Behavior*, ed. N. F. Stanley and R. A. Joske (New York: Academic Press, 1980), 115–28; Francis Black et al., "Genetic Correlates of Enhanced Measles Susceptibility in Amazon Indian," *Medical Anthropology* 6 (1982): 37–45; Neel, "Infectious Disease among Amerindians"; Robert J. Wolfe, "Alaska's Great Sickness, 1900: An Epidemic of Measles and Influenza in a Virgin Soil Population," *Proceedings of the American Philosophical Society* 126, No. 2 (1982): 91–121.

29. Ann Carmichael, "Infection, Hidden Hunger, and History," *Journal of Interdisciplinary History* 14, No. 2 (1983): 249–64; Nevin Scrimshaw, "Value of Contemporary Food and Nutrition Studies for Historians," *Journal of Interdisciplinary History* 14, No. 2 (1983): 529–34.

30. Shepard Krech III, "Disease, Starvation, and Northern Athapaskan Social Organization," *American Ethnologist* 5 (1978): 710–32; June Helm, "Female Infanticide, European Diseases, and Population Levels among the Mackenzie Dene," *American Ethnologist* 7 (1980): 259–85; Krech, "The Influence of Disease and the Fur Trade on Arctic Drainage Lowlands Dene, 1800–1850."

31. The antigens in the influenza A complex drift, which allows the development of new strains every several years, and shift, which results in a major change in antigenic profile—enabling the virus to "circumvent the protective effects of a patient's immune response." Influenza types B and C drift but do not shift (hence are less virulent). Today epidemiologists tend to classify the constantly evolving viral strains according to the types of hemagglutinin (H) and neuraminidase (N) antigens. E. D. Kilbourne, "The Influenza Viruses and Influenza—An Introduction," in *The Influenza Viruses and Influenza*, ed. E. D. Kilbourne (New York: Academic Press, 1975), 1–14; R. Gordon Douglas, "Influenza in Man," in *ibid.*, 395–447; E. D. Kilbourne, "Epidemiology of Influenza," in *ibid.*, 483–538; J. S. Mackenzie, "Possible Future Changes in the Epidemiology and Pathogenesis of Human Influenza A Virus Infections," in *Changing Disease Patterns and Human Behavior*, 129–49; Peter Palese and James F. Young, "Variation of Influenza A, B, and C Viruses," *Science* 215 (1982): 1468–74, p. 1468 ("circumvent the protective effects . . ."); Anderson and May, *Infectious Diseases of Humans*, 618–19. In 1928, influenza (A?) brought down the Mackenzie River by steamer spread rapidly to Indians, who were cared for by missionaries but went outside to convalesce and promptly caught chills that turned to pneumonia, from which many died in a few hours. In all, 1 in 10 perished. Influenza types B and C can be difficult to diagnose. In the 20th-century north, health workers identified influenza clinically in ailing people yet could not always confirm its presence in viral antibodies; and they failed to identify anything amiss clinically in 1 of every 3 individuals with influenza B in their antibodies. J. A. Hildes et al., "Surveys of Respiratory Virus Antibodies in an Arctic Indian Population," *Canadian Medical Association Journal* 93 (1965): 1015–18 ("something like influenza"); R. Ruggles Gates, "Blood Groups of Canadian Indians and Eskimos," *American Journal of Physical Anthropology* 12 (1929): 475–85.

32. One reason for variation is that people shed viruses at different rates over time, and

the course of influenza in a community depends on differences between shedders and nonshedders (Tyrrell, "Aspects of Infection in Isolated Communities," 145 ["not easy to predict"]). In the 18th-century epidemics of plague in France, deaths were distributed bimodally: In many towns, many died and in many other towns, few died. In 18th- to 19th-century Sweden, smallpox, dysentery, and cholera epidemics spread unevenly, concentrated in some locales but not in others. J.-N. Biraben, "Certain Demographic Characteristics of the Plague Epidemic in France, 1720–22," *Daedalus* 97 (1968): 536–45; A. Norberg et al., "Regional and Local Variations of Mortality in Sweden 1750–1900," in *The Fifth Scandinavian Demographic Symposium* (Oslo: The Scandinavian Demographic Society, 1979), 55–73.

33. For criticism of Dobyns's methodology in *Their Number Become Thinned* and other reactions, see William Cronon, "Review of *Their Number Become Thinned*," *Journal of American History* 71, No. 2 (1984): 374–75; Alfred Crosby, "Review of *Their Number Become Thinned*," *Pacific Historical Review* 53, No. 2 (1984): 219–20; James H. Merrell, "Playing the Indian Numbers Game," *Reviews in American History* 12 (1984): 354–58; Daniel K. Richter, "Review of *Their Number Become Thinned*," *William and Mary Quarterly* 41 (1984): 649–53; Russell Thornton, "But How Thick Were They?," *Contemporary Sociology* 13 (1984): 149–50; William C. Sturtevant, "Review of *Their Number Become Thinned*," *American Historical Review* 89 (1984): 1380–81; Douglas Ubelaker, "Review of *Their Number Become Thinned*," *Ethnohistory* 31 (1984): 303–5; David Henige, "Primary Source by Primary Source? On the Role of Epidemics in New World Depopulation," *Ethnohistory* 33 (1986): 293–312; Henige, "If Pigs Could Fly," 701–20; Snow and Lanphear, "European Contact and Indian Depopulation in the Northeast"; Dobyns, "More Methodological Perspectives on Historical Demography"; Snow and Lanphear "'More Methodological Perspectives'"; David Henige, "On the Current Devaluation of the Notion of Evidence: A Rejoinder to Dobyns," *Ethnohistory* 36 (1989): 304–7; Roberts, "Disease and Death in the New World"; David Henige, "Their Numbers Become Thick: Native American Historical Demography as Expiation," in *The Invented Indian: Cultural Fictions and Government Policies*, ed. James Clifton (New Brunswick: Transaction Publishers, 1990), 169–91; Henige, *Numbers from Nowhere*.

34. Dobyns's work rests methodologically on the analyses of Scott F. Cook and Woodrow W. Borah: Cook, *The Extent and Significance of Disease among the Indians of Baja California, 1697–1773* (Berkeley: University of California Press, 1937); Cook, *The Conflict between the California Indian and White Civilization. I–IV* (Berkeley: University of California Press, 1943); Borah and Cook, *The Population of Central Mexico in 1548* (Berkeley: University of California Press, 1960); Cook and Borah, *The Indian Population of Central Mexico, 1531–1610* (Berkeley: University of California Press, 1960); Borah and Cook, *The Aboriginal Population of Central Mexico on the Eve of the Spanish Contact* (Berkeley: University of California Press, 1963); Cook and Borah, *Essays in Population History: Mexico and the Caribbean*, Volume I (Berkeley: University of California Press, 1971); Cook, "The Significance of Disease in the Extinction of the New England Indians," *Human Biology* 45 (1973): 485–508; Cook and Borah, *Essays in Population History: Mexico and the Caribbean*, Volume II (Berkeley: University of California Press, 1974). Many have voiced skepticism over this work, especially the estimate of over 25 million people (2,000–3,000 people/sq mi) in Central Mexico in 1518, a population size regained only in 1969 following 5 decades of extraordinary growth: David Henige, "On the Contact Population of Hispaniola: History as Higher Mathematics," *Hispanic American Historical Review* 58 (1978): 217–37; Rudolph A. Zambardino, "Critique

of David Henige's 'On the Contact Population of Hispaniola: History as Higher Mathematics'," *Hispanic American Historical Review* 58 (1978): 700–708; Henige, "Reply," *Hispanic American Historical Review* 58 (1978): 709–12; Zambardino, "Mexico's Population in the Sixteenth Century: Demographic Anomaly or Mathematical Illusion?," *Journal of Interdisciplinary History* 11 (1980): 1–27; William T. Sanders, "The Population of the Central Mexican Symbiotic Region, the Basin of Mexico, and the Teotihuacán Valley in the Sixteenth Century," in *The Native Population of the Americas in 1492*, 85–150; Henige, *Numbers from Nowhere.*

35. Dobyns's method of estimating population size depends on the use of multipliers that result from separate estimations, and the errors inherent in them compound each other. The historian James Merrell derides the piling of "guess upon assumption on top of inference to construct a towering but tottering mathematical monument" and suggests that to go along with this "numbers game" one would need to "check one's ordinary critical faculties at the door." Even Alfred Crosby, a staunch supporter of high-end estimates, in frustration voiced skepticism that the hemispheric estimate will ever "be accurate to a tolerance of plus or minus 30–50 percent!" Merrell, "Playing the Indian Numbers Game," 355, 356; Alfred Crosby, "Summary on Population Size before and after Contact," in *Disease and Demography in the Americas*, 277–78, p. 278; Henige, *Numbers from Nowhere.*
36. On the behavior of populations following (or between) epidemics, see J.-N. Biraben, "Certain Demographic Characteristics"; Otto Andersen, "The Development in Danish Mortality 1735–1850," in *The Fifth Scandinavian Demographic Symposium*, 9–21; J.-N. Biraben, "Les Consequences Démographiques des Crises de Mortalité," in *The Great Mortalities: Methodological Studies of Demographic Crises in the Past*, ed. H. Charbonneau and A. Larose (Liege: Ordina, 1980), 345–56; Solvi Sogner, "Nature and Dynamics of Crises," in *ibid.*, 311–31; Fernand Braudel, *The Structures of Everyday Life* (New York: Harper & Row, 1981); Noble David Cook, "Eighteenth Century Population Change in Andean Peru," in *Studies in Spanish American Population History*, ed. David J. Robinson (Boulder: Westview Press, 1981); Noble David Cook, *The People of the Colca Valley: A Population Study* (Boulder: Westview Press, 1982); Russell Thornton, Tim Miller, and Jonathan Warren, "American Indian Population Recovery following Smallpox Epidemics," *American Anthropologist* 93 (1991): 28–45.
37. In the text and Table 3.2, California, Northwest Coast, Southwest, etc., refer to anthropological culture areas, that is, regions in which people are grouped because of shared subsistence and other superficial characteristics; culture areas correspond neatly to major biomes defined by dominant plants and animals. Table 3.2 is adapted from Ubelaker ("North American Indian Population Size," 291), whose estimate of 1,894,000 is the only one accompanied by substantial detail on all culture areas. Ubelaker's culture area total of 6.7 million sq mi is less than the estimated 7.5 million sq mi for the continental Canada and United States in other sources (e.g., *National Geographic Atlas of the World*, fifth edition [Washington, DC: National Geographic Society, 1981]; Colin McEvedy and Richard Jones, *Atlas of World Population History* [New York: Facts on File, 1978]).
38. For 4, 7, and 12 million people (the remaining three estimates), the average continental density would be 60, 105, and 179 people/100 sq mi, and the range by culture area would be 10–386, 18–689, and 30–1,164 people/100 sq mi, respectively. For New England regional differences, see Shepard Krech III, "Native Americans and the Environment," *Encyclopedia of New England Culture*, ed. Burt Feintuch and David Watters (New Haven: Yale University Press, in press).

39. These figures suggest crudely that the press of population was 30 to 45 times greater in Europe than in North America. Paul Demeny, "Population," in *The Earth as Transformed by Human Action: Global and Regional Changes in the Biosphere over the Past 300 Years,* ed. B. L. Turner et al. (Cambridge: Cambridge University Press, 1990), 41–54.
40. Densities are far better known for nations than for regions. In 1600, the densities in Europe ranged from 390 people/100 sq mi in Scandinavia and Finland to over 10,400 people/100 sq mi in the Netherlands and Italy; the average was 7,200–9,000 people/100 sq mi. In France and England they were as follows:

France and England, 1600-1850: Population Size and Density (Rounded).

	POPULATION SIZE	DENSITY (PEOPLE/ 100 SQ MI)
England 1600	4,100,000	8,800
England 1750	5,800,000	12,200
England 1850	16,000,000	34,400
France 1600	19,000,000	9,000
France 1750	25,000,000	11,900
France 1850	35,000,000	16,600

McEvedy and Jones, *Atlas of World Population History*; Fernand Braudel, *Civilization and Capitalism, 15th–18th Century. Volume I. The Structures of Everyday Life: The Limits of the Possible* (New York: Harper & Row, 1981), 51–103; Michael W. Flinn, *The European Demographic System, 1500–1820* (Baltimore: Johns Hopkins University Press, 1981); Michael Anderson, *Population Change in North-Western Europe, 1750–1850* (London: Macmillan, 1988); R. A. Houston, *The Population History of Britain and Ireland 1500–1750* (Cambridge: Cambridge University Press, 1992); Massimo Livi-Bacci, *A Concise History of World Population,* second edition (Malden, MA: Blackwell, 1997), 104–5; also Woodrow Borah, "The Mixing of Populations," in *First Images of America: The Impact of the New World on the Old*, 2 volumes, ed. Fredi Chiappelli (Berkeley: University of California Press, 1976), Volume 2, 707–22.
41. The range, 15–900, is from 8,800 people/100 sq mi compared to 689 people/100 sq mi, and 9,000 people/100 sq mi versus 10 people/100 sq mi.
42. Archie Clow, "The Influence of Technology on Environment," in *Ecology, The Shaping Inquiry: A Course Given at the Institute of Contemporary Arts,* ed. Jonathan Benthall (London: Longman, 1972), 50–80; Keith Thomas, *Man and the Natural World: A History of the Modern Sensibility* (New York: Pantheon Books, 1983), 242–302; Carolyn Merchant, *The Death of Nature: Women, Ecology and the Scientific Revolution* (New York: Harper & Row, 1983), 42–68; William Brandon, *New Worlds for Old* (Athens: University of Ohio Press, 1986), 74–81; Michael Williams, "Forests," in *The Earth as Transformed by Human Action,* 179–201; Clive Ponting, *A Green History of the World: The Environment and the Collapse of Great Civilizations* (New York: Penguin, 1991), 161–65.
43. Jim Potter, "The Growth of Population in America, 1700–1860," in *Population in History: Essays in Historical Demography*, ed. D. V. Glass and D. E. C. Eversley (Chicago: Aldine Publishing Company, 1965), 631–88; Daniel Scott Smith, "The Demographic History of Colonial New England," *Journal of Economic History* 1 (1972): 165–83; Richard A. Easterlin, "Population Issues in American Economic History: A Survey and Critique," in *Recent Developments in the Study of Business*

and Economic History: Essays in Memory of Herman E. Krooss, ed. Robert E. Gallman (Greenwich, CT: JAI Press, 1977), 131–58; Jim Potter, "Demographic Development and Family Structure," in *Colonial British America: Essays in the New History of the Early Modern Era*, ed. Jack P. Greene and J. R. Pole (Baltimore: Johns Hopkins University Press, 1984), 123–56; Peter H. Wood, "The Changing Population of the Colonial South: An Overview by Race and Region, 1685–1790," in *Powhatan's Mantle: Indians in the Colonial Southeast*, ed. Peter H. Wood, Gregory A. Waselkov, and M. Thomas Hatley (Lincoln: University of Nebraska Press, 1989); Demeny, "Population"; Ubelaker, "North American Indian Population Size, A.D. 1500 to 1985."

44. Williams, "Forests"; Robert L. Peters and Thomas E. Lovejoy, "Terrestrial Fauna," in *The Earth as Transformed by Human Action*, 353–69; Cronon, *Changes in the Land*; Timothy Silver, *New Face on the Countryside: Indians, Colonists and Slaves in South Atlantic Forests, 1500–1800* (Cambridge: Cambridge University Press, 1990); Carolyn Merchant, *Ecological Revolutions: Nature, Gender, and Science in New England* (Chapel Hill: University of North Carolina Press, 1989).
45. Robert W. Kates, B. L. Turner II, and William C. Clark, "The Great Transformation," in *The Earth as Transformed by Human Action*, 1–17, pp. 2, 11; Peters and Lovejoy ("Terrestrial Fauna," 359) stated that "where people are, animals generally are not," but given suitable habitats and protection, mammals like deer and beaver can reestablish themselves.
46. Daniel R. Headrick, "Technological Change," in *The Earth as Transformed by Human Action*, 55–67; John W. Bennett and Kenneth A. Dahlberg, "Institutions, Social Organization, and Cultural Values," in *ibid.*, 69–86; David Lowenthal, "Awareness of Human Impacts: Changing Attitudes and Emphases," in *ibid.*, 121–35; Carolyn Merchant, "The Realm of Social Relations: Production, Reproduction, and Gender in Environmental Transformations," in *ibid.*, 673–84; B. L. Turner II and William B. Meyer, "Environmental Change: The Human Factor," in *Humans as Components of Ecosystems*, 40–50 (subtle effects); Andrew P. Vayda, "Ecosystems and Human Actions," in *ibid.*, 61–71 (subtle and unintended human actions); Stephen Boyden, "The Human Component of Ecosystems," in *ibid.*, 72–77; Christine Padoch, "Part II: A Human Ecologist's Perspective," in *ibid.*, 303–5 ("poor predictor"); Michael Painter and William H. Durham, eds., *The Social Causes of Environmental Destruction in Latin America* (Ann Arbor: University of Michigan Press, 1995); William H. Durham, "Political Ecology and Environmental Destruction in Latin America," in *ibid.*, 249–64; Thomas C. Patterson, "Toward a Properly Historical Ecology," in *Historical Ecology: Cultural Knowledge and Changing Landscapes*, ed. Carole Crumley (Santa Fe: School of American Research Press, 1994), 223–41; Philip Sarre and John Blunden, eds., *An Overcrowded World?* (New York: Oxford University Press, 1995), 2–141; Livi-Bacci, *A Concise History of World Population*, 206–17.
47. William L. Thomas, Jr., ed., *Man's Role in Changing the Face of the Earth* (Chicago: University of Chicago Press, 1956), passim; Karl J. Narr, "Early Food-producing Populations," in *ibid.*, 134–51; Carl O. Sauer, "The Agency of Man on the Earth," in *ibid.*, 49–69; Paul B. Sears, "The Processes of Environmental Change by Man," in *ibid.*, 471–84; "Symposium Discussion: Retrospect," in *ibid.*, 401–48; C. D. Darlington, "The Impact of Man on Nature," in *Ecology, The Shaping Enquiry*, 36–49; Demeny, "Population"; Bennett and Dahlberg, "Institutions, Social Organization, and Cultural Values," 69–86; Headrick, "Technological Change," 55–67; Boyden, "The Human Component of Ecosystems"; Lowenthal, "Awareness

of Human Impacts: Changing Attitudes and Emphases," 121–35; Turner and Meyer, "Environmental Change: The Human Factor."

48. George Perkins Marsh, *Man and Nature; Or, Physical Geography as Modified by Human Action*, ed. David Lowenthal (Cambridge: Belknap Press of Harvard University Press, 1965); H. C. Darby, "The Clearing of the Woodland in Europe," in *Man's Role in Changing the Face of the Earth*, ed. William L. Thomas, Jr. (Chicago: University of Chicago Press, 1956), 183–216; I. G. Simmons, *Changing the Face of the Earth: Culture, Environment, History* (Oxford: Basil Blackwell, 1989), 29–195; Andrew Goudie, *The Human Impact on the Natural Environment* (Cambridge, MA: The MIT Press, 1990), 37–47; Peters and Lovejoy, "Terrestrial Fauna," 353–69, p. 363 ("extreme"); Williams, "Forests"; Turner and Meyer, "Environmental Change: The Human Factor"; Emilio Moran, "Nurturing the Forest: Strategies of Native Amazonians," in *Redefining Nature: Ecology, Culture and Domestication* (Oxford: Berg, 1996), 531–56, p. 549 ("notable transformations"); Sarre and Bunden, *An Overcrowded World?*, 26–28.
49. Daniel Hillel, *Out of the Earth: Civilization and the Life of the Soil* (Berkeley: University of California Press, 1991), 60, 69ff., and passim.
50. In 20th-century North America the population grew by almost 200 million; in May 1998, nearly 270 million people lived in the United States alone. In 1990 (see following table), 12 million people (the highest figure accepted here for aboriginal North America) lived in Florida or Pennsylvania, 7 million (the higher of two mid-range estimates) in New Jersey or New York City, 4 million (the lower of the two) in Alabama, and 2 million in Arkansas or Dade County, Florida. Alaska is the only state whose density falls into the range of 30–179 people/100 sq mi for populations of 2–12 million in aboriginal North America; the next least dense, Wyoming, is well beyond range. In 1990, comparable densities to AD 1500 were found only in specific census areas in Alaska, Montana, Nevada, Texas, Utah, and other western states. For 1990 population figures (all figures rounded), see
http://www.census.gov/population/censusdata/90den_stco.txt;
http://www.census.gov/population/censusdata/c1008090.txt.

United States, 1990: Population Size and Density of Selected Areas

CENSUS AREA	POPULATION	DENSITY (PEOPLE/ 100 SQ MI)
New Jersey	7,731,000	104,200
Dade County, FL	1,937,000	99,600
New York	17,990,000	38,100
Pennsylvania	11,882,000	26,510
Florida	12,938,000	23,900
Alabama	4,041,000	7,960
United States (continental)	247,601,000	6,900
Arkansas	2,351,000	4,510
Wyoming	454,000	470
Alaska	500,000	100
Garfield County, UT	3,980	80
Eureka County, NV	1,547	40
Bethel Census Area, AK	13,656	30

Chapter Four: Fire

1. Stephen J. Pyne's *Fire in America: A Cultural History of Wildland and Rural Fire* (Princeton: Princeton University Press, 1982), 72–83 and passim, and Michael Williams's *Americans & Their Forests: A Historical Geography* (Cambridge: Cambridge University Press, 1989), 22–49 and passim, are valuable works on the subject of fire. Stephen J. Pyne, "Indian Fires," *Natural History* 92 (February 1983): 6–11; David Pietersz. de Vries, *Voyages from Holland to America A.D. 1632–1644*, trans. Henry C. Murphy (New York, 1853), 31 ("smelt before it is seen"); Julian Harris Salomon, "Indians That Set the Woods on Fire," *Conservationist* 38 (March–April, 1984): 34–39; Timothy Silver, *New Face on the Countryside: Indians, Colonists and Slaves in South Atlantic Forests, 1500–1800* (Cambridge: Cambridge University Press, 1990), 59 (in 1524 off Carolina, Verrazzano smelled "the sweet fragrance [of smoke] a hundred leagues away" and saw Indians burning); Henry Wadsworth Longfellow, *The Song of Hiawatha* (New York: Grosset and Dunlap, n.d.), 9, 41, 131, 139, 140, 194, 255, 274, 275 ("interminable . . . gloomy" are his); Francis Parkman, *France and England in North America* (Boston: Little, Brown and Company, 1909), 179 ("shadows and gloom"); John Josselyn, *New England Rarities Discovered* (London: Printed for G. Widdowes, 1672), 4 ("infinite thick woods"); Gordon M. Day, "The Indian as an Ecological Factor in the Northeastern Forest," *Ecology* 34 (1953): 329–46; Roderick Nash, "Sorry, Bambi, but Man Must Enter the Forest: Perspectives on the Old Wilderness and the New," in *Proceedings—Symposium and Workshop on Wilderness Fire, Missoula, Montana, November 15–18, 1983*, General Technical Report INT-182 (Ogden, UT: Intermountain Forest and Range Experiment Station, Forest Service, U.S. Department of Agriculture, 1985), 264–68.
2. Omer Stewart was an early proponent of a significant Indian role in burning: Omer C. Stewart, "Burning and Natural Vegetation in the United States," *Geographical Review* 41 (1951): 317–20; "Forest Fires with a Purpose," *Southwestern Lore* 20 (1954): 42–46; "Why Were the Prairies Treeless?," *Southwestern Lore* 20 (1954): 59–64; "The Forgotten Side of Ethnogeography," in *Method and Perspective in Anthropology: Papers in Honor of Wilson D. Wallis*, ed. Robert F. Spencer (Minneapolis: University of Minnesota Press, 1954), 221–311; "Forest and Grass Burning in the Mountain West," *Southwestern Lore* 21 (June 1955): 5–9; "Fire as the First Great Force Employed by Man," in *Man's Role in Changing the Face of the Earth*, ed. William L. Thomas, Jr. (Chicago: University of Chicago Press, 1956), 115–33; "Barriers to Understanding the Influence of Use of Fire by Aborigines on Vegetation," in *Proceedings of the 2nd Annual Tall Timbers Fire Ecology Conference—March 14–15, 1963* (Tallahassee: Tall Timbers Research Station, 1963), 117–26.
3. Hu Maxwell, "The Use and Abuse of Forests by the Virginia Indians," *William and Mary Quarterly* 19 (1910): 73–103, pp. 86, 88 ("destructive," "savage"); Day, "The Indian as an Ecological Factor"; Stewart, "Forest Fires with a Purpose," 42–43 (Indians as conservationists); Clarence K. Collins, "Indian Firefighters of the Southwest," *Journal of Forestry* 60 (February 1962): 87–91 ("the one thing . . ."); Stewart, "Barriers to Understanding the Influence of Use of Fire by Aborigines on Vegetation," 119 ("small campfires"); Henry T. Lewis, *Patterns of Indian Burning in California: Ecology and Ethnohistory*, Ballena Press Anthropological Papers No. 1 (Ramona, CA: Ballena Press, 1973); L. T. Burcham, "Fire and Chaparral before European Settlement," in *Symposium on Living with the Chaparral Proceedings*, ed.

Murray Rosenthal (San Francisco: Sierra Club, 1974), 101–20, p. 115 ("the great master-scourge"); Henry T. Lewis, "Maskuta: The Ecology of Indian Fires in Northern Alberta," *Western Canadian Journal of Anthropology* 7, No. 1 (1977): 15–52; Pyne, *Fire in America*, 72–83, 176–80 (Smokey); Stephen J. Pyne, "Vestal Fires and Virgin Lands: A Historical Perspective on Fire and Wilderness," in *Proceedings—Symposium and Workshop on Wilderness Fire*, 254–62; Nash, "Sorry, Bambi, but Man Must Enter the Forest."

4. Early-16th-century southeastern Texas Indians and many Subarctic Indians deployed fire to keep insects away (Stewart, "Burning and Natural Vegetation"; Harold J. Lutz, *Aboriginal Man and White Man as Historical Causes of Fires in the Boreal Forest, with Particular Reference to Alaska*, Yale University, School of Forestry Bulletin No. 65 [New Haven: Yale University, 1959], 18–20).
5. William Wood, *New England's Prospect*, ed. Alden T. Vaughan (Amherst: University of Massachusetts Press, 1993), 38; Edward Johnson, *Johnson's Wonder-Working Providence 1628–1651*, ed. J. Franklin Jameson (New York: Charles Scribner's Sons, 1910), 85; Day, "The Indian as an Ecological Factor," 335; Stewart, "Fire as the First Great Force Employed by Man," 121; Daniel Q. Thompson and Ralph H. Smith, "The Forest Primeval in the Northeast—A Great Myth," in *Proceedings of the Tall Timbers Fire Ecology Conference* 10 (1970): 255–65; Calvin Martin, "Fire and Forest Structure in the Aboriginal Eastern Forest," *Indian Historian* 6, No. 4 (1973): 38–42, 54; Conrad Taylor Moore, *Man and Fire in the Central North American Grassland 1535–1890: A Documentary Historical Geography*, Ph.D. dissertation (University of California-Los Angeles, 1972), 75–76.
6. Maxwell, "The Use and Abuse of Forests," 89; Emma Helen Blair, *The Indian Tribes of the Upper Mississippi Valley and Region of the Great Lakes, as described by Nicolas Perrot . . .* , Volumes I–II (Cleveland: Arthur H. Clark Company, 1911), Volume I, 120, 122; Donald J. Lehmer, "The Plains Bison Hunt—Prehistoric and Historic," *Plains Anthropologist* 8, No. 22 (1963): 211–17 (Perrot); Henry R. Schoolcraft, *A Narrative Journal of Travel through the Northwestern Regions of the United States . . . in the Year 1820*, ed. Mentor L. Williams (East Lansing: Michigan State College Press, 1953), 185; Moore, *Man and Fire*, 20–21 (Schoolcraft); Lewis, *Patterns of Indian Burning in California*, 55; Emily W. B. Russell, "Indian-Set Fires in the Forests of the Northeastern United States," *Ecology* 64 (1983): 78–88.
7. Mark Catesby, *The Natural History of Carolina, Florida, and the Bahama Islands*, Volumes I–II (London, 1771), Volume II, xii; Moore, *Man and Fire*, 22, 67–69; Charles F. Cooper, "Changes in Vegetation, Structure, and Growth of Southwestern Pine Forests since White Settlement," *Ecological Monographs* 30, No. 2 (1960): 129–64, p. 138; J. G. Nelson and R. E. England, "Some Comments on the Causes and Effects of Fire in the Northern Grasslands Area of Canada and the Nearby United States, 1750–1900," in *Proceedings of the 1977 Rangeland Management and Fire Symposium*, prepared by Connie M. Bourassa and Arthur P. Brackebusch (Missoula: University of Montana School of Forestry, 1978), 39–47.
8. Richard Irving Dodge, *The Plains of the Great West and Their Inhabitants Being a Description of the Plains, Game, Indians, &c. of the Great North American Desert* (New York: G. P. Putnam's Sons, 1877), 29 (several "sagacious" men); Moore, *Man and Fire*, 22–23; Lewis, *Patterns of Indian Burning in California*, 73.
9. Frank Bergon, ed., *The Journals of Lewis and Clark* (New York: Penguin Books, 1989), 95; [John Palliser, James Hector, and others], *The Journals, Detailed Reports, and Observations Relative to the Exploration, by Captain Palliser, of That Portion of British America . . . during the Years 1857, 1858, 1859, and 1860* (London: Eyre and

Spottiswoode, 1863), 54; Joel A. Allen, *The American Bisons, Living and Extinct* (New York: Arno Press, 1974 [orig. 1876]), 202; Clark Wissler, "Material Culture of the Blackfoot Indians," *Anthropological Papers of the American Museum of Natural History*, Volume V, Part 1 (New York: American Museum of Natural History, 1910), 50; Joe Ben Wheat, "The Olsen-Chubbuck Site: A Paleo-Indian Bison Kill," *American Antiquity* 37 (1972): 1–169, p. 93; Moore, *Man and Fire*, 24–25, 74–75, 91; David A. Dary, *The Buffalo Book: The Full Saga of the American Animal* (Chicago: The Swallow Press, [1974]), 39–40; Nelson and England, "Some Comments on the Causes and Effects of Fire"; Eleanor Verbicky-Todd, *Communal Buffalo Hunting among the Plains Indians: An Ethnographic and Historic Review* (Alberta: Archaeological Survey of Alberta, 1984), 156.

10. Lewis, *Patterns of Indian Burning in California*, 66–69.
11. Maxwell, "The Use and Abuse of Forests."
12. Stewart, "Fire as the First Great Force," 120; Stewart, "Forest and Grass Burning in the Mountain West"; Lewis, *Patterns of Indian Burning in California*, 41, 50–53, 61–62; Harold Weaver, "Effects of Fire on Temperate Forests: Western United States," in *Fire and Ecosystems*, ed. T. T. Kozlowski and C. E. Ahlgren (New York: Academic Press, 1974), 279–319; Richard White, "Indian Land Use and Environmental Change: Island County, Washington, A Case Study," *Arizona and the West* 17, No. 4 (1975): 327–38; Helen H. Norton, "The Association between Anthropogenic Prairies and Important Food Plants in Western Washington," *Northwest Anthropological Research Notes* 13 (1979): 175–200. Tarweed is *Madia sativa.*
13. Moore, *Man and Fire*, 24, 75.
14. Day, "The Indian as an Ecological Factor"; Maxwell, "The Use and Abuse of Forests"; Moore, *Man and Fire*, 56.
15. Moore, *Man and Fire*, 18 (Murray), 16–96 passim; Mavis A. Loscheider, "Use of Fire in Interethnic and Intraethnic Relations on the Northern Plains," *Western Canadian Journal of Anthropology* 7, No. 4 (1977): 82–96; Gregory Thomas, "Fire and the Fur Trade: The Saskatchewan District 1790–1840," *Beaver* 308 (Autumn 1977): 34–39.
16. [Palliser, Hector, and others], *The Journals, Detailed Reports, and Observations*, 57, 89; Blair, *The Indian Tribes of the Upper Mississippi Valley and Region*, 336ff. (Bacqueville de la Potherie); Moore, *Man and Fire*, 12–16, 53–54, 67, 70–72 (Flathead, Sioux); Loscheider, "Use of Fire in Interethnic and Intraethnic Relations," 89; George E. Gruell, "Indian Fires in the Interior West: A Widespread Influence," in *Proceedings—Symposium and Workshop on Wilderness Fire*, 68–74; Lutz, *Aboriginal Man and White Man*, 4–11.
17. John P. Dempsey, *New English Canaan by Thomas Morton of "Merrymount": A Critical Edition*, Ph.D. dissertation (Department of English, Brown University, 1998), 49–50; Maxwell, "The Use and Abuse of Forests," 88–89 (Smith).
18. Stewart, "Burning and Natural Vegetation," 319 ("almost universal"); Pyne, *Fire in America*, 72–83; Stephen F. Arno, "Ecological Effects and Management Implications of Indian Fires," in *Proceedings—Symposium and Workshop on Wilderness Fire*, 81–86; James K. Agee, *Fire Ecology of Pacific Northwest Forests* (Washington, DC: Island Press, 1993), 53–57.
19. Moore, *Man and Fire*, 111–17; Loscheider, "Use of Fire in Interethnic and Intraethnic Relations"; Lewis, *Patterns of Indian Burning in California*, 64–65 (redwood); Burcham, "Fire and Chaparral before European Settlement"; Jan Timbrook, John R. Johnson, and David D. Earle, "Vegetation Burning by the Chumash," *Journal of California and Great Basin Anthropology* 4, No. 2 (1982): 163–86.

20. Day, "The Indian as an Ecological Factor"; Maxwell, "The Use and Abuse of Forests," 94 (Beverley); Silas Little, "Effects of Fires on Temperate Forests: Northeastern United States," in *Fire and Ecosystems*, 225–50; Thompson and Smith, "The Forest Primeval"; Julia E. Hammett, "The Shapes of Adaptation: Historical Ecology of Anthropogenic Landscapes in the Southeastern United States," *Landscape Ecology* 7 (1992): 121–35; Russell, "Indian-Set Fires"; William A. Patterson III and Kenneth E. Sassaman, "Indian Fires in the Prehistory of New England," in *Holocene Human Ecology in Northeastern North America*, ed. George P. Nicholas (New York: Plenum Press, 1988), 107–35 (fire and population), p. 115 ("alluring"—Timothy Dwight, 1823).
21. C. E. Ahlgren, "Effects of Fires on Temperate Forests: North Central United States," in *Fire and Ecosystems*, 195–223; H. G. Reynolds and J. W. Bohning, "Effects of Burning on a Desert Grass-Shrub Range in Southern Arizona," *Ecology* 37 (1956): 769–77; J. F. Bendell, "Effects of Fire on Birds and Mammals," in *Fire and Ecosystems*, 73–138.
22. E. I. Kotok, "Fire, A Major Ecological Factor in the Pine Region of California," *Fifth Pacific Science Congress, Proceedings* 5 (1933): 4017–22; H. H. Biswell, "Man and Fire in Ponderosa Pine in the Sierra Nevada of California," *Sierra Club Bulletin* 44, No. 7 (1959): 44–53; Roehajat Emon Soeriaatmadja, "Fire History of the Ponderosa Pine Forests of the Warm Springs Indian Reservation, Oregon," thesis (Oregon State University, 1966); Harold Weaver, "Ecological Changes in the Ponderosa Pine Forest of the Warm Springs Indian Reservation in Oregon," *Journal of Forestry* 57 (January 1959): 15–20; Cooper, "Changes in Vegetation, Structure, and Growth of Southwestern Pine Forests," pp. 129, 137 (Powell); Lewis, *Patterns of Indian Burning in California*, 71–80, pp. 74–80; Melissa Savage, "Structural Dynamics of a Southwestern Pine Forest under Chronic Human Influence," *Annals of the Association of American Geographers* 81 (1991): 271–89.
23. Harold H. Biswell, "Effects of Fire on Chaparral," in *Fire and Ecosystems*, 321–64; Lewis, *Patterns of Indian Burning in California*, 20–31, 50–59, 82–84; William O. Wirtz II, "Chaparral Wildlife and Fire Ecology," in *Symposium on Living with the Chaparral Proceedings*, 7–18; Burcham, "Fire and Chaparral before European Settlement."
24. Kenneth H. Garren, "Effects of Fire on Vegetation of the Southeastern United States," *Botanical Review* 9 (1943): 617–54; E. V. Komarek, "Effects of Fire on Temperate Forests and Related Ecosystems: Southeastern United States," in *Fire and Ecosystems*, 251–77.
25. W. Raymond Wood and Thomas D. Thiessen, *Early Fur Trade on the Northern Plains: Canadian Traders among the Mandan and Hidatsa Indians, 1738–1818* (Norman: University of Oklahoma Press, 1985), 230; Carl O. Sauer, "Grassland Climax, Fire, and Man," *Journal of Range Management* 3 (1950): 16–21; Stewart, "Why Were the Prairies Treeless?"; Stewart, "The Forgotten Side of Ethnogeography"; Stewart, "Fire as the First Great Force Employed by Man," 125–29; Waldo R. Wedel, "The Central North American Grassland: Man-Made or Natural?," *Social Science Monographs 3* (Washington, DC: Pan American Union, 1957), 39–69; Moore, *Man and Fire*, 34–38, 82–86, 119–122; Richard J. Vogl, "Effects of Fire on Grasslands," in *Fire and Ecosystems*, 139–94; Carl O. Sauer, "Man's Dominance by Use of Fire," *Geoscience and Man* 10 (April 20, 1975): 1–13; George W. Arthur, *An Introduction to the Ecology of Early Historic Communal Bison Hunting among the Northern Plains Indians* (Ottawa: National Museums of Canada, 1975), 10–30; George E. Gruell, "Fire on the Early Western Landscape: An

Annotated Record of Wildland Fires 1776–1900," *Northwest Science* 59, No. 2 (1985): 97–107.

26. Vogl, "Effects of Fire on Grasslands," 152–72; Gregory Thomas, "Fire and the Fur Trade"; Nelson and England, "Some Comments on the Causes and Effects of Fire"; Gruell, "Indian Fires in the Interior West"; Kenneth F. Higgins, *Interpretation and Compendium of Historical Fire Accounts in the Northern Great Plains*, Resource Publication No. 161 (Washington, DC: U.S. Department of the Interior, Fish and Wildlife Service, 1986).
27. Carl L. Johannessen, William A. Davenport, Artimus Millet, and Steven McWilliams, "The Vegetation of the Willamette Valley," *Annals of the Association of American Geographers* 61 (1971): 286–302; Robert Boyd, "Strategies of Indian Burning in the Willamette Valley," *Canadian Journal of Anthropology/Revue Canadienne d'Anthropologie* 5, No. 1 (Fall 1986): 65–86; Agee, *Fire Ecology of Pacific Northwest Forests*, 354–58.
28. Henry T. Lewis, "Maskuta: The Ecology of Indian Fires in Northern Alberta," *Western Canadian Journal of Anthropology* 7, No. 1 (1977): 15–52; Henry T. Lewis, "Indian Fires of Spring," *Natural History* 89 (1980): 76–78, 82, 83; Henry T. Lewis, *A Time for Burning*, Occasional Publication No. 17 (Edmonton, Alberta: The Boreal Institute for Northern Studies, The University of Alberta, 1982), 50 (Dunne-za quote); Henry T. Lewis, "Fire Technology and Resource Management in Aboriginal North America and Australia," in *Resource Managers: North American and Australian Hunter-Gatherers*, ed. Nancy M. Williams and Eugene S. Hunn (Boulder: Westview Press, 1982), 45–67; Henry T. Lewis, "Why Indians Burned: Specific Versus General Reasons," in *Proceedings—Symposium and Workshop on Wilderness Fire*, 75–80; Henry T. Lewis and Theresa A. Ferguson, "Yards, Corridors, and Mosaics: How to Burn a Boreal Forest," *Human Ecology* 16 (1988): 57–77; Richard White, "Indian Land Use and Environmental Change: Island County, Washington, a Case Study," *Arizona and the West* 17, No. 4 (1975): 327–38; John Dennis and Roland H. Wauer, "Role of Indian Burning in Wilderness Fire Planning," in *Proceedings—Symposium and Workshop on Wilderness Fire*, 296–98.
29. Franz Boas, *The Religion of the Kwakiutl Indians*, Parts I–II. Columbia University Contributions to Anthropology, Volume X (New York: Columbia University Press, 1930), Part II, 203 ("I have come . . ."); Nancy J. Turner, " 'Burning Mountain Sides for Better Crops': Aboriginal Landscape Burning in British Columbia," *Archaeology in Montana* 32, No. 2 (1991): 57–73; Carling Malouf, "The Coniferous Forests and Their Uses in the Northern Rocky Mountains through 9,000 Years of Prehistory," in *Coniferous Forests of the Northern Rocky Mountains: Proceedings of the 1968 Symposium, Center for Natural Resources, September 17–20, 1968*, ed. Richard D. Taber (Missoula: University of Montana Foundation, 1969), 271–90.
30. Henry Lewis, personal communication (e-mail), March 11, 1996; Lutz, *Aboriginal Man and White Man*, 18–20; K. G. Davies, ed., *Northern Quebec and Labrador Journals and Correspondence 1819–1835*, Volume 24 (London: The Hudson's Bay Record Society, 1963), 202–4, 223.
31. Stephen W. Barrett, "Indian Fires in the Pre-settlement Forests of Western Montana," in *Proceedings of the Fire History Workshop, October 20–24, 1980, Tucson, Arizona*, technical coordinators M. A. Stokes and J. H. Dietrich. General Technical Report RM-81, Rocky Mountain Forest and Range Experiment Station (Fort Collins, CO: Forest Service, U.S. Department of Agriculture, 1981), 35–41; Stephen W. Barrett, "Indians & Fire," *Western Wildlands* 6, No. 3 (1980): 17–21; Stephen W. Barrett, "Relationship of Indian-Caused Fires to the Ecology of

Western Montana Forests," M.S. thesis (University of Montana, 1981); Stephen W. Barrett and Stephen F. Arno, "Indian Fires as an Ecological Influence in the Northern Rockies," *Journal of Forestry* 80 (1982): 647–51.

32. "Careless" must be placed in a context in which white people construed the behavior of Indians derogatorily and in opposition to their own. J. B. Tyrrell, *David Thompson's Narrative of His Explorations in Western America, 1783–1812* (Toronto: Champlain Society, 1916), 137; Glyndwr Williams, ed., *Andrew Graham's Observations on Hudson's Bay 1767–91* (London: The Hudson's Bay Record Society, 1969), 270–71; Peter Fidler, "Journal of a Journey over Land from Buckingham House to the Rocky Mountains in 1792 & 3." Accession No. 79.269/89. Provincial Archives of Alberta, Edmonton, Alberta, 1–87, pp. 49–54; [Palliser, Hector, and others], *The Journals, Detailed Reports, and Observations*, 57; Moore, *Man and Fire*, 26–28, 54–55; Lutz, *Aboriginal Man and White Man*, 1–4, 13–16; Julian Harris Salomon, "Indians That Set the Woods on Fire," *Conservationist* 38 (March–April, 1984): 34–39; Conrad J. Bahre, "Wildfire in Southeastern Arizona between 1859 and 1890," *Desert Plants* 7, No. 4 (1985): 190–94.
33. Moore, *Man and Fire*, 38–42 (Alexander Henry, Daniel Harmon), 61–62; Wood and Thiessen, *Early Fur Trade on the Northern Plains*, 230 (Charles McKenzie); Nelson and England, "Some Comments on the Causes and Effects of Fire"; Dean A. Shinn, "Historical Perspectives on Range Burning in the Inland Pacific Northwest," *Journal of Range Management* 33, No. 6 (November 1980): 415–23 (beavers); Thomas, "Fire and the Fur Trade"; Gruell, "Indian Fires in the Interior West"; Higgins, *Interpretation and Compendium of Historical Fire Accounts in the Northern Great Plains*.
34. Along the Little Tennessee River, many species of plants consistent with disturbed, cleared lands induced or maintained by fire appeared some 1,500 years ago (Paul A. Delcourt, Hazel R. Delcourt, Patricia A. Cridlebaugh, and Jefferson Chapman, "Holocene Ethnobotanical and Paleoecological Record of Human Impact on Vegetation in the Little Tennessee River Valley, Tennessee," *Quaternary Research* 25 [1986]: 330–49; Jefferson Chapman, Hazel R. Delcourt, and Paul A. Delcourt, "Strawberry Fields, Almost Forever," *Natural History* 98 [September 1989]: 51–59). On the recent debate over wilderness and related matters, see Pyne, "Vestal Fires and Virgin Lands"; Nash, "Sorry, Bambi, but Man Must Enter the Forest"; Bruce M. Kilgore, "What Is 'Natural' in Wilderness Fire Management?," in *Proceedings—Symposium and Workshop on Wilderness Fire*, 57–67; Clinton B. Phillips, "The Relevance of Past Indian Fires to Current Fire Management Programs," in *ibid.*, 87–91; James K. Agee, "The Historical Role of Fire in Pacific Northwest Forests," in *Natural and Prescribed Fire in Pacific Northwest Forests*, ed. John D. Walstad, Steven R. Radosevich, and David V. Sandberg (Corvallis: Oregon State University Press, 1990), 25–38; Conrad Smith, "Yellowstone Media Myths: Print and Television Coverage of the 1988 Fires," in *Fire and the Environment: Ecological and Cultural Perspectives, Proceedings of an International Symposium*, Knoxville, Tennessee, March 20–24, 1990, ed. Stephen C. Nodvin and Thomas A. Waldrop (Asheville, NC: Southeastern Forest Experiment Station, 1991), 321–27; William Cronon, ed., *Uncommon Ground: Rethinking the Human Place in Nature* (New York: W. W. Norton & Company, 1995).

Chapter Five: Buffalo

1. I use the terms *buffalo* and *bison* interchangeably. "True" buffaloes, biologists and zoologists point out, are native to Asia and Africa, and the popular name buffalo for

the North American *Bison bison* is a misnomer. But it is also of long standing; see especially Jerry N. McDonald, *North American Bison: Their Classification and Evolution* (Berkeley: University of California Press, 1981). John F. Burns, "Head-Smashed-In Journal: In the Bison's Land, Pride Lives On," *New York Times*, August 10, 1990, A4; Nicole Bernshaw, "Head-Smashed-In Buffalo Jump," *American History Illustrated* 20 (March 1985): 38–41, p. 41; Ian Darragh, "The Killing Cliffs," *Canadian Geographic* 107 (1957): 55–61; Brian O. K. Reeves, "Head-Smashed-In: 5500 Years of Bison Jumping in the Alberta Plains," in *Bison Procurement and Utilization*, ed. Leslie B. Davis and Michael C. Wilson, in *Plains Anthropologist* 23, Memoir 14 (1978): 151–74; Brian O. K. Reeves, "Six Millenniums of Buffalo Kills," *Scientific American* 249 (October 1983): 120–35; Jack Brink, "Blackfoot and Buffalo Jumps: Native People and the Head-Smashed-In Project," in *Buffalo*, ed. John E. Foster, Dick Harrison, and I. S. MacLaren (Edmonton: University of Alberta Press, 1992), 19–43; Ed Sponholz, "Head-Smashed-In Buffalo Jump: A Centre for Cultural Preservation and Understanding," in *ibid.*, 45–59.

2. George Bird Grinnell, "The Last of the Buffalo," *Scribner's Magazine* 12 (1892): 267–86, p. 268 ("country was one robe"); Joe Ben Wheat, "The Olsen-Chubbuck Site: A Paleo-Indian Bison Kill," *American Antiquity* 37 (1972): 1–169, p. 87 ("multitude so great . . .").
3. Peter Fidler, "Journal of a Journey over Land from Buckingham House to the Rocky Mountains in 1792 & 3." Accession No. 79.269/89. Provincial Archives of Alberta, Edmonton, Alberta, 1–87, p. 69; J. G. MacGregor, *Peter Fidler: Canada's Forgotten Surveyor 1769–1822* (Toronto: McClelland and Stewart, 1966), 82; W. Raymond Wood and Thomas D. Thiessen, *Early Fur Trade on the Northern Plains: Canadian Traders among the Mandan and Hidatsa Indians, 1738–1818* (Norman: University of Oklahoma Press, 1985), 251, 277; Charles MacKenzie, "The Mississouri Indians: A Narrative of Four Trading Expeditions to the Mississouri 1804–1805–1806 for the North-West Company," in *Les Bourgeois de la Compagnie du Nord-Ouest*, Volume 1, ed. Louis Masson (Québec: L'Imprimerie Générale A Coté et Cie, 1889), 315–93, pp. 351–52; Duncan M'Gillivray, *The Journal of Duncan M'Gillivray of the Northwest Company at Fort George on the Saskatchewan, 1794–95*, ed. Arthur S. Morton (Toronto: Macmillan, 1929), 28.
4. Maria R. Audubon, *Audubon and His Journals*, 2 volumes, ed. Elliott Coues (Freeport, NY: Books for Libraries Press, 1972 [orig. 1897]), 2, 146; William Blackmore, "Introduction," in Richard Irving Dodge, *The Plains of the Great West* (New York: G. P. Putnam's Sons, 1877), xiv; Colonel Richard Irving Dodge, *Our Wild Indians: Thirty-three Years' Personal Experience among the Red Men of the Great West* (Freeport, NY: Books for Libraries Press, 1970 [orig. 1882]), 283–84; David A. Dary, *The Buffalo Book: The Full Saga of the American Animal* (Chicago: The Swallow Press, [1974]), 22–29.
5. Dary, *The Buffalo Book*, 27 ("they were afraid . . .").
6. Ernest Thompson Seton, *Life-histories of Northern Animals: An Account of the Mammals of Manitoba*, Volume 1: *Grass-Eaters* (New York: Charles Scribner's Sons, 1909), 247–303, pp. 258–60; Ernest Thompson Seton, *Lives of Game Animals* (Garden City: Doubleday, Doran & Company, 1927 [1909]), 639–717, pp. 654–56; William T. Hornaday, *The Extermination of the American Bison, with a Sketch of Its Discovery and Life History* (1887 Annual Report, Board of Regents, U.S. National Museum, Part 2, 1889), 367–548; Henry Poland, "Buffalo, or American Bison," in *Fur-bearing Animals in Nature and in Commerce* (London: Gurney &

Jackson, 1892), 290–99; Roger A. Caras, "A Symbol for All: The Mighty Bison," in *North American Mammals: Fur-bearing Animals of the United States and Canada* (New York: Meredith Press, 1967), 461–67; Frank Gilbert Roe, *The North American Buffalo: A Critical Study of the Species in Its Wild State* (Toronto: University of Toronto Press, 1970); Francis Haines, *The Buffalo* (New York: Thomas Y. Crowell, 1970); Tom McHugh, *The Time of the Buffalo* (New York: Alfred A. Knopf, 1972); Dary, *The Buffalo Book*, 28–29; A. W. F. Banfield, "American Bison or Buffalo," in *The Mammals of Canada* (Toronto: University of Toronto Press, 1974), 405–8.

7. Dan Flores, "Bison Ecology and Bison Diplomacy: The Southern Plains from 1800 to 1850," *Journal of American History* 78 (1991): 465–85; [John Palliser, James Hector, and others], *The Journals, Detailed Reports, and Observations Relative to the Exploration, by Captain Palliser, of That Portion of British America . . . during the Years 1857, 1858, 1859, and 1860* (London: Eyre and Spottiswoode, 1863), 54; Douglas B. Bamforth, "Historical Documents and Bison Ecology on the Great Plains," *Plains Anthropologist* 32 (1987): 1–16.
8. Hornaday, *The Extermination of the American Bison*, 376–86; Roe, *The North American Buffalo*, 26–93; Joel Asaph Allen, *The American Bisons, Living and Extinct* (New York: Arno Press, 1974), 72–191; Erhard Rostlund, "The Geographic Range of the Historic Bison in the Southeast," *Association of American Geographers* 50 (1960): 395–407; Dolores A. Gunnerson, "Man and Bison on the Plains in the Protohistoric Period," *Plains Anthropologist* 17 (February 1972): 1–10; D. W. Moodie and Arthur J. Ray, "Buffalo Migrations in the Canadian Plains," *Plains Anthropologist* 21 (February 1976): 45–52; R. Grace Morgan, "Bison Movement Patterns on the Canadian Plains: An Ecological Analysis," *Plains Anthropologist* 25 (May 1980): 144–60.
9. The lines are clearly drawn between Hornaday, *The Extermination of the American Bison*, 504–6, 527, and Roe, *The North American Buffalo*, 467–88.
10. Eleanor Verbicky-Todd, *Communal Buffalo Hunting among the Plains Indians: An Ethnographic and Historic Review* (Alberta: Archaeological Survey of Alberta, 1984), 168–84. This work is an important synthesis and discussion of archival and published materials.
11. John C. Ewers, *The Blackfeet: Raiders of the Northwestern Plains* (Norman: University of Oklahoma Press, 1958), 72–87; Verbicky-Todd, *Communal Buffalo Hunting*, 185–96; McHugh, *The Time of the Buffalo*, 109.
12. Frank Bergon, ed., *The Journals of Lewis and Clark* (New York: Penguin Books, 1989), 115, 120; Dodge, *Our Wild Indians*, 291–92; Dodge, *Plains of the Great West*, 119–20; Dary, *The Buffalo Book*, 12, 34–35; Claude E. Schaeffer, "The Bison Drive of the Blackfeet Indians," in *Bison Procurement and Utilization*, 243–48 (coffee and bacon). A hunter who lay flat on the ground and waved a handkerchief in the air at the end of his ramrod could easily attract antelope (H. M. Brackenridge, *Journal of a Voyage up the Missouri Performed in Eighteen Hundred and Eleven*, second edition, in *Early Western Travels 1748–1846*, ed. Reuben Gold Thwaites [Cleveland: Arthur H. Clark Company, 1904], 103).
13. Joseph Medicine Crow, "The Crow Indian Buffalo Jump Legends," in *Symposium on Buffalo Jumps*, ed. Carling Malouf and Stuart Conner. Montana Archaeological Society, Memoir No. 1 (Missoula: Montana Archaeological Society, 1962), 35–39; Joe Medicine Crow, "Notes on Crow Indian Buffalo Jump Traditions," in *Bison Procurement and Utilization*, 249–53; Joseph Medicine Crow, *From the Heart of the Crow Country: The Crow Indians' Own Stories* (New York: Orion Books, 1992), 86; George W. Arthur, *An Introduction to the Ecology of Early Historic Communal*

Bison Hunting among the Northern Plains Indians (Ottawa: National Museums of Canada, 1975); George W. Arthur, "A Re-analysis of the Early Historic Plains Indian Bison Drives," in *Bison Procurement and Utilization*, 236–42; Schaeffer, "The Bison Drive of the Blackfeet Indians"; Donald J. Lehmer, "The Plains Bison Hunt—Prehistoric and Historic," *Plains Anthropologist* 8 (1963): 211–17; George Bird Grinnell, *The Cheyenne Indians: Their History and Ways of Life*, 2 volumes (New Haven: Yale University Press, 1923); Verbicky-Todd, *Communal Buffalo Hunting*.

14. John C. Ewers, "The Last Bison Drives of the Blackfoot Indians," *Journal of the Washington Academy of Sciences* 39 (1949): 355–60, p. 359 ("Help me to fall . . ."); Edwin James, *Account of an Expedition from Pittsburgh to the Rocky Mountains Performed in the Years 1819, 1820*, Volume 14 in *Early Western Travels, 1748–1846*, ed. Reuben G. Thwaites (Cleveland: Arthur H. Clark, 1905–1906), 288–301 (Omaha ritual); Edwin Thompson Denig, *Indian Tribes of the Upper Missouri*, ed. J. N. B. Hewitt. Forty-sixth Annual Report of the Bureau of American Ethnology, 1928–1929 (Washington, DC: Smithsonian Institution, 1930), 375–628, pp. 532–33 (Assiniboine); Wood and Thiessen, *Early Fur Trade on the Northern Plains*, 91 ("My grandfather . . .")—cf., John McDonnell, "Some Account of the Red Deer River (about 1797) with Extracts from His Journal 1793–1795," in *Les Bourgeois de la Compagnie du Nord-Ouest*, 265–95, p. 280.
15. Milo Milton Quaife, ed., *Alexander Henry's Travels and Adventures in the Years 1760–1776* (Chicago: R. R. Donnelley & Sons, 1921), 284 ("their gestures . . ."); Claude E. Schaeffer, "The Bison Drive of the Blackfeet Indians," in *Symposium on Buffalo Jumps*, 28–34, p. 33; James Willard Schultz, *Apauk: Caller of Buffalo* (Boston: Houghton Mifflin, 1916); Verbicky-Todd, *Communal Buffalo Hunting*, 47, 71.
16. Verbicky-Todd, *Communal Buffalo Hunting*, 100 ("if it can be called hunting"); Dodge, *Plains of the Great West*, 103 ("scarcely considered game"); William Blackmore, "Introduction [to Dodge]," xv ("legitimate"); H. A. L. [Henry Astbury Levenson], *Sport in Many Lands: Europe, Asia, Africa and America, Etc., Etc.* (London: Frederick Warne and Co., 1890), 513–15 ("indiscriminate slaughter"); F. Trench Townshend, *Ten Thousand Miles of Travel, Sport, and Adventure* (London: Hurst and Blackett, 1869); Grantley F. Berkeley, *The English Sportsman in the Western Prairies* (London: Hurst and Blackett, 1861); John I. Merritt, *Baronets and Buffalo: The British Sportsman in the American West, 1833–1881* (Missoula, MT: Mountain Press Publishing Company, 1985).
17. J. Russell Harper, ed., *Paul Kane's Frontier* (Toronto: University of Toronto Press, 1971), 79; Audubon, *Audubon and His Journals*, Volume II, 144–46; George Catlin, *Letters and Notes on the Manners, Customs, and Conditions of the North American Indians*, 2 volumes (New York: Dover Publications, 1973), Volume I, 199–201; Henry Youle Hind, *Narrative of the Canadian Red River Exploring Expedition of 1857 and of the Assiniboine and Saskatchewan Exploring Expedition of 1858*, 2 volumes (London: Longman, Green, Longman, and Roberts, 1860), Volume I, 355–59, Volume II, 142–43; Rev. P. J. De Smet, *Western Missions and Missionaries: A Series of Letters* (New York: T. W. Strong, Late Edward Dunigan & Bro., Catholic Publishing House, 1859), 146–54; [Palliser, Hector, and others], *The Journals, Detailed Reports, and Observations*, 70–71; Verbicky-Todd, *Communal Buffalo Hunting*, 88, 139.
18. M'Gillivray, *The Journal of Duncan M'Gillivray*, 44; Fidler, "Journal of a Journey over Land," 28; Alice Kehoe, personal communication, September 23, 1997.
19. George Bird Grinnell, *Blackfoot Lodge Tales: The Story of a Prairie People*

(Lincoln: University of Nebraska Press, 1962 [orig. 1893]), 228–29 ("piskun"); Ewers, "The Last Bison Drives"; De Smet, *Western Missions and Missionaries*, 146–53; Denig, *Indian Tribes of the Upper Missouri*, 532–35; George C. Frison, *Prehistoric Hunters of the High Plains* (New York: Academic Press, 1978), 315–28; Wheat, "The Olsen-Chubbuck Site," 85–86, 107–13; Joe Ben Wheat, "A Paleo-Indian Bison Kill," *Scientific American* 216 (January 1967): 44–52, p. 52; Arthur J. Ray, "The Northern Great Plains: Pantry of the Northwestern Fur Trade, 1774–1885," *Prairie Forum* 9 (1984): 263–80, p. 272; Seton, *Life-histories*, 249; John C. Ewers, *The Horse in Blackfoot Indian Culture*, Bureau of American Ethnology, Bulletin No. 159 (Washington, DC: Smithsonian Institution, 1955), 160; E. Douglas Branch, *The Hunting of the Buffalo* (Lincoln: University of Nebraska Press, 1962), 35, 89–90; Verbicky-Todd, *Communal Buffalo Hunting*, 81–83, 174.

20. Alice Kehoe, personal communication, September 23, 1997 (tongues); Clark Wissler, *Material Culture of the Blackfoot Indians*, Anthropological Papers of the American Museum of Natural History, Volume 5, part 1 (New York: American Museum of Natural History, 1910), 42 (heavy and light butchering); Verbicky-Todd, *Communal Buffalo Hunting*, 168–84.
21. Audubon, *Audubon and His Journals*, Volume 1, 496–97; John McDonnell, "Some Account of the Red River," 294; Wood and Thiessen, *Early Fur Trade on the Northern Plains*, 239, 265; MacKenzie, "The Mississouri Indians," 337, 366.
22. James, *Account of an Expedition*, 301 ("every eatable part . . ."); Emma Helen Blair, *The Indian Tribes of the Upper Mississippi Valley and Region of the Great Lakes, as described by Nicolas Perrot*, Volume I (Cleveland: Arthur H. Clark Company, 1911), 124 (Perrot); De Smet, *Western Missions and Missionaries*, 148–53.
23. Fidler, "Journal of a Journey over Land," 50; Bergon, *Journals of Lewis and Clark*, 141; MacKenzie, "The Mississouri Indians," 366 (Mandans in 1805); Elliot Coues, ed., *New Light on the Early History of the Greater Northwest. The Manuscript Journals of Alexander Henry, Fur Trader, and David Thompson, Official Geographer and Explorer of the North West Company*, 3 volumes (New York: Francis P. Harper, 1897), 576–77; J. Russell Harper, ed., *Paul Kane's Frontier* (Toronto: University of Toronto Press, 1971), 79–82; Hind, *Narrative of the Canadian Red River Exploring Expedition of 1857*, Volume I, 340, 355–59; Verbicky-Todd, *Communal Buffalo Hunting*, 62, 87–89 ("strewn with . . ."). Other reports hint at the possibility of waste, including John Bradbury, *Travels in the Interior of America in the Years 1809, 1810, and 1811*, in *Early Western Travels 1748–1846*, Volume 5, ed. Reuben Gold Thwaites (Cleveland: Arthur H. Clark, 1904), 174 ("they often kill many more than they can possibly dispose of") and [Palliser, Hector, and others], *The Journals, Detailed Reports, and Observations*, 71 (who report a pound whose bottom "was strewn with fragments of carcases left from former slaughters").
24. Wood and Thiessen, *Early Fur Trade on the Northern Plains*, 209 (Larocque), 265, 282 (McKenzie); MacKenzie, "The Mississouri Indians," 331, 366; Fidler, "Journal of a Journey over Land," 66; Wheat, "The Olsen-Chubbuck Site," 100, 107; compare Bergon, *Journals of Lewis and Clark*, 82–83.
25. Flores, "Bison Ecology and Bison Diplomacy."
26. The basis for the difference between the two estimates is not yet published. Douglas H. Ubelaker, "Prehistoric New World Population Size: Historical Review and Current Appraisal of North American Estimates," *American Journal of Physical Anthropology* 45 (1976): 661–65; Douglas Ubelaker, "North American Indian Population Size, A.D. 1500 to 1985," *American Journal of Physical Anthropology* 77

(1988): 289–94; William M. Denevan, "Native American Populations in 1492: Recent Research and a Revised Hemispheric Estimate," in *The Native Population of the Americas in 1492*, second edition, ed. William M. Denevan (Madison: University of Wisconsin Press, 1992), xvii–xxix; Douglas H. Ubelaker, "The Sources and Methodology for Mooney's Estimates of North American Indian Populations," in *ibid.*, 243–88; John D. Daniels, "The Indian Population of North America in 1492," *William and Mary Quarterly* 49 (1992): 298–320. See also Chapter 3, "Eden."

27. Lists of Plains groups differ depending on the period, the definition of "tribe" or "nation," and the preferred ethnonym. Often included are the Sarcee, Blackfeet (Blood/Kainai, Siksika/Blackfeet, Piegan/Pikuni), Gros Ventres/Atsina, Plains Cree, Assiniboine, Plains Ojibwa, Crow, Hidatsa, Mandan, Arikara, Cheyenne, Shoshone, Arapahoe, various Sioux/Dakota groups (Teton/Lakota, Yankton/Nakota, Santee/Dakota), Pawnee, Ponca, Omaha, Iowa, Oto, Kansa, Osage, Missouri, Wichita, Kiowa, Comanche, Kiowa Apache, Quapaw, and Caddo. For ethnographic and historical background, see Alice B. Kehoe, *North American Indians: A Comprehensive Account* (Englewood Cliffs, NJ: Prentice Hall, 1992), 287–359; Elizabeth Grobsmith and Beth R. Ritter, "The Plains Culture Area," in *Native North Americans: An Ethnohistorical Approach*, second edition, ed. Molly R. Mignon and Daniel L. Boxberger (Dubuque, IA: Kendall Hunt, 1997), 199–252.
28. Ewers, *The Horse in Blackfoot Indian Culture;* Ewers, *The Blackfeet;* Verbicky-Todd, *Communal Buffalo Hunting*, 191.
29. Ubelaker, "North American Indian Population Size, A.D. 1500 to 1985" (120,000); cf., Ubelaker, "The Sources and Methodology." On consumption, see Irene M. Spry, *The Palliser Expedition: An Account of John Palliser's British North American Expedition 1857–1860* (Toronto: The Macmillan Company of Canada Limited, 1963), 177 (at Fort Edmonton in the mid–19th century, 150 men, women, and children ate 700 pounds of buffalo meat each day); Flores, "Bison Ecology and Bison Diplomacy," 479.
30. Flores's analysis for the southern Plains ("Bison Ecology and Bison Diplomacy") is important. See also Seton, *Life-histories*, 267–73; Roe, *The North American Buffalo*, 503–5; H. W. Reynolds, R. D. Glaholt, and A. W. L. Hawley, "Bison," in *Wild Mammals of North America*, ed. Joseph A. Chapman and George A. Feldhamer (Baltimore: Johns Hopkins University Press, 1982), 972–1007; Joel Berger and Carol Cunningham, *Bison: Mating and Conservation in Small Populations* (New York: Columbia University Press, 1994), 99–112 and passim. On buffalo deaths, see Dodge, *Plains of the Great West*, 130; Brackenridge, *Journal of a Voyage*, 36; Theodore R. Davis, "The Buffalo Range," *Harper's New Monthly Magazine* 38 (January 1869): 147–63.
31. Flores, "Bison Ecology and Bison Diplomacy," 469–70, 481–82; [Palliser, Hector, and others], *The Journals, Detailed Reports, and Observations*, 111 (disease); Frank G. Roe, "The Extermination of the Buffalo in Western Canada," *Canadian Historical Review* 15 (1934): 1–23, pp. 3–4 (disease); Frederic E. Clements and Ralph W. Chaney, *Environment and Life in the Great Plains* (Washington, DC: Carnegie Institution, 1937); Waldo R. Wedel, *Environment and Native Subsistence Economies in the Central Great Plains*, Smithsonian Miscellaneous Collections 101, No. 3 (Washington, DC: Smithsonian Institution, 1941); Philip V. Wells, "Historical Factors Controlling Vegetation Patterns and Floristic Distributions in the Central Plains Region of North America," in *Pleistocene and Recent Environments of the Central Great Plains*, ed. W. Dort, Jr., and J. K. Jones, Jr. (Lawrence: University Press of Kansas, 1970), 211–21; Merlin Paul Lawson, *The Climate of the Great American Desert*, University of

Nebraska Studies 46 (Lincoln: University of Nebraska, 1974). See also Chapter 4, "Fire."

32. Flores, "Bison Ecology and Bison Diplomacy," 481; Fidler, "Journal of a Journey over Land," 48; MacKenzie, "The Mississouri Indians," 338.

33. Conrad E. Heidenreich and Arthur J. Ray, *The Early Fur Trades: A Study in Cultural Interaction*, ed. John Wolforth and R. Cole Harris (Toronto: McClelland and Steward Limited, 1976), 34–43; Wood and Thiessen, *Early Fur Trade on the Northern Plains*, 3–74.

34. A key summary for the following discussion is William Swagerty, "Indian Trade in the Trans-Mississippi West to 1870," in *Handbook of North American Indians*, Volume 4 (Washington, DC: Smithsonian Institution, 1988), 351–74.

35. R. O. Merriam, "The Bison and the Fur Trade," *Queen's Quarterly* 34 (1926): 78–96; Wood and Thiessen, *Early Fur Trade on the Northern Plains*, 3–74; Mark Judy, "Powder Keg on the Upper Missouri: Sources of Blackfeet Hostility, 1730–1810," *American Indian Quarterly* 11 (1987): 127–44; Thomas F. Schilz and Donald E. Worcester, "The Spread of Firearms among the Indian Tribes of the Northern Frontier of New Spain," *American Indian Quarterly* 11 (1987): 1–10; Thomas F. Schilz and Jodye L. D. Schilz, "Beads, Bangles, and Buffalo Robes: The Rise and Fall of the Indian Fur Trade along the Missouri and Des Moines Rivers, 1700–1820," *Annals of Iowa* 49 (Summer–Fall 1987): 5–25; Francis Haines, *The Plains Indians* (New York: Thomas Y. Crowell Company, 1976), 16–69; Swagerty, "Indian Trade in the Trans-Mississippi West."

36. Henry H. Sibley, "Sport of Buffalo Hunting on the Open Plains of Pembina," in *Information Respecting the History, Condition and Prospects of the Indian Tribes of the United States: Collected and Prepared under the Direction of the Bureau of Indian Affairs*, by Henry R. Schoolcraft (Philadelphia: Lippincott, Grambo and Company, 1854), Volume IV, 94–110; Alexander Ross, *The Red River Settlement: Its Rise, Progress, and Present State* (London: Smith, Elder and Co., 1856), 235–74; Hind, *Narrative of the Canadian Red River Exploring Expedition*, Volume II, 103–44; Dodge, *Plains of the Great West*, 130–33; Maximilian, Prince of Wied, *Travels in the Interior of North America*, Volumes 22–24 in *Early Western Travels, 1748–1846*, ed. Reuben G. Thwaites (Cleveland: Arthur H. Clark, 1905–1906), Volume 22, 380, Volume 23, 246, and passim; Hornaday, *The Extermination of the American Bison*, 487–89; Seton, *Life-histories*, 292–93; John E. Sunder, *The Fur Trade on the Upper Missouri, 1840–1865* (Norman: University of Oklahoma Press, 1965), 16ff.; G. Herman Sprenger, "The Metis Nation: Buffalo Hunting Vs. Agriculture in the Red River Settlement (Circa 1810–1870)," *Western Canadian Journal of Anthropology* 3 (January 1972): 158–78; Dary, *The Buffalo Book*, 69–84; David J. Wishart, *The Fur Trade of the American West, 1807–1840* (Lincoln: University of Nebraska Press, 1992); Ray, "The Northern Great Plains"; Branch, *The Hunting of the Buffalo*, 66–126; John E. Foster, ed., "The Metis and the End of the Plains Buffalo in Alberta," in *Buffalo*, 61–77; Swagerty, "Indian Trade in the Trans-Mississippi West."

37. Hornaday, *The Extermination of the American Bison*, 490–525; Seton, *Life-histories*, 293–301; Seton, *Lives of Game Animals*, 662–69; John Hanner, "Government Response to the Buffalo Hide Trade, 1871–1883," *Journal of Law and Economics* 24 (1981): 239–71; Dodge, *Our Wild Indians*, 293–96; Dodge, *Plains of the Great West*, 133–44; Roe, "The Extermination of the Buffalo in Western Canada"; Branch, *The Hunting of the Buffalo*, 127–222; James L. Haley, "Prelude to War: The Slaughter of the Buffalo," *American Heritage* 27 (February 1976): 36–41, 82–87; John C. Ewers, "Ethnological Report on the Blackfeet and Gros Ventre Tribes of Indians,"

in *American Indian Ethnohistory: Plains Indians*, ed. David A. Horr (New York: Garland Publishing, 1974), 11; Ewers, *The Blackfeet*, 277–96 (on the Piegan); Dary, *The Buffalo Book*, 84–120.

38. Seton, *Lives of Game Animals*, passim; Branch, *The Hunting of the Buffalo*, 221–22; Michael C. Wilson, "Bison in Alberta: Paleontology, Evolution, and Relationships with Humans," in *Buffalo*, 1–17; Dary, *The Buffalo Book*, 121–43; Berger and Cunningham, *Bison*, 23–41.

39. Hanner, "Government Response to the Buffalo Hide Trade"; Dary, *The Buffalo Book*, 68 ("Where the Indian . . .").

40. James Willard Schultz, *Apauk: Caller of Buffalo* (Boston: Houghton Mifflin, 1916), 226. In another account—in which hunting for commodities is not mentioned—a Piegan named Many-Tail-Feathers says that jumps were no longer used after his father had a vision in the 1840s in which a buffalo bull said, "I must give you warning about something you and your kind are doing that is very wrong. It is that with your *piskans* you are rapidly killing off us buffalo. If you keep on doing it you will soon put an end to the very last ones of us. So I say: stop using your *piskans* if you would prevent something dreadful happening to all of your kind" (James W. Schultz, *Blackfeet and Buffalo*, ed. Keith C. Seele [Norman: University of Oklahoma Press, 1962], 306–19, p. 317).

41. Fidler, "Journal of a Journey over Land," 76; Audubon, *Audubon and His Journals*, 2, 145; David J. Wishart, "Cultures in Co-operation and Conflict: Indians in the Fur Trade on the Northern Great Plains, 1807–1840," *Journal of Historical Geography* 2 (1976): 311–28, pp. 320–21; Ray, "The Northern Great Plains," 273; Roe, *The North American Buffalo*, 404–9; Wood and Thiessen, *Early Fur Trade on the Northern Plains*, 3–74; Denig, *Indian Tribes of the Upper Missouri*, 461, 540–41, 582, and passim.

42. Because jump sites are near rivers (and riverine transport), the pemmican market could be ancient, antedating the arrival of Europeans, as Alice Kehoe (personal communication, September 23, 1997) and others suggest. On the archaeology of communal hunting, see Malouf and Conner, eds., *Symposium on Buffalo Jumps;* Frison, *Prehistoric Hunters of the High Plains;* Davis and Wilson, eds., *Bison Procurement and Utilization;* George C. Frison, "Prehistoric, Plains-Mountain, Large-Mammal, Communal Hunting Strategies," in *The Evolution of Human Hunting*, ed. Matthew H. Nitecki and Doris V. Nitecki (New York: Plenum Press, 1987), 177–223; George C. Frison, "Paleoindian Subsistence and Settlement during Post-Clovis Times on the Northwestern Plains, the Adjacent Mountain Ranges, and Intermontane Basins," in *Americans before Columbus: Ice-Age Origins*, ed. Ronald C. Carlisle (Pittsburgh: Department of Anthropology, University of Pittsburgh, 1988), 83–106; Liz Bryan, *The Buffalo People: Prehistoric Archaeology on the Canadian Plains* (Alberta, Canada: University of Alberta Press, 1991); Wilson, "Bison in Alberta: Paleontology, Evolution, and Relationships with Humans," 1–17. Also see references in notes 43 to 45.

43. George C. Frison, "Animal Population Studies and Cultural Inference," in *Bison Procurement and Utilization*, 44–52; George C. Frison, *The Wardell Buffalo Trap 48 SU 301: Communal Procurement in the Upper Green River Basin, Wyoming* (Ann Arbor: University of Michigan, 1973); Richard G. Forbis, *The Old Women's Buffalo Jump, Alberta*, National Museum of Canada Bulletin No. 180 (Contributions to Anthropology, 1960), Part 1 (Ottawa: Department of Northern Affairs and National Resources, 1962); Thomas F. Kehoe, *The Gull Lake Site: A Prehistoric Bison Drive in Southwestern Saskatchewan*, Milwaukee Public Museum Publications in

Anthropology and History 1 (Milwaukee: Milwaukee Public Museum, 1973); J. Michael Quigg, "Winter Bison Procurement in Southwestern Alberta," in *Bison Procurement and Utilization*, 53–57; Dennis J. Stanford, "The Jones-Miller Site: An Example of Hell Gap Bison Procurement Strategy," in *ibid.*, 90–97.

44. Leslie B. Davis, ed., "Panel Discussion: Symposium on Bison Procurement and Utilization," in *Bison Procurement and Utilization*, 287–311; Andrew Hill and Anna Kay Behrensmeyer, "Natural Disarticulation and Bison Butchery," *American Antiquity* 50 (January 1985): 141–45; Lawrence C. Todd, "Analysis of Kill-Butchery Bonebeds and Interpretation of Paleoindian Hunting," in *The Evolution of Human Hunting*, 225–66.
45. Wheat, "The Olsen-Chubbuck Site"; Wheat, "A Paleo-Indian Bison Kill"; Joe Ben Wheat, "Olsen-Chubbuck and Jurgens Sites: Four Aspects of Paleo-Indian Economy," in *Bison Procurement and Utilization*, 84–89.
46. Mary Weekes, "An Indian's Description of the Making of a Buffalo Pound," *Saskatchewan History* 1, No. 3 (1948): 14–17; Joseph Epes Brown, *Animals of the Soul: Sacred Animals of the Oglala Sioux* (Rockport, MA: Element, Inc., 1992), 15 ("everything was taken . . ."); Grinnell, *Blackfoot Lodge Tales*, 228–32; Verbicky-Todd, *Communal Buffalo Hunting*, 58, 68, 86.
47. Wissler, *Material Culture of the Blackfoot Indians*, 34 ("no effort of man . . .").
48. Barre Toelken, "Seeing with a Native Eye," in *Seeing with a Native Eye: Essays on Native American Religion*, ed. Walter Holden Capps (New York: Harper, 1976), 9–24.
49. Bradbury, *Travels in the Interior of America*, 141.
50. Raymond J. DeMallie, "Lakota Belief and Ritual in the Nineteenth Century," in *Sioux Indian Religion: Tradition and Innovation*, ed. Raymond J. DeMallie and Douglas R. Parks (Norman: University of Oklahoma Press, 1987), 25–43; Raymond J. DeMallie, "Kinship and Biology in Sioux Culture," in *North American Indian Anthropology: Essays on Society and Culture*, ed. Raymond J. DeMallie and Alfonso Ortiz (Norman: University of Oklahoma Press, 1995), 125–46; Howard L. Harrod, *Renewing the World: Plains Indian Religion and Morality* (Tucson: University of Arizona Press, 1987).
51. James R. Walker, *Lakota Belief and Ritual*, ed. Raymond J. DeMallie and Elaine A. Jahner (Lincoln: University of Nebraska Press, 1980), passim; Joseph Epes Brown, ed., *The Sacred Pipe: Black Elk's Account of the Seven Rites of the Oglala Sioux* (Baltimore: Penguin Books, 1971), 72; Grinnell, *Last of the Buffalo*, 278; Verbicky-Todd, *Communal Buffalo Hunting*, 197–245.
52. MacGregor, *Peter Fidler*, 68–69 ("always very anxious"); Fidler, "Journal of a Journey over Land," 23 ("at any future time . . ."); John McDougall, *Saddle, Sled and Snowshoe* (Toronto: William Briggs, 1896), 282 ("Not one buffalo . . ."); John McDougall, *Parsons on the Plains*, ed. Thomas Bredin (Ontario: Longman, Don Mills, 1971), 183; Verbicky-Todd, *Communal Buffalo Hunting*, 125.
53. Dodge, *Our Wild Indians*, 289; Kehoe, *The Gull Lake Site*, 185; Denig, *Indian Tribes of the Upper Missouri*, 457. In this context it is interesting that the interpretive program for visitors at Head-Smashed-In Buffalo Jump stresses that "all the animals had to be killed," and that this site's *Buffalo Bulletin* states that "Plains Indians had a different view of the natural world than man does today, believing any escaped animal would warn other herds of the deadly trap" ("Interpretative Program Matrix," unpublished document, Head-Smashed-In Buffalo Jump, Alberta, p. 37; *Buffalo Bulletin* [Summer 1994], p. 2, The Friends of Head-Smashed-In Buffalo Jump Society, Head-Smashed-In Buffalo Jump; compare "Buffalo Hunting in the

Alberta Plains," Alberta Culture; with thanks to Beth Hrychuk for these materials).

54. Dodge, *Our Wild Indians*, 286–87, 580–581; Flores, "Bison Ecology and Bison Diplomacy," 485.
55. Roe, *The North American Buffalo*, 643–44; Branch, *The Hunting of the Buffalo*, 2–3; Dary, *The Buffalo Book*, 54–55; Verbicky-Todd, *Communal Buffalo Hunting*, 198.
56. DeMallie, "Lakota Belief and Ritual in the Nineteenth Century," 32.

Chapter Six: Deer

1. Timothy Silver, *New Face on the Countryside: Indians, Colonists and Slaves in South Atlantic Forests, 1500–1800* (Cambridge: Cambridge University Press, 1990), 69 (Thomas Harriot); Joel W. Martin, "Southeastern Indians and the English Trade in Skins and Slaves," in *The Forgotten Centuries: Indians and Europeans in the American South 1521–1704*, ed. Charles Hudson and Carmen Chaves Tesser (Athens: University of Georgia Press, 1994), 304–23, p. 309 ("up to ye middle . . ."). On exchange see, inter alia, James H. Merrell, *The Indians' New World: Catawbas and Their Neighbors from European Contact through the Era of Removal* (Chapel Hill: University of North Carolina Press, 1989), 29, 35–36; also see Chapter 7, "Beaver," infra.
2. Several anthropologists and historians have argued for the inevitability of dependence and a forest proletariat; for example, see Harold Hickerson, "Fur Trade Colonialism and the North American Indians," *Journal of Ethnic Studies* 1 (1973): 15–44. But local culture and external factors greatly complicate the processes whereby people become dependent; Shepard Krech III, "The Hudson's Bay Company and Dependence among Subarctic Tribes before 1900," in *Overcoming Economic Dependency, Occasional Papers in Curriculum Series,* No. 9, D'Arcy McNickle Center (Chicago: The Newberry Library, 1988), 62–70. For the exchange in the South, see especially Merrell, *The Indians' New World;* Richard White, *The Roots of Dependency: Subsistence, Environment and Social Change among the Choctaws, Pawnees, and Navajos* (Lincoln: University of Nebraska Press, 1983), 1–146, 315–23; Daniel H. Usner, Jr., *Indians, Settlers, & Slaves in a Frontier Exchange Economy: The Lower Mississippi Valley before 1783* (Chapel Hill: University of North Carolina Press, 1992); Kathryn E. Holland Braund, *Deerskins & Duffels: The Creek Indian Trade with Anglo-America, 1685–1815* (Lincoln: University of Nebraska Press, 1993); and work of Gregory A. Waselkov cited in notes below.
3. David Wilcox, "Skins, Rum & Ruin," *Southern Exposure* 13 (1985): 57–60, p. 60 ("an ethos . . ."); James Axtell, *The Indians' New South: Cultural Change in the Colonial Southeast* (Baton Rouge: Louisiana State University Press, 1997), 69 ("omitted their religious obligations"). According to Margaret Z. Searcy ("Choctaw Subsistence, 1540–1830: Hunting, Fishing, Farming, and Gathering," in *The Choctaw before Removal*, ed. Carolyn Keller Reeves [Jackson: University Press of Mississippi, 1985], 32–54, p. 47), 19th-century Choctaws "taught conservation" through a myth that seems instead to provide guidance on how to kill as many deer as possible.
4. Ernest Thompson Seton, "The Northern Whitetail, Northern Whitetailed Deer, or Northern Virginian Deer," in *Life-histories of Northern Animals: An Account of the Mammals of Manitoba,* Volume 1 (New York: Charles Scribner's Sons, 1909), 68–113; John James Audubon and John Bachman, "Virginian Deer," in *The Quadrupeds of North America,* Volume 2 (New York: Arno Press, 1974), 220–39; Roger A. Caras, "Our Most Common Big-Game Animal: The Deer," in *North American Mammals:*

Fur-bearing Animals of the United States and Canada (New York: Meredith Press, 1967), 428–40; *White-Tailed Deer in the Southern Forest Habitat*, Proceedings of a Symposium at Nacogdoches, Texas (Southern Forest Experiment Station, Forest Service, U.S. Department of Agriculture et al., 1969); A. W. F. Banfield, "White-Tailed Deer," in *The Mammals of Canada* (Toronto: University of Toronto Press, 1974), 391–95; Leonard Lee Rue III, *The Deer of North America* (New York: Crown Publishers, Inc., 1978); William T. Hesselton and Ruth Ann Monson Hesselton, "White-tailed Deer," in *Wild Mammals of North America: Biology, Management, and Economics*, ed. Joseph A. Chapman and George A. Feldhamer (Baltimore: Johns Hopkins University Press, 1982), 878–901; Timothy Silver, personal communication, July 7, 1998 ("every conceivable habitat").

5. Muskogean speakers included the Creek, Chickasaw, and Choctaw; Iroquoian speakers, the Cherokee; and Siouan speakers, the Catawba; other Indians in Virginia and North Carolina spoke Algonquian tongues, and in Florida, Timucuan. For the South during this early post-European arrival period, see Charles Hudson, *The Southeastern Indians* (Knoxville: University of Tennessee Press, 1978); Merrell, *Indians' New World*, 8–48; Peter H. Wood, Gregory A. Waselkov, and M. Thomas Hatley, eds., *Powhatan's Mantle: Indians in the Colonial Southeast* (Lincoln: University of Nebraska Press, 1989); David Hurst Thomas, ed., *Columbian Consequences, Volume 2, Archaeological and Historical Perspectives on the Spanish Borderlands East* (Washington, DC: Smithsonian Institution Press, 1990); Hudson and Tesser, *The Forgotten Centuries*; David J. Weber, *The Spanish Frontier in North America* (New Haven: Yale University Press, 1992); Braund, *Deerskins & Duffels*, 3–9, 26–27; Patricia Galloway, *Choctaw Genesis, 1500–1700* (Lincoln: University of Nebraska Press, 1996).
6. Seton, "The Northern Whitetail," 106; Audubon and Bachman, "Virginian Deer"; Caras, "Our Most Common Big-Game Animal: The Deer"; *White-Tailed Deer in the Southern Forest Habitat;* Banfield, "White-Tailed Deer"; Hesselton and Hesselton, "White-tailed Deer"; Rue, *The Deer of North America*; Samuel Cole Williams, ed., *Adair's History of the American Indians* (Johnson City, TN: The Watuga Press, 1930), 139 ("swifter and more sagacious"); Alexander Moore, ed., *Nairne's Muskohegan Journals: The 1708 Expedition to the Mississippi River* (Jackson: University Press of Mississippi, 1988), 52; Bernard Romans, *A Concise Natural History of East and West Florida* (New Orleans: Pelican Publishing Company, 1961 [orig. 1775]), 44; White, *Roots of Dependency*, 26–27; Usner, *Indians, Settlers, & Slaves*, 151–54; Braund, *Deerskins & Duffels*, 62–67; Arlene Fradkin, *Cherokee Folk Zoology: The Animal World of a Native American People, 1700–1838* (New York: Garland Publishing, Inc., 1990), 253–61, 265, 365–66.
7. James Mooney, "Myths of the Cherokee," *Bureau of American Ethnology, Nineteenth Annual Report for 1897–98* (Washington, DC: Government Printing Office, 1900), 3–548, p. 263; Williams, *Adair's History*, 7–9; William Harlan Gilbert, Jr., "The Eastern Cherokees," *Smithsonian Institution, Bureau of American Ethnology, Bulletin No. 133, Anthropology Papers No. 3* (Washington, DC: Government Printing Office, 1943), 169–413, pp. 327f., 344; Bruce D. Smith, "Middle Mississippi Exploitation of Animal Populations: A Predictive Model," *American Antiquity* 39 (1974): 274–91; Gregory A. Waselkov, "Evolution of Deer Hunting in the Eastern Woodlands," *Mid-continental Journal of Archaeology* 3, No. 1 (1978): 15–34; Moore, ed., *Nairne's Muskohegan Journals*, 62; Fradkin, *Cherokee Folk Zoology*, 265–66, 309–11, 348–59; Braund, *Deerskins & Duffels*, 71; Hudson, *The Southeastern Indians*, 261–69.

8. The social displacements and demographic changes produced by Soto might also have contained the germ for new national formations like the Creek Confederacy, which would later embrace people speaking five or more languages. On the 16th and 17th centuries, see Marvin T. Smith, "Aboriginal Population Movements in the Early Historic Period Interior Southeast," in *Powhatan's Mantle*, 21–34; other essays in *Powhatan's Mantle;* Thomas, *Columbian Consequences;* Hudson and Tesser, *The Forgotten Centuries*; Gregory A. Waselkov, "Historic Creek Indian Responses to European Trade and the Rise of Political Factions," in *Ethnohistory and Archaeology: Approaches to Postcontact Change in the Americas*, ed. J. Daniel Rogers and Samuel M. Wilson (New York: Plenum Press, 1993), 123–31; Braund, *Deerskins & Duffels*, 4–5, 53–54. On the importance of economic (and political) factors in explaining the trade in the Southeast, see Charles M. Hudson, Jr., "Why the Southeastern Indians Slaughtered Deer," in *Indians, Animals, and the Fur Trade: A Critique of "Keepers of the Game,"* ed. Shepard Krech III (Athens: University of Georgia Press, 1981), 155–76.
9. John Lawson, *A New Voyage to Carolina*, ed. Hugh Talmage Lefler (Chapel Hill: University of North Carolina Press, 1967), 129. On the early trade, see especially Silver, *New Face on the Countryside*, 68–74; Braund, *Deerskins & Duffels*, 28; Gregory A. Waselkov, "Seventeenth-Century Trade in the Colonial Southeast," *Southeastern Archaeology* 8, No. 2 (1989): 117–33; Usner, *Indians, Settlers, & Slaves*, 244–75; Gregory A. Waselkov, "Changing Strategies of Indian Field Location in the Early Historic Southeast," in *People, Plants, and Landscapes: Studies in Paleoethnobotany*, ed. K. J. Gremillion (Tuscaloosa: University of Alabama Press, 1996); Waselkov, "Evolution of Deer Hunting."
10. Daniel H. Usner, Jr., "The Deerskin Trade in French Louisiana," *Proceedings of the Tenth Meeting of the French Colonial Historical Society, 1984*, ed. Philip Boucher (Washington, DC: University Press of America, 1985), 75–93; Usner, *Indians, Settlers, & Slaves*, 28, 244–75; Braund, *Deerskins & Duffels*, 42, 87–89.
11. Merrell, *The Indians' New World*, passim; Braund, *Deerskins & Duffels*, passim; Richard L. Haan, "The 'Trade Do's Not Flourish as Formerly': The Ecological Origins of the Yamassee War of 1715," *Ethnohistory* 28 (1982): 341–58.
12. One wonders if women lobbied to get traders to accept undressed skins. Dressing deerskins and preparing them for market was dependent on their labor, and the increased value of skins and acceptance of undressed skins in theory eased the pressure on women—but only if hunters continued to kill the same number of deer, which they did not. On this and other issues in these paragraphs, see W. Neil Franklin, "Virginia and the Cherokee Indian Trade, 1673–1752," *East Tennessee Historical Society's Publications* 4 (January 1932): 3–21; Peter A. Brannon, *The Southern Indian Trade: Being Particularly a Study of Material from the Tallapoosa River Valley of Alabama* (Montgomery: The Paragon Press, 1935), 50–51 and passim; Usner, "The Deerskin Trade in French Louisiana"; Charles E. Hanson, Jr., "The Southern Fur Trade: A Slightly Different Story," *The Museum of the Fur Trade Quarterly* 22 (Spring 1986): 1–9; Merrell, *The Indians' New World*, 32; Seymour Feiler, ed., *Jean-Bernard Bossu's Travels in the Interior of North America 1751–1762* (Norman: University of Oklahoma Press, 1962), 39 (for the Natchez quotation), 146 (hunters who kill up to 400 deer a year); Moore, ed., *Nairne's Muskohegan Journals*, 37; White, *Roots of Dependency*, 44–47, 57–59; Daniel H. Usner, Jr., "The Frontier Exchange Economy of the Lower Mississippi Valley in the Eighteenth Century," *William and Mary Quarterly* 44 (April 1987): 165–92; Usner, *Indians, Settlers, & Slaves*, 25–26, 252, 259–75; Braund, *Deerskins & Duffels*, 28–37, 68–71, 125 (Scottish

look), 121–38; Gregory A. Waselkov, "French Colonial Trade in the Upper Creek Country," in *Calumet and Fleur-de-Lys: Archaeology of Indian and French Contact in the Midcontinent*, ed. John A. Walthall and Thomas E. Emerson (Washington, DC: Smithsonian Institution Press, 1992), 35–53; Waselkov, "The Eighteenth-Century Anglo-Indian Trade." For a 1784 tariff, see William S. Coker and Thomas D. Watson, *Indian Traders of the Southeastern Spanish Borderlands: Panton, Leslie & Company and John Forbes & Company, 1783–1847* (Pensacola: University of West Florida Press, 1986), 60.

13. Romans, *Concise Natural History*, 46, 51, 55, 64; White, *Roots of Dependency*, 57–58 (on alcohol and the "inelastic" market), 75, 82–86; Usner, *Indians, Settlers, & Slaves*, 120, 126–27, 255; Braund, *Deerskins & Duffels*, 50, 57, 103–7 (Charles Stuart, 105), 125–27, 131, 137; Wilcox, "Skins, Rum & Ruin"; Martin, "Southeastern Indians and the English Trade in Skins and Slaves," 318. In the 1770s, when the spirits and dry goods trades were both booming, the Quaker naturalist William Bartram remarked (with clearly offended sensibilities), using a familiar metaphor for the day, that to obtain goods the Creeks "wage eternal war against deer and bear." He thought that Creeks hunted "to an unreasonable and perhaps criminal excess" because traders "have dazzled their senses with foreign superfluities" including alcohol (Francis Harper, ed., *The Travels of William Bartram* [New Haven: Yale University Press, 1958], 135).
14. Estimating the number of deerskins traded and exported requires occasional conversion of weight (usually pounds or tons) to skins. Skins ranged in weight from under 1 to over 3 pounds depending on the deer's age and sex and the condition and preparation of the skin. I adopt here an arbitrary 2 pounds unless there is explicit reason (deriving from skin preparation, for example) to use a higher or lower estimate. Verner W. Crane, *The Southern Frontier 1670–1732* (Ann Arbor: University of Michigan Press, 1956 [orig. 1929]), 108–36 and passim; Franklin, "Virginia and the Cherokee Indian Trade, 1673–1752"; Brannon, *The Southern Indian Trade*, 51–55; Romans, *Concise Natural History*, 74–75; Wilcox, "Skins, Rum & Ruin"; Hanson, "The Southern Fur Trade"; White, *Roots of Dependency*, 92; Usner, "The Deerskin Trade in French Louisiana"; Daniel H. Usner, Jr., "The Frontier Exchange Economy of the Lower Mississippi Valley in the Eighteenth Century," *William and Mary Quarterly* 44 (1987): 165–92; Usner, *Indians, Settlers, & Slaves*, 119, 246–47; Braund, *Deerskins & Duffels*, 29, 36, 70–72, 88–89, 97–99; Silver, *New Face on the Countryside*, 90–97; Martin, "Southeastern Indians and the English Trade in Skins and Slaves," 313 (for 1707); Waselkov, "French Colonial Trade in the Upper Creek Country"; Gregory A. Waselkov, "The Eighteenth-Century Anglo-Indian Trade in Southeastern North America," paper presented at Seventh North American Fur Trade Conference, Halifax, Nova Scotia, 1995. For export figures, see also *White-Tailed Deer in the Southern Forest Habitat*, p. 1: In 1755–73, Savannah shipped 2.6 million pounds of deerskins from an estimated 600,000 deer; in 1753, North Carolina exported 30,000 deerskins; in 1771, Pensacola and Mobile shipped 250,000 pounds of deerskins and St. Augustine another 4,000 pounds; and in 1765–73, Georgia exported annually over 200,000 pounds of skins.
15. Romans, *Concise Natural History*, 82–126; White, *Roots of Dependency*, 57–59, 95–146, 316; Daniel H. Usner, Jr., "American Indians on the Cotton Frontier: Changing Economic Relations with Citizens and Slaves in the Mississippi Territory," *Journal of American History* 72 (September 1985): 297–317; Merrell, *The Indians' New World*, 39–40; Usner, *Indians, Settlers, & Slaves*, 244–75; Braund, *Deerskins & Duffels*, 99, 150, 153, 165–79.

16. Crane, *The Southern Frontier*, 111 ("infinite Herds"); Louis De Vorsey, Jr., ed., *De Brahm's Report of the General Survey in the Southern District of North America* (Columbia: University of South Carolina Press, 1971), 110–11, 153 (the deerskin-rum trade); Haan, "The 'Trade Do's Not Flourish as Formerly' "; White, *Roots of Dependency*, 8–11, 87, 92–94; Usner, *Indians, Settlers, & Slaves*, 173–74; Braund, *Deerskins & Duffels*, 34, 67–72 ("are becoming scarce"—the Mortar of Okchai), 132; Merrell, *The Indians' New World*, 129–37; Silver, *New Face on the Countryside*, 54, 69–70, 89–97 (Catesby, Mad Dog, Benjamin Hawkins, and colonial statutes); Axtell, *The Indians' New South*, 69 (killing deer for skins only); M. Thomas Hatley, "The Eighteenth-Century Tallapoosa Landscape Re-visited," in Gregory A. Waselkov, John W. Cottier, and Craig T. Sheldon, Jr., *Archaeological Investigations at the Early Historic Creek Indian Town of Fusihatchee (Phase I, 1988–1989)*. A Report to the National Science Foundation, Grant No. BNS-8718934, May 1990, 77–107; Waselkov, "Changing Strategies of Indian Field Location in the Early Historic Southeast"; Waselkov, "Eighteenth-Century Anglo-Indian Trade"; Wilcox, "Skins, Rum & Ruin"; Usner, "The Deerskin Trade in French Louisiana"; Waselkov, "French Colonial Trade in the Upper Creek Country"; Martin, "Southeastern Indians and the English Trade in Skins and Slaves," 319 (Virginia's closed season).
17. On population, see Peter Wood, "The Changing Population of the Colonial South: An Overview by Race and Region, 1685–1790," in *Powhatan's Mantle*, 35–103; Braund, *Deerskins & Duffels*, 133, 158. On war, peace, and deer: Richard White (*Roots of Dependency*, 9–10, 27, 32, 66–67, 70, 94, 317) concludes correctly that "although cultural demands for blood revenge were not designed to keep game abundant, by stimulating warfare they often created borderland havens for game." But if he implies that conscious motivation is involved when he remarks that war was a "cultural mechanism used . . . to maintain borderland hunting grounds," then this is surely debatable. Renewed hunting of deer was no doubt one incentive for peace, but people did not necessarily wage war to conserve deer.
18. Braund, *Deerskins & Duffels*, 67–71 (one million); Silver, *New Face on the Countryside*, 89, 97; Gregory A. Waselkov, "Introduction: Part Two, Politics and Economics," in *Powhatan's Mantle*, 129–33, p. 132.
19. Mooney, "Myths of the Cherokee," 229–31, 250–52; James Mooney, "The Sacred Formulas of the Cherokees," *Smithsonian Institution, Bureau of American Ethnology, Seventh Annual Report for 1885–1886* (Washington, DC: Government Printing Office, 1891), 301–97, pp. 319–22; Fradkin, *Cherokee Folk Zoology*, 112–13, 201–3, 289–95.
20. Charles Hudson, "Cherokee Concept of Natural Balance," *Indian Historian* 3, No. 4 (1970): 51–54, pp. 52, 54. On harmony and equilibrium in Cherokee religion and ritual, see also Raymond D. Fogelson, "Change, Persistence, and Accommodation in Cherokee Medico-magical Beliefs," in *Symposium on Cherokee and Iroquois Culture, Smithsonian Institution, Bureau of American Ethnology, Bulletin No. 180*, ed. William N. Fenton and John Gulick (Washington, DC: Government Printing Office, 1961), 215–25; Catherine L. Albanese, "Exploring Regional Religion: A Case Study of the Eastern Cherokee," *History of Religions* 23 (1984): 344–71; Lee Irwin, "Cherokee Healing: Myth, Dreams, and Medicine," *American Indian Quarterly* 16 (Spring 1992): 237–57, p. 240.
21. For *idi:gawé:sdi* and *dida:hnvwi:sg(i)*, "curers of them" or medicine men, see Mooney, "Sacred Formulas"; James Mooney and Frans M. Olbrechts, "The Swimmer Manuscript: Cherokee Sacred Formulas and Medicinal Prescriptions," *Smithsonian Institution, Bureau of American Ethnology, Bulletin No. 99*

(Washington, DC: Government Printing Office, 1932); Jack Frederick Kilpatrick and Anna Gritts Kilpatrick, *Walk in Your Soul: Love Incantations of the Oklahoma Cherokees* (Dallas: Southern Methodist University Press, 1965), 4–5; Jack Frederick Kilpatrick and Anna Gritts Kilpatrick, *Run toward the Nightland: Magic of the Oklahoma Cherokees* (Dallas: Southern Methodist University Press, 1967), 4–7; Fogelson, "Change, Persistence, and Accommodation"; Raymond D. Fogelson, "An Analysis of Cherokee Sorcery and Witchcraft," in *Four Centuries of Southern Indians*, ed. Charles M. Hudson (Athens: University of Georgia Press, 1975), 113–31; Fradkin, *Cherokee Folk Zoology*, 296–302; Charles M. Hudson, *Elements of Southeastern Indian Religion* (Leiden: E. J. Brill, 1984), 12–16.

22. Mooney, "Myths of the Cherokee," 248, 435; Mooney, "Sacred Formulas," 311; Mooney and Olbrechts, "The Swimmer Manuscript," 146–47, 153, 156. See also Frank G. Speck and Leonard Broom in collaboration with Will West Long, *Cherokee Dance and Drama* (Norman: University of Oklahoma Press, 1983), 84–85, 89–92. On *idi:gawé:sdi* structure, "the powers resident in the minor sacred numeral four or major sacred numeral seven," and Mooney's apparent neglect of "sacred numerology," see Kilpatrick and Kilpatrick, *Walk in Your Soul*, 7.
23. Albert S. Gatschet, *A Migration Legend of the Creek Indians, with a Linguistic, Historic, and Ethnographic Introduction, Volume I* (New York: AMS Press, 1969 [orig. 1884]), 79–80. In putting this song to printed page, I have literally followed Gatschet, who stated that the "song-lines are repeated thrice, in a slow and plaintive tune, except the refrain, which is sung or rather spoken in a quicker measure, and *once* only." See also Mooney, "Myths of the Cherokee," 435; John R. Swanton, "Social Organization and Social Usages of the Indians of the Creek Confederacy," *Forty-Second Annual Report of the Bureau of American Ethnology, Smithsonian Institution, 1924–1925* (Washington DC: Government Printing Office, 1928), 23–472, pp. 444–45; Braund, *Deerskins & Duffels*, 63.
24. Mooney, "Sacred Formulas," 369–71; Mooney and Olbrechts, "The Swimmer Manuscript," 15–16, 23, 159; Gilbert, "The Eastern Cherokees," 297; Kilpatrick and Kilpatrick, *Run toward the Nightland*, 11; Kilpatrick and Kilpatrick, *Walk in Your Soul*, 25; Speck, Broom, and Long, *Cherokee Dance and Drama*, 85–86, 89–92.
25. Obviously great care should be taken projecting 20th-century Oklahoma Muskogean songs to the Cherokee past. Kilpatrick and Kilpatrick, *Walk in Your Soul*, 75; Jack Frederick Kilpatrick and Anna Gritts Kilpatrick, "Muskogean Charm Songs among the Oklahoma Cherokees," *Smithsonian Contributions to Anthropology* 2, No. 3 (1967): 29–40. According to Olbrechts (Mooney and Olbrechts, "The Swimmer Manuscript," 90, 163), Cherokee knowledge of deer anatomy was scant even though one formula mentions seven different kinds of deer; Cherokees killed few deer when he was living with them.
26. Mooney, "Myths of the Cherokee," 251, 263–64.
27. This particular medicine man invoked spirits in the early 20th century. Jack Frederick Kilpatrick and Anna Gritts Kilpatrick, "Notes of a Cherokee Shaman," *Smithsonian Contributions to Anthropology* 2, No. 6 (1970): 83–125, pp. 87–88, 114–15; Kilpatrick and Kilpatrick, *Walk in Your Soul*, 8; Mooney "Sacred Formulas," 345–51; Mooney and Olbrechts, "The Swimmer Manuscript," 19, 25–26, 43, 51–54, 57, 69, 196, 202–8, 291–94, 301–2; Fradkin, *Cherokee Folk Zoology*, 300–301.
28. Lawson, *A New Voyage to Carolina*, 58, 219; Williams, *Adair's History*, 122–24, 138, 144; Moore, *Nairne's Muskohegan Journals*, 43; Braund, *Deerskins & Duffels*, 63–64; Mooney, "Myths of the Cherokee," 447; John R. Swanton, "Religious Beliefs and Medical Practices of the Creek Indians," *Bureau of American Ethnology, Bulletin*

No. 42 (Washington, DC: Government Printing Office, 1928), 473–672, pp. 498, 502–3, 517, 637–39, 654, 660.

29. Williams, *Adair's History*, 124 ("religious oeconomy"). Adair's remark follows a general comment on an Indian hunter "sacrific[ing]" part of or an entire buck to powers that had granted him success, and his subsequent "purification" in water protecting him from future misfortune. See also Mooney, "Sacred Formulas," 309, 374; Fogelson, "Change, Persistence, and Accommodation" (on atrophy of hunting formula knowledge as game decreased); Gilbert, "The Eastern Cherokees," 188, 367–70.
30. Silver, *New Face on the Countryside*, 53 (Ralph Hamor); Helen C. Rountree, *The Powhatan Indians of Virginia: Their Traditional Culture* (Norman: University of Oklahoma Press, 1990), 40–41 (William Strachey); Rountree concludes that the Powhatan hunted deer and other animals without regard for conservation.
31. Mooney, "Myths of the Cherokee," 261–62 (my emphasis); Mooney and Olbrechts, "The Swimmer Manuscript," 27–29; Speck, Broom, and Long, *Cherokee Dance and Drama*, 84. According to Fradkin (*Cherokee Folk Zoology*, 361), "successive animations were primarily associated with the bear." She bases this conclusion largely on one of Olbrechts's consultants in the 1920s. But deer were then scarce, *idi:gawé:sdi* directed at influence over them had atrophied greatly, Olbrechts admits to great difficulty obtaining information on what Mooney discovered four decades before, and even though Mooney had difficulty obtaining information on deer, he contradicts Fradkin's conclusion (Mooney and Olbrechts, "The Swimmer Manuscript," 77, 112, 140, 146). For the number seven, see Mooney and Olbrechts, "The Swimmer Manuscript," 52; Kilpatrick and Kilpatrick, *Walk in Your Soul*, 5.
32. *White-Tailed Deer in the Southern Forest Habitat*, 1–5; Silver, *New Face on the Countryside*, 94–97; Robert L. Downing, "Success Story: White-Tailed Deer," in *Restoring America's Wildlife*, ed. Harmon Kallman et al. (Washington, DC: U.S. Department of the Interior, Fish and Wildlife Service, 1987), 47–57; "Bambi the Pest," *New York Times*, July 26, 1997, 20; Andrew C. Revkin, "Coming to the Suburbs: A Hit Squad for Deer," *New York Times*, November 30, 1998, A1, 25. In November and December 1996, and on June 29, 1997, *60 Minutes* and a national nightly newscast dedicated segments to the adverse impact of exploding deer populations on suburban Long Island, New York, and Michigan farmlands.

Chapter Seven: Beaver

1. The most pervasive commodification is associated with capitalism and the West. On commodities, which in economic shorthand possess "use" and "exchange" value simultaneously—commodities are goods that have value in relation to other goods—and commodification, see Igor Kopytoff, "The Cultural Biography of Things: Commoditization as Process," in *The Social Life of Things: Commodities in Cultural Perspective*, ed. Arjun Appadurai (New York: Cambridge University Press, 1986), 64–91, and other essays in this volume. John P. Dempsey, *New English Canaan by Thomas Morton of "Merrymount": A Critical Edition*, Volumes I–II, Ph.D. dissertation (Brown University, 1998), Volume I, 59–108; William Wood, *New England's Prospect*, ed. Alden T. Vaughan (Amherst: University of Massachusetts Press, 1993), 37, 38, 72; John Lawson, *A New Voyage to Carolina*, ed. Hugh Talmage Lefler (Chapel Hill: University of North Carolina Press, 1967), passim.
2. Dempsey, *New English Canaan*, 78.
3. Lewis Henry Morgan, *The American Beaver: A Classic of Natural History and*

Ecology (New York: Dover Publications, 1986 [orig. 1868]); John Richardson, "Castor fiber, Americanus. The American Beaver," in *Fauna Boreali-Americana; or the Zoology of the Northern Parts of British America. Part First Containing The Quadrupeds* (New York: Arno Press, 1974 [orig. 1829–1837]), 105–13; John James Audubon and John Bachman, "American Beaver," in *The Quadrupeds of North America*, Volume 1 (New York: Arno Press, 1974 [orig. 1846]), 347–59; J. A. Allen, *Monographs of North American Rodentia. No. VI. Castoridae*, by Elliott Coues and Joel Asaph Allen, Department of the Interior, U.S. Geological Survey of the Territories, Report 11, No. 6 (1877), 427–54; Horace T. Martin, *Castorologia or the History and Traditions of the Canadian Beaver* (Montreal: William Drysdale and Company, 1892); Ernest Thompson Seton, "Canadian Beaver," in *Life-histories of Northern Animals: An Account of the Mammals of Manitoba*, Volume 1 (New York: Charles Scribner's Sons, 1909), 447–79; Edward Royal Warren, *The Beaver: Its Work and Its Ways* (Baltimore: The Williams & Wilkins Company, 1927), 20–21 and passim; Leonard Lee Rue III, *The World of the Beaver* (Philadelphia: J. B. Lippincott Co., 1964); A. W. F. Banfield, "Beavers," in *The Mammals of Canada* (Toronto: University of Toronto Press, 1974), 157–62; Edward P. Hill, "Beaver," in *Wild Mammals of North America: Biology, Management, and Economics*, ed. Joseph A. Chapman and George A. Feldhamer (Baltimore: Johns Hopkins University Press, 1982), 256–81; Milan Novak, "Beaver," in *Wild Furbearer Management and Conservation in North America*, ed. Milan Novak et al. (Ontario: Ministry of Natural Resources, 1987), 282–312.

4. Reuben Gold Thwaites, ed., *The Jesuit Relations and Allied Documents: Travels and Explorations of the Jesuit Missionaries in New France 1610–1791* (Cleveland: Burrows Brothers, 1897), Volume 6, 297, 299 ("the English . . . "); Jean Elizabeth Murray, *The Fur Trade in New France and New Netherland prior to 1645*, Ph.D. dissertation (University of Chicago, 1936), 1–23 and passim; Eleanor Leacock, "The Montagnais 'Hunting Territory' and the Fur Trade," *Memoirs of the American Anthropological Association* No. 78 (Menasha, WI, 1954), 1–59, pp. 10–12 (Champlain); Dean R. Snow, "Abenaki Fur Trade in the Sixteenth Century," *Western Canadian Journal of Anthropology* 6, No. 1 (1976): 3–11; Herbert C. Kraft, "Sixteenth and Seventeenth Century Indian/White Trade Relations in the Middle Atlantic and Northeast Regions," *Archaeology of Northeastern North America* 17 (1989): 1–29; Arthur J. Ray and Donald Freeman, *'Give Us Good Measure': An Economic Analysis of Relations between the Indians and the Hudson's Bay Company before 1763* (Toronto: University of Toronto Press, 1978), 19ff.

5. Martin, *Castorologia*, passim; Warren, *The Beaver*, 19; Rue, *The World of the Beaver*, 135; Novak, "Beaver"; Harold A. Innis, *The Fur Trade in Canada: An Introduction to Canadian Economic History*, revised edition (Toronto: University of Toronto Press, 1970), 386–96 and passim; Murray G. Lawson, *Fur: A Study in English Mercantilism, 1700–1775* (Toronto: University of Toronto Press, 1943); Murray G. Lawson, "The Beaver Hat and the North American Fur Trade," in *People and Pelts*, Selected Papers of the Second North American Fur Trade Conference, ed. Malvina Bolus (Winnipeg: Peguis Publishers, 1972), 27–37.

6. For example, Harold Hickerson, "Fur Trade Colonialism and the North American Indians," *Journal of Ethnic Studies* 1 (1973): 15–44, p. 24. Toby Morantz was an early proponent of the idea that there was not one but many trades. See Toby Morantz, "The Fur Trade and the Cree of James Bay," in *Old Trails and New Directions: Papers of the Third North American Fur Trade Conference*, ed. Carol M. Judd and Arthur J. Ray (Toronto: University of Toronto Press, 1980), 39–58;

Shepard Krech III, ed., *The Subarctic Fur Trade: Native Social and Economic Adaptations* (Vancouver: University of British Columbia Press, 1984); Jacqueline Peterson and John Afinson, "The Indian and the Fur Trade: A Review of Recent Literature," *Manitoba History* 10 (1988): 10–18; Ray and Freeman, *'Give Us Good Measure,'* 20.

7. William I. Roberts III, *The Fur Trade of New England in the Seventeenth Century*, Ph.D. dissertation (University of Pennsylvania, 1958); Peter A. Thomas, "The Fur Trade, Indian Land and the Need to Define Adequate 'Environmental' Parameters," *Ethnohistory* 28 (Fall 1981): 359–79; Neal Salisbury, *Manitou and Providence: Indians, Europeans, and the Making of New England, 1500–1643* (New York: Oxford University Press, 1982).
8. Bruce G. Trigger, "Ontario Native People and the Epidemics of 1634–1640," in *Indians, Animals, and the Fur Trade: A Critique of "Keepers of the Game,"* ed. Shepard Krech III (Athens: University of Georgia Press, 1981), 19–38; Bruce G. Trigger, "The Road to Affluence: A Reassessment of Early Huron Responses to European Contact," in *Out of the Background: Readings on Canadian Native History*, ed. Robin Fisher and Kenneth Coates (Toronto: Copp Clark Pitman Ltd., 1988), 88–101; Conrad Heidenreich, *Huronia: A History and Geography of the Huron Indians 1600–1650* (Toronto: Historical Sites Branch, Ontario Ministry of Natural Resources, McClelland and Stewart Ltd., 1971), 207–8; Conrad E. Heidenreich and Arthur J. Ray, *The Early Fur Trades: A Study in Cultural Interaction*, ed. John Wolforth and R. Cole Harris (Toronto: McClelland and Stewart Ltd., 1976), 27–28 (Sagard), 63–65; Murray, *The Fur Trade in New France and New Netherland*, 103–12, 184–85; Paul Chrisler Phillips, *The Fur Trade*, Volume 1 (Norman: University of Oklahoma Press, 1961).
9. Long before 1670, the Iroquois were said to have "absolutely exhausted" the south side of Lake Ontario, and as a consequence roamed north and west to fight the Illinois and Miami who had poached on Iroquois lands. In light of the Iroquois' role in the eradication of beavers in their own lands, their report to Baron de Lahontan that "contrary to the custom of all the Savages" the Illinois and Miami "have carried off whole Stocks, both Male and Female" seems self-serving. Allen W. Trelease, "The Iroquois and the Western Fur Trade: A Problem in Interpretation," *Mississippi Valley Historical Review* 49 (June 1992): 32–51, p. 43; Thwaites, *The Jesuit Relations*, Volume 40, 211–15; Innis, *The Fur Trade in Canada*, 21, 36–37, 51 ("absolutely exhausted"), 54–55; Bruce Alden Cox, "Indian Middlemen and the Early Fur Trade: Reconsidering the Position of the Hudson's Bay Company's 'Trading Indians,'" in *Rendezvous, Selected Papers of the Fourth North American Fur Trade Conference, 1981*, ed. Thomas C. Buckley (St. Paul: North American Fur Trade Conference, 1984), 93–99; George T. Hunt, *The Wars of the Iroquois: A Study in Intertribal Trade Relations* (Madison: University of Wisconsin Press, 1968); Thomas Elliot Norton, *The Fur Trade in Colonial New York 1686–1776* (Madison: University of Wisconsin Press, 1974).
10. Peter Fidler, a Hudson's Bay Company surveyor and trader, said that the Piegan were "so full of superstition" in the 1790s that they would not bring dead beavers inside their tipis, or touch or eat them. Perhaps the aversion was linked to the significance of beavers, at least among the closely related Blackfeet, in sacred ceremonies, medicine bundles, and ritual conducive to success hunting buffaloes. Peter Fidler, "Journal of a Journey over Land from Buckingham House to the Rocky Mountains in 1792 & 3." Accession No. 79.269/89. Provincial Archives of Alberta, Edmonton, Alberta, 11. For the Plains and Upper Midwest, see Annie Heloise Abel,

ed., *Tabeau's Narrative of Loisel's Expedition to the Upper Missouri* (Norman: University of Oklahoma Press, 1939), 83–88; Oscar Lewis, *The Effects of White Contact upon Blackfoot Culture with Special Reference to the Role of the Fur Trade,* Monographs of the American Ethnological Society, Volume 6 (Seattle: University of Washington Press, 1942); Joseph Jablow, *The Cheyenne in Plains Indian Trade Relations 1795–1840,* Monographs of the American Ethnological Society, Volume 19 (Seattle: University of Washington Press, 1950); John E. Sunder, *The Fur Trade on the Upper Missouri, 1840–1865* (Norman: University of Oklahoma Press, 1965); James L. Clayton, "The Growth and Economic Significance of the American Fur Trade, 1790–1890," in *Aspects of the Fur Trade,* Selected Papers of the 1965 North American Fur Trade Conference (St. Paul: Minnesota Historical Society, 1967), 62–72; Josiah Gregg, *Commerce of the Prairies,* ed. Max L. Moorhead (Norman: University of Oklahoma Press, 1974); Jeanne Kay, "Wisconsin Indian Hunting Patterns, 1634–1836," *Annals of the Association of American Geographers* 69, No. 3 (1979): 402–18; Robert A. Trennert, Jr., *Indian Traders on the Middle Border: The House of Ewing, 1827–54* (Lincoln: University of Nebraska Press, 1981); Jeanne Kay, "Native Americans in the Fur Trade and Wildlife Depletion," *Environmental Review* 9 (1985): 118–30; Fred R. Gowans, *Rocky Mountain Rendezvous: A History of the Fur Trade Rendezvous, 1825–1840* (Layton, UT: Gibbs M. Smith, Inc., 1985); Hiram Martin Chittenden, *The American Fur Trade of the Far West,* Volumes 1–2 (Lincoln: University of Nebraska Press, 1986); David J. Wishart, *The Fur Trade of the American West 1807–1840* (Lincoln: University of Nebraska Press, 1992); R. Grace Morgan, *Beaver Ecology/Beaver Mythology,* Ph.D. thesis (Department of Anthropology, University of Alberta, 1991), 1–13, 45–47, 102–4, 172–90, and passim; Robert Glass Cleland, *This Reckless Breed of Men: The Trappers and Fur Traders of the Southwest* (Lincoln: University of Nebraska Press, 1992); Mary K. Whelan, "Dakota Indian Economics and the Nineteenth-Century Fur Trade," *Ethnohistory* 40 (Spring 1993): 246–76.

11. In the 1820s, Sewell Newhouse began making traps at Oneida Community, which five decades later produced 300,000 annually. On castoreum and the steel trap: Richard Glover, ed., *David Thompson's Narrative 1784–1812* (Toronto: The Champlain Society, 1962), 204–5; Innis, *The Fur Trade in Canada,* 263–64; A. W. Schorger, "A Brief History of the Steel Trap and Its Use in North America," *Wisconsin Academy of Sciences, Arts and Letters* (1951): 171–99; Carl P. Russell, *Firearms, Traps, & Tools of the Mountain Men* (New York: Alfred A. Knopf, 1967), 97–163; Robin F. Wells, "Castoreum and Steel Traps in Eastern North America," *American Anthropologist* 74 (June 1972): 479–83; Christian F. Feest, "More on Castoreum and Traps in Eastern North America," *American Anthropologist* 77 (September 1975): 603; Richardson, "Castor fiber, Americanus. The American Beaver," 108; Martin, *Castorologia,* 147 (Iroquois); Warren, *The Beaver,* 19; Rue, *The World of the Beaver,* 135 (mountain men).

12. James A. Tober, *Who Owns the Wildlife? The Political Economy of Conservation in Nineteenth-Century America* (Westport, CT: Greenwood Press, 1981); John F. Reiger, *American Sportsmen and the Origins of Conservation,* revised edition (Norman: University of Oklahoma Press, 1986); R. MacFarlane, "Notes on Mammals Collected and Observed in the Northern Mackenzie River District, Northwest Territories of Canada, with Remarks on Explorers and Explorations of the Far North," *Proceedings U. S. National Museum* 28, No. 1405 (1905): 673–764, p. 743; William T. Hornaday, "The Fur Trade and the Wild Animals," *Zoological Society Bulletin* 24, No. 2 (1921): 29–52, p. 29 ("craze," "mad rush"); Martin, *Castorologia,* 50–59,

143–45; Seton, "Canadian Beaver"; Ernest A. Sterling, "The Return of the Beaver to the Adirondacks," *American Forests* 19, No. 5 (1913): 292–99; G. B. Heath, "The Beaver Coming Back," *Fins, Feathers and Fur* 6 (1916): 3–5; Robert B. Peck, "The Renaissance of the Beaver," *Forest and Stream* 91 (April 1921): 152–54, 182–87, p. 184 ("interesting but destructive"); Vernon Bailey, "Beaver Habits, Beaver Control, and Possibilities in Beaver Farming," *U.S. Department of Agriculture*, Bulletin No. 1078 (Washington, DC, 1922): 1–29; Lee E. Yeager, "Trouble in the High Country—Beaver Mismanagement," *Colorado Conservation* 3, No. 4 (1954): 11–15; Lee E. Yeager, "Let's Argue . . . about Beaver!" *Hunting & Fishing* 31, No. 10 (1954): 22–25, 66–67; Rue, *The World of the Beaver*, 138–43; Julius F. Wolff, Jr., "Hot Fur," in *Rendezvous*, 215–30; Novak, "Beaver"; Martyn E. Obbard et al., "Furbearer Harvests in North America," in *Wild Furbearer Management and Conservation in North America*, 1007–34; Milan Novak et al., *Furbearer Harvests in North America, 1600–1984*, supplement to *ibid.*

13. John R. Luoma, "Back to Stay," *Audubon* 98 (January–February 1996): 53–58; Elizabeth Bumiller, "Besieged by Beavers in Rural New York," *New York Times* September 3, 1996, B1; Todd Shields, "Busy Beavers Gnaw on Suburban Nerves," *Washington Post*, December 14, 1996, A1; Robert Whitcomb, "We Humans Subdivide Nature at Our Own Whim," *Providence Sunday Journal*, July 27, 1997.

14. Linguistic classification and ethnonymy are complex in this region. Following expansion, various Ojibwa-speaking people—ethnonyms from *Handbook of North American Indians*—lived in Ontario (the Algonquin, Nipissing, Northern Ojibwa, Southeastern Ojibwa, Southwestern Chippewa, Ottawa, and Saulteaux), Manitoba (the Saulteaux), Michigan (the Ottawa), Wisconsin (the Southwestern Chippewa and Ottawa), and Minnesota (the Southwestern Chippewa). (The exact linguistic relationship of Ottawa and Algonquin to "Ojibwa" is under discussion.) For the Montagnais, Naskapi, East Cree, Attikamek, Eastern and Western Swampy Cree, Woods Cree, Ottawa, Saulteaux, Severn Ojibwa, Central Southern Ojibwa, and Eastern Ojibwa languages in the Algonquian (or more broadly, Algic) language family, see Ives Goddard, "Introduction," in *Handbook of North American Indians, Volume 17, Languages* (Washington, DC: Smithsonian Institution, 1996), 1–16; Ives Goddard, "Native Languages and Language Families of North America," in *ibid.*, endmap; Michael K. Foster, "Language and the Culture History of North America," in *ibid.*, 64–110, pp. 97–100. On ethnonymy, see Bruce Trigger, ed., *Handbook of North American Indians, Volume 15, Northeast* (Washington, DC: Smithsonian Institution, 1978); Ives Goddard, "Synonymy," in "Southeastern Ojibwa" by Edward S. Rogers, in *ibid.*, 760–71, pp. 768–71 ("puckered up"); June Helm, ed., *Handbook of North American Indians, Volume 6, Subarctic* (Washington, DC: Smithsonian Institution, 1981); Daniel Francis and Toby Morantz, *Partners in Furs: A History of the Fur Trade in Eastern James Bay 1600–1870* (Kingston: McGill-Queen's University Press, 1983), 11–13; Charles A. Bishop, *The Northern Ojibwa and the Fur Trade: An Historical and Ecological Study* (Toronto: Holt, Rinehart and Winston of Canada, Ltd., 1974), 305–39; Charles A. Bishop, "Ojibwa, Cree, and the Hudson's Bay Company in Northern Ontario: Culture and Conflict in the Eighteenth Century," in *Western Canada: Past and Present*, ed. Anthony W. Rasporich (University of Calgary, 1975), 150–62; Shepard Krech III, "The Subarctic Culture Area," in *Native North Americans: An Ethnohistorical Approach*, second edition, ed. Molly Mignon and Daniel Boxberger (Dubuque, IA: Kendall Hunt, 1997), 85–112.

15. The debate over family hunting territories extends over eight decades. See Adrian

Tanner, "The Significance of Hunting Territories Today," in *Cultural Ecology: Readings on the Canadian Indians and Eskimos*, ed. Bruce Cox (Toronto: McClelland and Stewart Ltd., 1973), 101–14; Charles A. Bishop and Toby Morantz, eds., "A Qui Appartient Le Castor? Les Régimes Fonciers Algonquins Du Nord Remis En Cause/Who Owns the Beaver? Northern Algonquian Land Tenure Reconsidered," *Anthropologica* 28, Nos. 1–2 (1986): 1–220; Colin Scott, "Property, Power, and Aboriginal Rights among Quebec Cree Hunters," in *Hunters and Gatherers 2: Property, Power, and Ideology*, ed. Tim Ingold, David Riches, and James Woodburn (New York: Berg, 1988), 35–51.

16. Le Jeune remarked that this man "was making sport of us Europeans, who have such a fondness for the skin of this animal and who fight to see who will give the most to these Barbarians, to get it; they carry this to such an extent my host said to me one day, showing me a beautiful knife, 'The English have no sense; they give us twenty knives like this for one Beaver skin.'" Thwaites, *The Jesuit Relations,* Volume 6, 297, 299. On these Montagnais, see also John M. Cooper, *The Northern Algonquian Supreme Being*, Catholic University of America Anthropological Series No. 2 (Washington, DC: Catholic University of America, 1934), 60–61. Later that century, Father Chrétien Le Clercq, a Récollet missionary to the Mi'kmaq in northern New Brunswick (across the St. Lawrence from the Montagnais) echoed Le Jeune when he reported being "unable to keep from laughing on overhearing an Indian" say "in banter" as follows, "In truth, my brother, the Beaver does everything to perfection. He makes for us kettles, axes, swords, knives, and gives us drink and food without the trouble of cultivating the ground" (see Innis, *The Fur Trade in Canada*, 27–28; Leacock, "The Montagnais 'Hunting Territory,' " 11–12; compare John M. Cooper, "Is the Algonquian Family Hunting Ground System Pre-Columbian?," *American Anthropologist* 41 [1939]: 66–90).
17. Thwaites, *The Jesuit Relations,* Volume 8, 57; Innis, *The Fur Trade in Canada*, 28.
18. Thwaites, *The Jesuit Relations,* Volume 8, 57, Volume 7, 171, Volume 31, 209, Volume 32, 269, 271, Volume 59, 29. On Le Jeune, see, for example, Leacock, "The Montagnais 'Hunting Territory,' " 14–15; Cooper, "Is the Algonquian Family Hunting Ground System Pre-Columbian?," 76; Frank G. Speck and Loren C. Eiseley, "Significance of Hunting Territory Systems of the Algonkian in Social Theory," *American Anthropologist* 41 (1939): 269–80, pp. 271, 274–75. Toby Morantz (personal communication, June 7, 1998) rightly cautions about generalizing beyond Le Jeune given the equivocal nature of evidence at his time.
19. There is no indication that Indians deliberately left beavers alive (Thwaites, *The Jesuit Relations,* Volume 8, 57, 59, Volume 6, 299–303; see also Leacock, "The Montagnais 'Hunting Territory,' " 3; Thomas L. Altherr, " 'Flesh Is the Paradise of a Man of Flesh': Cultural Conflict over Indian Hunting Beliefs and Rituals in New France as Recorded in *The Jesuit Relations,*" *Canadian Historical Review* 64 [1983]: 267–76, p. 276; Heidenreich and Ray, *The Early Fur Trades*, 65). On Denys and his remark that the Mi'kmaq saved "few" beavers (which does not necessarily contradict other things that he said), see Calvin Martin, "The European Impact on the Culture of a Northeastern Algonquian Tribe: An Ecological Interpretation," *William and Mary Quarterly* 31 (1974): 3–26, pp. 4, 11, 16. Following Denys, Martin stated that the Mi'kmaq formerly took only what they needed for subsistence, and that the taking was governed by "spiritual consideration." But is there evidence for this or for Martin's thesis that "overkill of wildlife would have been resented by the animal kingdom as an act comparable to genocide" in any sources prior to the 20th century? See note 56. For a recent account of Mi'kmaq history, see

Harald E. L. Prins, *The Mi'kmaq: Resistance, Accommodation, and Cultural Survival* (Fort Worth: Harcourt Brace, 1996).

20. Thwaites, *The Jesuit Relations,* Volume 8, 57, 59.
21. The Rupert House account is reported by J. Oldmixon in 1741 from a journal of Thomas Gorst dated 1670–75. See Diamond Jenness, *The Ojibwa Indians of Parry Island, Their Social and Religious Life*, Canada Department of Mines, National Museum of Canada, Bulletin No. 78, Anthropological Series No. 17, (Ottawa: National Museum of Canada, 1935), 5; Toby Morantz, "Old Texts, Old Questions: Another Look at the Issue of Continuity and the Early Fur-Trade Period," *Canadian Historical Review* 73 (1992): 166–93, p. 184; Cooper, "Is the Algonquian Family Hunting Ground System Pre-Columbian?," 77–78; Leacock, "The Montagnais 'Hunting Territory,' " 16; Bishop, "Ojibwa, Cree, and the Hudson's Bay Company in Northern Ontario," 153–54.
22. Additional problems stem from Radisson's still-debated claims to have reached James Bay and other places. Arthur T. Adams, ed., *The Explorations of Pierre Esprit Radisson*, (Minneapolis: Ross and Haines, 1961), 88, 95, 147; Charles A. Bishop, "The Western James Bay Cree: Aboriginal and Early Historic Adaptations," *Prairie Forum* 8 (1983): 147–55; Robert A. Brightman, "Conservation and Resource Depletion: The Case of the Boreal Forest Algonquians," in *The Question of the Commons: The Culture and Ecology of Communal Resources* (Tucson: University of Arizona Press, 1987), 121–41, p. 123; Murray, *The Fur Trade in New France and New Netherland*, 8; Francis and Morantz, *Partners in Furs*, 22; Germaine Warkentin, personal communication (e-mail), June 2, 1998. The evidence for conservation or hunting territories elsewhere in this era is thin. Le Clercq (also see note 16) mentioned that the Mi'kmaq elders and a chief determined (in 1675–87) how territories should be assigned to hunters the following season (Frank G. Speck, "Family Hunting Territories of the Lake St. John Montagnais and Neighboring Bands," *Anthropos* 22 [1927]: 387–403, p. 392; Cooper, "Is the Algonquian Family Hunting Ground System Pre-Columbian?," 78–79). In 1689, Baron de Lahontan remarked that each fall the Algonquian Fox agreed to the allotment of hunting grounds, each with fur-bearing resources, and not to trespass, but Cooper ("Is the Algonquian Family Hunting Ground System Pre-Columbian?," 75) and others wonder whether Lahontan is dependable.
23. Thwaites, *The Jesuit Relations*, Volume 68, 109, Volume 69, 113 ("asking The Impossible"); Edward S. Rogers, "The Hunting Group-Hunting Territory Complex among the Misstassini Indians," National Museum of Canada, Bulletin No. 195, Anthropological Series No. 63 (Ottawa: National Museum of Canada, 1963); Toby Morantz, "The Probability of Family Hunting Territories in Eighteenth Century James Bay: Old Evidence Newly Presented," in *Papers of the Ninth Algonquian Conference*, ed. William Cowan (Ottawa: Carleton University, 1978), 224–36, p. 233; Francis and Morantz, *Partners in Furs*, 33–64, 96 ("in one anothers Leiberty"); Charles A. Bishop, "Demography, Ecology and Trade among the Northern Ojibwa and Swampy Cree," *Western Canadian Journal of Anthropology* 3 (1972): 58–71 (Fort Albany). Toby Morantz (personal communication, June 7, 1998) emphasizes that evidence for hunting territories increased in the 18th century.
24. Discussion is confined to the Cree who traded at York Factory—generalization beyond would be hazardous—at a period selected because three York Factory residents left reports: James Isham, present except for several years from the late 1730s to 1761; T. F. Drage, who spent one winter with Isham in the late 1740s; and Andrew Graham, at York Factory from 1753 to 1774. Their accounts are not inde-

pendent and require careful reading. E. E. Rich, ed., *James Isham's Observations on Hudsons Bay, 1743* (London: The Champlain Society for the Hudson's Bay Record Society, 1949); T. F. Drage, "An Ethnographic Account of the Northern Cree, 1748," *Manitoba Archeological Quarterly* 6, No. 1 (1982): 1–40; Glyndwr Williams, ed., *Andrew Graham's Observations on Hudson's Bay 1767–91* (London: The Hudson's Bay Record Society, 1969).

25. Williams, *Andrew Graham's Observations*, 263, 275–77; E. E. Rich, "Trade Habits and Economic Motivation among the Indians of North America," *Canadian Journal of Economics and Political Science* 26 (1960): 35–53; Heidenreich and Ray, *The Early Fur Trades*, 76–87; Arthur J. Ray, "Competition and Conservation in the Early Subarctic Fur Trade," *Ethnohistory* 25 (1978): 347–57; Ray and Freeman, '*Give Us Good Measure*,' 125–74, 223–28, and passim. Ray and Freeman reveal beaver trade fluctuations at HBC posts on Hudson Bay in 1700–1760, the era of French-English competition. At Fort Albany and Eastmain, the value of beaver pelts (expressed as a percent of the total return) declined from roughly 80 percent to 50 percent, then recovered to 70 to 80 percent. Elsewhere the change in value was in one direction: down. At Moose Factory the value shot down from 80 to 50 percent and at York Factory, from 70 to 94 to under 50 percent, and notable declines in value occurred at Eastmain in the 1730s to 1740s, Fort Albany in the 1750s, and Moose Factory and York Factory in the 1760s.

26. Graham drew on Isham for his depiction of caribou hunting. Rich, *James Isham's Observations*, 81, 116, 143, 147; Williams, *Andrew Graham's Observations*, xiv, 10–11, 15–16, 154, 280–81; Drage, "Ethnographic Account," 18–21; J. B. Tyrrell, ed., "Letters of la Potherie," in *Documents Relating to the Early History of Hudson Bay* (Toronto: The Champlain Society, 1931), 143–370, pp. 233–36, 341–42; Brightman, "Conservation and Resource Depletion: The Case of the Boreal Forest Algonquians," 123; Bishop, "The Western James Bay Cree," 147–55. According to Bishop ("Ojibwa, Cree, and the Hudson's Bay Company in Northern Ontario," 159), the Fort Albany Cree "were taught conservation measures" but it is unclear when or by whom. It is difficult to know what to make of the report that the Illinois Indians angered Canadian Indians because they "killed or carried off both male and female beavers," which "the tribes who trade beaver skins for supplies with the Europeans" considered "criminal and cowardly" (Seymour Feiler, ed., *Jean-Bernard Bossu's Travels in the Interior of North America 1751–1762* [Norman: University of Oklahoma Press, 1962], 77).

27. For the 1750–1830 era and Simpson's policy, see Innis, *The Fur Trade in Canada*, 261–80, 326–35, p. 261 ("great scarcity of Beaver"); E. E. Rich, *The Fur Trade and the Northwest to 1857* (Toronto: McClelland and Stewart Ltd., 1967); Frederick Merk, ed., *Fur Trade and Empire: George Simpson's Journal*, revised edition (Cambridge: Belknap Press of Harvard University Press, 1968); Arthur J. Ray, *Indians in the Fur Trade: Their Role as Trappers, Hunters, and Middlemen in the Lands Southwest of Hudson Bay, 1660–1870* (Toronto: University of Toronto Press, 1974), 117–24, 195–204; Arthur J. Ray, "Some Conservation Schemes of the Hudson's Bay Company, 1821–50: An Examination of the Problems of Resource Management in the Fur Trade," *Journal of Historical Geography* 1 (1975): 49–68, pp. 51, 54, 57, 64, 67; Ray, "Competition and Conservation in the Early Subarctic Fur Trade"; Bishop, *The Northern Ojibwa and the Fur Trade*, 124–28, 184, 210–11 (quotes from Simpson), 245–49, 284; Calvin Martin, *Keepers of the Game: Indian-Animal Relationships and the Fur Trade* (Berkeley: University of California Press, 1978), 136–43 ("red and bloody"—the description was John Tanner's and may have

referred to tularemia); Ann M. Carlos, *The North American Fur Trade, 1804–1821: A Study in the Life-cycle of a Duopoly* (New York: Garland Publishing, Inc., 1986), 140–41, 155–64, 177.

28. As Glover remarks, the date on this particular account (1797) may well be incorrect (Glover, *David Thompson's Narrative*, 154–57); see also Martin, *Castorologia*, 144–46. For Kihcimanitōw and Wīsahkēcāhk, see Jennifer S. H. Brown and Robert Brightman, *"The Orders of the Dreamed": George Nelson on Cree and Northern Ojibwa Religion and Myth, 1823* (St. Paul: Minnesota Historical Society Press, 1988), 107–8, 119–38. According to a story reported by Alexander Henry, beavers once possessed speech but Nanabozho/Great Hare/the Great Spirit took it away from them "lest they should grow superior in understanding to mankind." In different versions, animals conspired against men but by stripping from them the power of speech, the Great Hare ensured that men would continue to exist. Alexander Henry, *Travels and Adventures in Canada and the Indian Territories* (Rutland, VT: Charles E. Tuttle, 1969), 126, 205–6. For castoreum and steel, see note 11.
29. Paul S. Thistle, *Indian-European Trade Relations in the Lower Saskatchewan River Region to 1840* (Winnipeg: University of Manitoba Press, 1986), 63–64, 72–73, 77, 88 ("dispersed all over . . ."; "Sacrificing . . .").
30. Julius Lips, "Naskapi Law," *Transactions of the American Philosophical Society* NS Volume 37, Part 4 (Philadelphia: American Philosophical Society, 1947), 379–492, pp. 433–34, 458; Morantz, "The Probability of Family Hunting Territories," 226, 234; Francis and Morantz, *Partners in Furs*, 97, 125–32; compare Rolf Knight, "A Re-examination of Hunting, Trapping, and Territoriality among the Northeastern Algonkian Indians," in *Man, Culture, and Animals: The Role of Animals in Human Ecological Adjustments*, ed. Anthony Leeds and Andrew P. Vayda (Washington, DC: American Association for the Advancement of Science, 1965), 27–42, p. 32.
31. With minor exceptions, quotations are from Charles A. Bishop, "The Emergence of Hunting Territories among the Northern Ojibwa," *Ethnology* 9 (January 1970): 1–15; Bishop, *The Northern Ojibwa and the Fur Trade*, 11–12, 108–10, 245–49, 277; Bishop, "Ojibwa, Cree, and the Hudson's Bay Company in Northern Ontario," 160. See also Innis, *The Fur Trade in Canada*, 91 ("so plentiful" etc.—La Verendrye); Ray and Freeman, *'Give Us Good Measure,'* 35f.
32. Bishop, "The Emergence of Hunting Territories," 4–5, 11; Bishop, *The Northern Ojibwa and the Fur Trade*, 11–12, 110–11, 124–28, 184, 206–20, 245–49, 284, 289–96; Edward S. Rogers, "Cultural Adaptations: The Northern Ojibwa of the Boreal Forest 1670–1980," in *Boreal Forest Adaptations: The Northern Algonkians*, ed. A. Theodore Steegman (New York: Plenum Press, 1983), 85–141; Harold Hickerson, "Land Tenure of the Rainy Lake Chippewa at the Beginning of the 19th Century," *Smithsonian Contributions to Anthropology 2* (Washington, DC: Smithsonian Institution, 1967), 37–63, pp. 58–59. In 1826, Mattagamis who lived 240 miles southwest of James Bay had family "allotments" in part hunted and in part rested in a given year (Bishop, *The Northern Ojibwa and the Fur Trade*, 212).
33. Bishop, *The Northern Ojibwa and the Fur Trade*, 94–95, 124–28, 184, 196–97. Perhaps "encroachment" was broadly common; in 1885 some Mistassini Crees and Lac St. Jean Montagnais evidently sought to conserve beavers but others poached if they could get away with it (Lips, "Naskapi Law," 402–3).
34. On variation within the region, see A. Irving Hallowell, "The Size of Algonkian Hunting Territories: A Function of Ecological Adjustment," *American Anthropologist* 51 (1949): 35–45; Hickerson, "Land Tenure of the Rainy Lake Chippewa," 42; Edward S. Rogers, "Subsistence Areas of the Cree-Ojibwa of the

Eastern Subarctic: A Preliminary Study," *Contributions to Ethnology V*, National Museum of Canada, Bulletin No. 204, Anthropological Series No. 70 (Ottawa: National Museum of Canada, 1967), 59–90. Toby Morantz (personal communication, June 7, 1998) suggests that at Abitibi in 1823, the Cree left beavers to breed if the numbers were sufficient; that Indians who were "poor" trapped out their own lands and then poached on their neighbors' lands; and that conservation, poaching, etc. might always have depended on how easy or difficult it was to obtain food and basic supplies.

35. There are possible links elsewhere between population pressure, competition, game depletions, and territoriality and conservation: In the 1690s the Ottawa evidently tried to leave some beavers alive in lodges; in 1700 the Algonquin apparently marked beaver lodges yet allowed others to have access to meat; in the 1760s the Algonquin possessed territories descending within families and punished trespass severely and Southeastern Ojibwa families had exclusive rights to territories; and in 1800 the Southwestern Ojibwa hunted beavers in roving bands or areas alloted informally to them by a leader for the season (Alexander Henry, *Travels and Adventures in Canada and the Indian Territories* [Rutland, VT: Charles E. Tuttle, 1969], 23; Cooper, "Is the Algonquian Family Hunting Ground System Pre-Columbian?," 73; Leacock, "The Montagnais 'Hunting Territory,' " 15–16; Harold Hickerson, "The Southwestern Chippewa: An Ethnohistorical Study," *Memoirs of the American Anthropological Association*, No. 92 [Menasha, WI, 1962], 14, 40–45; W. Vernon Kinietz, *The Indians of the Western Great Lakes 1615–1760* [Ann Arbor: University of Michigan Press, 1965 (orig. 1940)], 237; Brightman, "Conservation and Resource Depletion: The Case of the Boreal Forest Algonquians," 123 [for Baron de Lahontan].

36. The "Abenaki" (perhaps including the Penobscot, Passamaquoddy, Maliseet, and others) reportedly possessed and defended family hunting territories against trespass in 1710 (Cooper, "Is the Algonquian Family Hunting Ground System Pre-Columbian?," 73–74 [A. Raudot]); the Penobscot reported in the 1760s that "their hunting ground and streams were all parcelled out to certain families, time out of mind" but that "it was their rule to hunt every third year and kill two-thirds of the beaver, leaving the other third part to breed, and that their Beavers were as much their stock for a living as Englishman's cattle was his living; that since the late war English hunters kill all the Beaver they find on said streams, which had not only empoverished many Indian families, but destroyed the breed of Beavers, etc." Disentangling their complaint against the English from the rest of this statement is difficult (Dean R. Snow, "Wabanaki Family Hunting Territories," *American Anthropologist* 70 [1968]: 1143–51, p. 1149 [Joseph Chadwick]).

37. Frank G. Speck, "The Family Hunting Band as the Basis of Algonkian Social Organization," *American Anthropologist* 17 (1915): 289–305, pp. 294–96; Speck, "Family Hunting Territories and Social Life of Various Algonkian Bands of the Ottawa Valley," *Canada Department of Mines, Geological Survey, Memoir* 70, No. 8 (Ottawa: Government Printing Bureau, 1915), 5 and passim; Speck, "Mistassini Hunting Territories in the Labrador Peninsula," *American Anthropologist* 25 (1923): 452–71; Speck, "Family Hunting Territories of the Lake St. John Montagnais and Neighboring Bands"; Frank G. Speck and Loren C. Eiseley, "Montagnais-Naskapi Bands and Family Hunting Districts of the Central and Southeastern Labrador Peninsula," *Proceedings of the American Philosophical Society* 85 (1942): 215–42, p. 231.

38. Harvey A. Feit, "The Construction of Algonquian Hunting Territories: Private Property as Moral Lesson, Policy Advocacy, and Ethnographic Error," in *Colonial*

Situations: Essays on the Contextualization of Ethnographic Knowledge, ed. George W. Stocking, Jr. (Madison: University of Wisconsin Press, 1991), 109–34. In the mid-1920s, all Grand Lake Algonquin hunters reported from minor to severe poaching on their lands (see Hallowell, "The Size of Algonkian Hunting Territories," 43–44).

39. Speck, "The Family Hunting Band," 294–95, 297–99; Speck, "Family Hunting Territories and Social Life," 11–30; Feit, "The Construction of Algonquian Hunting Territories," 116–18; Scott, "Property, Power, and Aboriginal Rights."

40. The Watts' scheme saw instant success at Rupert House and elsewhere, but in the long run was apparently compromised in part by hunting pressure and noncompliance. Cooper, "Is the Algonquian Family Hunting Ground System Pre-Columbian?," 68–69 (Attikameks); Lips, "Naskapi Law," 435 (1930s); Leacock, "The Montagnais 'Hunting Territory,' " 31 (mid-century Western and Natashquan Montagnais); D. E. Denmark, "James Bay Beaver Conservation," *Beaver* 279 (September 1948): 38–43; Rolf Knight, "A Re-examination of Hunting, Trapping, and Territoriality," 27–42; Knight, "Ecological Factors in Changing Economy and Social Organization among the Rupert House Cree," *National Museum of Canada, Anthropology Papers*, No. 15 (Ottawa: National Museum of Canada, 1967): 26–31; William H. Metcalfe, "How the Beaver Have Come Back," *Canadian Geographic Journal* 89 (December 1971): 28–33; Adrian Tanner, "Game Shortage and the Inland Fur Trade in Northern Québec, 1915 to 1940," in *Papers of the Ninth Algonquian Conference*, ed. William Cowan (Ottawa: Carleton University, 1978), 146–59; Francis and Morantz, *Partners in Furs*, 129; Colin Scott, "Ideology of Reciprocity between the James Bay Cree and the Whiteman State," in *Outwitting the State*, *Political Anthropology*, Volume 7, ed. Peter Skalnik (New Brunswick: Transaction Publishers, 1989), 81–108, pp. 95–97.

41. Harvey A. Feit, "Twilight of the Cree Hunting Nation," *Natural History* 82 (August–September 1973): 48–57, 72; Paul Charest, "Hydroelectric Dam Construction and the Foraging Activities of Eastern Quebec Montagnais," in *Politics and History in Band Societies*, ed. Eleanor Leacock and Richard Lee (Cambridge: Cambridge University Press, 1982), 413–26; Sylvie Vincent, "Background and Beginnings," in *Baie James et Nord Québécois: Dix Ans Après/James Bay and Northern Quebec: Ten Years After*, ed. Sylvie Vincent and Garry Powers (*Recherches Amérindiennes au Québec*, Quebec, 1988), 211–38; Sylvie Vincent, "Hydroelectricity and Its Lessons," in *ibid.*, 245–50; Larry Lack, "All Is Not Well in Cree Country," *Whole Earth Review* 58 (Spring 1988): 58–65; André Picard, "James Bay II," *Amicus Journal* 12, No. 4 (Fall 1990): 1–16; Harry Thurston, "Power in a Land of Remembrance," *Audubon* 93 (November–December 1991): 52–59; Sam Howe Verhovek, "Power Struggle: A Massive Hydroelectric Project Could Help Light New York but May Also Obliterate a Way of Life in Quebec," *New York Times Magazine* (January 12, 1992): 16–21, 26–27; John Bowermaster, "Sacrificial People: Will Quebec's Indians Be Driven from Their Land?," *Condé Nast Traveler* (May 1993): 94–99, 169, 174–76.

42. When Diamond proposed removing James Watt's name from the Rupert House community house (Watt was the HBC manager who pushed measures leading to the recovery of beavers in the 1930s), he overreached. Rupert House Cree elders recalled cautiously that, as one said, it was Watt "who brought back the beaver, to make sure it did not go extinct." The Cree did their part, to be sure, complying to beaver recovery measures during trying times for them. Boyce Richardson, *Strangers Devour the Land* (Post Mills, VT: Chelsea Green Publishing Company, 1991 [orig. 1976]), 109

("who brought back the beaver . . ."), 151 ("the Whiteman . . ."); Harvey A. Feit, "Negotiating Recognition of Aboriginal Rights: History, Strategies and Reactions to the James Bay and Northern Quebec Agreement," *Canadian Journal of Anthropology* 1, No. 2 (1980): 159–70, p. 167 (Billy Diamond); Thurston, "Power in a Land of Remembrance," 55 ("Here, nothing is wasted"); Matthew Coon-Come, letter on behalf of NRDC, April 1994; Scott, "Ideology of Reciprocity," 99; Morantz, personal communication, June 7, 1998.

43. Harvey A. Feit, "The Ethno-Ecology of the Waswanipi Cree; or How Hunters Can Manage Their Resources," in *Cultural Ecology*, 115–25, pp. 116–18; Feit, "Twilight of the Cree Hunting Nation," 54, 56, 72; Harvey A. Feit, "Political Articulations of Hunters to the State: Means of Resisting Threats to Subsistence Production in the James Bay and Northern Quebec Agreement," *Etudes/Inuit/Studies* 3 (1979): 37–52, pp. 41–42; Feit, "Negotiating Recognition of Aboriginal Rights," 167 (Billy Diamond); Harvey A. Feit, "The Income Security Program for Cree Hunters in Quebec: An Experiment in Increasing the Autonomy of Hunters in a Developed Nation State," *Canadian Journal of Anthropology* 3, No. 1 (Fall 1982): 57–70; Harvey A. Feit, "The Future of Hunters within Nation-States: Anthropology and the James Bay Cree," in *Politics and History in Band Societies,* 373–411, pp. 377, 386–87, 390; Harvey A. Feit, "Self-Management and State-Management: Forms of Knowing and Managing Northern Wildlife," in *Traditional Knowledge and Renewable Resource Management in Northern Regions*, ed. Milton M. R. Freeman and Ludwig N. Carbyn, Occasional Publication No. 23 (Edmonton: IUCN Commission on Ecology and the Boreal Institute for Northern Studies, University of Alberta, 1988), 72–91, pp. 77–78, 81; Harvey A. Feit, "The Power and the Responsibility: Implementation of the Wildlife and Hunting Provisions of the James Bay and Northern Quebec Agreement," in *Baie James et Nord Québécois,* 74–88, pp. 78, 80–81, 83–84; Harvey A. Feit, "James Bay Cree Self-governance and Land Management," in *We Are Here: Politics of Aboriginal Land Tenure*, ed. Edwin N. Wilmsen (Berkeley: University of California Press, 1989), 68–98, pp. 77, 80; Fikret Berkes, "Environmental Philosophy of the Chisasibi Cree People of James Bay," in *Traditional Knowledge and Renewable Resource Management*, 7–21; Scott, "Property, Power, and Aboriginal Rights."

44. Henry's report continues after "grandmother . . .": "and requesting her not to lay the fault upon them, since it was truly an Englishman that had put her to death" (Bruce M. White, " 'Give Us a Little Milk': The Social and Cultural Significance of Gift Giving in the Lake Superior Fur Trade," in *Rendezvous*, 185–98; p. 187). On the variety of thoughts about animals in 17th–18th-century England, see Keith Thomas, *Man and the Natural World: A History of the Modern Sensibility* (New York: Pantheon Books, 1983).

45. Thwaites, *The Jesuit Relations*, Volume 5, 165, 179, Volume 6, 211, 213, 215. In the 1720s to 1730s, the Mistassini kept bones from dogs by throwing them in the fire or in water (*ibid.*, Volume 68, 47). According to Father Chrétien Le Clercq (*New Relation of Gaspesia, with the Customs and Religion of the Gaspesian Indians*, ed. and trans. William F. Ganong [Toronto, 1910], 225–29 as reported in Martin, "European Impact," 13–14), the Mi'kmaq held similar taboos; if they did not heed them, the "spirit of the bones . . . would promptly carry the news to the other beavers, which would desert the country in order to escape the same misfortune."

46. Jenness, *The Ojibwa Indians of Parry Island*, 21–25, 80; A. Irving Hallowell, *Contributions to Anthropology: Selected Papers of A. Irving Hallowell*, intro. Raymond D. Fogelson et al., (Chicago: University of Chicago Press, 1976), 356–90,

401–44, pp. 385, 401, 405, 411–12, 419, 426; A. Irving Hallowell, *Culture and Experience* (New York: Schocken Books, 1967 [orig. 1955]), 178–80; Mary B. Black, "Ojibwa Taxonomy and Percept Ambiguity," *Ethos* 5 (1977): 90–118.

47. Thomas W. Overholt and J. Baird Callicott, *Clothed-in-Fur and Other Tales: An Introduction to an Ojibwa World View* (Lanham, MD: University Press of America, 1982), 74–75, 146–47.
48. Speck, "Mistassini Hunting Territories," 464; Frank G. Speck, *Naskapi: The Savage Hunters of the Labrador Peninsula*, revised edition (Norman: University of Oklahoma Press, 1977), 102, 113–17, 165–67.
49. Adrian Tanner, *Bringing Home Animals: Religious Ideology and Mode of Production of the Mistassini Cree Hunters* (New York: St. Martin's Press, 1979), 122, 130, 136–81; Tanner, "The Significance of Hunting Territories Today"; Lips, "Naskapi Law," 389 and passim.
50. James Axtell, *The European and the Indian: Essays in the Ethnohistory of Colonial North America* (New York: Oxford University Press, 1981), 261; cf., James Axtell, *The Indians' New South: Cultural Change in the Colonial Southeast* (Baton Rouge: Louisiana State University Press, 1997), 69. Axtell seems to follow Calvin Martin's argument in *Keepers of the Game;* but see notes 19 and 56, and note 3 in Chapter 6, "Deer."
51. Robert A. Brightman, *Grateful Prey: Rock Cree Human-Animal Relationships* (Berkeley: University of California Press, 1993), 287–88. Morantz suggests (personal communication, June 7, 1998)—and I agree—that neither the failure of Jesuits (whose thoughts on indigenous religion were wanting) to mention rules, nor people's behavior contrary to rules necessarily meant that there were no rules.
52. Brightman, *Grateful Prey*, 288–91.
53. Jenness, *The Ojibwa Indians of Parry Island*, 21–25, 80.
54. Speck, *Naskapi*, 123; Tanner, *Bringing Home Animals*, 136–81; Feit, "Self-Management and State-Management," 77; Berkes, "Environmental Philosophy of the Chisasibi Cree People."
55. Speck, *Naskapi*, 78–82, 87–91, 118–20; William H. Mechling, "The Malecite Indians, with Notes on the Micmacs, 1916," *Anthropologica* 7–8 (1958–59): 1–274, pp. 199–200; K. G. Davies, ed., *Northern Quebec and Labrador Journals and Correspondence 1819–1835*, Volume 24 (London: The Hudson's Bay Record Society, 1963), 54–56.
56. Bishop, *The Northern Ojibwa and the Fur Trade*, 35–36; Brightman, "Conservation and Resource Depletion"; Brightman, *Grateful Prey*. Despite starting from the same premise as Martin in *Keepers of the Game*—that to comprehend the beaver pelt trade fully we need to understand native thought—my argument here departs notably from his. I find reasons for the trade and local exterminations in the conjunction of desires for manufactured goods and the belief that one could not kill too many beavers treated properly because they always returned. Martin's idea that hunters took revenge on animals because they blamed them for diseases is largely unsupported by historical evidence. The evidence is slim or nonexistent prior to the late 19th century for his argument (*Keepers of the Game*, 74, 83, and passim) that killing too many animals for the population to support was a sign of lack of respect. The specific link he asserts between animals and disease is also largely unsubstantiated in Algonquian ethnomedicine. People blamed themselves, others nearby, or sorcerers—not animals—for most maladies. The prominence given to men "warring" on animals as somehow a significant call to battle is belied by the commonness of this metaphor for hunting. For the debate, see Martin, "European Impact"; Calvin Martin, "Subarctic Indians and Wildlife," in *Old Trails and New Directions:*

Papers of the Third North American Fur Trade Conference, ed. Carol M. Judd and Arthur J. Ray (Toronto: University of Toronto Press, 1980), 73–81; Richard White, review of *Keepers of the Game . . .* , *Journal of Ethnic Studies* 7, No. 2 (1979): 115–17; Shepard Krech III, ed., *Indians, Animals, and the Fur Trade: A Critique of "Keepers of the Game"* (Athens: University of Georgia Press, 1981); Francis Jennings, review of *Indians, Animals, and the Fur Trade . . .* , *Journal of American History* 69 (1982): 415–16; Edward Rogers, review of *Indians, Animals, and the Fur Trade . . .* , *American Ethnologist* 10 (1983): 403–04; Adrian Tanner, review of *Indians, Animals, and the Fur Trade . . .* , *American Anthropologist* 85 (1983): 204–5; Brightman, "Conservation and Resource Depletion"; Brightman, *Grateful Prey*, 284ff. Also see note 19 above.

57. Sylvie Vincent and José Mailhot, "Montagnais Land Tenure," trans. Mary Stark and Marguerite Mackenzie, *Interculture* 15, Nos. 75–76 (April–September 1982): 61–69.

58. Colin H. Scott, "Property, Power, and Aboriginal Rights"; Colin H. Scott, "Knowledge Construction among Cree Hunters: Metaphors and Literal Understanding," *Journal de la Société des Américanistes* 75 (1989): 193–208; Colin H. Scott, "The Socio-economic Significance of Waterfowl among Canada's Aboriginal Cree: Native Use and Local Management," in *The Value of Birds*, ICBP Technical Publication No. 6, ed. A. W. Diamon and F. L. Filion (Kingston, Ontario: ICBP, 1987); Charles A. Drolet, "Land Claim Settlements and the Management of Migratory Birds, a Case History: The James Bay and Northern Quebec Agreement," in *Transactions of the 51st North American Wildlife and Natural Resources Conference* (Washington, DC: Wildlife Management Institute, 1986): 511–15; Charles A. Drolet, Austin Reed, Mimi Breton, and Fikret Berkes, "Sharing Wildlife Management Responsibilities with Native Groups: Case Histories in Northern Quebec," in *Transactions of the 52nd North American Wildlife and Natural Resources Conference* (Washington, DC: Wildlife Management Institute, 1987): 389–98. Also see Fikret Berkes, "James Bay: The Cree Indian Coastal Fishery," *Canadian Geographic Journal* 93 (1976): 60–65; Fikret Berkes, "An Investigation of Cree Indian Domestic Fisheries in Northern Quebec," *Arctic* 32 (1979): 46–70; Fikret Berkes, "Waterfowl Management and Northern Native Peoples with Reference to Cree Hunters of James Bay," *Musk-Ox* 30 (1982): 23–35.

59. Milton M. R. Freeman, "Appeal to Tradition: Different Perspectives on Arctic Wildlife Management," in *Native Power: The Quest for Autonomy and Nationhood of Indigenous Peoples*, ed. Jens Brøsted et al. (Bergen: Universitetsforlaget As, 1985), 265–81; Fikret Berkes, "Fishermen and 'The Tragedy of the Commons,'" *Environmental Conservation* 12, No. 3 (1985): 199–206; Fikret Berkes and M. M. R. Freeman, "Human Ecology and Resource Use," in *Canadian Inland Seas*, ed. I. P. Martini (Amsterdam: Elsevier, 1986), 425–55; Peter J. Usher, "Indigenous Management Systems and the Conservation of Wildlife in the Canadian North," *Alternatives* 14, No. 1 (1987): 3–9; Gail Osherenko, "Wildlife Management in the North American Arctic: The Case for Co-management," in *Traditional Knowledge and Renewable Resource Management*, 92–104; Polly Wheeler, "State and Indigenous Fisheries Management: The Alaska Context," in *ibid.*, 38–47; Feit, "Self-Management and State-Management: Forms of Knowing and Managing Northern Wildlife"; Feit, "James Bay Cree Self-governance and Land Management," 79–85 and passim; Fikret Berkes, Peter George, and Richard J. Preston, "Co-management: The Evolution in Theory and Practice of the Joint Administration of Living Resources," *Alternatives* 18, No. 2 (1991): 12–18, 92–104; Gail Osherenko, "Human/Nature Relations in the Arctic: Changing Perspectives,"

Polar Record 28, No. 167 (1992): 277–84; cf., John B. Theberge, "Commentary: Conservation in the North—An Ecological Perspective," *Arctic* 34, No. 4 (December 1981): 281–85; Tanner, *Bringing Home Animals,* 144.

Epilogue

1. For the Yup'ik as for others, conservation management problems in light of these beliefs are obvious—even though the Yup'ik today increasingly construct waste of meat as "untraditional" (Ann Fienup-Riordan, "Original Ecologists?: The Relationship between Yup'ik Eskimos and Animals," in *Eskimo Essays: Yup'ik Lives and How We See Them* [New Brunswick: Rutgers University Press, 1990], 167–91). In former days, motivated by desires for safe hunts for the tastiest large animals, the Eskimo widely killed suckling and young whales. No matter how appalling their choice of prey to contemporary whale lovers, they might actually have been practicing a form of "fortuitous ecology"—to use Igor Krupnik's phrase—in that the survival of adult whales is crucial for the perpetuation of the herds (Igor Krupnik, "Prehistoric Eskimo Whaling in the Arctic: Slaughter of Calves or Fortuitous Ecology," *Arctic Anthropology* 30, No. 1 [1993]: 1–12). On reincarnation, see Antonia Mills, "Reincarnation Belief among North American Indians and Inuit: Context, Distribution, and Variation," in *Amerindian Rebirth: Reincarnation Belief among North American Indians and Inuit*, ed. Antonia Mills and Richard Slobodin (Toronto: University of Toronto Press, 1994), 15–37.
2. American Indians often subscribe to the Ecological Indian regardless of their political beliefs. For example, Russell Means, cofounder of the American Indian Movement and a Lakota born on Pine Ridge Reservation, spoke in 1980 of "the traditional Lakota way and the ways of the other American Indian Peoples" to thousands gathered in the Black Hills. This is "the way," he said, "that knows that humans do not have the right to degrade Mother Earth, that there are forces beyond anything the European mind has conceived, that humans must be in harmony with *all* relations or the relations will eventually eliminate the disharmony." And David Lester, then executive director of the Council of Energy Resources Tribes, a mainstream economic development consortium formed so that tribes might deal directly with energy companies, called American Indians "truly people of the land. It is we who belong to the land in a spiritual sense much more than it belongs to us, in any material sense." Land, water, and air, Lester maintained, constitute life, and "the harmony of these three elements is crucial to the cultural, spiritual, aesthetic, physical, and economic health of the tribes that live on America's reservations. Non-Indians are just now awakening to the importance of a harmonious relationship with nature. . . . What few people stop to realize is that Indians have been advocating environmentalism for time out of mind. We are the original environmentalists." Both Means and Lester are invested in the Ecological Indian. Russell Means, "Fighting words on the future of the earth," *Mother Jones* 5 (December 1980): 22–31, 36–38, p. 30A; David Lester, "The environment from an Indian perspective," *EPA Journal* 12 (January/February 1986): 27–28, p. 27.
3. How can one doubt the affinity to nature of indigenous people who chant about "becom[ing] part of" trees, mountains, mists, or clouds; or who sing about the sea, the sky, and moving "as a weed"; or who pray for "love, compassion, and honor" in order to "heal the earth" (Elizabeth Rogers and Elias Amadon, eds., *Earth Prayers: From around the World, 365 Prayers, Poems, and Invocations for Honoring the Earth* [New York: Harper San Francisco, 1991], 5, 21, 95).

4. The Lakota poet Gilbert Walking Bull writes in his poem "Rocks Not Happy in Sacks" of rocks that are sacred and are people (Paula Gunn Allen, ed., *Studies in American Indian Literature: Critical Essays and Course Designs* [New York: The Modern Language Association of America, 1983], 69 and passim); Chief Dan George, *My Heart Soars* (Blaine, WA: Hancock House, 1989 [orig. 1974]), 14, 37, and passim; Carol Cornelius, "This Land Is Our Land," *Progressive* 47 (December 1983): 18.
5. Ed McGaa, Eagle Man, *Native Wisdom: Perceptions of the Natural Way* (Minneapolis: Four Directions Publishing, 1995); Steven McFadden, *Profiles in Wisdom: Native Elders Speak about the Earth* (Santa Fe: Bear and Co., 1991), 21–22, 137–38 (Sun Bear; the Iroquois *Basic Call to Consciousness* [1977]). For a skeptical view of Sun Bear's knowledge—but not his blood—see Wendy Rose, "The Great Pretenders," in *The State of Native America: Genocide, Colonization, and Resistance,* ed. M. Annette Jaimes (Boston: South End Press, 1992); reprinted in *Native American Voices: A Reader*, ed. Susan Lobo and Steve Talbot (New York: Longman, 1998), 296–308, p. 303.
6. Rudolf Kaiser, "A Fifth Gospel, Almost: Chief Seattle's Speeches. American Origins and European Reception," in *Indians and Europe*, ed. Christian Feest (Aachen, Germany: Edition Herodot, 1987), 175–93; Rudolf Kaiser, "Chief Seattle's Speech(es): American Origins and European Reception," in *Recovering the Word: Essays on Native American Literature*, eds. Brian Swann and Arnold Krupat (Berkeley: University of California Press, 1987), 497–536; [Chief Seattle], *How Can One Sell The Air?: Chief Seattle's Vision* (Summertown, TN: The Book Publishing Company, 1992); Albert Furtwangler, *Answering Chief Seattle* (Seattle: University of Washington Press, 1997).
7. Vine Deloria, Jr., *We Talk, You Listen: New Tribes, New Turf* (New York: Macmillan, 1970), 186 (italics in original); Alison Anderson, "An Expendable People," *Ecologist* 5, No. 7 (1975): 237–40; Ward Churchill, "Radioactive Colonization and the Native American," *Socialist Review* 81 (May–June 1985): 95–119; Winona LaDuke and Ward Churchill, "Native America: The Political Economy of Radioactive Colonialism," *Journal of Ethnic Studies* 13 (1985): 107–32; Ward Churchill and Winona LaDuke, "Native North America: The Political Economy of Radioactive Colonialism," in *The State of Native America*, 241–66; Ward Churchill, *Struggle for the Land: Indigenous Resistance to Genocide, Ecocide and Expropriation in Contemporary North America* (Monroe, ME: Common Courage Press, 1993); Robert D. Bullard, ed., *Confronting Environmental Racism: Voices from the Grassroots* (Boston: South End Press, 1993).
8. "Common Terns Get Uncommon Good Turn at Mille Lacs," *Aitken Independent Age*, May 12, 1993; Duane Noriyuki, "Sacred Ground," *Saint Paul Pioneer Press*, June 14, 1993, 1B–2B; Lou Cannon, " 'Low-Tech' Effort Aims to Return Massive Trout to Nevada Waters, *Washington Post*, April 19, 1998, A3; Kathleen O'Reilly, "Wild Rice Restoration," *Audubon* 99, No. 6 (November–December 1997), 116–17; Lisa Prevost, "Economics or Exploitation?: Waste Industry Courting Indian Nations," *New Paper*, March 8, 1990, 1, 4; Christopher Rowland, "Hazardous-waste Firms Wooing Indian Tribes," *Providence Journal*, February 25, 1990, A1, 11; Kathie Durbin, "Reports—Rediscovering the Lost Coast: California's Sinkyone Indians Plan to Restore the Land of Their Ancestors," *Audubon* 98, No. 2 (March–April 1996): 18–20; Colin Chisholm, "A Victory for the Natives," *Audubon* 99, No. 3 (May–June 1997), 19; Jim Robbins, "In the West, a Matter of the Spirit," *New York Times*, January 21, 1997; Colman McCarthy, "The Buffalo Is Back,"

Washington Post, September 14, 1996, A25; Jim Robbins, "Slaughter of Errant Bison to Begin near Yellowstone," *New York Times*, December 29, 1996; Deborah Frazier, "New Home New Status for Buffalo," *Rocky Mountain News*, January 23, 1997, 12A; Paul Hutchinson, "Meetings No Help to Bison, Dispute Might Be Too Tough to Find Solution," *Denver Post*, March 24, 1997, B1; Gregg Bourland, "Reunite the Plains Tribes and Their Bison," *Christian Science Monitor*, April 4, 1997, 19; Doug Peacock, "The Yellowstone Massacre," *Audubon* 99, No. 3 (May–June 1997), 40–49, 102–3, 106–10; Mark Matthews, "Battle Grows over Where the Yellowstone Buffalo Roam; Activists Try to Halt Montana's Slaughter of Diseased Bison Despite Danger to Livestock," *Washington Post*, November 29, 1997, A16; Kit Miniclier, "Judge Restricts Bison Killings outside Yellowstone," *Denver Post*, December 17, 1997, B1.

9. Julianne Labreche, "An Island Unfit for Man or Beast," *Maclean's* 92 (July 30, 1979): 40–41; Janet Raloff, "The St. Regis Syndrome," *Science News* 118 (July 19, 1980): 42–43; Elizabeth Gray, "Island of Woe," *Maclean's* 93 (November 3, 1980): 17, 19–20; John E. Milich, "Contaminant Cove: Where Polluters Defile Mohawk Land," *Progressive* 53 (January 1989): 23–25; Donald A. Grinde and Bruce E. Johansen, *Ecocide of Native America* (Santa Fe: Clear Light Publishers, 1995), 171–201; Aaron Derfel, "Dredging Plan Worries Local Environmentalist, Mohawks," *Gazette* (Montreal), June 29, 1995, A8; Deborah Tetley, "Fish Farm Fights Diabetes," *Gazette* (Montreal), April 23, 1997, C4.

10. Alvin M. Josephy, Jr., "The Murder of the Southwest," *Audubon* 80 (July 1971): 52–67; Alvin M. Josephy, Jr., "Kaiparowits: The Ultimate Obscenity," *Audubon* 78 (March 1976): 64–67, 69–70, 72–78, 84, 87–90; Hanna J. Cortner, "The Navajo Environmental Protection Commission: Developing the Capabilities for Environmental Impact Assessment and Regulation," *Indian Historian* 9 (Fall 1976): 32–37; Richard O. Clemmer, "Black Mesa and the Hopi," in *Native Americans and Energy Development*, eds. Joseph G. Jorgensen et al. (Cambridge, MA: Anthropology Resource Center, 1978), 17–34; Lynn A. Robbins, "Energy Developments and the Navajo Nation," in *ibid.*, 35–48; Becky J. Miles Viers, "Environmental Law: Uranium Mining on the Navajo Reservation," *American Indian Law Review* 7 (1979): 115–24; Tom Barry, "Navajo Legal Services and Friends of the Earth Sue Six Federal Agencies over Alleged Careless Uranium Mining Policies," *American Indian Journal* 2, No. 5 (February 1979): 3–7; David Harris, "Last Stand for an Ancient Indian Way," *New York Times Magazine* (March 16, 1980): 38–41, 63–64, 66, 68, 70–74, 76, 78–79; Thomas W. Pew, Jr., "Summit Powwow at Canyon de Chelly: So Lives Will Not Waste Away Like Water on Sand," *American West* 21 (November/December 1984): 38–44; Richard O. Clemmer, "Effects of the Energy Economy on Pueblo Peoples," in *Native Americans and Energy Development II*, eds. Joseph G. Jorgensen et al. (Cambridge, MA: Anthropology Resource Center and Seventh Generation Fund, 1984), 79–115; Lynn A. Robbins, "Energy Developments and the Navajo Nation: An Update, in *ibid.*, 116–45; Sandra D. Atchison, "Suddenly Peter MacDonald Is Business' Best Friend: The Controversial Navajo Leader Is Courting Companies," *Business Week* (August 10, 1987): 64; Mark Allen, "Native American Control of Tribal Natural Resource Development in the Context of the Federal Trust and Tribal Self-determination," *Boston College Environmental Affairs Law Review* 16 (1989): 857–95; Sandra D. Atchison, "The Navajos May Generate Juice—and Even Power: A Utility Deal Should Bring in Electricity, Money, and Respect," *Business Week* (November 11, 1991): 162.

11. William Booth, "Indian Wars of 1990s Fought over the Everglades," *Washington*

Post, October 3, 1996, A1, 16; Todd Wilkenson, "Native Americans Challenge Park Agency for Land Rights," *Christian Science Monitor*, October 22, 1996, 1, 14; John Weiss, "Elk Massacre in Montana," *Outdoor Life* 65 (June 1980): 28; Lonnie Williamson, "No Laws for the Indians," *Outdoor Life* 73 (May 1984): 33, 36, 41, 144; John G. Mitchell, "Where Have All the Tuttu Gone?," *Audubon* 79, No. 2 (March 1977): 2–15; David Parmentier, "Mississippi of the North," *Humanist* 49, No. 5 (September/October 1989): 17–19, 38; Paul Schneider, "Other People's Trash," *Audubon* 93, No. 4 (July–August 1991), 108–19, p. 116 ("concerned about Mother Earth"); Trebbe Johnson, "Caring for the Earth: New Activism among Hopi Traditionals," *Amicus Journal* 13, No. 1 (Winter 1991): 22–27, p. 25 ("gifts of Mother Earth"); James Brooke, "Battle of What May Be the West's Last Big Dam," *New York Times*, September 20, 1997, A7.

12. Timothy Egan, "New Prosperity Brings New Conflict to Indian Country," *New York Times*, March 8, 1998, 1, 24.
13. Al Gedicks, "Exxon, Copper, and Sokaogon," *Progressive* 44, No. 2 (February 1980): 43–46; Keith Schneider, "Concerned about Pollution from Proposed Mine, Wisconsin Tribe Takes on a Giant," *New York Times*, December 26, 1994, 12; Will Fantle, "Mining Plans Poison Town," *Progressive* 61, No. 6 (June 1997): 15; Al Gedicks, "Update: The Exxon/Rio Algom Mine Controversy," http://www.menominee.com/nomining/alg1.html; http://www.earthwins.com/home.html#recent.
14. Sharon Metz, "American Indian Treaty Rights Attacked in Wisconsin: A Legacy of Broken Promises," *Sojourners* 19, No. 5 (June 1990): 16–20; "The Wisconsin Fishing War," *Sports Illustrated* (May 15, 1989): 16; Parmentier, "Mississippi of the North," 17–19, 38; Glenn Emery, "Indians' Fishing Rights Net Big Trouble in Wisconsin," *Insight* 5 (November 13, 1989): 22–23; Jim Oberly, "Race and Class Warfare: Spearing Fish, Playing 'Chicken,'" *Nation* 248 (June 19, 1989): 844–45, 848; Weston Kosova, "Indian Fishing Rights and Wrongs: Race Baiting," *New Republic* 202 (June 11, 1990): 16–17; "Walleye War: Indians and Sportsmen Clash over Fishing Rights," *Time* (April 30, 1990): 36; Mike Beno, "Treaty Troubles," *Audubon* 93 (May 1991): 102–14; William E. Schmidt, "Wisconsin Spring: New Fishing Season, Old Strife," *New York Times*, April 5, 1990, 20; Bob Secter, "As Walleyes Spawn, Whites Battle Indians over Special Fishing Rights," *Providence Journal-Bulletin*, May 2, 1989, A6; "Clashes on Indian Fishing Are Down in Wisconsin," *New York Times*, April 20, 1990, A11; Don Terry, "Indian Treaty Accord in Wisconsin," *New York Times*, May 21, 1991, A12; *A Guide to Understanding Chippewa Treaty Rights* (Odanah, WI: Great Lakes Indian Fish & Wildlife Commission, 1991); Jim Thannum, *1991 Chippewa Spearing Season: Building Cooperation and Bridging Conflicts* (Odanah, WI: Great Lakes Indian Fish & Wildlife Commission); *Casting Light upon the Waters: A Joint Fishery Assessment of the Wisconsin Ceded Territory* (Minneapolis: U.S. Department of the Interior, Bureau of Indian Affairs, 1991); *Chippewa Treaty Harvest of Natural Resources: Wisconsin, 1983–1991* (Odanah, WI: Biological Services Division, Great Lakes Indian Fish and Wildlife Commission); *Masinaigan, A Publication of the Great Lakes Indian Fish and Wildlife Commission* (Summer 1992); Rick Whaley with Walter Bresette, *Walleye Warriors: An Effective Alliance against Racism and for the Earth* (Philadelphia: New Society Publishers, 1994).
15. James Bruggers, "The Salish-Kootenai Comeback," *Sierra Club Bulletin* 72 (July/August 1987): 22–23, 26.
16. Daniel Gibson, "Cutting through a Sacred Forest," *Sierra* 72, No. 1 (January–February 1987): 135–36; Michael Kantor, "Wilderness and Worship—or Wells?," *Sierra* 72, No. 3

(May/June 1987): 67–68; James Bruggers, "Forest Service Steps on Blackfeet," *Progressive* 51 (April 1987): 14; Keith Ervin, "Spirit Dancers and the Law," *Sierra Club Bulletin* 73 (November/December 1988): 106–7.

17. "A Crow Indian Threat to Western Strip Mines," *Business Week* (October 13, 1975): 37.
18. Fred and La Donna Harris, "Indians, Coal, and the Big Sky," *Progressive* 38 (November 1974): 22–26; Alvin M. Josephy, Jr., "Agony of the Northern Plains," *Audubon* 75 (July 1973): 66–88, 90, 92, 94, 96, 98–101.
19. "The Cheyennes Drive for Clean-Air Rights," *Business Week* (April 4, 1977): 29.
20. William J. Broad, "The Osage Oil Cover-up," *Science* 208 (April 4, 1980): 32–35.
21. "A Daring Comanche Foray into Oil," *Business Week* (January 10, 1983): 29–30.
22. Daniel Cohen, "Tribal Enterprise," *Atlantic* 264, No. 4 (October 1989): 32–33, 35–36, 38, 40, 43.
23. Schneider, "Other People's Trash," 115 (over 300 billion pounds of garbage); Mary Hager et al., "Dances with Garbage," *Newsweek* 117 (April 29, 1991): 36.
24. Robert Reinhold, "Indians and Neighbors Are at Odds over Waste Dump on Reservation," *New York Times*, January 8, 1990, A1, C4; Keith Schneider, "Grants Open Doors for Nuclear Waste," *New York Times*, January 9, 1992, A14; "Oklahoma Tribe Sees Riches in Storing Nuclear Waste," *Providence Sunday Journal*, June 24, 1994.
25. Schneider, "Other People's Trash"; Katrin Snow, "Tribes' Activism Poses Hazard to Waste Industry's Health," *National Catholic Reporter* 28, No. 6 (December 6, 1991): 13–14, p. 13; Conger Beasley, Jr., "Dances with Garbage," *E: The Environmental Magazine* 2 (November–December 1991): 38–41, 58; Eugene L. Meyer, "Environmental Racism," *Audubon* 94 (January–February 1992): 30–32.
26. I wish to thank Patricia Galloway for press clippings on hazardous waste and the Choctaw. Conger Beasley, Jr., "Of Landfill Reservations," *Buzzworm: The Environmental Journal* 3, No. 5 (September–October 1991), 36–42; Mary Hager et al., "Dances with Garbage"; Robert Allen Warrior, "Dancing with Wastes," *Christianity and Crisis* 51 (July 15, 1991): 216–18; Ronald Smothers, "Future in Mind, Choctaws Reject Plan for Landfill," *New York Times*, April 21, 1991, 22; Sharon Stallworth, "State 'Anxious' about Proposed Choctaw Waste Site," *Clarion-Ledger*, November 24, 1990, A1, 11; Sharon Stallworth, "Choctaws Pursuing Hazardous Waste Landfill," *Clarion-Ledger*, February 6, 1991, A1, 6; Sharon Stallworth, "Choctaws Vote Down Hazardous-Waste Landfill," *Clarion-Ledger*, April 20, 1991, A1; Sharon Stallworth, "Hazardous Waste: Where Does It Go from Here?," *Clarion-Ledger*, June 2, 1991, A1, 15; Johna Rodgers, "Indian Land Eyed for Incinerator?: Location Might Shield Waste Disposal Firm from State Regulations," *Meridian Star*, January 10, 1991, A1, 13; Johna Rodgers, "Protests Meet Choctaw Tour of Waste Site," *Meridian Star*, January 30, 1991, A1, 9; Johna Rodgers, "Chief Martin Lauds Choctaw Landfill Venture," *Meridian Star*, February 6, 1991, A1, 7; Johna Rodgers, "Land Deal Gives Unique Twist to Area Issue," *Meridian Star*, March 24, 1991, A1, 9; Johna Rodgers, "State: Can't Block Choctaw Landfill," *Meridian Star*, April 1, 1991, A1, 7; Johna Rodgers, "Noxubee Landfill May Not Fulfill Law: Emelle Site Threatened?," *Meridian Star*, April 7, 1991, A1, 11; Johna Rodgers, "Woman's Tenacity in Struggle Piqued Nation's Curiosity," *Meridian Star*, April 28, 1991, A1, 9; Phillip Martin, "Choctaw Waste Proposal Is Sound in Every Respect," *Meridian Star*, April 11, 1991.
27. Keith Schneider, "Nuclear Complex Threatens Indians," *New York Times*, September 3, 1990, 9; Schneider, "Concerned about Pollution"; Keith Schneider,

"Idaho Tribe Stops Nuclear Waste Truck," *New York Times*, October 17, 1991, A18; Monika Bauerlein, "Nukes on the Reservation," *Progressive* 55 (November 1991): 14.

28. Fred C. Shapiro, "Radwaste in the Indians' Backyards," *Nation* 236 (1983): 573–75; Schneider, "Other People's Trash"; Matthew L. Wald, "Nuclear Storage Divides Apaches and Neighbors," *New York Times*, November 11, 1993, A18; Erik Eckholm, "The Native—and Not So Native—Way: The Apaches," *New York Times Magazine*, February 27, 1994, 45–48; "Letters," *Washington Post*, October 4, 1995, A24; George Johnson, "Nuclear Waste Dump Gets Tribe's Approval in Re-vote," *New York Times*, March 11, 1995, 6; Michael Satchell, "Dances with Nuclear Waste," *U.S. News & World Report* (January 8, 1996): 29–30.
29. "Eskimos: Native Rites," *Economist* (November 5, 1977): 40, 42; Craig Van Note, "IWC Slashes Quotas, Bans Eskimo Hunt," *Audubon* 79, No. 5 (September 1977): 141–42; John R. Bockstoce, "An Issue of Survival: Bowhead Vs. Tradition," *Audubon* 79, No. 5 (September 1977): 142–45; John Bockstoce, "Battle of the Bowheads," *Natural History* 89, No. 5 (May 1980): 52–61; Edward Mitchell and Randall R. Reeves, "The Alaska Bowhead Problem: A Commentary," *Arctic* 33, No. 4 (December 1980): 686–723; Sam W. Stoker and Igor I. Krupnik, "Subsistence Whaling," in *The Bowhead Whale*, ed. John J. Burns, J. Jerome Montague, and Cleveland J. Cowles, Special Publication No. 2 (Lawrence, KS: The Society for Marine Mammalogy, 1993), 579–629.
30. Nora Underwood, "The Whales of Alaska: A Desperate Rescue Effort in the Arctic," *Maclean's* 101 (October 31, 1988): 46–47; Jerry Adler, "Just One Mammal Helping Another," *Newsweek* (October 31, 1988): 74–75, 77; Roger Rosenblatt, "Looking at Them Looking at Us," *U.S. News & World Report* (November 7, 1988): 8–9; James S. Kunen and Maria Wilhelm, "To Save the Whales," *People Weekly* (November 7, 1988); Charles Colson, "Save the Wails," *Christianity Today* 35 (July 14, 1989): 72; "Saving Grays," *People Weekly* (March 28, 1988); Andrea Dorfman, "Free at Last! Bon Voyage!: The Whales Finally Escape Their Icy Arctic Prison," *Time* (November 7, 1988): 130; Eugene Linden, "Helping Out Putu, Siku and Kanik," *Time* (October 31, 1988): 76–77; Randall R. Reeves, "Tales of Leviathan (review of *Whales*, by Jacques Cousteau and Yves Paccalet)," *Natural History* 98 (March 1989): 76–81.
31. Watson is a noted radical environmentalist responsible for sending Icelandic and Norwegian ships down in earlier actions. Timothy Egan, "A Tribe Sees Hope in Whale Hunting, but U.S. Is Worried," *New York Times*, June 4, 1995, 1, 34; "Tribe Seeks International Okay to Resume its Whaling Hunts," *Providence Journal-Bulletin*, October 23, 1997, A6; "Commission Grants Tribe Right to Hunt Gray Whales," *Providence Journal-Bulletin*, October 24, 1997, A9; Robert Sullivan, "Permission Granted to Kill a Whale. Now What?," *New York Times Magazine* (August 9, 1998): 30–33; Richard Blow, "The Great American Whale Hunt," *Mother Jones* 23, No. 5 (September–October 1998): 49–53, 86–87.
32. Mike Miller, "Alaska's Tongass Suit—The 'Exercise' at Juneau," *American Forests* 77, No. 2 (March 1971): 28–31, 50–52; Philip L. Fradkin, "Southeast: Not Enough Land to Go Around," *Audubon* 80 (1978): 16–25; Jim Rearden, "The Chilkat Miracle," *Audubon* 86 (1984): 41–54; Bill Richards, "Alaska's Southeast: A Place Apart," *National Geographic* 165, No. 1 (January 1984): 50–59, 61–87; William Least Heat Moon, "The Native Son," *Esquire* 102, No. 6 (December 1984): 502–4, 506, 507; Peeter Kopvillem, "The Law and the Forest," *Maclean's* 98 (April 8, 1985): 52; John Goddard, "War of the Worlds," *Saturday Night* 101, No. 4 (April 1986): 42–53; Marcus Gee, "The South Moresby War," *Maclean's* 100 (July 8, 1987): 12; George Laycock, "Trashing the Tongass," *Audubon* 89 (November 1987): 110–27;

Lisa Drew, "Native Timber Cuts Run Deep," *National Wildlife* 20, No. 4 (June–July 1990): 29; Hal Quinn, "A Split Decision: A Forestry Compromise Angers Both Sides," *Maclean's* 103 (April 23, 1990): 53; Timothy Egan, "Space Photos Show Forests in Pacific Northwest Are in Peril, Scientists Say," *New York Times*, June 11, 1992, A13; Ted Williams, "Tearing at the Tongass," *Audubon* 97 (July–August 1995): 26–32, pp. 29–30 ("hush money"); Mark Kurlansky, "Icy Bay," *Audubon* 97 (November–December 1995): 48–55, p. 51 ("This is America."); "A Poor Deal for the Tongass," *New York Times*, June 8, 1997, 14.

33. Joby Warrick, "King Cove's Relentless Road War," *Washington Post*, May 27, 1998, A3; Bruce Babbitt, "Road to Ruin," *New York Times*, June 25, 1998, A23.
34. Eugene Linden, "A Tale of Two Villages," *Time* (April 17, 1989): 62; Martha Peale, "Beating the Drum for Caribou," *Sierra Club Bulletin* 74, No. 3 (May/June 1989): 32, 36, 38, 40, pp. 36 ("to meet . . ."), 38 ("thumbs up . . ."); Matthew L. Wald, "Eskimo Company Attacks Indians on Oil Drilling," *New York Times*, November 15, 1991, D19; Colman McCarthy, "Saved in Alaska," *Washington Post*, November 9, 1991, A27; "Caribou Petrol," *Economist* (July 20, 1991): 33; Timothy Egan, "The Great Alaska Debate: Can Oil and Wilderness Mix?," *New York Times Magazine*, August 4, 1991, 20–27, p. 25 ("Oil is the future"); Michael Bedford, "Saving a Refuge," *Cultural Survival Quarterly* 16 (Spring 1992): 38–42; Norma Kassi, "Gwich'in Alert," at fyre@web.apc.org, June 1, 1995; Carey Goldberg, "Turmoil beneath a Land's Tranquility," *New York Times*, July 13, 1997, 12 NE; John G. Mitchell, "Oil on Ice," *National Geographic* 191, No. 4 (April 1997): 104–31; Weston Kosova, "Alaska: The Oil Pressure Rises," *Audubon* 99, No. 6 (November–December 1997): 66–74.
35. Dennis Martinez, "First People, Firsthand Knowledge," *Sierra* 81, No. 6 (November/December 1996): 50–51, 70–71; Winona LaDuke, "Social Justice, Racism and the Environmental Movement," University of Colorado at Boulder, September 28, 1993.
36. Daniel Cohen, "Tribal Enterprise," *Atlantic* 264, No. 4 (October 1989): 32–34, 36, 38, 40, 43, p. 33.
37. Robert H. White, *Tribal Assets: The Rebirth of Native America* (New York: Henry Holt and Company, 1990), 112–13.
38. Stuart Elliott, "Advertising," *New York Times*, April 22, 1998, D6.

Index